Driven by a collection of gripping self-narratives, Johns tells an old story in a powerful, original way, tracking the bleak journey from the existential isolation of the prison to the existential isolation of release, always from the perspective of ex-prisoners themselves. The reader is left wondering where does 'risk' reside? In the people released from prison or in the communities that sent them there to begin with?

– **Shadd Maruna, Professor of Criminology,**
University of Manchester, UK, and author of *Making*
Good: How Ex-Convicts Reform and Rebuild Their Lives

'Liminality is experienced as not quite fitting in, not belonging, no longer a prisoner but not entirely free either.' So writes Diana Johns in the final chapter of her brilliant book. Through in-depth interviews with ex-prisoners and post-release workers (some of whom are themselves ex-prisoners), Johns deftly and empathetically brings to light the personal struggles to emerge from the stigma of imprisonment. More than this, she shows how such struggles are always already social – that 'moving on' after serving single or multiple periods in prison requires not only individual effort but transformation in the ways that communities 'receive' and conceive ex-prisoners. The book is filled with just the right mix of hard-hitting narrative excerpts and theoretically sophisticated analyses. In short, *Being and Becoming an Ex-Prisoner* makes a major contribution to criminological thought.

– **Mark Halsey, Professor of Criminology,**
Flinders University, Australia

Taking a phenomenological perspective on the experience of prisoner reentry, Diana Johns challenges popular notions of the 'post-release' experience by offering detailed narratives that capture the intense personal confusion, fear and isolation of released former prisoners. Johns reveals a subaltern mix of challenges facing stigmatized citizens never fully integrated into society prior to prison – but then expected to adapt while facing challenges of mental illness, institutionalization, addiction, and poverty. The unsuitability of prisons and their progeny for truly helping people comes to the fore. Johns' professional experience in the field prior to becoming an academic sets the stage. Required reading.

– **Michael Hallett, Professor of Criminology and**
Criminal Justice, University of North Florida, USA

Being and Becoming an Ex-Prisoner

Despite broad scholarship documenting the compounding effects and self-reproducing character of incarceration, ways of conceptualising imprisonment and the post-prison experience have scarcely changed in over a century. Contemporary correctional thinking has congealed around notions of risk and management. This book aims to cast new light on men's experience of release from prison.

Drawing on research conducted in Australia, it speaks to the challenges facing people leaving prison and seeking acceptance amongst the non-imprisoned around the world. Johns reveals the complexity of the post-prison experience, which is frequently masked by constructions of risk that individualise responsibility for reoffending and reimprisonment. This book highlights the important role of community in ex-prisoner integration, in providing opportunities for participation and acceptance. Johns shows that the process of becoming an 'ex'-prisoner is not simply one of individual choice or larger structural forces, but occurs in the spaces in between.

Being and Becoming an Ex-Prisoner reveals the complex interplay between internal and external meanings and practices that causes men to feel neither locked up, nor wholly free. It will appeal to scholars and students interested in desistance, criminology, criminological or penological theory, sociology and qualitative research methods.

Diana F. Johns is Lecturer in Criminology in the School of Social and Political Sciences at the University of Melbourne, Australia.

International Series on Desistance and Rehabilitation

The *International Series on Desistance and Rehabilitation* aims to provide a forum for critical debate and discussion surrounding the topics of why people stop offending and how they can be more effectively reintegrated into the communities and societies from which they came. The books published in the series will be international in outlook, but tightly focused on the unique, specific contexts and processes associated with desistance, rehabilitation and reform. Each book in the series will stand as an attempt to advance knowledge or theorising about the topics at hand, rather than being merely an extended report of specific a research project. As such, it is anticipated that some of the books included in the series will be primarily theoretical, whilst others will be more tightly focused on the sorts of initiatives which could be employed to encourage desistance. It is not our intention that books published in the series be limited to the contemporary period, as good studies of desistance, rehabilitation and reform undertaken by historians of crime are also welcome. In terms of authorship, we would welcome excellent PhD work, as well as contributions from more established academics and research teams. Most books are expected to be monographs, but edited collections are also encouraged.

General Editor
Stephen Farrall, University of Sheffield

Editorial Board
Ros Burnett, University of Oxford
Thomas LeBel, University of Wisconsin-Milwaukee, USA
Mark Halsey, Flinders University, Australia
Fergus McNeill, Glasgow University
Shadd Maruna, Rutgers University, USA
Gwen Robinson, Sheffield University
Barry Godfrey, University of Liverpool

Being and Becoming an Ex-Prisoner

Diana F. Johns

Routledge
Taylor & Francis Group

LONDON AND NEW YORK

First published 2018
by Routledge
2 Park Square, Milton Park, Abingdon, Oxon OX14 4RN

and by Routledge
711 Third Avenue, New York, NY 10017

Routledge is an imprint of the Taylor & Francis Group, an informa business

British Library Cataloguing in Publication Data
A catalogue record for this book is available from the British Library

Library of Congress Cataloging in Publication Data
Names: Johns, Diana F., author
Title: Being and becoming an ex-prisoner / Diana F. Johns.
Description: Abingdon, Oxon ; New York, NY : Routledge, 2018. | Series:
    International series on desistance and rehabilitation ; 11 | Includes
    bibliographical references and index.
Identifiers: LCCN 2017009818| ISBN 9781138665897 (hardback) |
    ISBN 9781315619637 (ebook)
Subjects: LCSH: Prisoners—Australia. | Prisoners—Deinstitutionalization. |
    Ex-convicts—Australia.
Classification: LCC HV9872 .J64 2018 | DDC 364.80994—dc23
LC record available at https://lccn.loc.gov/2017009818

ISBN: 978-1-138-66589-7 (hbk)
ISBN: 978-1-315-61963-7 (ebk)

Typeset in Times New Roman
by Swales & Willis Ltd, Exeter, Devon, UK

MIX
Paper from
responsible sources
FSC
www.fsc.org   FSC® C013985

Printed in the United Kingdom
by Henry Ling Limited

This book is dedicated to people leaving prison everywhere, and becoming.

Contents

General editor's introduction

The *International Series on Desistance and Rehabilitation* aims to provide a forum for critical debate and discussion surrounding the topics of why people stop offending and how they can be more effectively reintegrated into the communities and societies from which they came. The books published in the series will be international in outlook, but tightly focused on the unique, specific contexts and processes associated with desistance, rehabilitation and reform. Each book in the series will stand as an attempt to advance knowledge or theorising about the topics at hand, rather than being merely an extended report of a specific research project. As such, it is anticipated that some of the books included in the series will be primarily theoretical, whereas others will be more tightly focused on the sorts of initiative that could be employed to encourage desistance. It is not our intention that books published in the series be limited to the contemporary period, as good studies of desistance, rehabilitation and reform undertaken by historians of crime are also welcome. In terms of authorship, we would welcome excellent PhD work, as well as contributions from more established academics and research teams. Most books are expected to be monographs, but edited collections are also encouraged.

I am delighted to welcome Diana Johns' book into the series. Based on a series of interviews with men formerly imprisoned and leaving prison in Victoria, Australia, and the support workers who worked with this client group, Johns is able to throw further light on their experiences of release and the profound shock that this provokes. As one might well imagine, she finds that housing, employment and drug use feature prominently in their accounts of release. However, Johns goes further than this and explores the ways in which cultural processes shape and hinder successful release, concluding that:

> The reincarceration assemblage comprises lines radiating from the prison out into the community and back again, in iterative loops. The recursive processes by which men are ensnared in these lines arise from identities forged within prison culture. These prison habits, skills, styles and ways of being provide men with the toolkit from which they construct their ways of being and acting in the community. Replacing these tools with more pro-social strategies demands either the difficult process of cultural retooling, or the

reliance on pre-existing resources undiminished by prisonisation processes. Each of these possibilities requires the support of an understanding and accepting community. Such resources are beyond the reach of men brought up in the system. [. . .] These men's 'ex-prisoner' identities have congealed around the 'dis-habilitation' that their experience of institutionalisation and imprisonment has engendered. In this way, the prison culture is seen as both product and producer of the reincarceration assemblage.

Diana Johns' book adds to existing literature on both the effects of imprisonment on human lives, and the thorny issue of efforts to desist from crime against the backdrop of (often) repeated periods of incarceration.Her book contributes to a broader conceptualisation of the problems of prison release, problems that include the subjectivity and daily practices of those released. In so doing, she adds to the growing critical studies of the imprisonment–release–reimprisonment phenomenon. Although Johns' research shows the 'dark side' of desistance – the difficulties of ceasing offending within contexts of impoverishment and exclusion – it helps to illuminate how such barriers may be overcome and, as such, represents a key reading for all interested in desistance, imprisonment and life after release. I welcome the book's inclusion in the series.

Stephen Farrall,
Sheffield,
February 2017

Acknowledgements

This book is the result of my PhD work, which was made possible with the support of many people. My warmest gratitude goes to my supervisors, Dr Mark Brown and Dr Stuart Ross, for their continued support, guidance and friendship. To Professor Mark Halsey and Dr Thomas LeBel for their generous comments on the original thesis. To Dr Marg Liddell for her ready eye and ear, and constant encouragement. To my colleagues in Law and Criminology at Aberystwyth University for their helpful feedback on my initial ideas for the structure of the book. And to the wonderful team at the University of Melbourne, for the luxury of time to finish writing.

My PhD research was supported by a 3-year scholarship awarded by the Australian Prisons Project, which was funded by an Australian Research Council Discovery Projects grant (DP0877331). I am ever grateful for the opportunity to have been part of the Australian Prisons Project, for the financial support and even more for the chance to participate in the workings of such an esteemed academic team – not only experts in the penal field, but also a great bunch of people: Chris Cunneen, Eileen Baldry, David Brown, Mark Brown, Alex Steel, Melanie Schwartz and (my Sydney counterpart) Maggie Hall. Thank you for your trust and generosity, your goodwill and inspiration.

I am truly indebted to the twelve men who participated in this research, who allowed me to delve into the shadows of their lives, to hear their stories, and to interpret their deeply personal experiences of being imprisoned and released. I am grateful, too, to the men and women working to support ex-prisoners, who gave up their time to be interviewed: the Link Out and Konnect staff at ACSO, the Brosnan Centre, the Salvation Army, and VACRO; the Ex-offender Employment Program staff at WISE Employment; and the Five8s. Thank you for sharing your insights and experience.

I reserve my deepest gratitude for my friends and my family, without whose love and support I could not have made this journey. To my parents for helping beyond measure, thank you. To Craig, my rock, thank you for bearing the load and keeping everything together. To my beautiful girls, who tolerated my absences with such patience, I hope you are inspired to pursue passions of your own.

1   What's the post-release problem?

'Scott'

The last day of autumn. I am driving under a leaden sky through outer-suburban Melbourne to meet my first ex-prisoner interviewee, 'Scott'. That's not his real name. But, to those who've spent time in Victoria's prisons, he is well known, having spent much of his adult life behind bars.

We've arranged to meet in a pub on a busy corner. It's quiet, late morning. I find a seat near the door, through which he soon bursts, tilting towards the bar. He hasn't slept for three days, he tells me, he's been injecting amphetamines. I try humour – so coffee's unnecessary then? – and offer to buy him a coke. His reluctant acceptance seems part chagrin at having no money, part old-fashioned ideas about chivalry and gender roles. Ideas steeped in prison thinking, I wonder, as we sit down to talk.

Scott is 34, turning 35. He has around 220 convictions, mainly for property and drug-related offences. Since his first adult custodial sentence at 18, he has been imprisoned and released at least fifteen times. His last release date was just over six-and-a-half months ago, which is the longest he's been out that he can remember. Other times, it's been two days, five days, and he's back inside. This time, he was sentenced to 15 months, with a minimum of 7, but they kept him in for 12 and then let him out on 3 months' intensive parole because, as he tells me, 'the more you go to jail the less they trust you on the street'.

This time, for the first time, he has support – and an address: for 3 months, while on parole, he stayed with his sister, sleeping on the couch in the two-bedroom unit she shares with her two small children. Now, his transitional support case-worker has helped him find accommodation: a self-contained 'studio apartment' in a boarding house. It's small, but it's home, for now.

He also has his Mum, though her support is limited. Her boyfriend – his stepfather – died a few weeks after Scott's release, so he's had to be there for her as she's gone 'a bit weird in the head'. It's his niece and nephew – his 'bubbas' – who are the main motivation for him to stay out of jail. And the fact that he's 'sick of living like a crumb' and of people dying around him.

He's been trying to moderate his drug use, not using every day, trying to manage his money so he doesn't feel tempted to go and do 'burgs' to get money to buy more drugs. He's trying to leave the 'old days' behind: the days of thieving and burglary to pay for his drug habits, and of being flush with thousands of dollars in his pocket from selling heroin. It was 'an exciting life', but he admits it was risky too: 'I've had thirty thousand dollars stolen off me . . . people have tried to overdose me to steal money off me, and . . . I've woken up in the . . . hospital that many times'.

He uses anything: heroin, speed, ice, cocaine. And he's on methadone, which he hates because 'it's wrecking me teeth', but at least he's not 'doing illegal stuff to get it'. Though he does still 'shoot up' his methadone. When I ask him why, he explains that, if you take a handful of Valium tablets and then shoot up, you get something like a 'heroin stone' – 'that instant kick where you're straight one minute and then you're like . . . ' (he slumps).

Most days, he carries a box cutter and an ice pick on him, just in case, just like you do in jail, except in jail you make them yourself. His preferred weapon inside was a modified toothbrush: you shave all the bristles off with a razor, then melt razor blades into the head, in different directions, so it doesn't matter which way you cut someone, it'll cut them. And when it does, it opens up two wounds, so it's harder to stitch up. Across the face is best, so that every day they look in the mirror, they remember it was you who cut them. He'd never start it, but he'd do it if he had to . . . It's all about respect.

He had to appear in court last week for charges dating from last year. He received a 6-month suspended sentence that, together with the 3-month suspended he's already serving, means that, if he breaches, he'll be locked up for 9 months. He doesn't want to go back to prison, although he does confess some days he wouldn't mind, some days he just can't face getting out of bed, just wants to sleep the day away, and the night, and the next day . . .

In jail he slept a lot: he'd get up early, about 8 o'clock, to have his methadone; he'd have a nap from around 1 till about 5, then get up to walk and talk with mates until lockdown, then he'd be back to sleep about 8.30, 9 o'clock. Perhaps it's all the medication he's on – antidepressant, antipsychotic, anti-epilepsy drugs, methadone – he just has no energy most of the time. When he was younger, he was always up and about, at the gym, playing basketball, walking, walking. Lately, he can't even get himself to the gym. His Mum's happy, though, because he's still the weight he was when he was released – 80 kilos – when normally, by now, he'd be down to 45. He puts that down to his favourite meal: vanilla ice cream with a few spoonfuls of Nutella, warmed for about 15 seconds in the microwave so it goes all soupy.

Since being out, having secured stable accommodation, he's been focused on trying to manage his money and his drug use and avoid criminal associates that he knows he would end up following 'like a sheep'. He is also struggling with his personal identity – who he is and how others see him. He has seen people that he has known for years, and respected, who are now so 'fucked up' and he reflects that, 'maybe that's how people see me'. He would like to find a girlfriend – lamenting 'I've been out six months and I haven't even been with a girl' – but, he adds despondently, 'it makes me just think that I'm not really worthy, not worth it'.

During the hour and a half I spend with Scott, we become 'sort of friends', as he puts it: 'I might be a thief but mate because I know you, you could leave your purse there with five grand in it and I wouldn't touch a cent because I know you. And we're sort of friends now, you know?'.

Driving home, I am aware of a clinging sense of wretchedness. I feel heavy with the weight of Scott's story and with what it means to be his 'friend'. This feeling will return as I gather stories of what it means to be – and to become – an ex-prisoner.

Since the birth of the modern prison, despite countless innovations and reforms, a question persists: Why do so many men released from prison return to prison? This book seeks to explore and understand the social space inhabited by ex-prisoners, from which some manage to integrate back into society and yet where many seem to linger, neither locked up nor wholly free. It focuses on the experience of men, as prison is largely a male domain: more than 90 per cent of prisoners are men, and male prisoners' higher proportion of prior imprisonment suggests that men face particular reintegrative difficulties. Beyond this pragmatic concern, however, lies a deeper rationale: the fundamental issue of maleness and masculinity. In the closed male domain of the prison, masculinities are negotiated, performed, reproduced. Patriarchal norms are enacted, exaggerated, reinforced through modes of domination and intimidation. This book explores connections between ways of 'doing' masculinity and ways of being in prison – and how these leak out into the post-prison realm. It seeks to foreground this gendered aspect of prison life and prisoner subjectivity that research tends to treat as incidental.

'Scott' is one of twelve men whose stories are the warp and weft of this book. Their understandings and perspectives form the backdrop against which I have tried to make sense of the different ways men experience their return to the community following release from prison. Their voices and experiences are the yarns that give the book its colour and texture. Central to this book is the idea that prison is part of a penal apparatus that functions to reproduce itself. Prison produces the post-prison, in that men's experience is shaped and shadowed by their experience of being imprisoned. This idea builds on the work of Halsey (2006, 2007) and Arrigo and Milovanovic (2009) and the concept of the 'carceral assemblage'. The post-prison is seen as a social space characterised by risks – of homelessness, social isolation, family and relationship breakdown, poverty, unemployment, mental ill-health, substance abuse and reimprisonment. Each time a man returns to prison, he will be released with fewer resources and less capacity for social integration. Each release magnifies the post-prison risks he faces. The rise of the 'risk' paradigm, the punitive turn and increasing numbers of people imprisoned and released have exacerbated this situation. Risk thinking conceives reoffending risk in terms of individual failings and typically deems ex-prisoners 'risky until proven innocent' (Maruna, LeBel, Mitchell & Naples, 2004: 272). Such logic dominates post-prison thinking.

This book seeks to reconceptualise the social space inhabited by released prisoners by applying a theoretical lens that can 'see into' that space. This lens comprises three concepts: *assemblage*, *culture* and *liminality*. By exploring the ways in which prisoners understand and experience release, and drawing these together with the conceptions of post-release support workers, this lens casts new light on how and why prison shadows persist in men's lives and make (re) integration[1] difficult. I explain these concepts – and how and why I have used them in this book – below. First, though, I describe the study – its conception, its aims and the questions at its heart. The research context provides a brief account of the historical and non-governmental roots of post-release support, and a snapshot of imprisonment and release in Victoria, Australia, as background to the study. This leads into the scope and setting of the research, its contribution to post-prison knowledge, and an outline of the structure of the book.

The conception of the study

Prior to undertaking this research, I worked as a Personal Support Program[2] (PSP) caseworker. PSP participants were referred for many reasons, including, for some, a history of offending and imprisonment. One young man commenced the programme upon release from prison. Aged 21, he reported a history of foster care, family estrangement, drug abuse and associated mental health problems. His abuse of the drug 'ice' had left him with lasting cognitive impairment. In prison, he was stable, 'medicated' and contained. Released without links to ongoing medical or psychiatric care, and homeless, within weeks he was reimprisoned. As his sole support in the community, I felt largely ineffective, having little capacity to interrupt the cycle of homelessness and offending in which he seemed caught. Another 'client', imprisoned briefly while on the programme, spent the rest of the 2 years failing to appear in court and having hearings repeatedly adjourned in a bid to avoid reimprisonment, while nevertheless continuing to offend through his drug use. He admitted he'd never waste a hundred bucks on 'speed' if he'd worked hard for the money, but, as the government was giving it to him for nothing, he didn't mind. It was something to do.

The experience of working with these men and others provided insight into the invisible worlds they inhabit, the difficulty engaging meaningfully with those worlds, and the problem of a lack of support available to recognise their particular needs. Inspired by that work, this study was driven by the desire to understand the subjective experience of inhabiting a social space largely invisible to non-imprisoned society. The opportunity presented itself when a national prison research project,[3] funded by the Australian Research Council (ARC), advertised a PhD scholarship, for which I applied, successfully. My study's post-release focus fitted the larger research on Australian penal policy and practice and its impact on vulnerable populations. The number of men returning to custody attests to the vulnerability of people caught in offending cycles and the problems associated with efforts to foster and sustain so-called reintegration.

The notion of reintegration is particularly problematic for prisoners with no previous experience of effective integration into a law-abiding community. Rather than *re*integration, the issue is one of working towards integration as a new and continuing process. This can entail ongoing social learning and reacculturation:

acquiring and absorbing information about how to live a law-abiding life; trying to assimilate the norms and mores associated with such a lifestyle; and, at the same time, struggling to unlearn or repress the ways of being when 'doing crime' or in prison. Along with the ex-prisoner's participatory efforts, the reintegrative aim of social inclusion implies reciprocity, mutual tolerance and a degree of community acceptance. This poses a dilemma: if a man[4] can live in the community independently, with a legal source of income and avoiding crime, and yet still feels an outsider, is he 'reintegrated'? Out of such dilemmas, the myriad difficulties of engaging ex-prisoners and facilitating integration and the lack of knowledge about the experience of released prisoners in Australia grew the seeds of the research and, subsequently, this book.

The study and its aims   40% recidivism.

Over 50,000 people are released from prison in Australia every year,[5] of which 20,000 are likely to be reimprisoned within 2 years, either for committing further crime or for breaching conditions of their release. This is a familiar cycle, mapped in statistical detail by correctional authorities and recited and analysed by policymakers, critics and criminologists. A fuller understanding of this cycle and its contributing factors, however, requires listening to the subjective experience of ex-prisoners and workers in the field. These voices, scarcely heard, are potentially a rich source of insight into the nature and characteristics of the sociocultural space between prison and the community. This book delves into this knowledge, exploring its layers of meaning and perspective, to bring to light the lived experience of release.

The book is concerned with meanings and conceptions of imprisonment and release, and how these coalesce into stories and shared understandings when exchanged and reproduced. It seeks to trace the lines of these stories, to find out how and why different perspectives and experiences give rise to conflicting views and perceptions of the imprisonment–release phenomenon. Its starting point is the sense that there is something missing from explanations of and solutions to the problem of post-prison integration. Missing from individualist, risk-factor accounts is the prison itself and the role the experience of imprisonment has in shaping the post-prison landscape, both in men's inner worlds and externally in the social spaces they find themselves inhabiting. The way I have used the book's conceptual tools to explore the dimensions of this landscape is briefly summarised here.

Assemblage (Deleuze & Guattari, 1987; DeLanda, 2006) permits a focus on multiplicities as a way to shift or dislodge linear, dominant or hierarchical perspectives. Assemblage of different perspectives enables reconceptualisation of the 'custodial subject' as comprising component parts and (re)incarceration as a 'collective event' or process (Halsey, 2007: 1249). *Culture*, when taken to mean semiotic practices (Wedeen, 2002), offers a way to analyse the interrelationship between signs/meanings and actions/behaviour. Building on Swidler's (1986) conception of a 'cultural toolkit', I conceive culture here, not as a fixed frame or social entity into which its participants enter, but as an analytical dimension of social relations (Garland, 2006). *Liminality* describes states of post-release transition.[6] In terms of rites-of-passage theory (Van Gennep, 1909; Turner, 1967), liminality reveals how states of 'in-betweenness' may persist or be brought to an end, thus explaining processes of social exclusion and (re)integration. The layering of these conceptual tools evokes the idea of collectivity, or multi-strandedness, which is a theoretical keystone and methodological theme of this book. This involved gathering threads of meaning via in-depth, semi-structured interviews and weaving these together to qualitatively map the subjective experiences, understandings and expectations of life after release from prison.

The aim of this book is to understand the experience of prisoners' release into the community: how it is conceptualised and understood by releasees themselves, and how these understandings relate to those of post-release support practitioners. In foregrounding the subjective and applying its unique theoretical lens, it takes a critical perspective on the post-release terrain. Its conceptual tools are employed with particular aims in mind: (1) assemblage, to draw together different threads of meaning and perspective and see them in relationship with each other; (2) culture, to explain how and why the prison inflects and shapes the post-release experience; and (3) liminality, to characterise the internal and external features of the post-prison social landscape. The book aims to construct a layered depiction of what it means for men to be released from prison, and what it means to facilitate and sustain life in the community under the rubric of reintegration.

This idea of 'construction' refers to putting together or assembling elements in a way that makes sense, as a coherent whole. The methodological approach and conceptual framework are built around this aim and around its focus on meanings, understandings, shared and divergent experiences and the language and signifiers by which these are expressed and exchanged. The notion of construction describes the process whereby meanings coalesce into storylines that, through repetition and reproduction, become 'knowledge' and sociocultural narratives, ways of explaining 'how things are'. These meaning-narratives may be examined by separating and teasing out their component lines. In this way, the book aims to investigate different constructions of release from prison and what it means to be a released prisoner: their sources of meaning, the variations in perspective and experience, and what holds them together.

The research questions

Seeking to assemble and understand how meanings and symbols intersect with post-release practices, and the lived experience of release, gives rise to the question(s) at the heart of the study:

> *How is men's prison release (and post-release life) constructed?*
> *And how do these constructions conflict and cohere?*

And sub-questions:

- What are the qualitatively different ways men experience release from prison?
- How is post-release support conceived and experienced?
- How does culture flow from and feed into the reincarceration assemblage?
- How is post-release liminality experienced? What are its interior and exterior dimensions, and how do these facilitate or impede community (re)integration?

Together, these questions yield insights into the post-prison realm and how it is experienced and conceived by those most intimately acquainted with its terrain. The concepts shaping this enquiry enable a perspective not otherwise afforded by risk-based accounts or those emphasising dualistic notions of offenders/non-offenders, agency/structure or the prison as separate from the community. That is, they allow a view of the prison and its post-prison ramifications as a web of interconnected lines and flows, which together constitute the carceral assemblage.

The research context

This section outlines the history and development of community-based post-release support in Victoria, Australia, and briefly summarises men's imprisonment and release in this state.

Historical roots of post-release support in Victoria

The 1850s and 60s saw an imprisonment boom in Victoria. In the wake of rapid, gold-fuelled population increases, new prisons were built at Ballarat, Bendigo, Beechworth and Castlemaine. The overcrowded Melbourne Gaol was extended, and Pentridge Prison was transformed from a wooden penal stockade in 1850 to a Pentonville-style bluestone prison by the mid 1860s (Lynn & Armstrong, 1996). The idea and practice of post-release support similarly have colonial roots, embedded in the tradition of Christian charitable work (Norden, 2008). In 1871, with imprisonment rates at 210 per 100,000 adult population, a Royal Commission into the Penal Establishments and Gaols and a report of the Inspector-General of Penal Establishments called for the introduction of a body to provide assistance to released prisoners. The Discharged Prisoners' Aid Society of Victoria began in 1872. An article in *The Argus*[7] newspaper describes the penal/judicial milieu of mid-nineteenth-century Victoria, where:

> prisoners on their release received but a very little money, and nothing was done further for their benefit. . . . It was a constant source of anxiety to judges and magistrates when they reflected on what prisoners would or could do on emerging from gaol.
>
> (*The Argus*, 1 August 1872: 3)

At that time, according to Mr Castieau, Governor of Melbourne Gaol:

> Victoria was not a very hospitable country even for persons of decent reputation, if they had no money and no friends; it was still more inhospitable in the case of persons with a gaol reputation.
>
> *(The Argus,* 1 August 1872: 3)

Reflecting a nascent welfarist ethos, the first prisoners' aid society was established in England in 1857, with similar schemes emerging in Ireland, Wales, Europe, Canada and some states of America, 'with signal success' *(The Argus,* 1872: 3). 'In advocating the usefulness of such societies', the chairman of the Board of Directors of Prisons in Ireland suggested, 'the discharged prisoner is not so much in want of money as the advice, assistance, and patronage of a society' *(The Argus,* 1872: 3). He evokes the importance of the community's support, acceptance and investment in the reintegration of released prisoners, echoed a century later in Father John Brosnan's counsel: 'Three things are needed by people upon their release from prison: a place to live that is decent; a job that they can handle; and friendship, and the hardest to provide is friendship.'

Community-based post-release support in Victoria

Contemporary models of community-based ex-prisoner support mirror the early societies whose members:

> visited convicts previous to their discharge, ascertained their necessities and wishes, furnished them, when necessary, with clothing, procured railroad tickets . . . and in general gave such good counsel and assistance as seemed suited to their need.
>
> *(The Argus,* 1872: 3)

The Discharged Prisoners' Aid Society of Victoria was later to become the Victorian Association for the Care and Resettlement of Offenders (VACRO), and, although its commitment to released prisoners remains, recent decades have seen the shadow of nineteenth-century paternalism diminish in the light of a focus on human rights and dignity (Norden, 2008). A non-government, non-denominational organisation, VACRO is dedicated to providing support and information to prisoners and their families, and people charged with a criminal offence.

In 1977, a young Jesuit-in-training, Peter Norden, set up a halfway house for young men leaving custody. In 1987, it was named the Brosnan Centre to honour the work of Father Brosnan, who served as Pentridge Prison chaplain for 30 years. From its early days as a small team dedicated to helping young people manage day to day after exiting jail, the Brosnan Centre has continued to grow and expand its range of programmes,[8] including an intensive pre- and post-release support programme for men deemed at high risk of reoffending, which, at the time of the study, was called Link Out. Funded by the Victorian Department of Justice, Link

Out comprised a consortium of agencies: VACRO, ACSO, the Brosnan Centre and the Salvation Army.

In response to the continued growth in prisoner numbers, the Victorian government's (2002) Corrections Long Term Management Strategy committed to building new prisons, expanding community corrections and improving rehabilitation programmes. Between 2000 and 2007, the Department of Justice also funded a range of pilot programmes aimed at addressing the high rate of return to custody. Specific eligibility criteria precluded participation in more than one programme, however, 'preventing a holistic approach to transitional support' (Link Out, 2008: 3). In 2007, therefore, these became Link Out (for men) and the Women's Integrated Support Program (WISP). This period signalled the movement to a privatised model of post-release service provision in Victoria, which has not diminished the importance of non-government services but has rendered their foothold more tenuous, as they have become reliant on government funding to survive. Nevertheless, faith-based programmes such as Five8 (prison slang for 'my mate') embodied the persistent ethos and role of community-based support. Based on the Canadian model of Circles of Support and Accountability (COSA), Five8 – a small programme at an inner-suburban church in Melbourne – built 'micro-communities' of volunteer supports around individual released prisoners. Contrasts between this approach to post-release support and a case management model are drawn in Chapter 7. The following provides the context of prison release in Victoria at the time of the research.

Imprisonment and release in Victoria

In 2001, Victoria's Corrections Minister, Andre Haermeyer, noted the state government's woeful post-release expenditure: 'we have spent more than \$55,000 a year to keep a person in prison and less than \$300 to stop them coming back'. Subsequent investment in various prisoner rehabilitation strategies reflects efforts to break the cycle of reoffending and reimprisonment, through prison programmes and increased transitional support. Over a decade later, the costs of imprisoning an individual had risen to more than \$90,000 per year (SCRGSP, 2012), prison numbers had swollen, and post-release support remained under-provided, with four out of five prisoners released straight into the community without any ongoing support.

Over 20 years, 1987–2007, Australia's adult imprisonment[9] rate increased by more than 68 per cent, from 100.8 to 169.4 per 100,000 adult population (Carcach & Grant, 1999; ABS, 2008). The total number of prisoners grew by a third in the decade since 2000 (ABS, 2010, 2012). Victoria's imprisonment rate, consistently lower than other Australian states, has steadily increased. In 2010–11, Victoria's average daily adult prison population was 4,586 people: 4,271 men and 315 women (SCRGSP, 2012). In 2014–15, this had risen to 6,350: 5,915 men and 435 women (SCRGSP, 2016). Almost half all male prisoners have previously served an adult prison sentence (ABS 2012). Victoria has a reimprisonment rate of 44 per cent, up from a low of 35 per cent in 2011–12

(SCRGSP, 2016). These figures underscore this book's concern with the perpetual functioning of the penal machine. Despite reforms and efforts to interrupt the cycle, a reduction of the reincarceration rate to below (approximately) one in three imprisoned men appears impossible.

At the time of the study, roughly a third of prisoners were released on parole (Adult Parole Board, 2009, 2012). Most relevant to the research is the high rate of men on 'straight release': 2010–11 saw 4,966 discharges of male prisoners in Victoria, with 1,623 releases on parole, indicating 3,343 straight releases (Corrections Victoria, 2011; Adult Parole Board, 2012). Albeit this figure includes men released more than once, it indicates around 3,000 men discharged on straight release from Victorian prisons each year. Since parole reforms in Victoria, post-2013, this number has increased. The implications for the accessibility and provision of post-release support are clear: there are far more prisoners released than there are services to cater for their particular needs.

The scope and setting of the research

This study's gendered, state-based focus, and the range of post-release support available to men leaving prison in Victoria, delimited its scope. Link Out represented the largest post-release service segment, and, hence, the agencies comprising the Link Out consortium were the starting point for the research, with the Indigenous programme, Konnect, and WISE Employment's Ex-offender Program included later. I sourced post-release support workers for interviews via these programmes. These workers enabled contact with a small number of ex-prisoner interviewees, including 'Scott'. Subsequent contact with Five8 led to additional interviews.

Ethics process constraints meant that Link Out/Konnect clients on parole were ineligible for inclusion in the study. As the majority of the Link Out/Konnect clients were on parole, this significantly reduced the pool of potential interviewees, which meant I relied upon informal referral processes to find research participants. At WISE Employment, I briefed workers about the research and posted information sheets in their offices to invite released prisoners to participate in the study; I recruited several in this way. Interviews with workers took place at their agencies. Interviews with ex-prisoners took place either on agency premises or at mutually convenient public venues such as cafés, with one at a boarding house. The research thus took place in – or as close as possible to – the physical landscape of its participants.

What does this book add to what we already know?

The important contribution of this book is its unique perspective on issues that have persisted over a century, despite broad scholarship documenting the compounding effects and self-reproducing character of incarceration. It highlights that, despite this knowledge, ways of conceptualising imprisonment and the post-prison experience have scarcely changed. Contemporary correctional thinking has congealed around notions of risk and management. Theories about reoffending, rehabilitation and desistance offer explanations for why and how the formerly imprisoned manage (or not) to stay out of prison. Perspectives of prisoners themselves have provided insight into their worlds, and experience of workers in the field has lent empirical weight to our understanding. Yet questions remain, such as why – after all this time and acquisition of knowledge – do men return to prison at such a rate? And why does this rate seem so unalterable?

This book contributes a broader conceptualisation of the post-release problem, one that encompasses ex-prisoner subjectivity as well as post-release practice perspectives. This adds to critical work[10] on the imprisonment–release–reimprisonment phenomenon. Other writers[11] have exposed the social–structural and economic injustices of hyperincarceration and its twin, 'transcarceration'; of expanding punishment through mechanisms of control that extend beyond the penal realm; and the nature and recursive effects of social exclusion, all seen as arising from risk-obsessed policies and practices and the construction of the risk subject. This book respectfully adds to this important body of work. In exploring the nature and implications of post-prison liminality, the book builds on burgeoning scholarship[12] on this theme. It also adds a sociocultural dimension to work on the psychological effects of imprisonment and how these shadow ex-prisoners' lives and communities (see Haney, 2003), to explain the persistence of liminality and barriers to social reintegration. Lastly, it attests – empirically and theoretically – to the need for communities to provide reintegrative opportunities and rituals to facilitate ex-prisoner reintegration.[13]

Chapter outline

The men's stories, individually or thematically, punctuate the chapters. In this respect, I have sacrificed methodological conformity to bring the text to life. In Chapter 2, I review post-release research (with a focus on Australia) and find it lacking an overarching theoretical or policy narrative. As ex-prisoners are contained and defined within and by distinct political discourses and policy models, Chapter 3 traces the key assumptions and logics of these by examining how we conceive the post-release problem, its subject and solutions. This chapter highlights important theoretical threads that I pick up in later chapters. Chapter 4 builds a conceptual framework for the study: I explain the theories of assemblage, culture and liminality, how they fit together as a 'theoretical lens', and how this lens connects to and supports the methodological structure. Chapter 5 outlines the methodology I chose, why and how I used phenomenography, my methods, sampling strategy and how I collected and analysed data. Ethical and access issues are discussed here too.

Chapter 6 draws on interviews with formerly imprisoned men to portray the lived experience of release. The emphasis is on variation, on different ways of experiencing and conceptualising release from prison. In Chapter 7 I explore post-release support perspectives, drawing on interviews with workers. In Chapter 8, I apply the assemblage–culture–liminality lens to the analysis of these findings.

This chapter goes beyond description to explain the implications for men leaving prison and the communities to which they return. I conclude, in Chapter 9, that ex-prisoners emerge diminished by the experience of imprisonment, acculturated to norms functional within prison society but dysfunctional in the wider community, and entangled in webs of meaning that constrain and compel their behaviour.

Notes

1. Throughout this book '(re)integration' is used to highlight the problem with the term 'reintegration', which assumes a degree of integration to be resumed or rekindled, when, for many prisoners, the experience of ever having been integrated into a law-abiding community is alien.
2. The Personal Support Program (PSP) was funded by the Australian government between July 2001 and June 2009 to assist unemployed people facing multiple personal barriers to employment and social participation. The PSP offered individual case management over 2 years, with the aim of linking participants into services and community supports to help overcome their problems.
3. The Australian Prisons Project was funded by Australian Research Council (ARC) Discovery Projects grant DP0877331, between 2008 and 2011.
4. A 'man' as this book focuses on the experience of men.
5. Baldry, 2007; AIHW, 2010; Halsey 2010.
6. See, for example, Douglas, 1966; Jewkes, 2005b; Baldry, 2009; Healy, 2010.
7. *The Argus* was a newspaper in Melbourne, Victoria, from 1848 to 1954.
8. See www.jss.org.au
9. The period 2010–11 saw a daily average of 28,711 people in prison in Australia, with $2.3 billion spent on prisons (SCRGSP 2012).
10. See Halsey, 2006, 2007; Arrigo & Milovanovic 2009.
11. See Rose, 1989, 2000; Wacquant, 2001, 2002; Patillo, Weiman & Western, 2004; Armstrong, 2004, 2006; Hannah-Moffat, 2005; Maurutto & Hannah-Moffat, 2006; Western, 2002, 2008a, 2008b; Harcourt, 2008, 2011.
12. See Jewkes, 2005b; Baldry et al., 2006; Baldry et al., 2008; Peacock, 2008; Baldry, 2009; Healy, 2010.
13. See Douglas, 1966; Maruna & LeBel 2003; Maruna 2005, 2006, 2011a, 2011b.

2 A catalogue of post-prison disadvantage

'Tom'

'Tom' is 22, nearly 23, a young Aboriginal man from coastal New South Wales, recently released from prison. This is the second time he's got out – when he was 18 he 'done two months for a car theft'. He's just got back from NSW – his grandmother passed away, and he went back for the funeral. He has lots of family there, though his mother lives in regional Victoria with his younger half-brothers. He tells me that all of his uncles, as well as one of his three sisters, have spent time in prison.

Since getting out, this time, he doesn't associate with many people in Melbourne anymore – ''cos all they do is get you into trouble'– so he just has 'a few friends' now and tries to 'be happy with them' and to stay out of trouble, avoiding 'the idiots [he] used to hang around with'. He admits his drug use is 'still a bit of a problem, smoking marijuana and drinking', and, though he doesn't drink as much, he admits that he smokes 'a lot'.

His 'few friends' appear to include the staff at the agency where I meet him. He has a Link Out worker – 'my worker' – and he says that, 'all the workers here have given me support . . . they all like me . . . and people are happy', suggesting that the experience of being liked and being around 'happy' people is important, and perhaps novel. He reveals that, 'this place helped me stay out of jail actually once . . . by being up there with me at court', and that, 'having my workers around me' will help him stay out this time, indicating the degree of trust and support he feels here. A sense of belonging, too, is discernible in his reference to the agency's rooming house as 'home'. He's been staying there for a while.

Tom was a Ward of the State for most of his life, first in New South Wales and then, 'they gave up after a while when I kept coming back to Victoria, so they just made me a Ward of the State of Victoria'. He claims to have lived by himself, affirming (when I seek to clarify) that he had a worker who helped look after him. I get the strong feeling that having a worker around is a normal part of life for Tom.

During his 14-and-a-half months in prison, Tom was assessed for and spent time in the intellectual disability unit. He has recently undergone a second assessment and is awaiting the results. His degree of disability is not immediately apparent during our interview, however. He is able to reflect on his experience, describing what it felt like to have his freedom back: 'when I got out it felt strange, real strange . . . my body took two weeks to adjust to the environment again, yeah, it feels heaps strange when you get out'.

When I ask about going back to prison, Tom laughs nervously: 'I really don't want to go back'. When I ask if he thinks he will go back, he pauses, then says quietly, 'Probably, yeah'. What will make it hard to stay out of trouble is 'hanging around the wrong people . . . getting into the same things again – it's not good, and that's why I try and stay away from the people I used to hang around'.

He has hopes and plans, though. He has started a course, which is 5 days a week, though he's missed 3 or 4 weeks owing to his grandmother's death and subsequent funeral. Once he's sorted things out in Melbourne, he wants to 'do the course and get a job and then go back to New South Wales', because he's 'sick of getting into trouble'. Notwithstanding his seeming casual confidence, it is unclear how feasible his hopes of getting a job and staying out of trouble really are.

Australian post-release literature is dominated by studies of specific programmes, jurisdictional issues and the particular disadvantages of ex-prisoners. This chapter examines this work thematically, identifying the most salient issues emerging from research on prisoners' release in Australia. Although this catalogue of disadvantage accords with global knowledge about the post-imprisonment experience, it reveals a lack of an overarching narrative, with research attention largely directed towards the 'needs, deeds and demographic characteristics' (McNeill et al., 2005: 9) of state-based populations. The post-release problem is seen in terms of multiple factors militating against ex-prisoners' social integration, but, in localised contexts, highlighting the fragmentation of Australia's post-release landscape. The chapter begins with an overview of this landscape, and then explores its emergent themes in detail. In the last section, I consider prison culture and institutionalisation as key aspects of post-release disadvantage that, perhaps surprisingly, remain implicit in much research.

Australia's post-release landscape

Despite Australia mirroring the global phenomenon of burgeoning prison populations, and the consequent increase in the numbers of prisoners released and returning to prison each year, several authors note the paucity of Australian research into post-release experiences and outcomes. Borzycki (2005), for instance, in her extensive report on crime prevention, urged a systematic account of the returning prisoner population and the service delivery apparatus. Among other issues, she highlighted the need to examine whether prisoners in Australia face similar post-release challenges to those identified abroad. Although it is assumed that the problems faced by prisoners released in Victoria, Australia, are 'essentially no different from those faced by prisoners in comparable jurisdictions' (Ross, 2003: 19) – in that they reflect lives marked by precariousness and disadvantage – there are limited data showing how these problems manifest in the lives of released prisoners, their families and communities, and how they relate to the cycle of reimprisonment.

From this lack of attention, two issues stand out. First, that, between release from prison and return to custody, ex-prisoners inhabit an invisible space; in liminal states such as post-release transition, 'the subject [is] structurally, if not physically, "invisible"' (Turner, 1967: 95). As a population, they are not reflected, reported or recorded in statistics. Apart from those released on parole, and the small proportion who participate in post-release programmes, their trajectories are not mapped. A fragmented picture of their pathways may be traced in the findings of broader investigations, such as the Drug Use Monitoring in Australia[1] (DUMA) programme. Second, services providing support for released prisoners typically do so in isolation, without a cohesive policy framework or coordination across organisations. Victoria's more integrated approach has been notable as an exception among Australian states and territories. Post-release services are often subsumed under generic welfare services, whose staff may lack training and resources specific to the needs of released prisoners, or skills to engage them. These factors make an accurate picture of the range, efficacy and outcomes of post-release service provision difficult to capture.

Borzycki (2005) provides the most comprehensive account of the state of transitional support for prisoners leaving custody in Australia. Canvassing 185 post-release programmes, Borzycki found varied interpretations and implementation of 'throughcare'. Over half of government correctional agencies characterised their post-release services as 'integrated throughcare' (Borzycki, 2005: 126), and yet fewer reported having both pre-release and post-release components, and hardly any began at reception into custody. Half the programmes commenced prior to release, and around three-quarters involved post-release support focused on the 'whole offender' and their social context. This research highlighted ambiguity and variation in the conceptualisation and delivery of post-release support and throughcare across Australia.

As Borzycki (2005) points out, the purpose of post-release services beyond simply reducing recidivism is 'offender reintegration' – 'active and productive community participation' (p. xv) – in which correctional authorities are not the only investors. Reintegrative efforts require the coordinated involvement of government and non-government agencies, businesses and the community. As planning post-prison adjustment ideally begins prior to a prisoner's release, however, it is the prison system that holds the largest stake in this process. This can pose challenges to existing ways of managing prisoners, as it demands a commitment to case management, continuous care and a partnerships approach antithetical to traditional correctional systems.

Lamenting the lack of local research and evaluation of correctional programming, Borzycki highlights the need for research that takes into account our unique history, geography and cultural mix and Australia's multifarious state-based justice and welfare systems. Specific research areas she identifies include: the issues facing Indigenous individuals and communities; whether the consequences are the same for prisoners returning to metropolitan, regional or rural and remote communities; how to service remote locations; whether post-release issues are the same in different jurisdictions; and how to best meet the needs of vulnerable groups of prisoners, including women, young people and those with mental health or addiction issues.

A broad understanding of the post-release experience of Australian prisoners first requires accurate and ongoing recording of prisoner and programme information, collated nationally. Belcher and Al Yaman (2007), highlighting the limited and state-based scope of research on post-prison mortality, suggested that national data be gathered using the National Coroners Information System (NCIS). As post-release death is most commonly caused by injury, drug overdose or suicide, and often in the weeks following release, this strategy would likely capture a significant proportion of such deaths. Such a national focus has been lacking in Australia and arguably characterises post-release research generally. Rather than taking a national view, research in Australia has tended to focus on particular programmes, individual states or jurisdictions, or populations such as sex offenders. The range and complexity of post-release factors and what is known about them in an Australian context is explored below.

A catalogue of disadvantage

This analysis is based on a thematic categorisation that broadly identifies the main issues emerging from the post-release literature, in Australia and internationally. Universally, stable accommodation and the risk of homelessness are identified as among the most critical factors influencing outcomes for released prisoners.

Housing and homelessness

The most cited Australian study of ex-prisoner housing and homelessness is by Baldry, McDonnell, Maplestone and Peeters (2003) on the impact of various accommodation options on released prisoners' social reintegration in Victoria and New South Wales (NSW). The researchers interviewed 339 prisoners just prior to their release, after which post-release interviews were sought at 3, 6 and 9 months. The study found several factors associated with reimprisonment, including homelessness and a lack of effective housing support, increased drug and alcohol abuse, being in debt and being Aboriginal or Torres Strait Islander. Most significantly, being highly transient was found to be predictive of return to prison. Of 226 respondents followed up post-release, half reported having to move at least twice in the 3 months between interviews, and, after 9 months, over half of these had returned to prison. Ross (2003) reported similarly high levels of post-prison transience.

Baldry and her colleagues (2003) linked the following factors to staying out of prison: moving only once, or not at all, in a 3-month period; living with a partner, parents or close family; being engaged in education, training or employment; and reporting a positive experience with a post-release support service. Significant differences emerged between Victoria and NSW, with higher numbers of Victorian releasees staying with parents and close family and being employed. Although all the participants came from, returned to and moved between socially disadvantaged areas, these were more highly concentrated geographically in NSW, with particularly strong clustering among Indigenous respondents. Although the authors point to Victoria's lower incarceration rate, housing costs and greater investment in post-release support to account for such differences, these factors alone lack explanatory power and are indeed suggestive of deeper cultural issues at play that remain unexplained.[2] More striking is the observation of 'a progressive stripping away of things that promote social attachment . . . each time a person is incarcerated' (Baldry et al. 2003: ii) – the 'serial depletion' (p. 26) of prisoners' resources whereby their disadvantage is compounded each time they are imprisoned and released. This phenomenon, consistently confirmed by international findings and long recognised as a causal factor in the cycle of reimprisonment, remains of critical importance in understanding post-release processes and ex-prisoner integration.

Although it is difficult to assemble a complete picture of the post-release experience, owing in part to the invisibility of its subjects, DUMA findings attest to this serial depletion of resources by highlighting factors associated with prison release, homelessness and rearrest. Between 1999 and 2006, 24,936 police detainees were surveyed: 1,689 reported being homeless at the time of their arrest – that is, living on the street, having no fixed address or living in crisis accommodation (AIC, 2008). Almost a third of this group had been imprisoned in the past 12 months, compared with a fifth of non-homeless detainees. A third reported having been admitted to a psychiatric hospital, twice as many as non-homeless detainees. Homeless detainees' dependence on drugs and alcohol exceeded that of the non-homeless, as did their reliance on welfare payments or illegal income sources; the latter double that of the non-homeless (AIC, 2008). These findings reveal something about the pathways of released prisoners, in that the proportion of released prisoners among homeless arrestees is significantly higher than among the non-homeless. The links between homelessness and mental illness, drug and alcohol dependence, poverty and offending illuminate the processes and events that stem from the difficulties released prisoners face in securing stable accommodation. These processes are mutually reinforcing (Gowan, 2002). The incarceration–reincarceration cycle is also characterised by elements that are harder to quantify.

Hinton (2004), for instance, gives voice to the 'hardening' experience of being imprisoned and its impact on ex-prisoners' capacity to trust and to seek/accept help. Hinton highlights the difficulty estimating the extent of post-release homelessness, due in large part to the way the need is assessed. Correctional authorities' data only account for prisoners who identify as homeless and/or seek housing support while in prison. Although paroled prisoners are required to provide an identified address, there is no information routinely collected about post-release accommodation for the majority of prisoners released straight into the community. Similarly, the number of people for whom housing arrangements break down following their release is unquantified. Hinton (2004) concludes that the numbers of prisoners facing post-release housing difficulties is likely to be much greater than those officially recorded. Her study reports that nearly half of the thirty-eight prisoners interviewed about their pre-/post-prison housing needs were living in temporary accommodation, with six identifying as homeless, which accords with officially recorded figures. She brings to light, however, a degree of non-reporting evidenced by the fact that, of twelve people with access to post-release housing who stated they did not face any post-release housing challenges, one was homeless, and three were in short-term accommodation prior to their imprisonment. This seems to underscore ex-prisoners' unwillingness to trust and/or seek assistance.

Hinton (2004) highlights the exacerbation of such difficulties for prisoners serving short sentences. Lack of knowledge surrounding their release dates makes exit planning problematic and increases the likelihood of homelessness upon release. This group has the highest rates of reconviction and reimprisonment, a cycle constantly militating against any form of housing security. Baldry et al. (2003) emphasise this problem for prisoners on remand, of whom half may routinely be released directly from court, without advance warning, rendering their post-release housing situation particularly precarious, as housing support agencies require a release date. These issues are intensified for Indigenous prisoners, for whom reimprisonment, release without conviction following remand, and shorter sentences are more likely (Willis, 2008). An additional structural impediment is that prisoners are not deemed 'homeless' while they are incarcerated, and are, therefore, ineligible to apply for public housing until they are released (Baldry et al., 2003). Many prisoners face debts upon release for rent defaults incurred while locked up (Baldry et al., 2002; Keyzer & Cole, 2009). Ross (2003) notes a 2-year wait for public housing for releasees, even those deemed high priority.

Such circumstances exemplify the service limbo in which many released prisoners find themselves when generic service systems lack coordination and resources to meet their needs. Perhaps, as Ross (2003) observes, the problem is not so much a lack of services as the many barriers faced by ex-prisoners in their access to services. In Victoria, to address this situation, a partnership between the Office of the Correctional Services Commissioner, the Office of Housing and registered housing agencies resulted in the Transitional Housing Management–Corrections Housing Pathways Initiative (THM–CHPI), a collaborative approach to reducing homelessness and recidivism among people released from prison. The THM–CHPI was introduced as a 2-year pilot in three prisons and was subsequently established as an ongoing programme providing supported housing placements for exiting prisoners, with housing information and referral now available in all Victorian prisons.

Bartholomew et al. (2004) evaluated the THM–CHPI and found that the initiative was successful in targeting a sector of the prison population at high risk of post-release homelessness. Almost half the sample gained stable post-release housing, and nearly a third were referred to short-term or crisis accommodation. Noteworthy was a decrease in the pre-prison to post-release rate of participants' homelessness. Comparing outcomes with findings from the same Victorian prisons (Baldry et al., 2003), Bartholomew et al. (2004) found the THM–CHPI participants in stable accommodation were less likely to reoffend and were significantly less likely to be reimprisoned. Perhaps homelessness is indeed criminogenic, crime as a 'survival strategy' (Snow, 1989, in McCarthy & Hagan, 1991: 408) amid poverty and isolation. As Baldry et al. (2002: 1) note, prison provides 'a form of secure, affordable housing for many prisoners' for whom stable accommodation remains out of reach. Little wonder that, for many, life is easier inside than out.

Building on the findings of Baldry et al. (2003) and Hinton (2004), Willis (2004) explored the issue of post-release housing insecurity and homelessness, highlighting barriers to housing faced by prisoners returning to the community, and the link between incarceration, increasing homelessness and reincarceration. As well as agency workers, Willis interviewed ex-prisoners to give voice to their experience in an Australian context. Most linked their offending with difficulty securing and maintaining accommodation. Supporting Hinton's (2004) findings, Willis noted 'worse post-release outcomes' (p. 179) for prisoners on short sentences, remand or released without supervision. Short-term imprisonment can cause housing disruption, property loss and relationship breakdown and can also preclude support-programme eligibility, thus increasing short-termers' post-release vulnerability. Willis (2004) emphasised the importance of secure, stable accommodation for ex-prisoners' 'successful' return to the community, and the need for specialised post-release support. Disadvantage associated with ex-prisoners' ill health, education/literacy, unemployment, poverty and aboriginality was linked to housing insecurity.

Unemployment, education and poverty

Unemployment, economic disadvantage and financial insecurity underpin the limited range of housing options available to ex-prisoners: as international findings attest,[3] released prisoners typically face the problem of a lack of income. High rates of poverty and unemployment characterise many communities to which ex-prisoners return (Victorian Ombudsman, 2015). In Australia, prisoners are released with their 'set aside' money – a percentage of their weekly income accumulated throughout their sentence – which can add up to a substantial amount over several years, but is more often a few hundred dollars at most. For example, if 20 per cent of weekly earnings – at an average of $35 a week – are set aside, after 6 years, a prisoner may receive $2,184 upon release. After 6 months, however, he would have $184. Although the 'set aside' system is designed to provide for immediate post-release needs, such as clothing and toiletries, it is manifestly insufficient to enable access to secure accommodation. Hartley and Baraka (2007) emphasise the inadequacy of Centrelink's crisis payment,[4] and, if a prisoner is not already registered, the problem of acquiring proof of identification can delay access to payments.[5]

Employment and job stability can curb offending (Sampson & Laub, 1993; Makkai & Payne, 2003), or at least prolong crime-free periods (Tripodi, Kim & Bender, 2010). Yet prison populations are characterised by high levels of pre-prison unemployment: two-thirds of male prisoners in Victoria were unemployed prior to imprisonment (Corrections Victoria, 2011). Prisoners can acquire qualifications and experience through work and education programmes in prison, but the prison environment is conducive to neither real-life workplace skills nor a strong work ethic. Prison time and a criminal record are impediments to post-release employment, not least because employment services lack specialist knowledge or understanding of post-release issues. Anecdotally, despite the transferability of prison-gained skills, ex-prisoners commonly report having 'done nothing' that could be included on a résumé, leaving gaps that generalist employment consultants are at a loss to fill.

Although the negative impact of imprisonment on employability and economic mobility has been examined in the US (Western, 2008b; Pew, 2010), such research is lacking in Australia, apart from some work on criminal records.[6] Nevertheless, local data confirm international findings[7] of prisoners' severe educational disadvantage, manifest in low levels of pre-prison employment. Just a quarter of prison entrants hold a non-school qualification, most commonly a trade certificate (AIHW, 2010). Only 6 per cent of male prisoners in Victoria have completed secondary, trade or tertiary education at the time of their imprisonment (Corrections Victoria, 2011). The National Prisoner Health Census (2009) showed prison entrants were six times more likely than the general population to have Year 9 as their highest educational level, with significantly lower educational attainment among Indigenous prisoners (AIHW, 2010), echoing racialised disparities in the US (Western, 2002, 2008a; Pew, 2010) and New Zealand (Nadesu, 2009). Prisoners' level of education significantly affects their capacity to resolve legal issues and extract themselves from the web of debts, charges and outstanding warrants in which many become entangled.

Legal problems

Grunseit, Forell and McCarron (2008) highlight the range of legal problems besetting prisoners and ex-prisoners, which typically include debts, unpaid fines and unresolved family law matters. Other problems arise out of being suddenly removed from ordinary life: the rupturing effects of imprisonment on prisoners' housing, child custody and parenting arrangements, employment and business, for instance. Parole conditions and discrimination may thwart prisoners' housing or employment options post-release. Grunseit et al. (2008) also highlight the impact of charges and warrants incurred pre-custody or during imprisonment. Their study delves into an area subject to little previous research and, importantly, illustrates the extent to which prisoners' access to justice is impeded. Despite the opportunities for prisoners to obtain legal advice, information and assistance, various factors relating to the prison environment, including prison culture and prisoners' personal capacity, constrain these opportunities.

These findings are relevant here as prisoners' capacity to access justice and resolve legal issues directly impinges on their post-release experience and likelihood of return to prison. Grunseit et al. (2008) suggest that, together with limited financial resources and inadequate documentation, prisoners' lack of awareness of the extent of their legal problems exacerbates the reimprisonment risk.

Incarceration itself serves to reduce prisoners' confidence and ability to effectively resolve legal issues in the community. Men's 'bravado or disinterest' may mask illiteracy, unwillingness to seek legal help, distrust or anxiety about the law and legal process (Grunseit et al. 2008: 4). These authors identify prison culture as constraining prisoners' access to justice: not reporting prison assaults, for instance, owing to the stigma of 'lagging'. The depletion of skills and resources, through repeat incarceration, 'may cumulatively erode inmates' capacity to address their legal needs on their own behalf even when released' (Grunseit et al. 2008: 6). The combination of these issues manifests as marginalisation from formal legal processes.

Grunseit et al. (2008) identify the range of legal issues to be negotiated post-release, including: parole compliance; social security, housing and other debt; and custody of children. They characterise the typical environment released prisoners are likely to find themselves in and the barriers men face. One common factor, implicit in the findings of ex-prisoners' legal problems, is the importance of social support: the significance of personal relationships and connection to children and family.

Fatherhood and family

Several Australian studies have focused on the particular post-release needs of women prisoners in relation to their children and broader care-giving or familial roles.[8] International research into the challenges facing imprisoned parents is largely focused on mothers (Tudball, 2000; Tomkin, 2009). Less is written about the experience of men and the fracturing of relationships with family and children through their imprisonment, notwithstanding that many imprisoned 'fathers . . . were the primary carers of children prior to incarceration' (Standing Committee on Social Issues, 1997: 145).

Bartholomew et al. (2004: 41) found that 42 per cent of male THM–CHPI participants expected to have access to their children post-release, compared with 58 per cent of females. The proportion of male parent caregivers is significant. Between 2005 and 2009, in Victoria, the proportion of single or never-married male prisoners increased slightly; one in four were partnered at their reception into prison, and around 10 per cent were separated or divorced (Corrections Victoria, 2009). Perhaps such figures diminish the significance of men's fathering and family relationships as a research priority. Woodward (2003: 5) noted that, on any given day, there were 11,000 children in NSW with a parent in prison. She highlighted that the overwhelming majority of female prisoners are mothers, but gave little indication of the extent of fatherhood among male prisoners in Australia. In 2011, however, NSW Corrective Services reported that half of male prisoners had their own children, with more than a third living with them prior to incarceration (in Brown and O'Sullivan, 2013: 14).

Tudball et al. (2000) estimated that 3,000 Victorian children[9] had a primary carer in prison. Quilty (2005) suggested that nearly one in twenty Australian children and one in five Indigenous children have had a parent imprisoned (in Hannon, 2006: 15).

Yet data about male prisoners' parenting is not routinely collected (Healy, Foley & Walsh, 2000). This could be owing in part to an assumption that the care of children is disrupted less by the removal of the father than the mother, as the children of male prisoners are more likely to be cared for by the non-imprisoned parent than children of female inmates (Howard, 2000; Cunningham, 2001; Hannon, 2006).[10] The impact of parental incarceration may be shaped by the nature of the pre-existing relationship between parent and child (Rosenberg, 2009), implying that, the closer the bond, the greater the trauma of separation caused by imprisonment (Howard, 2000). Nevertheless, children remain hidden, 'secondary victims' of parental incarceration (Howard, 2000: 2).

As primary caregivers, fathers are largely ignored in prison policy (Woodward, 2003). Indeed, Victoria is the only Australian state 'whose [correctional] policy does not exclude fathers from applying to have their child(ren) with them: the policy refers throughout to "parents" and children, rather than "mothers" and children as . . . in other states' (Standing Committee on Social Issues, 1997: 25). Provision is made for children to live with their mothers in prison; in theory, 'children may reside with their fathers in prison if it is in their best interests to do so', but, in reality, this is unlikely to occur (Standing Committee on Social Issues, 1997: 25). Although some prisons allow children to live with their fathers – in Denmark and Bolivia, for example (Rosenberg, 2009; Tomkin, 2009) – generally fathers must seek alternative means to maintain contact with their children. Relationship-building programmes in prison acknowledge the impact of family fracturing on men's post-prison reintegration, and the importance of 'repairing or maintaining relationships with their children' among older prisoners in particular (Vinson & Tehan, 2001: 65).

Permitting prisoners to have contact with their children is frequently construed as a privilege in the prison system, when, in fact, as Woodward (2003: 15) argues, 'it is the child's right to maintain contact and preserve their relationship with a parent'. The problem of relationships between men and their children disrupted and damaged by the experience of imprisonment remains largely invisible in Australia. International knowledge, such as the generative potential of fatherhood (Walker, 2010), is just beginning to accumulate – for instance, that men closely connected to their children show better employment and substance abuse outcomes (Visher, Debus-Sherrill & Yahner, 2008; La Vigne, Shollenberger & Debus, 2009).

It is important to understand paternal imprisonment in terms of harm to children and the role of family in sustaining men's reintegration.[11] Rosenberg (2009) documents mothers' 'gatekeeping' (p. 7) affecting children's contact with their imprisoned fathers, creating power imbalance and excluding and restricting paternal involvement. She identifies the economic disadvantage experienced by imprisoned fathers and their children, the health and behavioural impacts on children, and fathers' fear of modelling criminal behaviour, particularly to sons. She highlights the ambiguity of paternal identity and men's feelings of helplessness in knowing how to be a father while in prison; one response can be withdrawal or abandonment of this role/identity. Another risk arises in men's idealisation of

their paternal role and relationships while imprisoned, which can lead to alienation from and conflict with children post-release. Rosenberg (2009) illuminates
issues of powerlessness and prisonisation as having significant effects on men's
capacity to father from behind bars, 'hangover identities' (p. 22) which inevitably
impinge on their post-release fathering ability and connection to their children.
The health and behavioural impacts on fathers, as well as their children, are under-
researched. Ex-prisoners' mental and physical health is mainly conceived in terms
of post-release morbidity and mortality, as examined below.

Prisoner health and post-release morbidity

Until recently, national knowledge of prisoner health in Australia has been scant.
An AIHW (2010) report fills this gap, presenting a detailed national picture of
the health of prisoners upon entry and their use of health services in prison,
from which much can be inferred about post-release health issues. As well as
significantly higher rates of hepatitis B and C than in the general population,
the AIHW report attests to higher rates of smoking, alcohol and illicit drug use
among prison entrants. In addition, nearly half of prisoners reported taking prescribed medication. Mental health issues, more prevalent among non-Indigenous
prisoners, affected two-fifths of the sample. Hepatitis B, hepatitis C, and alcohol
abuse were more common among Indigenous prison entrants. One in four prison
entrants reported a chronic health condition, including asthma, arthritis, diabetes
and cancer (AIHW, 2010).

Prior to the AIHW report, prisoner health data were predominantly state-based.
Modelled on the NSW Inmate Health Survey (1996 and 2001), Deloitte Consulting
(2003) conducted the first general health survey of prisoners in Victoria. This
report indicated prisoners' significantly higher levels of: hepatitis A, B and C;
asthma; depression; insomnia; dental problems and gum disease; sexually transmitted diseases; self-inflicted harm and injury; suicidal ideation and attempts;
history of emotional, physical and sexual abuse; and hospitalisation. Indig et al.
(2010) found multiple health problems among NSW prisoners, with a quarter of
men reporting four or more conditions. The most prevalent were poor eyesight,
asthma and back problems, at much higher rates than among other Australians.
Reported psychological assessment or treatment increased steadily between 1996
and 2009; the proportion of women remains higher than men, but this gender gap
has shrunk. The most common mental issues reported were depression, anxiety
and drug or alcohol dependence.

Hepatitis C has a national prevalence of less than 1 per cent of the Australian
population; it is estimated to affect nearly half the prisoner population (Deloitte
Consulting, 2003; AIHW, 2010). Significant differences in infection rates of
Aboriginal and non-aboriginal prisoners for A and B types, yet virtually no difference
for hepatitis C, suggest its higher rate of transmission within the prison population (Deloitte Consulting, 2003). The alarming rate of prisoners' hepatitis C
infection has generated a stream of research focused on blood-borne virus
transmission through sharing injecting equipment and tattooing (AIHW, 2010).

One Australian study found injecting drug users (IDUs) in prison to be twenty-four times more likely to contract hepatitis C than non-IDUs (Vescio et al., 2008, in AIHW, 2010: 35). Promisingly, Indig et al. (2010) report a substantial decline from 2001 to 2009 in the rate of injecting drug use and hepatitis C seropositivity among NSW prisoners.[12]

Hellard, Hocking and Crofts (2004) surveyed 630 Victorian prisoners: more than half tested positive for hepatitis C; two-thirds of prisoners reported having injected drugs before; and more than half reported injecting in prison. Tattooing in prison is an additional risk factor in hepatitis C transmission, as prison tattooists, mostly untrained, use home-made, non-sterile equipment. Hellard, Aitken and Hocking (2007) report frequent sharing of needles and ink in Victoria's prisons; tattooed prisoners testing positive for hepatitis C were more likely to have been tattooed in prison than those without the virus. Hepatitis C infection has significant post-release health implications for ex-prisoners, particularly those with reduced access to medical care in the community (Kariminia, Butler & Levy, 2007b).

In terms of post-release morbidity, the risks for Indigenous people are significantly higher than for non-aboriginal people, reflecting higher rates of criminal justice involvement and general ill-health associated with social disadvantage.[13] In Western Australia (WA), rates of hospitalisation for mental disorders, injury and poisoning are twice as high among Aboriginal male ex-prisoners and three times as high among Aboriginal female ex-prisoners than in the broader Indigenous population (Hobbs et al., 2006), signifying the heightened post-release vulnerability for Aboriginal releasees returning to their communities. The impact of higher rates of disease – including diabetes (Gilles et al. 2008) – is exacerbated by Indigenous releasees' poorer access to post-release medical treatment. Kariminia et al. (2007b) studied the comparative health of prisoners in NSW and found increased use of and access to medical services among Aboriginal men and women while in prison, compared with outside. This included drug and alcohol treatment, as dependence on drugs, including alcohol, is 'the single largest factor affecting the lives of offenders' (Anderson, in VAADA, 2003: 3).

Drug use and addiction

Australian prison/post-prison populations are characterised by high rates of drug use.[14] A Queensland study found that more than half of released prisoners resumed illicit drug use within a month of their release, with nearly a third injecting drugs; by 4 months, nearly half were engaged in harmful drinking; and, by 6 months, a fifth had been reimprisoned (Kinner, 2006a, 2006b). The risk of reincarceration was highest for men, IDUs and those who indicated in prison that they expected to use drugs post-release (Kinner, 2008). The 2009 NSW Inmate Health Survey found nearly two-thirds of male prisoners had engaged in hazardous, harmful or dependent alcohol consumption in the year preceding their incarceration (Indig et al. 2010). These findings show the extent to which problem drinking is associated more with men than women. Prisoners' use of drugs, predictably, is higher than among the general community (Indig et al. 2010). Makkai and Payne (2003) highlight the extent of cannabis, amphetamine, heroin and cocaine use among prisoners: nearly two-thirds report regular drug use in the 6 months prior to incarceration; a third of prisoners identify as poly-drug users.

Drug users are vulnerable, not only to physical and psychological effects, but also to stigmatisation. Common misconceptions about drug use give rise to widespread discrimination against drug users, further compounded by the stigma of imprisonment. An annual Australia-wide survey of IDUs reports a history of imprisonment for typically half of this group (Kinner, 2006a). A similar proportion of police detainees report pre-arrest drug use, and urinalysis revealed up to 60 per cent of those incarcerated in the last 12 months had used opiates, amphetamines or cocaine (Makkai & McGregor, 2003; Kinner, 2006a). Prison is acknowledged as a high-risk environment – for blood-borne virus transmission, for example – yet, as Kelsall (2009) argues, concern for drug-dependent prisoners' human rights does not register on the social barometer. Despite the known level of intravenous drug use among prison entrants, and the recommendations for needle exchange and opioid substitution programmes to combat the spread of hepatitis B and C,[15] prisons do not provide needle exchange. Methadone and buprenorphine are available to prisoners in Victoria; however, clean syringes are not. In light of the high risk of prisoners contracting hepatitis C virus through tattooing in prison, trials of safe, legal tattooing are recommended (Hellard et al. 2007).

Stoové et al. (2010) explore the post-release experiences of prisoners with a history of IDU, in relation to health services and risk behaviours. Two-thirds of participants had been imprisoned at least three times, a third more than five times. Stoové et al. report a low rate of engagement with mental health services. Nearly half participants' income was spent on substances – mainly heroin, benzodiazepines, alcohol and methadone – suggesting a degree of self-medication. The research describes the inadequacy of housing support and availability. 'Unsuitable accommodation' was found to be 'a major barrier to avoiding ongoing [drug use] and criminal behaviour', as one participant explains, 'boarding houses are often worse than jail . . . filled with drunks and drug addicts . . . you set yourself up for failure straight away' (in Stoové et al., 2010: 3). The study finds that continued IDU in prison and after release is 'the norm', identifying 'social and structural drivers of post-release substance use' (p. 6), which link to Halsey's (2007) idea of 'risky systems'. Though conceding that opioid substitution therapies (OST) can help reduce 'problematic IDU' (Stoové et al., 2010: 6), the high rate of post-release overdose underscores the importance of understanding the many factors impinging upon the experience of release from prison and the risks of reimprisonment.

Despite the recognition that drug abuse and dependency characterise prison and ex-prisoner populations, the literature is missing any theorisation of the causes and effects of this phenomenon. Neurophysiological tools and concepts applied in the broader addiction literature[16] are absent in conceptualisations of prisoners' experience. For example, the concept of 'allostasis'[17] describes the physiology of adaptation to change in terms of humans' reacting to and anticipating psychosocial challenges and adverse environments. Repeated allostatic cycles can reduce the efficiency of the body's responses and result in 'chronic overactivity of regulatory systems [which] render one vulnerable' to disease (Schulkin, 2011: 112). Such conceptualisation can explain men's maladjustment and morbidity and could enable deeper understanding of post-release problems and cycles of offending. Yet no such links are made in the post-release literature. Instead, studies are more focused on particular post-prison factors, not least of which is the risk of death following release.

Post-release mortality

Recently released prisoners are at far greater risk of fatal (and non-fatal) drug overdose than others in the community. Cook and Davies (2000), in their study of the deaths of ninety-three women released from prison in Victoria, found the majority were drug-related, with around a quarter resulting from violence, car accidents and suicide. Biles, Harding and Walker (1999) confirmed a higher death rate among Victorians serving community corrections orders than those in custody, with parole orders linked to the highest death rate. In 2008–09, eighty-nine people died while under Community Corrections Services (CCS) jurisdiction in Victoria, nineteen of whom were on parole, and nearly half of these deaths were drug-related or suicide (Department of Justice, 2009).

The majority of prisoners are released straight to the community, however, and, recognising the lack of empirical knowledge about this group's risk of post-release mortality, Graham (2003) investigated the unnatural deaths of 820 Victorian prisoners released between 1990 and 2000. Linking prisoner information with coronial data, she found the rate of death among ex-prisoners – due largely to homicide, suicide and accident – was around ten times that of the general Victorian population. Approximately 60 per cent of ex-prisoner deaths were caused by drug toxicity, with male ex-prisoners around seven times more likely to die unnaturally than other Victorian men (Graham, 2003). Kariminia et al. (2007a) report similar findings in NSW. Among heroin users in particular, McGregor et al. (2002) identify recent release from prison as a mortality risk factor.

Stewart et al. (2004) found that, although the mortality risk was higher for all released prisoners in WA, Aboriginal prisoners were most at risk. Hobbs et al. (2006), echoing Graham's (2003) results, found injury, poisoning or the effects of drug or alcohol abuse caused two-thirds of ex-prisoner deaths in WA, with the risk of dying being four times higher in the 6 months post-release than after 1 year (Hobbs et al. 2006). Kariminia et al. (2007a) examined the risk and cause of death of more than 85,000 adults who had experienced full-time custody in NSW between 1987 and 2002. Of 5,137 recorded deaths, 94 per cent occurred following release from prison, mainly owing to accidents or drug overdose, most commonly heroin. For prisoners with multiple incarcerations, the risk of dying increases with each subsequent release (Hobbs et al., 2006; Kariminia et al., 2007a), suggesting that the cyclic experience of incarceration, release and reincarceration has a compounding effect on mortality risk factors such as drug abuse: evidence of the serial erosion of prisoners' resources and capacity to manage life outside prison.

The risk of an ex-prisoner dying unnaturally is highest in the first week, month and year following their release, with one in four post-release deaths occurring within 1 month (Graham, 2003). Kariminia et al. (2007c) examined whether, in Australia, the first few weeks after release are associated with an increased risk, as studies have shown in the US, UK and Scotland.[18] Among NSW ex-prisoners, 86 per cent of suicides and 97 per cent of overdose deaths occurred post-release (Kariminia et al., 2007c). Men's suicide rate, both in prison and post-prison, was higher than women's, and the male rate of suicide within 2 weeks of release was nearly four times higher than after 6 months. Men's drug-related mortality was nine times higher after 2 weeks than at 6 months after release. This finding supports international evidence of the increased risk of post-release mortality in the weeks immediately following release from prison.

A meta-analysis of post-release mortality studies in Europe, the US and Australia (Merrall et al., 2010) focused on drug overdose and showed that increased risk of drug-related death in the first 2 weeks remains high until at least the fourth week post-release. Merrall et al. (2010) found notable differences between countries, with one US and two Australian studies[19] showing markedly lower mortality risk in the 2-week post-release period than the other US and two UK studies. In addition, Kariminia et al. (2007c) found no Aboriginal suicides recorded in the 2-week post-release period. Notwithstanding this variation, the risk is highest within 2 weeks and remains elevated until 4 weeks, compared with the subsequent 8 weeks following release from prison (Merrall et al., 2010). Possible explanations include reduced tolerance through less frequent use while imprisoned, together with prisoners' propensity for 'celebration' upon release (Shewan et al., 2000; Merrall et al., 2010). Merrall et al. (2010) emphasise the contingency of both factors on regional and cultural factors, such as drug-use behaviours and patterns, and the availability and use of drugs and drug treatment in prisons. NSW prisons introduced methadone maintenance from the 1980s, for example, compared with 2003 in Scotland. The increased availability and purity of heroin in Australia in the late 1990s, and the subsequent 'heroin drought' at the end of 2000, inevitably complicate drug-related mortality figures.[20]

In commenting on the Merrall et al. study, Kinner (2010) makes some important observations: that, as 41 per cent of post-release deaths are not drug-related, research needs to focus on additional causes and related factors, such as the impact of mental illness on suicide risk; also that the focus of research ought not to be limited to the immediate post-release period, when studies[21] have shown the increased mortality risk may persist for years owing to chronic health conditions such as liver and cardio-vascular disease, or cancer. Notwithstanding the urgent need for strategies to reduce drug-related deaths among ex-prisoners, Kinner (2010) advocates for broad-based transitional programmes, as well as longitudinal qualitative research to help build an evidence base that may help reduce morbidity and mortality among 'this profoundly disadvantaged, at-risk group'

(Kinner, 2010: 1556). Andrews and Kinner (2012) similarly emphasise the need to analyse drug-related death in the broader context of post-prison experience, to inform such intervention.

Mental disorders and cognitive impairment

Post-release drug death and suicide are linked to ex-prisoners' diminished capacity to manage life outside prison, which is exacerbated by mental illness and/or cognitive impairment. The prevalence of mental health disorders in Australian prison populations is well-established.[22] Prisoners' mental health problems manifest 'before, during and after their incarceration' (Kinner, 2006a: 10) and are often associated with drug and/or alcohol abuse (Stoové et al., 2010), though substance abuse alone does not account for the extent of mental disorder among inmates. The incidence of major mental illness, including depression and schizophrenia, is three to five times more prevalent among prison populations than the wider community, with an even higher rate among unsentenced prisoners (Ogloff et al., 2007).

Butler and Allnutt's (2003) study of NSW prisoners found substantially higher prevalence of psychiatric disorders among inmates (74 per cent) than in the general community (22 per cent). Almost half of reception prisoners and more than one-third of sentenced inmates had suffered psychosis, affective or anxiety disorders in the previous 12 months, and two-thirds of reception prisoners had a substance use disorder. Anxiety disorders, particularly post-traumatic stress disorder (PTSD), were most commonly reported. Prisoners with a psychiatric diagnosis also manifest higher degrees of disability. Butler and Alnutt (2003) found nearly half of male prison entrants were found to have lost consciousness as a result of a blow to the head, indicative of possible traumatic brain injury (TBI). In prison, high rates of TBI and mental illness and the pressure of prison life combine to increase the likelihood of further injury and impairment (Belcher & Al Yaman, 2007).

Holland et al. (2007) examined the characteristics of male prisoners with an intellectual disability (ID), released from prison in Victoria between 2003 and 2006, compared with a sample of prisoners without ID released in the same period. Holland et al. found that, although the prevalence of intellectual disability in Australian prison populations was only marginally higher than in the general population, it was significantly higher among Indigenous prisoners. Overall, prisoners with ID had experienced youth detention three times more than non-ID inmates and had a higher number of community corrections orders and previous terms of imprisonment, both sentenced and remand, and they spent a longer time on remand. ID prisoners were more likely to have parole denied or delayed, most commonly owing to a lack of suitable accommodation. A further disparity emerged in the security classification of prisoners, with considerably more ID prisoners classified as medium security and notably fewer classified as minimum security at release. Incidents of self-harm and attempted suicide were higher among the ID cohort. The most marked differences between the ID and non-ID prisoners were significantly higher literacy needs and homelessness. Although Holland et al. (2007) note the general consistency of their results with those of earlier Australian studies,[23] some inconsistent findings emerged: Victoria did not manifest the extent of over-representation of people with ID in prison populations that others have observed. Nevertheless, Holland et al. (2007) lamented the lack of pre-release preparation via minimum security pathways and, in light of the higher recidivism rates for ID prisoners, highlighted the need for coordinated pre-/post-release service provision, most clearly in relation to housing.

Baldry (2009) highlights that comorbidity – cognitive disabilities (CD)[24] with mental illness, or a dual diagnosis of CD together with alcohol or other drug dependency – heightens the risk of criminalisation and imprisonment. People with mental health disorders (MHD) and CD are commonly imprisoned for lower-level offences – theft, traffic and vehicle regulatory offences, breaching of orders and acts intended to cause injury – and charges of public order and alcohol-related offences are common for people with CD (Dowse, Baldry & Snoyman, 2009). Their experience is marked by high numbers of convictions and yet short sentences, which means they 'cycle in and out of prison quickly' (Baldry et al. 2008: 38; Baldry, 2009: 21). Indigenous prisoners with an intellectual disability are over-represented to an even greater degree than non-ID Aboriginal prisoners, whose already significant over-representation is firmly established.

Among all prisoner populations, owing to the limitations of custodial databases, the extent of intellectual disability is likely to be underestimated. Although prisoners with an identified ID are flagged on offender management systems, many jurisdictions rely on other agencies for the identification, and, as data on borderline intellectual impairments are not recorded, estimates are simply that (Belcher & Al Yaman, 2007). Stigmatisation by service systems, in and outside prison, further contributes to the social and political invisibility of people with mental disorders and/or cognitive impairment (Baldry et al. 2008). To truly grasp the experience of 'this chronically marginalised and unwell group' (Kinner, 2010: 1), Wacquant's (2002) urging for a revival of prison ethnography appears apposite.

Prison acculturation

This catalogue of post-prison problems underscores the effects of imprisonment on men's existing disadvantage and the serial depletion of resources that accompanies cyclic imprisonment. One contributing factor is prison culture, and yet surprisingly few post-release researchers explicitly acknowledge its effects. This section explores the role of prison culture and penal institutionalisation in shaping men's post-release experience.

Prison culture

Prison culture has been depicted and analysed exhaustively from within and outside the walls of the hyper-regulated prison environment.[25] Contemporary portrayals mirror early accounts of prison codes, whereby 'prisoners lift weights compulsively, adopt the meanest stare they can muster, and keep their fears and their pain carefully hidden beneath a well-rehearsed tough-guy posture' (Sabo, Kupers & London, 2001: 10–11). Clemmer (1940) used the lens of social assimilation (borrowed from the immigrant experience) to explore how the prison shaped the attitudes and behaviour of prisoners, via experiences that made them part of the prison community. Conceding that acculturation occurs by degrees, Clemmer argued that every prisoner undergoes, to some extent, what he called 'prisonisation', if only in terms of assuming the status of prisoner and learning to navigate the day-to-day patterns of prison life. He identified the factors most significant in hastening or slowing prisonisation, including an inmate's pre-prison personality, the nature and extent of relationships, the associations imposed by in-prison proximity, and the degree of internal acceptance of prison codes and mores.

Clemmer theorised that the longer the sentence, the higher the likelihood of 'prisonisation'. Many years in prison, even for men who managed to insulate themselves from its worst effects, would make 'a happy adjustment in any community . . . next to impossible' (1940: 300). Short-termers would have fewer difficulties. Although Clemmer failed to address directly the post-release impact of prisonisation, in terms of the length of its shadow or its bearing on reoffending, he implies that the experience of imprisonment significantly affects a prisoner's thinking and social behaviour. Effective reintegration depends upon how 'prisonised' the inmate becomes, as Haney (2003) suggests in his account of the psychological effects of imprisonment and the implications for the released prisoner. Although the prisonisation thesis tends to individualise its effects on prisoners, the significance in terms of post-release integration is clear. It is in society, after all, that released prisoners need to function to avoid reimprisonment.

Whereas Clemmer took for granted the existence of prison culture, other theorists sought to address its origins. Sykes (1958)[26] described the 'pains of imprisonment' as chiefly comprising five 'deprivations' to which inmates must respond/adapt. These include being deprived of liberty and social acceptance, goods and services or material possessions, heterosexual relationships, personal autonomy and personal security. Sykes noted the loss of liberty was exemplified in the ways the restriction and monitoring of contact with family and friends 'frustrated' prisoners' capacity to maintain social bonds. In terms of the loss of autonomy or self-determination, he identified as particularly 'galling', from an inmate perspective, 'the triviality of much of the officials' control', which aroused not only irritation and cynicism but 'intense hostility' (p. 73). Sykes (1958) posited that a man's self-concept was tied to his sense of masculinity, which, in an all-male prison environment, was under constant challenge. A prisoner's manhood, self-concept and physical well-being hinged on his reaction and ability to cope with this pervasive sense of insecurity.

The most realistic way prisoners might survive the pains of imprisonment, Sykes reasoned, was through 'adaptive endurance', or adopting the patterned social interaction characterising the 'society of captives', which swung between 'collectivistic' and 'individualistic' extremes (1958: 82–3). A 'collectivist orientation' (p. 83) lessened the pains of imprisonment through heightened inmate solidarity and stronger observance of the inmate code, by which staunchness and honour were established among other prisoners. An 'individualistic orientation' described verbal rather than actual adherence to the code, the violation of which took various forms. These were reflected in the ascription of 'argot roles' representing behaviours performed and labelled by prisoners, which Sykes used as 'a map of the inmate social system' (1958: 84).

Whereas Sykes saw inmate culture and its processes of meaning-making as originating within the prison walls, Irwin and Cressey (1962) perceived its characteristics as imported from outside the prison. According to this 'importation model', the prison comprised multiple competing normative systems arising in and regulating external subcultures. To illustrate their theory, Irwin and Cressey (1962: 146–8) identified two conflicting inmate subcultures – 'thief' and 'convict' – and a third group, 'oriented to "legitimate" subcultures', who rejects both. The thief subculture consisted of men considered trustworthy and dependable, reflecting the familiar maxim 'honour amongst thieves' underpinning the subculture outside prison. Their self-image aligned with a criminal life but not necessarily a prison life; they served their time with a minimum of conflict. The convict subculture emerged in response to Sykes' material and physical deprivations, and yet was rooted in the prison hierarchy, in using violence, manipulating power and seeking status within the prison walls. The third or 'legitimate' subculture – the 'straights' – in contrast, subscribed to prosocial attitudes and behaviours on the outside and inside prison and largely comprised 'accidental criminals' who shared none of the values of the two previous groups; they were the most likely to actively seek out ways of improving their chances of rehabilitation and release, via legitimate means of education, work and programmes.

Within each of these groupings, the nature of prisoners' ties to the outside world (which Clemmer, 1940, identified as significant in determining 'prisonisation') implies the effectiveness of reintegration. Irwin and Cressey used their typology to gauge the effect of rehabilitative attempts and the likelihood of reoffending post-release. If thieves maintained links to the thief-criminal subculture in and outside prison, and if 'convict-prisoners' relied wholly on their prison associations, then trying to instil new moral codes could present enormous challenges. Unsurprisingly, and echoing Clemmer's conclusion, Irwin and Cressey (1962) found that identification with the legitimate subculture correlated positively with rehabilitative potential, whereas those identifying with the convict-prison culture showed the least potential. For these prisoners, release was merely 'a short vacation from prison life' (p. 154); for the thief-criminals, prison was a 'pitfall', a disruption to outside life. Irwin (1970) later wrote about the ways prisoners 'do their time': either by 'doing time', 'jailing' or 'gleaning', types that correspond closely to the subcultures above. Importantly, Irwin argued that all prisoners assume a 'convict identity', acquired by degrees, yet permanently ingrained.

Recalling Clemmer's (1940) assumption that the longer the sentence, the greater the risk of prisonisation, some research indicates a different, yet equally disorienting, outcome for prisoners serving short sentences, particularly those with a high rate of return to custody. Schmid and Jones (1993) observe that, for short-term prisoners, identification with the outside world may inhibit their gaining of prison cultural entry or status, resulting in an ambivalence that directly shapes their adaptation and survival strategies in prison. The subsequent experience of marginalisation from prison life, although potentially shielding this group from the effects of prisonisation, may serve to redouble their sense of alienation and social isolation – thereby further militating against community integration – following their release. Hinton's research (2004) indicates that 'short-termers' are the 'hardest to work with' from a post-release support perspective (p. 24). If the meaning of prison for this group is predominantly one of temporary dislocation and disorientation, then this is the experience in which they become habituated and skilled.

Part of the process of social cohesion – in which prisoners participate to a greater or lesser extent – involves the specific use of an encoded and nuanced vocabulary, reflecting the culture of the prison and embodying the meaning-making practices used to make sense of the imprisonment experience. Prisoners use language to neutralise and communicate their experience of prison life and to foster or resist social alliances. Prison argot operates to designate strict social and behavioural mores, to reinforce hierarchy and to subvert the authority of the penal institution.[27] Prisoner institutionalisation implies a more comprehensive and enduring acculturation to prison ways and norms than simply adopting the idiom, however.

Penal institutionalisation

Institutionalisation is a long-established human response to confinement in 'total institutions' (Goffman, 1961). At one extreme, prisoners unable to cope with the pains of imprisonment may experience Goffman's (1961) 'mortification of the self', may even succumb to psychosis and suicide. For most prisoners, the process of institutionalisation has a less fatal, yet nonetheless persistent, impact on their capacity to identify, connect and engage with the wider community and their ability to function independently and productively within its bounds. For instance, Grunseit et al. (2008: 5) observe that the passivity learnt via institutional norms of compliance, obedience and perceived lack of worthiness inhibits civic activity or engagement post-release, even insofar as seeking or accepting help. They identify aspects of prison culture as undermining prisoners' access to justice and reinforcing their alienation from legal processes. These factors combine to give a sense of belonging in prison – a settling-in, based on familiarity with norms and expectations – that is reinforced by the concomitant sense of alienation from the world outside prison.

Penal institutionalisation does not only occur at the individual level. Arrigo and Milovanovic (2009) offer a broader perspective on the pains of imprisonment. They conceive the 'pains of release' (p. 86) as penal harm, 'maintained, legitimised, and reified by the recursive activities . . . [and] discursive work of prisoners, correctional officers, government officials or other administrators, and the general public' (p. 101), all investing in and sustaining the prison machine.

This, they argue, has the social effect of inhibiting 'human flourishing and becoming for *all* concerned. . . . This is what is meant by the pains of imprisonment' (p. 101). Their construal of Sykes' descriptor locates the social world of the prison squarely within the wider community, dissolving the perceived boundary between the two. 'Instead there is continuity', they argue, 'between what occurs within the prison environment and what occurs outside of it' (Arrigo & Milovanovic, 2009: 39). This continuity occurs through prisoners' connections with other prisoners, prison workers, and family and friends in the outside world. Prison economies such as drugs trade, for example, require sustained external links. Families and friends of prisoners suffer as 'collateral casualties' of prison. Families can become institutionalised.

Comfort's (2002) study of such 'collateral' effects seeks 'to document how the incarceration of a partner infiltrates and systematically distorts women's personal, domestic and social worlds', tracing the way the wives, fiancées, girlfriends of imprisoned men try to counteract and neutralise the effects of incarceration by transforming the prison visit into a 'domestic satellite' (p. 470). However, in doing so, Comfort argues, 'they partake in the paradoxical "institutionalization" of their own family life and thus extend the reach and intensity of the transformative affects of the carceral apparatus' (2002: 471). In her interviews with fifty female partners of male prisoners in the US, Comfort asked what the women meant by institutionalisation: One replied, '[for] some people – this is home, and *getting out* is a vacation' (p. 470), echoing Irwin and Cressey's (1962) finding decades earlier.

Comfort observed that 'women use food as a tool to "domesticize" the carceral environment' (p. 480). During 3-day family visits, wives (the most frequent participants) fabricate:

> a romanticised 'home' environment . . . which in fact *surpasses* that which exists away from the prison walls and which – despite the powerful constraints of forced confinement and strict surveillance – offers women idealized versions of domestic tranquillity . . . not available to them under their regular . . . circumstances.
>
> (p. 489–90)

Comfort warns against misconstruing this normalisation as a 'social pathology' of the 'underclass' (p. 491). She argues that, in the midst of mass incarceration and welfare reduction, 'the prison stands out as the most prominent, powerful, and "reliable" state institution in the lives of the poor and dispossessed' (Comfort, 2002: 491). This example of penal institutionalisation on a broader social scale, beyond individual prisoners, resonates with recent work on the rise and repositioning of the prison as a social institution in the US,[28] and in Australia.[29] A dichotomy emerges between the normalisation of imprisonment as a broadly accepted strategy of control (Garland, 2001) and the normalisation Comfort observes among those over whom the penal shadow looms large. Both constitute Arrigo and Milovanovic's (2009) penal harm.

Conclusion

This chapter has highlighted the lack of a national focus or depth of critical analysis about ex-prisoner reintegration, or a common logic to post-release practice in Australia. Although there is a clear picture of disadvantage characterising ex-prisoner populations, suggesting that prisoners in Australia do face similar challenges to those in the UK and US, an overarching theoretical narrative framing this post-prison landscape is missing. For most men, any rehabilitative support largely ends at the prison gate. Tailored post-release assistance is limited, and policy responses to broader social disadvantage such as health or housing, in ignoring issues of accessibility and exclusion, fail to meet the needs of released prisoners who remain 'a largely forgotten group, at least until they reoffend' (Kinner, Lennox & Taylor, 2009: 73). As prison populations expand, the profile of prisoners remains unchanged, Indigenous over-representation being emblematic of broader marginalisation, socio-economic disadvantage and ill-health. Knowledge of the challenges facing these groups is increasing, and yet post-release policy still lacks a strong, local evidence base. The institutionalising effects of imprisonment are barely considered. The most striking lacuna, though, is any depth of analysis of these issues at a societal level. Notwithstanding notable exceptions,[30] concerns are overwhelmingly programme- and policy-focused, with little theoretical critique. Critical consideration of how the post-release problem and its subject are constructed or conceived as the focus of intervention, for instance, scarcely features in the Australian literature. Before turning to these issues, the stories of two 'invisible' men I met in the netherworld of a Melbourne boarding house illustrate the complex disadvantage catalogued above.

Notes

1 The Drug Use Monitoring in Australia (DUMA) programme began in 1999 and collects drug use information from police detainees at nine sites across Australia.
2 A study of differences between Vic, NSW, WA and SA points to cultural/local effects on penal practice and yet is still unable to account for persistent differences between these states (see Tubex et al. 2015).
3 See, for example, Western, 2002; Kuppens & Ferwerda, 2008; Lockhart, Ullmann & Chant, 2008; Nugent, 2008; Visher, Debus & Yahner, 2008, 2010; Pew, 2010; Lösel, 2012.
4 Under Newstart Allowance for a single male without children, at the time of the study, 1 week's payment amounted to a maximum of AU$231.40 (Centrelink, 2010).
5 Similar issues prevail in Europe (Kuppens and Ferwerda, 2008) and the US (Visher et al. 2010).
6 Naylor, Paterson & Pittard, 2009; Naylor, 2011; Paterson & Naylor, 2011; Saliba, 2012.
7 Lynch & Sabol, 2001; Western, 2002, 2008b; Pew, 2010.
8 Easteal, 1992, 2001; Cook & Davies, 2000; Slowinski, 2001; Sisters Inside, 2005; Ross, Brown & Henry, 2006; Baldry, Ruddock & Taylor, 2008; Peacock, 2008; Willis & Moore, 2008; Carlton & Segrave, 2009; Brown & Ross 2010a and 2010b.
9 At that time, Victoria's prison population comprised 2,970 men and 183 women.
10 A US study found that most imprisoned fathers had their children cared for by a parent, step-parent or grandparent, with less than 1 per cent in foster care, whereas nearly a fifth of mothers had children in foster care (Hirschfield, Katzenstein & Fellner, 2002, in Hannon, 2006: 64).

11 See Mills & Codd, 2008; Rosenberg, 2009; Tomkin 2009; Walker 2010; Lösel, 2012.
12 Similar declines in drug-related mortality in NSW in 1989–90 and 2001–02, how-ever, may be attributable to legislative change and the 'heroin drought' of that period (Kariminia et al., 2007a).
13 See Hobbs et al., 2006; Krieg, 2006; Kariminia et al., 2007a; Gilles et al., 2008; Willis & Moore, 2008; AIHW, 2010.
14 See Butler et al., 2003; Butler & Milner 2003; Deloitte Consulting, 2003; Makkai & Payne, 2003; AIHW, 2010.
15 See Hunt & Saab, 2009; Jurgens, Ball & Verster, 2009; AIHW 2010: 61–2.
16 Koob and Volkow (2012) describe the 'neurocircuitry of addiction' in terms of an addiction cycle that offers insight into offending cycles. Logrip, Zorrilla and Koob (2012) link extreme stress responses to substance abuse and dependence in a way that has implications for understanding the effects of imprisonment and post-release morbidity.
17 Sterling & Eyer, 1988; McEwen & Stellar, 1993, McEwen & Seeman, 2009; Schulkin, 2011.
18 See Binswanger et al., 2007; Seaman, Brettle & Gore, 1998; Shewan et al., 2000; Bird & Hutchison, 2003; Pratt et al., 2006.
19 Hobbs et al., 2006; Kariminia et al., 2007a.
20 Darke et al., 2002, and Day et al., 2003, cited in Merrall et al. 2010: 1552.
21 Stewart et al. 2004; Kariminia et al. 2007a.
22 Butler & Allnutt, 2003; Butler & Milner, 2003; Deloitte Consulting, 2003; Senate Select Committee on Mental Health, 2006; Ogloff et al., 2007; AIHW, 2010; Indig et al., 2010.
23 For examples, Glaser & Deane 1999; Cockram, 2005d, cited in Holland et al., 2007).
24 Cognitive disabilities include mental illness, intellectual disability (ID), borderline intellectual disability (BID), acquired brain injury (ABI), dementia, neurological dis-orders and autism spectrum disorders, as well as encompassing dual diagnoses such as mental illness–intellectual disability (Oliver & O'Brien, 2003: 7; Baldry, Dowse & Clarence, 2010: 3).
25 See Clemmer, 1940; Sykes, 1958; Goffman, 1961; Irwin & Cressey, 1962; Cohen & Taylor 1972.
26 In his book, *The Society of Captives*, Gresham Sykes (1958) documented his study of the effects of the prison environment on the self-concept and thinking of inmates in the New Jersey State Maximum Security Prison, through participant observation and interviews with inmates.
27 See, for example: Sykes, 1958: 85–6; Foster, 1982; Cardozo-Freeman & Delorme, 1984: 28–9; Wittenberg, 1996; Einat & Einat, 2000; Hensley et al., 2003: 290–1; Awofeso, 2004: 4.
28 See Wacquant, 2001, 2002; Western, 2002; Harcourt, 2008.
29 See, for example, Baldry, 2009.
30 Such as Halsey, 2006, 2007, and Baldry, 2009.

3   The post-release problem

'Paul' and 'Rob'

The house, once grand, now crumbling, evokes a long-forgotten dignity. Like its inhabitants, it occupies a nether-space between the street and the respectable houses nearby. I peer inside the open door and call out – 'hello?' – tentatively. No one appears. The interior exudes a shabby desperation. Daylight dissolves into shadow. There is a sense of unease, of imminent threat. Here live the people of the street and the night. Some appear at the doorway – a man and a woman – as I wait for 'Paul'. They're looking for someone, to buy or sell them something, they're nervous, it's urgent, they leave.

When Paul finally does arrive – it's not clear whether he was expecting me – he invites me inside to do the interview, where it's a bit more comfortable . . . Warning lights flash in my brain – I conduct interviews in public places – but I trust my instincts and follow my host into the small living room. A large television blares in the corner, dark sofas collapse against two walls. The window admits little light, a too-close fence walling in a large dog outside. There is a man on the other sofa who doesn't meet my eye. He's recently got out too, Paul explains, but he doesn't talk much, 'he's a very angry man'. Another man I'd interviewed ('Dale') had given me Paul's number, suggesting he'd like to talk – he was right. Paul's voice rumbles gently through the next two and a half hours, sometimes ranting, sometimes thoughtful, occasionally interrupted by comings and goings of the house . . .

Paul is 30. He got out of jail nearly 2 years ago after serving 3 months on remand, 9 months after his release following a 17-month sentence. Since that time he has moved around between different locations, in and around Melbourne and rural Victoria, though, for the past 3 months, he has been living in this inner-city boarding house, home to seven or eight other residents of similar transience, including other ex-prisoners.

Paul has a history of youth offending: his first offence at the age of 11 resulted in a probation order at 12; when he was 16, he spent 2 years in a youth training centre. At 18, he got a community-based order, which he breached, was given a suspended sentence and, at 20, he ended up in adult prison. Though ordered to attend drug rehabilitation, he 'didn't fit in there that well', and, though 'everybody thought cannabis was the problem, it was alcohol'. This sense of being misunder-stood, misdiagnosed, mistreated – by police, magistrates, his grandparents, prison 'psychs', parole officers – seems to pervade his story.

Paul's grandparents, with whom he grew up 'on and off' in the same country town as his parents, he describes as 'good value'. Although his father is 'not too bad . . . trying to get his own life together', he no longer speaks with his mother, who is 'quite dangerous . . . She's a very good manipulator'.

Paul is a father of two. He is embroiled in family court matters over the wel-fare and custody of his 6-year-old daughter, mainly against his ex-partner's father whom he describes with intense animosity. Nevertheless, he asserts confidently, 'everything will get sorted there . . . I've just gotta wait'. Paul also has a 13-year-old son by another ex-partner. He has some contact with his son, observing he is 'a good kid, he's intelligent . . . He's got a different sort of mind to me, not all over the joint'. Testament to this, his reflections on people, social relations and injustices range from philosophical musings to rambling remonstrations.

His main 'problem', he explains, is 'stress': 'I handle stress alright, but once I'm stressed out to the point where I lose it then I just lose it'. Though he clarifies, 'I don't lose it for no reason', evoking again the sense of being misunderstood: 'I've got this problem, my voice must resonate and people keep telling me can't you be quiet and it's like, I'm not being loud. I've always had a deep voice'. He hints at the instability of his interpersonal relationships and interactions, despite his appar-ently calm, measured demeanour. He emphasises that his overriding concern in his life is to find stability. This will enable him to 'sort things out' with his ex and his daughter. He has embarked on different courses – in horticulture and fitness – since leaving prison, and he plans to complete his fitness instructor training once he can find somewhere stable to live.

During our interview, the door suddenly bursts open, and a man lurches in, dark-haired and imposing, wanting to know what I'm doing. He fires information about his own situation and sense of grievance at the world, and we agree to meet and do an interview, after he's been to get his methadone. This is 'Rob' – we meet later at the boarding house and walk together to a nearby café.

Rob, also 30, was first locked up at the age of 10 or 11 for stealing a car. Prior to that, he had been 'charged with drunk and disorderly, committing a public nuisance, all little stuff'. One of six children, his mother and stepfather were vari-ously arrested and imprisoned for drug offences. At 13, when his stepfather died, Rob's mother informed him that his 'real father' was alive and in jail. In reaction, Rob stopped talking: 'I didn't talk for a couple of years . . . she'd lied to me my whole life'. A picture began to emerge of a childhood marked by dysfunction, drug use and trauma: 'my parents didn't give a shit about me'.

Rob is now living in the boarding house with Paul and other ex-prisoners. He has been jailed at least ten times, mostly for being what he describes as 'a very, very bad public nuisance', or 'for shit I haven't done'. More often than not, he has been imprisoned on remand, which means 'every time I've been released they don't find housing or fix up Centrelink or anything, they just dump me on the street'. Rob implies his familiarity with recurring homelessness: 'I've been on the streets, just knock about until I find somewhere to live'. Uncertainty and instability seem to characterise his day-to-day experience:

> I've always got it in the back of my head that the police could pull me up at any given point in time and lock me up for something I haven't done . . . it's happened so many times that you sort of get used to it.

Despite having worked in various roles, outstanding 'legal issues' and being known to police means Rob feels unable to commit to a job: 'I told myself I won't work again until I beat this case. It's too head-fucking. And . . . I can't guarantee a boss that I'll live long enough to work for them'. On a disability pension 'because of jail-related issues', he seems caught in a loop of social and economic exclusion, as he explains:

> Some jobs I can't work in anymore because I don't like people telling me what to do after a year and a half of it [in prison] . . . It's anxiety, panic attacks . . . A fear of everything and nothing.

His anxiety disorder 'sort of started when I done a runner with [criminal colleagues'] money, and it got worse when I went to jail for something I didn't do'. He describes his subsequent methadone dependency as 'prison induced': 'In jail . . . I was that anxious I had to get on something to relax myself . . . And then you get out with a [methadone] habit'. This aspect of his life seems to shape his social interactions, in that 'most people coming out of jail are on methadone as well, so just lining up to get my methadone there could be ten people in the line that I know from jail'. This means, as he laments, that 'no matter how hard I try you can't get away from it'. Thus constrained are the possibilities of his integration into a life beyond 'prison world', a life of 'mixing, living and hanging with jailbirds, yeah. You can't get away from them'.

Estranged from his family, Rob is socially isolated: 'I don't have many friends at all . . . and the ones I do have, half the time I don't even know if they're my friends'. His 'fear of everything and nothing' is increasingly evident as he admits, 'I don't trust many people anymore. That's basically because of jail'. One person he does feel supported by, however, is the pharmacist who dispenses his methadone: 'He's like a drug counsellor . . . he's really nice. . . . And he's changed my whole life, I think'. He attributes being on his way to 'getting better' to this man, in whom he apparently has an almost child-like faith.

Rob seems to inhabit a nether space between prison and the community, a space characterised by a sense of waiting . . . As he says, waiting 'until they find something else to lock me up for'. He describes a recurrent dream that seems to echo his experience: 'It's like I'm stuck in prison world. And once I do get out I always get caught and taken back. . . . It's a horrible dream, I've been having it for years'.

This chapter explores the problem of prisoners' return to society in broader terms, by critically examining how 'the problem' is constructed, how its subject is construed as the focus of intervention, and the types of response these construc-tions engender. The purpose is to build a picture of the sociopolitical discursive milieu against which post-prison shadows are cast, and within which the lived experience of ex-prisoners' disadvantage and marginalisation may be understood. This chapter draws on post-release knowledge and debate prevailing in Australia and the US and UK in the mid to late 2000s, identifying particular themes that will anchor later chapters' discussion.

The previous chapter characterised the post-release landscape in Australia as missing a central storyline, an overarching sociopolitical-historical account of post-release theory and practice. The Australian literature is marked by a lack of consistency in practice and coherent framing of responses to the problem of post-prison integration. Nevertheless, ex-prisoners are contained within and defined by distinct political discourses and policy narratives, two of which are traced here: 're-entry' in the US and 'resettlement' in the UK. I examine how each construes the post-release problem and conceives its subject. The underlying theme of risk is explored: the risk invested in the released subject, and the risk embedded in the penal system and its broader social-cultural context. Different ways of responding to the post-release problem are then considered, and their assumptions and under-pinning philosophies are brought to light.

Constructing the post-release problem

Although the discussion thus far has characterised Australian research as largely administrative and/or policy-oriented, more striking is the lack of a unifying nar-rative framing post-release policy and practice in Australia. In the US and UK, which dominate the international literature, the terms 're-entry' and 'resettlement', respectively, frame an apparently robust response to the problem of how to foster ex-prisoners' social and economic (re)integration. Post-release programmes have proliferated in these nations, particularly where the numbers of people released from prison each year have reached historical peaks. The renewed focus on re-entry, resettlement and reintegration reflects concern over emerging public safety and fiscal implications. Although the universality of post-prison problems emerges throughout this chapter, the purpose is to canvas what is missing in Australia: national recognition of and response to the post-release problem. The chapter now turns to ways this problem is identified and discussed. The labels 're-entry' and 'resettlement' and their theoretical underpinnings and policy implications are briefly examined.

'Re-entry' as a public safety issue

In the decade since the US Department of Justice published *But They All Come Back: Rethinking Prisoner Reentry* (Travis, 2000), a veritable re-entry industry has developed to address the problem of prisoners' return to American communi-ties. In January 2011, US Attorney General Eric Holder convened the inaugural meeting of the cabinet-level 'Reentry Council' in Washington, an inter-agency gathering with a threefold mission: 'to make communities safer by reducing recid-ivism and victimization; to assist those returning from prison and jail in becoming productive, tax paying citizens; and to save taxpayer dollars by lowering the direct and collateral costs of incarceration' (US DoJ, 2011: 1). This federal initiative represented the US government's substantial investment – fiscal and political – in the re-entry business, which the sheer scale of the carceral machinery and its human parts has necessitated. As Holder affirmed: 'More than two million people are behind bars, and 95 percent of them will be released back into their communi-ties. By developing effective, evidence-based re-entry programs, we can improve public safety and community well-being' (US DoJ, 2011: 1).

'Re-entry' describes the 'process of managing the transition from the status of 'imprisoned offender' to the status of 'released ex-offender'' (Travis, 2000: 1). Over the past decade in particular, as Ward and Maruna (2007) observe, these 'buzzwords' have emerged as new ways of conceiving an old problem: 'newer shinier terms' (p. 4) replacing the outmoded notion of 'rehabilitation'. Whereas strategies centred on education, job training and work release were certainly the focus of past rehabilitative efforts, the 'new dialogue is more focused on program-matic, evidence-based solutions' (Visher, 2007: 1). The new lexis reflects and aligns with important shifts in penal thinking: 'The rise of correctional manage-rialism, the associated rise and sustained influence of offender risk as a concept structuring correctional practice, and the development of a market in punishment through prison privatisation' (Brown, 2005: 115–6). Without irony, for exam-ple, 'the language of the assembly line' is invoked to describe the struggle of American communities 'to manage the higher production of released prisoners' (Travis & Petersilia, 2001: 293). Perhaps, as Ward and Maruna (2007: 3–5) sug-gest, re-entry has gained momentum in spite of – indeed, because of – its lack of definition or connotations, its mechanistic simplicity fitting with the industrial imagery of the carceral machine.

This use of language is significant in terms of how the problem is constructed. Ostensibly self-evident, 're-entry' implies a coming or going back in, transit through a point of ingress to an earlier or former location, as when a spacecraft re-enters the Earth's atmosphere. It is, first, 'a landing – a matter of just getting the [releasee] from prison to a resting place safely' (Ball, Weisberg & Dansky, 2008: 23). If this analogy is pursued, however, the term masks the intensity and complexity of the re-entry experience and, curiously, belies the immense forces exerted upon the human body during the process: return from a remote, surreal environment separated from and uninterrupted by the pressures and distractions of everyday life; through a brief period of searing intensity and then a sudden jud-dering, jolting return to familiar surroundings; to feeling one's own weight again and the heaviness of the world. 'Re-entry' condenses the process to a moment, a point in time after which normalcy is resumed; the transition from one world to another reduced to the act of stepping through a doorway.

Re-entry is passive, neutral, benign; as ordinary as a pass-out from a football match readmitting its holder to the ground; 'intentionally vague, largely descrip-tive' (Moore, 2012: 133), it is a term unencumbered by human agency or impact;

a blank, objective noun. In contrast, rehabilitation, resettlement and reintegration are replete with verb-ness: the doing of rehabilitating, resettling, reintegrating of people by people; invoking interaction, process, complexity and change. These terms, moreover, imply a temporal dimension missing from their American counterpart. And, despite their (often ill-founded) assumption of a pre-existing state of wholeness or wellness, they embody an ideal, an aspiration, and imply a social contract, an expectation of community participation and/or responsibility, for which re-entry leaves no room.

Rather, re-entry denotes a straightforward, national public-safety issue unadorned by any welfarist connotations (Moore, 2012). It is thus able to garner bipartisan support in the form of US federal government initiatives.[1] This legislative commitment to funding for literacy programmes, drug treatment and other services for prisoners and ex-prisoners represents a significant step in the broader movement towards improving prisoner re-entry policy in the US (Western, 2008a and 2008b). This culminated in the US Justice Department (in 2010) announcing US$110 million for a Justice Reinvestment Initiative, re-entry grants and a new Project Reentry initiative. Such policy was informed by research, such as undertaken by the Urban Institute since 2000, and partnerships with organisations such as the Reentry Policy Council and the Council of State Governments. This collaborative work aimed to build knowledge about the challenges facing ex-prisoners, their social integration and the costs of incarceration to individuals, families and communities, producing evidence to underpin policy.

Evidence-based policy

The Urban Institute's principal research, *Returning Home: Understanding the Challenges of Prisoner Reentry*, is a longitudinal study tracking ex-prisoners' pathways in four states and documenting challenges to reintegration across five dimensions: individual, family, peer, community and state. Visher, Yahner and La Vigne (2010), for instance, report on findings from pre-release and post-release interviews with 652 men, mainly African American or Latino, with multiple convictions and previous imprisonment, mirroring Australia's cycle of Aboriginal and Torres Strait Islander (ATSI) over-representation. The results show that, despite a high degree of programme participation in prison, a third of participants felt they were unable to access programmes they needed. Such is the experience of prisoners – particularly remandees – in Australia. Highlighted, too, is the issue of post-prison housing instability: few men secured lasting accommodation post-release, as Baldry et al. (2003) found. Family relationships were found to provide important material and emotional resources, and, despite the finding of many family members' drug use and/or imprisonment, the quality of these relationships and the support they provided were rated highly (Visher et al., 2010). Despite the ubiquitous challenges – lack of identification, significant debts and employment opportunities hampered by criminal convictions – nearly half the men were employed 7 months after their release, perhaps partly related to the lack of government income support available in the US.

A notable finding of the Returning Home study is the interviewees' optimism about their ability to remain drug- and crime-free post-release (Visher et al., 2008; Yahner, Visher & Solomon, 2008; La Vigne et al., 2009). Despite this, many return to crime and prison in the first year, many for violating their supervision (Visher et al., 2010). Most significantly, the study identifies the strongest predictors of reintegration outcomes: in-prison job training and education assisted post-release employment in the first year, as did pre-prison employment, securing work pre-release and using former employers to find work post-release (Visher et al., 2008; La Vigne et al., 2009). Yahner et al. (2008) link release on parole to higher employment and lower substance abuse among participants; conversely, although it had a negligible impact on self-reported crime or rearrest, parole increased the likelihood of reincarceration, mainly due to technical violations. Early post-release drug treatment and substantial family support are shown to reduce the risk of substance abuse in the first year (Kohl et al., 2008; La Vigne et al., 2009). Men with strong ties to their children showed better employment and drug use outcomes, married men reported higher employment levels 8 months after release, and men employed soon after release were less likely to be reimprisoned 1 year out (Visher et al., 2008; La Vigne et al., 2009).

The Returning Home study highlights challenges faced by male prisoners returning to certain large urban American communities, and the factors – such as job training, employment assistance, housing, drug treatment and family support – likely to promote reintegration. Although nearly half the men interviewed had found work in the year following their release, most were reliant upon the financial and housing support of family. Interesting to note is that the normalisation of crime and drug use within families appeared to strengthen – rather than diminish – reintegrative prospects (Visher et al., 2010). Identifying the hope and optimism of released prisoners and acknowledging the high risk of return to prison in the early post-release period, Visher at al. (2010) suggest that policies giving released prisoners immediate access to housing and support services are most likely to 'translate their desire for successful reintegration into prosocial activities and behaviours' (p. 6). Implied is the universality of this desire, a potential well of reintegrative capital that is frequently omitted from the re-entry discourse.

Another example of the Urban Institute's large-scale research, the Massachusetts Recidivism Study (Kohl et al., 2008) combines correctional data with parole officer focus groups and interviews with men returning to custody. The finding that two-fifths of the 1,786 men released in 2002 were reimprisoned within 3 years mirrors an earlier national recidivism study that found that more than two-thirds of prisoners released in 1994 were rearrested within 3 years, and half of these were reimprisoned (Langan & Levin, 2002, in Western, 2008b: 6). Kohl et al. (2008: 10) found that recidivists were younger (under 35), served shorter sentences and were less likely to be married. This latter finding supports previous research linking marriage to desistance from crime (Sampson & Laub, 1993; Sampson & Laub, 2005; Warr, 1998). In the Massachusetts study, African-American men returned to prison at a higher rate than other racial groups, and recidivism was associated with longer criminal histories and prior incarcerations (Kohl et al., 2008). Two-thirds of the men were released 'to the street' at the end of their sentence, and a third were paroled; the recidivism rate was significantly higher among the parolees compared with the 'street' group (p. 21). This finding suggests the supervisory and compliance aspects of parole exacerbate the risk of reimprisonment.

Kohl et al. (2008) note the perception that violent crime is predictive of a higher reoffending risk, despite evidence to the contrary, suggesting public fear is fuelled by media misrepresentations and the promotion of 'risk' messages, examined further below. In fact, repeat incarceration is a far stronger predictor. Notably, nearly three-quarters of the release cohort had been imprisoned at least once before. Hence, the authors urge that 'failures in the community' be addressed (Kohl et al., 2008: 31). Such findings have inspired restorative and community engagement approaches to tackle the issue of cyclic imprisonment, such as public education, offender employment and mentoring programmes (Rodriguez, 2011).

The 2008 Stanford Executive Sessions on Sentencing and Corrections (Ball et al., 2008) focused on the first 72 hours following a prisoner's release in California. Thinking narrowly about this critical period, they reason, can generate pragmatic solutions to specific issues and a lens through which to examine larger re-entry issues. Underscoring the first 3 days as a crucial period to connect releasees to resources, this project highlighted the benefits of 'choreographing' (Ball et al., 2008: 6) this period and harnessing potential 'participants in reentry' (families, police; p. 7). Such collaborative approaches challenge the prevailing fixation on public safety and the risk management approach to re-entry that it engenders.

An obsession with safety

Increasingly strict parole regimes have made re-entry 'a more difficult and precarious transition than ever before' (Maruna & LeBel, 2003: 91). Parole's emphasis on 'supervision over rehabilitation' has contributed to increasing rates of reincarceration (Lindquist, Hardison & Lattimore, 2003). In the US, 1 in 30 men aged 20–34 and 1 in 9 black men is behind bars (Pew, 2008). Further, with more than 5 million Americans on probation or parole, 'a stunning 1 in 31 adults . . . is under some form of correctional control' (Pew, 2009: 1). As Perata declared in 2007: 'we have fallen in love with one of the most undocumented beliefs: That somehow you get safer if you put more people in jail' (in Pew, 2008: 11). He encapsulates the problem as one of unfounded obsession with public safety. This fixation means that the overarching flavour of the penal and re-entry narrative remains firmly risk-based.

Critical of this prevailing theme, Wacquant (2001) examines the 'function of the criminal justice system as instrument for the management of dispossessed and dishonoured groups' (p. 95). Echoing Wacquant's concerns, Western (2008a, 2008b) writes about the social costs of mass imprisonment in terms of citizenship and inequality, highlighting that no other social indicator matches the racial disparity of 'the seven to one black–white ratio in incarceration rates' (2008b: 8). Recognising the impact of incarceration on employability, and the high rates of unemployment in communities to which ex-prisoners return, Western proposes a national re-entry programme focused on increasing employment, which would ultimately lead to 'sustainable public safety' (2008b: 5) Post-prison employment benefits families and neighbourhoods (Western, 2008b: 6), which, in turn, reduces reimprisonment risk (Visher et al., 2008; La Vigne et al., 2009). Conversely, the costs of ex-prisoners' economic exclusion are borne by families and communities (Pew, 2010). The impact of incarceration is thus intergenerational.

Findings such as these – although not exhaustive – are nevertheless indicative of the work informing evidence-based re-entry policies in the US. Though driven by competing social and fiscal concerns, they appear to coalesce in a flow of re-entry policy aimed at managing the effects of the penal regime by improving integrative outcomes for ex-prisoners. Moreover, although practices vary across states, information and resources are centralised and disseminated[2] in a way that is underdeveloped in Australia. Also lacking is a consolidated Australian research commitment to the post-release problem, as Australia's fragmented policies and practices suggest. In the UK, as in the US, a robust research commitment and evidence-gathering focus characterise the post-prison landscape. Policies are similarly driven by competing fiscal and social concerns, and risk thinking predominates, and yet the narrative has different emphases.

'Resettlement' as social inclusion

In the UK, the term resettlement variously embodies efforts by prison and probation services, and voluntary agencies, to help prepare prisoners and their families for life after prison. Hedderman (2007) explores the contested nature of the term and the implications of how differing interpretations shape practice and interventions. Her Majesty's Inspectorates of Prisons and Probation (HMIP&P, 2001) note preference for the use of the word resettlement and yet acknowledge doubts about the 'tendency to introduce less tender or morally more neutral language', or its implication of the 'restoration of a condition that never was' (HMIP&P, 2001: 3). The term is favoured because 'it focuses attention on the desired outcome as well as the processes which allegedly promote the outcome', and it 'implies a more modest assumption regarding prisoners' prior condition' (HMIP&P, 2001: 3).

The UK Association of Chief Officers of Probation defines resettlement as:

> A systematic and evidence-based process by which actions are taken to work with the offender in custody and on release, so that communities are better protected from harm and reoffending is significantly reduced. It encompasses the totality of work with prisoners, their families and significant others in partnership with statutory and voluntary organisations.
>
> (in HMIP&P, 2001: 12)

The nature, strength and extent of such 'partnership' could substantially influence the way 'resettlement' may be experienced, however, as this prisoner's experience suggests:

I have contacted approximately 70 organisations that indicate they have involvement with resettlement, yet none of them seem able to offer any help and/or advice on just what they consider a resettlement plan to be.

(in Maruna, 2006: 25)

Rhetoric can obscure the gap between theory and practice. This disparity is felt in the lives of prisoners and the families and communities to which they return, highlighting the importance of subjective accounts to give voice to the complexity of the post-release experience.

The need to integrate pre-and post-release planning and support is frequently emphasised. Fox et al. (2005) specifically highlight the need for release planning to commence upon entry to custody, and for collaborative practices and responsive processes to continue post-release. Their findings reflect systemic and procedural limitations to the provision of adequate support for people leaving custody. The UK government's Social Exclusion Unit (2002) identified nine key factors influencing reoffending among released prisoners: education, employment, drug and alcohol misuse, mental and physical health, attitudes and self-control, institutionalisation and life skills, housing, financial support and debt, and family networks. These well-documented disadvantages underpin the construction of released prisoners' risk of recidivism as the foremost problem to be addressed in England and Wales, and public protection as the purpose of post-release intervention. In contrast, Scotland accentuates rehabilitation as the primary aim (McNeill et al., 2005), reflecting recognition of the intrinsic and instrumental value of ex-prisoners' social inclusion. Such policy variation underscores the post-release problem as constructed, not a given.

Since the mid 1990s, when Home Secretary Michael Howard's claim that 'prison works'[3] validated the supposed deterrent value of imprisonment, British policy tides have turned, with rehabilitation gaining political momentum (Moore, 2012). The Commission on English Prisons Today (CEPT, 2009) identified a 'crisis of penal excess' (p. 7) in England and Wales, arising from 'criminal justice hyperactivity', which has resulted in 'unrealistic expectations about the role prison can play in securing a safer society' (pp. 7, 19). According to the CEPT (2009), evidence of the multiple failures of prison as an institution is 'incontrovertible': 'Prison fails to reform, fails to deter, fails to assuage public concern and fails to make communities safe' (p. 13). Short-term prisoners – being most numerous and most likely to be reconvicted – are symptomatic of this crisis:

The social harm they cause may not be grave in each individual case but the incremental, corrosive harm of unprevented volume crime is great. It promotes mistrust, fear and anger and contributes to the widespread public perception that the criminal justice system fails to protect.

(HMIP&P, 2001: 5)

The Scottish Executive (2004) expressed similar concerns about short-term sentences failing to protect the public (McNeill et al., 2005: 7). Advocating 'penal moderation', the CEPT argued for twin strategies of justice reinvestment and restorative justice to bring about fundamental reforms in the use of imprisonment. Nevertheless, governments appear 'determined to build [their] way out of crisis . . . a crisis which will only be exacerbated by yet more expansion of imprisonment' (CEPT, 2009: 14). The tension is clear: political commitment to penal expansionism despite consistent evidence of its dangers.

The international literature is shaped by largely pragmatic concerns around the increasing scale of the carceral machine and the social and fiscal costs associated with rising numbers of (predominantly) men returning to communities following imprisonment. Political responses reflect a dual rationale: on one hand, a commitment to addressing the causal factors associated with reoffending, via correctional and community-based programmatic approaches; on the other, a blind adherence to the belief that 'prison works', if only as a means of punishment and (often short-term) incapacitation. These conflicting currents serve to perpetuate both a sense of decisive action amid insecurity and an unwillingness to challenge or dismantle the penal structure, as some commentators urge (see Western, 2008a; CEPT, 2009). This contradictory construction of the problem has parallels in Australia, where penal expansionism mirrors that of the UK and US. But, it also distinguishes the international debate from its local counterpart, in highlighting the lack of coordination and conceptualisation of policy and practice in Australia, where the problem remains largely invisible. The following discussion illustrates how the construction of the problem generates particular subjects.

Constructing the post-release subject

This theme examines the construction of the subject of post-release intervention in terms of the notion of *risk*: risk embedded in the designation of offenders as 'clients'; and ex-prisoners' vulnerability to risks inhering in post-release systems of administration. These constructions emerge out of the confluence of political themes explored above. The way the post-release problem is constructed is seen to produce a particular type of subject. Increased imprisonment not only results in 'the higher production of released prisoners' (Travis and Petersilia, 2001: 293), but also brings forth a post-imprisoned incarnation of the reformed or reforming (or unreformable) citizen. The following illustrates how these discursive flows generate different constructions, beginning with the idea of 'risky individuals' constituting a 'risky population'.

A risky population

Over the last three decades, notions of risk assessment, management and individual responsibility have infused the language of corrections and penal policy. The prevailing view of offenders is of 'a risky population to be efficiently and prudently managed' (Hannah-Moffat, 2005: 30; drawing on Feeley & Simon, 1992; Garland, 2001). Reflecting the undertows of modern 'risk society' (Beck, 1992; Giddens, 1999), the assessment and management of (re)offending risk is also seen to bring together two distinct conceptions of risk: as a continuum, along which people may be at risk, individuals susceptible to the effects of various factors upon their behaviour; and risky individuals, who 'present a future risk to others' (Rose, 2010: 80), the latter drawing on psychiatric risk thinking in binary, oppositional terms of normal/abnormal, desirable/undesirable. The implications of such thinking are examined here, beginning with an example illustrating how prisoners, as a risky population, are invested with danger and undesirability.

Risky people

Combessie's (1998, 2002) research, on the interaction between four French prisons and the outside world, depicted the clientele of bars and cafés close to prison grounds as dichotomous – divided between prison guards and the families and visitors of prisoners. He described how proprietors navigated these relations and the stigma of the prison seeping into their business, showing that, 'the prison both radiates and exports the stigma it is assumed to contain' (2002: 535). The danger and undesirability of its inhabitants leak out beyond the prison walls. Combessie described the 'radical cleavage between "good" and "evil" people', these divisions 'materialised in the very bodies of prisoners by their penal confinement' (2002: 552). Treating prisoners 'as the "enemy of the interior"', he argued, makes it 'difficult [for them] to reintegrate into society' (2002: 553). They remain excluded.

Combessie (1998, 2002) highlights the infection of prisoners' families and communities with undesirability, which evokes Rose's (2000: 324) social 'circuits of exclusion'. In contrast, Combessie's 'ordinary clientele' (1998: 4) clearly inhabit circuits of inclusion. Café and bar owners emerge as checkpoints in these circuits, manifesting control 'through conditional access to circuits of consumption and civility: constant scrutiny of the right of individuals to access certain kinds of flows of consumption goods' and services (Rose, 2000: 326). By accommodating prisoners' families 'at a distance from the "ordinary" clientele' (Combessie, 1998: 4), or having two entrances to an inn 'to avoid clashes' (Combessie, 2002: 550), for instance, proprietors quite literally 'seek to manage these anti-citizens and marginal spaces through measures which seek to neutralise the dangers they pose' (Rose, 2000: 330). The extension of risk beyond offenders and into their social ecology, even the physical environment, is illustrated. As Combessie (1998: 7) puts it, 'the prison imparts on its host locality a stigma similar to that which affects the prisoners'. Risky populations thus constitute social, cultural and physical 'zones of exclusion' existing 'outside the circuits of inclusion – in "marginalized" space' (Rose, 2000: 331).

Control strategies directed towards these zones of exclusion include the 'securitization of identity' (Rose, 2000: 327) and the patterning and management of urban space, which serve to heighten 'the perceived riskiness of other unprotected zones' (pp. 329–30). Beyond individuals, factors 'associated with an increased likelihood of undesirable conduct (housing conditions, employment history, abuse of alcohol or drugs, family circumstances) . . . become the focus of the risk gaze' (Rose, 2000: 332).[4] Various professionals are rendered agents of control – police, social workers, doctors, mental health workers – gathering, inscribing, accumulating and distributing information in a 'perpetually failing endeavour to minimize the riskiness of the most risky' (Rose, 2000: 333). Their targets are the repeatedly imprisoned, 'dysfunctional families' (Garside, 2009: 3), the mentally ill, welfare recipients and street people, who constitute:

> An array of micro-circuits, micro-cultures of non-citizens, failed citizens, anti-citizens, comprised of those who are unable or unwilling to . . . manage their own risk, incapable of exercising responsible self-government, either attached to no moral community or to a community of anti-morality.
>
> (Rose, 2000: 331)

Ironically, risk management of 'the destitute, the disreputable and the dangerous, and all those who chafe in the lower regions of social space' (Wacquant, 2002: 382) functions through 'a regime of surveillance which actually constitutes them all as actually or potentially "risky" individuals' (Rose, 2000: 333). Farrington's (2007) acknowledgement that, typically, 'prospective prediction . . . is poor but retrospective prediction . . . is good' (in Garside, 2009: 8) renders risk a wholly unreliable predictive tool, better 'suited to generalisations about groups' (Armstrong, 2006: 272). As Visher (2007) notes, despite the heterogeneity of ex-prisoners as a group, perceptions of them may be shaped by experiences with particular sub-groups, particularly those deemed 'difficult'. Thus arising from the construction of the post-release subject as a population of risky individuals to be 'managed' is the notion of the 'offender/client'.

Offender/clients

Rose (1989: 213) notes the 'spectacular expansion of the psychotherapeutic domain' and its impact on the 'rationales and techniques of government'. Psychology has similarly shaped correctional interventions, such as cognitive skills, anger management, and sex offender treatment programmes (Donohue & Moore, 2009; Moore, 2012). Psychotherapeutic approaches establish a specific transactional relationship between practitioners and the subject of their intervention: the client. Donohue and Moore (2009) argue that the translation of offenders into criminal justice 'clients', spawned by the union of managerial and consumerist discourses, serves to recast subjects as active agents in the delivery of justice outcomes: 'Clients are consumers of the social services offered (mandated) through the criminal justice system. They are active participants in their own punishment and correction because they are choice making, free subjects' (Donohue & Moore, 2009: 320).

Offenders reconstructed as 'choice makers' fits with the psychotherapeutic rationale, 'to restore to individuals the capacity to function as autonomous beings in the contractual society of the self' (Rose, 1989: 227). Thus evoked are classical notions of freedom, choice and social contract as justification for punishment, the objects of which are 'wanton and hopeless, better warehoused on account of their dangerousness' (Donohue & Moore, 2009: 319). Yet offenders' transformative potential is prescribed in their designation as 'clients': 'Offenders are law breakers, clients are risky subjects in need of assistance' (p. 322), the assistance taking the form of strategies whereby the 'offender' is 'managed from dependence and mal-adjustment to autonomy and responsibility' (Rose, 1989: 214). The offender thus constitutes the 'transformative risk subject' (Hannah-Moffat, 2005) of 'bureaucratic control logic' (Arrigo & Milovanovic, 2009: 152).

The dual process of 'autonomisation' and 'responsibilisation' (Rose, 2000; Moore, 2012) evokes nineteenth-century ideals of moral reform through reflective self-scrutiny and endeavour (Hudson, 2003), though inflected with 'risk thinking' permeating modern 'risk society' (Beck, 1992; Giddens, 1999). Risk is linked to safety and security, and to responsibility, which denotes agency and accountability as well as obligation or liability. The latter, Giddens (1999: 8) suggests, is the most interesting counterpoint to risk and clearly tied to the notion of offender 'responsi-bilisation'. As Rose (1989) observes, 'the modern self is institutionally required to construct a life through the exercise of choice from among alternatives' (p. 227). For law-breakers, the obligation is upon them to choose a better way, to change. In facilitating this transformation, the goal of responsibilisation is 'to reconstruct self-reliance' in 'the excluded', such as ex-prisoners (Rose, 2000: 334). Thus, risk management is the management of exclusion.

'Offender' identities, however, are not fixed but fluid: contingent, localised and temporally defined; when offenders 'morph into empowered [moral] agents', their 'transformations are embodied in the client' (Donohue & Moore, 2009: 321). Translating offenders into clients involves identifying their pathologies – mental health problems, drug addiction, sexual deviance – as problems that can be solved with professional therapeutic intervention (Donohue & Moore, 2009). Ostensibly, 'clients' assume the capacity to free themselves. This is 'autonomisation' real-ised: autonomy is 'represented in terms of personal power and the capacity to accept responsibility . . . to recognise your own collusion in that which prevents you from being yourself, and . . . overcome it' (Rose, 2000: 334). This language of empowerment 'codes the subjective substrate of exclusion as lack of self-esteem, self-worth and the skills of self-management necessary to steer oneself as an active individual in the empire of choice' (Rose, 2000: 334); these deficits become the target of 'professional reconstruction' (p. 334).

Arrigo and Milovanovic (2009) illustrate how the 'empowerment' paradigm engenders a 'situated and finite being', a subject whose 'becoming, evolving, and transforming' (p. 141) is thereby limited:

> identifying with the idealized image of a recovering subject in a particular rehabilitation agency offers access to new reward structures . . . and/or to an alternative vocabulary (taking responsibility for personal deficits, 'owning' recovery, pursuing a 'good life') in which (illusory) empowerment may result.
>
> (p. 142)

Yet, this identity is contingent on one particular context that may connect or con-flict with other forces in the person's social field, forces that, through repetition, can lock the subject into fixed 'molar' identities of client, offender, parolee or recovering subject, for instance. Offenders embody a particular sort of exclusion, according to Rose (2000), 'not a psychological subjectivity with social determinants, as in welfare regimes . . . [but] an ethical subjectivity, and a cultural subjectivity' (p. 335). The implications for rehabilitative and reintegrative efforts are that:

It is through moral reformation, through ethical reconstruction, that the excluded citizen is to be reattached to a virtuous community . . . so that the individual can be reinserted into family, work and consumption, and hence into the continuous circuits and flows of control society.

(Rose, 2000: 335)

Those who resist this process, 'who refuse to become responsible, to govern themselves ethically, have also refused the offer to become members of our moral community . . . [C]itizenship becomes conditional upon conduct' (Rose, 2000: 335). Thus, increasingly punitive control and containment strategies are justified for the most dangerous and intractable. Those unable to be 'responsibilised' become the targets for ongoing control via administration and surveillance by professionals. These are 'difficult clients' (Slowinski, 2001: 53), perpetual offenders inhabiting 'circuits of exclusion' (Rose, 2000: 333); risky individuals, indeed 'risky brains' (Rose, 2010), governed through regimes of control informed by psychiatric/psychological modes of thinking. Evoking Foucault (1979), Rose (2010: 97) describes this as the 'emerging logic for the conduct of conduct: not so much "discipline and punish", but "screen and intervene"'.

Particular assumptions about offenders, prisoners and ex-prisoners underpin and shape the nature of post-release intervention and delimit the reintegrative possibilities of men so constructed. While psychotherapeutic modes dominate prison programmes and construct the post-release subject as self-transforming, barely acknowledged is 'the psychological residue of institutionalisation' (Haney, 2003: 59), or the fact that released prisoners face 'personal, social, and structural challenges for which they have neither the ability nor the resources to overcome entirely on their own' (p. 59). The post-prison environment can thus militate against the very ideal of rehabilitation or reintegration – of fitting in – towards which released prisoners and post-release support systems ostensibly aspire.

Risky systems

Whereas the preceding sections centre on the post-release subject as invested with risk, my focus now shifts to the extent to which penal processes themselves are infused with risk, an idea that subverts the prevailing view of offenders as a risky population. 'Risky systems' draws on Halsey's (2006, 2007) conception of the conditions that give rise to the cycle of imprisonment, release and reimprisonment. This theme sees the post-release subject as enmeshed in lines of risk inhering in the prison environment itself, and in the administrative systems and practices framing the post-prison terrain. These lines constitute and perpetuate the carceral assemblage. The following explores these ideas, starting with the criminogenic effects of incarceration.

Effects of imprisonment

'Detention causes recidivism', wrote Foucault (1979: 265), reminding us that nineteenth-century critiques of the prison as a criminogenic institution persist virtually unchanged: in 1831, Monsieur de Rochefoucauld reported to the French Parliament that 38 per cent of released prisoners were reconvicted. In Australia, nearly two centuries later, the figure was almost identical (SCRGSP, 2012). The self-perpetuating nature of the cycle of imprisonment and release is thus well established, a cycle amplified by increasing numbers of people imprisoned, released and returning to custody. Victoria's Sentencing Advisory Council (2013) found that people sentenced to imprisonment are more likely to reoffend and be reimprisoned than people on non-custodial sentences. Weatherburn (2010) also found 'evidence that prison increases the risk of reoffending' (p. 1), and Wan et al. (2012) conclude that longer sentences do not reduce offending. These findings highlight the capacity of the prison to assemble the conditions for reoffending and imply its criminogenic effects (see Brown, 2010). The everyday risks faced by released prisoners are clear, arising both from the imprisonment experience itself and the effects of stigmatisation and social alienation.

The effects of imprisonment are well documented in Liebling and Maruna's (2005) edited volume, in which Haney outlines prisons' criminogenic effects on prisoners and their communities. Haney (2005) observes the extent to which social context is largely ignored in penal policy and correctional practice, with prison programming clinging to outdated modes of psychological individualism. He underscores the irony that psychological theory holds such a central place in correctional practice, with penal programmes framed as 'an antidote to essentialised psychological and criminogenic tendencies' (Carlen, 2005: 427), whereas the most important of psychology's contemporary lessons – that 'context matters' (Haney, 2005: 78) – is sidelined by the focus on punishment. Haney (2003) describes the psychological effects of incarceration, highlighting the 'normal adaptations' prisoners make in response to the 'abnormal conditions of prison life' (p. 38), which become problematic when they impede post-prison adjustment. Prisoners manifest these to varying degrees: dependence on institutional structure and contingencies; hypervigilance, interpersonal distrust and suspicion; emotional over-control, alienation and psychological distancing; social withdrawal and isolation; the incorporation of exploitative norms of prison culture; a diminished sense of self-worth and personal value; and post-traumatic stress reactions to the pains of imprisonment (2003: 40–6). These are exacerbated for prisoners returning to 'difficult and stressful circumstances lacking supportive structure and services . . . [who] may be forced by social and economic disadvantage to live at the margins of society and, as a result, are more vulnerable to . . . reoffending' (p. 47).

The criminogenic character of the prison seems self-evident in light of consistent findings that penal institutionalisation serves to entrench and exacerbate existing aspects and levels of social and economic disadvantage, as documented in the previous chapter. The effects of incarceration are magnified for individuals already struggling with cognitive disabilities, including mental illness (Haney, 2003; Oliver & O'Brien, 2003), further stripping already depleted resources. As Grunseit et al. (2008) summarise: 'Each time [a] person cycles through the justice system personal supports are strained, skills become atrophied, financial resources are depleted and the capacity to operate well "on the outside" and without resort to unlawful means is further diminished' (p. 279). So, although imprisonment and release generate risk, the primary penal function has emerged as the containment of risk (Rose, 2000; Armstrong, 2004). Ex-prisoners' disadvantage, psychological damage and exclusion are thus both symptoms of and the rationale for the expansion of the penal-welfare complex.[5]

Arrigo and Milovanovic (2009) conceive of risk as abiding in and emanating and reissuing from every aspect of the penal system, in prison and post-release. They argue that the recursive cycle of penal harm is manifest in the iterative 'incarceration–release–reincarceration machine' (Halsey, 2007: 1249). Arrigo and Milovanovic (2009) foreground the iteration of dominant binaries in constructions of the imprisoned and released subject, which they see arising from the lack of a 'fully developed theory of the subject, of the "stranger"' (p. 86), 'relegated to the status of a mere shadow' (p. 133). The way to disrupt the cycle of penal harm, they argue, is with reference to the 'criminology of the shadow' and its transforming subject, the 'criminological stranger' (p. 86), conceptions that seek to transcend the agency–structure duality at the cycle's root, to find new ways of becoming. This perspective encompasses Halsey's (2007) notion of the 'reincarceration assemblage' and its implications for its subject.

The reincarceration assemblage

The idea of 'risky systems' – conceiving risk as systemic rather than located in the offender – challenges the dominant risk paradigm and goes to the heart of the current correctional view of offenders as a 'risky population'. Although based on research with young offenders, Halsey's (2007) notion of 'risky systems of post-release administration [which] assemble the conditions for recidivism and repeat incarceration' (p. 1212) casts a new light on the nature and functioning of what he terms the 'incarceration–release–reincarceration machine' (p. 1249), equally relevant in the adult domain. Rather than focusing on individuals' behaviour and circumstances as the root of offending cycles, Halsey urges an interrogation of the 'practices and philosophies which frame the custodial and post-release landscape' (p. 1248), and a recognition of the prison as functioning 'perfectly well', which 'is precisely the problem' (p. 1249). Without a restructuring and re-imagining of the 'reincarceration assemblage' (p. 1249), Halsey warns, its effects will persist.

Halsey (2007) highlights the importance of attending to the subjective post-release experience, specifically in relation to three key issues: the myth of deterrence and conflicting perceptions of risk, judging 'success' in the post-release context, and the rupture between the custodial and desired societal subjects. Robbers' (2009) findings, that formal and informal post-release sanctions impede the reintegrative prospects of released sex offenders, are illustrative. The exclusionary effects of being labelled a sex offender – ongoing harassment, continual job loss, family breakdown and erroneous rearrest, for example (Robbers, 2009: 21–2) – reinforced by legislative restrictions, reveal the sort of societal reactions encompassed in the reincarceration assemblage. As Robbers argues, the consequences include 'feelings of worthlessness that may translate to future offending' (2009: 22). These themes illuminate a cultural dissonance with which this book seeks to engage: the different ways meanings are constructed and experienced by prison releasees and support workers, and the relationships between these.

Additional aspects of the reincarceration assemblage emerge as sites of conflicting meaning, expectation and interpretation, and manifest as areas of systemic risk, setting ex-prisoners up to fail. Parole is one example: In remote communities particularly, as Willis (2008) notes, requiring compliance and reliability from an inherently unreliable group increases the likelihood of breach and thus the risk of reimprisonment. Holland et al. (2007: 6) find that prisoners with an intellectual disability, compared with their non-impaired counterparts, are more likely to have parole applications denied and are less likely to be paroled at their 'earliest eligibility date', the most commonly cited reason for denial and delay being a 'lack of suitable accommodation'. The mutually reinforcing dynamics of homelessness and reincarceration are well documented (Gowan, 2002) and form iterative cycles of imprisonment from which escape becomes increasingly difficult.

Grunseit et al. (2008: 284) identify 'vulnerabilities in access to justice' as issues confounding the resolution of released prisoners' legal needs, which can increase their risk of reimprisonment. These risks are magnified for vulnerable groups, such as people on remand, in protection or segregation, or those with comprehension difficulties. As well as previous charges to contend with upon release, legal issues can arise for prisoners during their current incarceration; in prison, non-criminal matters are given a low priority, which means these problems are more likely to persist post-release (Grunseit et al., 2008). The longer they remain unaddressed, the greater the risk of being returned to custody. Ex-prisoners' social exclusion is an inherently vulnerable state, in that, as Rose (2000: 336) observes:

> Exclusion itself is effectively criminalized, as crime control agencies home in on those very violations that enable survival in the circuits of exclusion: petty theft, drinking alcohol in public, loitering, drugs and so forth. These new circuits cycle individuals from probation to prison because of probation violations, from prison to parole, and back to prison . . .

In this way, a 'penal grid . . . defines zones of exclusion' (Rose, 2000: 337), solidifying the currents of stigma and division evoked by Combessie (1998, 2002) that hamper ex-prisoners' integrative capacity. The 'penal grid' metaphor accentuates the lines framing and underpinning the risky systems to which released prisoners are subject.

Summing up, the image of 'failed citizens, anti-citizens' (Rose, 2000: 331) is brought to life upon consideration of how the post-release subject is constructed. Not only is the released prisoner himself invested with risk, his world is contaminated: he is surveilled, assessed, monitored, excluded, stigmatised as 'offender'. When his transformation is foreshadowed by the designation 'client', he is expected to transcend this subjectivity and assume that of 'recovering subject'. Yet, this framing belies the enclosing reality of penal and post-release processes, which serve to perpetuate exclusion and indeed constitute risk. The extent to which post-release approaches either augment or seek to circumvent these processes is variously reflected in different modes of post-release intervention, as examined below.

Responses to the post-release problem

How the post-release problem and its subjects are conceived shapes the solution, its scope and remedy. This section explores different ways of responding to the post-release problem and its subject, via different models of practice. Arrigo and Milovanovic (2009) identify three such approaches: the deficit model, desistance models, and their 'transdesistance' model of post-release intervention. These, and their divergent implications for released subjects and their communities, frame the discussion below.

Deficit models

Under the banner of 'what works', much offender treatment literature since 1990 has centred on reducing offending behaviour, usually measured as rearrest or reimprisonment, with a predominant focus on risk/need assessment.[6] This approach is grounded firmly in the work of Andrews and Bonta (1998). Their notion of 'criminogenic needs' differentiates dynamic risk factors that are mutable (such as attitudes, associates, substance abuse, skills deficits) from static risk factors (such as offending history) that cannot be changed. From this perspective, risk is associated chiefly with the 'likelihood of reoffending *by the already convicted*' (Sparks, 2001: 160, original emphasis). Critics have expressed doubt about the importance of individual differences, the reliability of measuring changeable factors. Gendreau, Little and Goggin (1996: 576) argue, however, that dynamic variables are central to the reclassification process routinely required of correctional officials, and their utility is thus undeniable. Despite the oxymoronic appellation, then, a focus on criminogenic needs has emerged as the favoured and empirically verified way of identifying and describing targets for treatment and training, in Australia, Canada, NZ and the UK[7] at least. The assumption is that addressing problem areas in an offender's life identified as predictive of further offending – filling the gaps, as it were – will promote law-abidance.

As Gelb (2007) points out, the 'prediction of risk of reoffending is notoriously difficult and is often inaccurate' (p. 30), and constructions of risk based on actuarial assessments may overlie erroneous assumptions about the nature of offending

and offender types. It is a misconception, for instance, that sex offenders constitute a stable and homogeneous group; to attribute a degree of risk as inhering in
this population belies the diversity and heterogeneity of this group. Gelb (2007)
cites extensive research that casts doubt on the efficacy and usefulness of interventions such as sex offender registration and continued detention for reducing
rates of sexual offences. These findings highlight consistently lower reoffending
rates for sex offences than for violent, property or public-order offences, lack of
specialisation among sexual offenders, and the small proportion of serial rapists
or child molesters among these offenders. Indeed, such preventative strategies
ignore the far greater risk of sexual victimisation by family members or acquaint-
ances (Gelb, 2007). Misconstruing the risks associated with sexual offending can
undermine efforts to reintegrate sex offenders in the community and negate the
chances of reducing their recidivism (Robbers, 2009), chances that are otherwise
quite high (Lievore, 2004, in Gelb, 2007: 37).

Maurutto and Hannah-Moffat (2006) have shown risk to be a fluid concept,
embodying various tensions and inconsistencies often belied by its objective
and reliable guise. For example, the effect, in practice, of 'differing risk priori-
ties' (HMIP&P, 2001: 109) inevitably undermines the UK probation and prison
services' joint responsibilities. Probation is geared towards managing the 'risk
of harm in the community', whereas prisons are concerned with 'maintaining
security and control', which, in 'high-risk' cases, means the duty to prevent
escapes overshadows prisoners' resettlement needs (HMIP&P, 2001: 109). This
disparity highlights problems with the correctional focus on risk management
as its overarching objective. Risk is conceived as an objective, neutral, meas-
urable phenomenon, whereas the above example demonstrates its contingent
nature. Further, the potential to misconstrue risk based on underlying misconceptions makes the reliance on actuarial instruments for predictive, assessment
and management purposes inherently problematic. Despite confidence in the
supposed scientific, objective and apolitical nature of actuarial justice, risk/need
assessment tools are simply that – tools, useful in predicting the likelihood of
recidivism, but never wholly accurate or foolproof.

As Rose (2000: 332) contends, the 'techniques of calculation that are pervading
the work of control professions may be probabilistic, but they are seldom actuarial, and are often only weakly numericized'. They are more reflective of 'risk
thinking' (p. 332) than actuarial control. Far from being objective and morally
neutral, as Hannah-Moffat argues (2005), such tools emphasise professional discretion and subjective judgement in a way that masks their inherent moralistic and
normative elements, rendering 'invisible and hence incontestable, the complex
array of judgements and decisions that go into a scale and a number' (Rose, 1998
in Hannah-Moffat, 2005: 37). Risk and need are measured according to 'highly
gendered and racialized' middle-class mores and assumptions (Hannah-Moffat,
2005: 37–8). Just as risk can be seen as culturally constructed and located, so too
the definition of needs reflects political and institutional imperatives. Offenders'
problems are only ranked as 'needs' insofar as they relate directly to their risk of
reoffending and their 'intervenability' (Hannah-Moffat, 2005: 39).

The failure to contextualise such variables in relation to broader life circumstances can result in post-release implications, including programme irrelevance (Halsey, 2006, 2007), clash of values and understandings (Farrall, 2002), and misplaced targets (Sutherland, 2005). Support services may limit their substance and availability according to assessments that do not accurately reflect an individual's true or self-identified needs (Aubrey & Hough, 1997). The resultant mismatch between programme and participant engenders inefficacy and ex-prisoners' disengagement with services. The deficit model of rehabilitation and desistance emphasises 'failings or transgressions of *offenders* rather than . . . the strengths and progressions of . . . *persons*' (Halsey, 2006: 167, original emphasis). Notwithstanding its ascendancy in correctional circles, this approach is being shadowed by issues of effective practice and a trend towards more positive, strengths-based approaches (Burnett & Maruna, 2006), models with roots in positive psychology (Ward & Brown, 2004; Wormith et al., 2007). This shift towards a more holistic orientation has significant implications for wider post-release policy and practice. Concepts such as 'well-being' or 'a meaningful life' scarcely accord with current penal attitudes and approaches (Wormith et al., 2007) and yet feature strongly in new rehabilitative conceptualisations and the language of reintegration and desistance. Key themes in the desistance literature and models of practice are now explored.

Desistance models

Despite their varying emphases, the common theme uniting discourses of rehabilitation, desistance and reintegration is the time-honoured notion of 'going straight' (Farrall & Calverley, 2006). The desistance literature, largely informed by life course research (Sampson & Laub, 1993; Laub & Sampson, 2001), draws together agency, maturation, social bonds and narrative theories (Maruna, 2001; McNeill et al., 2005). It has evolved from an emphasis on the individual to see offending and its curtailment as a social issue, embedded in webs of interaction and connected to a whole set of social, economic and political factors (Farrall et al., 2011; McNeill, 2012). Altogether, strengths-based approaches to rehabilitation and desistance – what we might call the new rehabilitative paradigm – are better equipped than risk/need assessments to take into account the 'long shadow of the prison' (Combessie, 2002) and other sources of stigma and exclusion.

Desistance approaches highlight the importance of the social context of 'risk factors' such as unemployment and housing instability, as shown by Lösel's (2012) finding that 'employment, accommodation and financial problems . . . were not only related to a lack of material resources, but also to a lack of social resources such as quality of family relationships and contact during imprisonment' (p. 12). Ward (2002) and Maruna and LeBel (2003) similarly emphasise the contextual and relationship context of desistance (also in McNeill, Raynor & Trotter, 2010). McNeill et al. (2005) accentuate desistance as 'a process which is commonly characterised by ambivalence and vacillation. It is not an event' (p. 30). They argue that its relationship to life events is contingent upon their personal meaning,

that 'someone "believing in" the offender' may be a catalyst, and that it encompasses 'change in narrative identities (or self-stories)' (p. 30). They emphasise
the layers that desistance entails: 'agency ... first discovered and then exercised', in a process that 'requires social capital (opportunities) as well as human
capital (capacities)', possibly realising 'purpose through "generative activities"'
(McNeill et al., 2005: 31). Desistance from crime requires, not just individual psychological change, but also that social, moral and legal barriers to ex-prisoners'
reintegration be addressed (McNeill, 2012).

Opportunities for generativity, through 'caring for others or creative pursuits'
(Healy & O'Donnell, 2008: 27), are seen as ripe with integrative potential. A focus
on future generations enables individuals to transcend immediate self-interest,
evoking the rehabilitative dictum of leading a 'productive' life. Drawing on
Erikson's (1950) seventh stage of human development, generativity may be conceived as 'the commitment toward or practice of caring for self, other and future'
(Halsey & Harris, 2011: 74), the lack of which can engender '*stagnation*, boredom and self-impoverishment' (Erikson, 1968: 138, original italics, in Halsey &
Harris, 2011: 74). Erikson (1968) saw creativity and productivity as synonymous
with generativity (Halsey & Harris, 2011: 87). As a developing concept in the
desistance literature, generativity overlaps with long-established notions of 'giving back' (McNeill & Maruna, 2007), 'helping others' (Burnett & Maruna, 2006;
LeBel, 2007, 2009), 'commonality' (Toch, 2000b) and the transformative power
of parenthood (Sampson & Laub, 1993; Walker, 2010). Drawing on Toch (2000a),
Burnett and Maruna (2006: 84–5) note the 'alleged benefits of assuming the role
of helper, for offenders, include a sense of accomplishment, grounded increments
in self-esteem, meaningful purposiveness and a cognitive restructuring towards
responsibility'. The revival of such an approach has accompanied growing interest
in restorative justice (Burnett & Maruna, 2006).

The ethos of restorative justice has seeped into the pre-and post-release realm
in the recognition that restorative practices in prisons can pave the way for
prisoners' return to their communities and post-release reintegration.[8] Models
such as COSA,[9] by which Five8 is inspired, have grown across the US and UK,
recognising ex-prisoners' frequent social isolation and lack of social support
(Kemshall, 2002). Gray (2005), however, argues that risk thinking has co-opted
restorative principles, emphasising young offenders' 'responsibilisation' over
reintegration and thereby reinforcing their social exclusion. Gray shows that, by
privileging certain principles, ostensibly reintegrative approaches can serve to
constitute and perpetuate the risks they purport to reduce, exemplifying Halsey's
'risky systems'.

More optimistically, Maruna and LeBel (2003) consider a range of strengths-
based correctional and drug treatment practices and envision a re-entry court based
on these restorative principles. Maruna (2006) proposes a cooperative model of
'restorative reintegration' distinguished by four key features: it is community-led,
reparation-based and symbolically rich and leads eventually to 'wiping the slate
clean' through a 'de-labelling' process[10] (p. 31). From Burnett and Maruna's case

study (2006) of a strengths-based reintegration project involving prisoners volunteering at a Citizens' Advice Bureau, two important themes emerge: the perception of prisoners as a positive labour market resource, and the value of using the 'helping principle' for ex-prisoners to develop 'pro-social self-concepts and identity' (p. 102). Strengths-based and restorative activities are distinguished from traditional forms of prisoner labour or community service by putting 'offenders in visible, community-oriented "helping" or leadership roles' (Burnett & Maruna, 2006: 87), which foster a prosocial identity, thus providing opportunities for social and moral reintegration (McNeill, 2012).

Approaches to building human and social capital through mentoring and personal relationships are similarly strengths-based and 'person-centred' (Burnett, 2007). The most influential of these is the Good Lives Model (GLM), which takes a risk/needs approach as its point of departure and argues for 'an enriched concept of need embedded in the notion of human wellbeing' (Ward and Stewart, 2003: 125). This model rests on the assumption that the most effective way to reduce reoffending is 'to equip individuals with the tools to live more fulfilling lives rather than to simply develop increasingly sophisticated risk management measures and strategies' (Ward & Brown, 2004: 244). These tools enable ex-prisoners to improve their functioning and well-being 'in socially acceptable and personally meaningful ways' (Ward, 2002: 173). The GLM focuses on identity and well-being in an individual's social context (Ward, 2002, 2010).

Farrall (2004) emphasises the importance of social context in terms of social capital, the 'social interactions between individuals and other[s]' (p. 61) that give rise to individuals' connectedness and social participation. He identifies family and work as key reintegrative factors that function 'as *both* the precursors and the outcomes' of social capital (Farrall, 2004, original emphasis, in Brown & Ross, 2010a: 38). Mills and Codd (2008) explore the role of prisoners' families and how they may be 'mobilised' as a source of social capital. Reflecting on the value of 'relationship-based practice', Burnett (2007) highlights the importance of relationship in working with 'ex-offenders' and in building their connections with family, friends and other social networks, in the integrative process. McNeill et al. (2005) similarly underline the significance of relationship in desistance-focused interventions and point to the critical role of 'extra-therapeutic factors' (p. 23), including social support.

The significance of relationship is the key assumption underpinning mentoring programmes, matching volunteer mentors with socially isolated ex-prisoners. Brown and Ross (2010a, 2010b) found that mentors, in 'activating' their own social capital for the benefit of mentees, provided practical assistance as well as building trust and emotional support (social capital), from which human capital (capacity) could develop. In a similar capacity-building vein, the Australian 'Passports' model (Kinner, 2008) is a health-based approach relying on advocacy and referral for post-release support. Though more instrumental in its focus, linking ex-prisoners to health and community services, this model addresses the social context of offending and imprisonment cycles in order to promote social integration.

As Maruna (2001) illustrates, a key element of desistance is the role and transformation of 'narrative identities' (McNeill et al., 2005: 31) into 'redemption scripts' (Maruna & Roy, 2006: 17). Central to a future-focused self-story is hope. Exploring the role of hope in desistance, Burnett and Maruna (2004) find a link between hope and expectations of success and goal realisation. Halsey (2007) notes the interconnectedness of hope and despair: that one arises out of the other. Perhaps the finding that prisoners' optimistic forecasts of post-release success were largely unrealistic when compared with their reconviction rates (Dhami et al., 2006) reflects this. Perhaps repeatedly encountering social and structural barriers to desistance undermines hope.

Martin and Stermac (2010) link increased levels of hope to reduced risk of reoffending. Conversely, Halsey (2007: 16) observes that young men he interviewed exhibited roles characterised by learned helplessness, which may have developed during or prior to their incarceration, and yet have manifest implications for their capacity to integrate into a non-criminal community following their release. Indirectly related are prisoners' post-release expectations of continuity of in-prison support. Gideon (2009) describes the bewilderment and confusion of addicts who have undergone drug treatment in prison, likening their experience to that of 'immigrants that have just arrived in a foreign land' (p. 44). Gideon highlights an aspect of release that Haney (2003) also observes: how institutional dependence is experienced by released addicts who have 'been able to remain clean [in prison] . . . by depending heavily on the institution to limit and control their behaviour' (Haney, 2003: 49). Their 'stress is magnified during early stages of reentry' (Gideon, 2009: 44), underscoring the need for post-release services to maintain the 'momentum' (p. 44) of prison programmes.

Healy and O'Donnell (2008) identify a gap in knowledge about the early stages of desistance, crucial given that so many research subjects 'are in this transitional phase of reform' (p. 28). Maruna, LeBel and Lanier (2004) suggest that the internalisation of generativity through positive interactions represents the incipient stages of 'rehabilitation' and therefore desistance. Admittedly, how this process unfolds is inaccessible to most researchers (Healy & O'Donnell, 2008: 28). Nevertheless, we need to understand the different phases of transition when thinking about men's experience of release and liminality, explored later on. Drawing together the threads of desistance research reveals theoretical emphases on maturation, life transitions, social bonds, and subjectivities/identities and, increasingly, the interrelationship of these domains (McNeill, 2011). Now, to explore this interaction from a broader philosophical and societal perspective.

'Transdesistance' models

Arrigo and Milovanovic's (2009) 'transdesistance' is a postmodern concept, and yet it connects with arguments for broad-based reforms to address structural barriers to reintegration (Armstrong, 2004, 2006; Garside, 2009), in that both seek to challenge the form and operation of the penal apparatus. Although transdesistance offers little practical guidance for post-release intervention, their critical perspective is nevertheless an important lens through which to conceive and appraise existing policy and practices, as 'a vision of change rather than a blueprint for reform' (Arrigo & Milovanovic, 2009: 120).

Transdesistance builds on desistance models but goes further, challenging assumptions about the role of work, the nature of family and aspirations of freedom, arguing instead for multiple, non-normative constructions of self, family, work, hope and success. At the heart of Arrigo and Milovanovic's (2009) dense and elaborate theorisation, the 'subject-in-process' embodies notions of 'subjectivity' and 'becoming', central to their transformative thesis. In proposing a shift in how the post-release support role and the released subject are conceived, they argue for 'a transition from what is (. . . homeless/confined, poor, black . . .) to what could be (. . . a person yet to come)' (p. 151). They describe a process of 'becoming' whereby a person formerly consigned to being a 'stranger' may be 'resuscitated' (pp. 120, 152), in 'relational contexts' (p. 134). There is a clear overlap with Toch's (2000b) notion of 'commonality', seeing the 'relatedness' between the ex-prisoner, the 'keepers' who confine/monitor and the punitive public – implicating all in 'the recursive cycle of the pains of imprisonment, the pains of release, and the pains of imprisonment' (Arrigo & Milovanovic, 2009: 120).

This idea links to the construction of the post-release subject, explored above, though it is considered here in terms of its implications for post-release support. Arrigo and Milovanovic (2009) imply that, by responding to pre-ordained constructions and continuities, workers unwittingly participate in the repetitive reduction of 'client' 'identities to singularities, imaging [each] as nothing more or other than a client/offender indistinguishable from all others . . . [thus] rending the becoming self inaccessible, unrecognizable, and unspeakable' (p. 151). It is argued that 'the imagery, logic and language of the deficit and desistance models exemplify these status quo conditions' (p. 151), and that 'techniques of resistance', 'strategies of transformation', are needed to negate 'the harms of repression/reduction' (p. 152). Arrigo and Milovanovic imagine a fearless, unfettered kind of personal engagement, based not on a professional–client dynamic but on authentic human interaction. Only then, they posit, can the post-release subject be 'liberated from the agency/structure duality that repetitively fosters harm, essentialises prison discourse, and reifies the correctional edifice that stands above both' (2009: 120).

Consistent with a transdesistance approach, Halsey (2006, 2007) considers possibilities for transformation and becoming, extending horizons foreshortened by a desistance focus. He highlights the 'absurdity of the "chicken-or-egg" type' (2007: 1246) agency/structure characterisations dominating desistance approaches, endorsing instead LeBel et al.'s (2008) 'subjective-social model' (Halsey, 2007: 1247) and emphasising 'shared responsibility' for desistance (p. 1257). Toch's (2000b) emphasis on 'commonality' over difference resonates with this thinking. Halsey (2006) argues, moreover, for desistance to be conceived as a 'process to be negotiated . . . despite the occasional, or even more frequent, transgression' (p. 167). From this perspective, 'failure' is accommodated – indeed anticipated – rather than punished.

Like Halsey, Armstrong (2004, 2006) and Garside (2009) reflect on risk in relation to young people. Their critique of risk-based policies and practices is equally pertinent in the adult domain. Armstrong (2004) argues that preventative and reintegrative policy built on risk-factor identification results in the stigmatisation of already marginalised groups and the further imposition of 'mechanisms of governmentality' upon them, recalling Rose's (2000) 'circuits of exclusion'. Garside (2009: 3) highlights the flawed risk logic, aspiring to 'fewer criminals and less crime', that underpins overbearing interventions into families' and individuals' lives. A risk-based approach generates policy that shifts responsibility for systemic failings away from the system and on to the individual, rather than attempting meaningful social reform. As Armstrong (2006: 272) asserts: 'poverty, although recognised as a factor associated with high risk, is countered not by economic redistribution but by interventions aimed at supporting individuals . . . with the management of their own risk', evoking earlier discussion of offender/client constructions. Individuals are deemed responsible for their own salvation and/or transformation.

Transdesistance, and the 'risky systems' perspective it encompasses, envisions social reform via structural changes to risk-generating practices and processes. Decentring the 'offender' from risk equations, by focusing on systemic risks, makes room for economic arguments for reintegrative reform. Garside (2009) draws on Marmot and Wilkinson's (2006) work on risk factors relating to poor health outcomes to highlight an alternative perspective on risk analysis, one that focuses on the 'causes of the causes'. This approach views micro risk factors in terms of 'the macro social, economic and political context within which these micro factors unfold and shape the lives of individuals' (Garside, 2009: 12). Such a perspective casts light on the interplay of risk factors in determining post-release outcomes. For example, the risk of homelessness among released prisoners may be seen as relating to the limited availability of public housing, housing policy and prioritisation of need, and inadequate income support (Baldry et al., 2006; Hartley & Baraka, 2007).

Policy arising from attempts to identify risky individuals is inherently problematic and 'ultimately futile' (Garside, 2009: 11). The challenge, Garside (2009) argues, drawing on Armstrong's (2004, 2006) logic, is to craft a response that recognises the disproportionate levels of risk experienced by different population groups, and that addresses underlying inequalities and dysfunctions, rather than requiring individuals to manage their own risk. For instance, the risk of economic exclusion has increased with the rise in criminal-record checking by employers (Saliba, 2012). Victoria leads many Australian states in its post-release initiatives, and yet it is the only Australian jurisdiction without a statutory spent conviction scheme (Naylor, 2011; Paterson & Naylor, 2011). Although limited legal protections against discrimination exist, they do little to mitigate ex-prisoners' experience of labour-market exclusion (Naylor, 2011). Spent conviction laws embody the possibility of structural reform shifting the focus away from risk-based approaches. Yet the rehabilitative aim of expunging criminal records, explicit in France's 'judicial rehabilitation' (Herzog-Evans, 2011), contrasts sharply with

Australia's 'economic penal narrative' – convictions are spent, dues are paid – emblematic of a culture 'remarkably reluctant to forgive' (Naylor, 2011: 80). Naylor observes little scope for the kind of institutionalised rituals that Maruna (2001, 2011a) envisions to actively promote redemption and reintegration.

Prison's 'collateral consequences' (Mauer & Chesney-Lind, 2003) encompass the range of exclusionary practices affecting families and communities. Wacquant (2002) argues that the military metaphor 'collateral damage', in downplaying the extensive social and economic ramifications of imprisonment, is inadequate and misleading. It suggests that prison 'acts alone' (p. 388), negating the complex interplay with other institutions. It assumes the prison is 'external to social space' (p. 388), when it is deeply interwoven into the lives of whole social populations. It implies that the prison is necessarily and 'wholly negative', which denies its 'stabilizing and restorative' functions, such as removing violent men from families, interrupting addiction and providing health care (Wacquant, 2002: 388). Kariminia et al. (2007b) and Brown (2009) attest to these 'positive' effects of imprisonment among Australian Indigenous communities. Wacquant (2002: 388) concludes that the metaphor masks the prison's role as 'a perverse agency for the delivery of human services to the social refuse of the market society'.

This sociopolitical repositioning of the prison (Harcourt, 2008; Baldry, 2009) has prompted Wacquant's (2002) urging 'to *investigate the varied linkages between the prison and its surrounding institutions on the ground*, as they actually exist and operate . . . capturing process, nuance, and contradiction' (p. 387–8, original emphasis). It is these linkages and their nuances and contradictions that this book seeks to explore, to understand how 'the recursive cycle of the pains of imprisonment [and] release' unfolds (Arrigo & Milovanovic, 2009: 120). This requires listening to the subjective experience of those imprisoned and released.

Conclusion

This chapter depicts the sociopolitical, discursive milieu against/within which post-prison shadows are cast and ex-prisoners' lived experience may be understood. The implications of post-prison disadvantage are manifest in the released subject's ongoing exclusion and constitution as 'risky' while being ensnared in recursive patterns of penal/social harm: poverty, homelessness and criminalisation. Contributing systemic factors are overshadowed by the ascription of risk to individuals. 'Offenders' are constructed as responsible for their own problems and problematic behaviour and their own transformation. These broader themes have shaped this chapter's focus and structure. I have highlighted conflicting elements in the construction of the post-release problem: an obsession with public safety and risk management, and concern over ex-prisoners' socio-economic exclusion. I have shown how conceiving the released subject as 'risky' or 'at risk' engenders different ways of responding to (and imagining solutions to) the post-prison problem. These themes provide a theoretical context for policy and practice in Australia, where an overarching re-entry /reintegration narrative is missing. This context supports the book's focus on how post-release constraints are experienced, and their ramifications for (re)integration. The following chapter builds a conceptual framework within which we may understand prison release as a multilayered phenomenon.

Notes

1 Including the Bush Administration's Serious and Violent Offender Reentry Initiative (SVORI) in 2001, and the Second Chance Act (2008) under which the Prisoner Reentry Initiative and National Reentry Resource Centre were established in 2009.
2 By the Council of State Governments' online National Reentry Resource Centre, the National Institute of Corrections, and the National Governors' Association, for instance.
3 The Home Secretary's proclamation at a Conservative Party Conference in 1995 became the theme associated with the rise of 'popular punitiveness' or 'penal populism'.
4 See also Armstrong, 2004, 2006; Garside, 2009.
5 Rose, 2000; Wacquant, 2001, 2002; Patillo, Weiman & Western, 2004; Western, 2008a, 2008b; Harcourt, 2008, 2011; Baldry, 2009.
6 McGuire, 2002; Ward & Stewart, 2003; Day, Howells & Rickwood, 2003; Brown, 2005; Hannah-Moffat, 2005; Wormith et al., 2007; Willis & Moore, 2008.
7 Andrews et al., 1990; Ward & Stewart, 2003; McGuire, 2002; Ward & Brown, 2004; Wormith et al., 2007.
8 Liebmann & Braithwaite, 1999; Newell, 2003, 2002; Van Ness, 2005.
9 Circles of Support and Accountability, a Canadian model of offender reintegration.
10 A form of destigmatisation (Braithwaite, 1989; Braithwaite & Mugford, 1994).

4   Assemblage, culture, liminality

'Matt' and 'Eddie'

'Matt' is 27. He was 19, with no prior convictions, when he became involved in a series of incidents that culminated in a home invasion, abduction and failed extortion attempt. Sentenced to 12 years imprisonment, he was released after 7 years. An eloquent, softly spoken man, he relates his experience candidly yet with a polite reserve. He takes pride in his Middle Eastern heritage and language, and describes his family as close and bound by strong faith. Their culture of hospitality and respect for others, moreover, intensifies the remorse he feels for the crime he committed, 'a one-off': 'I was 19 at the time, no criminal history, nothing, not even a shoplift, nothing. No one in the history of my family had any drug history or drug problems, nothing like that.'

Intelligent and thoughtful, he observed prison life and the different ways men inhabit the prison social world with the keen eye of an outsider. He talked about having 'a lot of support from my family and from prison authorities', which meant his experience contrasted to that of men with cyclic experience of imprisonment. His insights into the different characters and interactions revealed his ability to blend skilfully into the background, as well as take an active role in pursuing his own interests and opportunities as they arose. He describes being at an open prison for his last 2 years, where:

> I was doing bush gang [work in the community], I was the librarian there, I was running the canteen, the cafeteria there. . . . In my last year I participated in the leave program, so I was getting leaves every 28 days. . . . While I was in there I finished a Diploma of Arts [in pottery]. I did various offending behaviour specific courses . . .

He admits he 'did it very easy' in prison, in that he 'did all the normal functional things a person would do every day'. He sums up the attitude that shaped his experience of imprisonment:

> The system is what you make of it. If you sit back and feel sorry for yourself and [think] 'everyone is against me', you're not going to get anywhere. It's how you use it and how much you push yourself and strive to get what you need or what you think is beneficial for you.

He referred to his crime, his reason for being in prison, firmly in the past:

> All the years that I was in there, I never wanted to come back to prison. I never wanted that to be my life. It's something that I did in my life, I made a mistake, I did something stupid which I took account for and did my time. I wanted to move on from that.

His account is punctuated with the phrase, 'I was fortunate', acknowledging how his experience contrasted with that of the majority of men in jail. He had the support of family and close friends, which allowed him to sustain his hope and confidence and his focus on the future. Since his release, he has engaged with the WISE ex-offender employment programme and has found work: 'It's amazing how everything fell into place. I've been pretty lucky the jobs that I've had . . . in the last few months'. Matt is realistic about having a criminal record and its potential constraints on getting long-term work. But he is confident and definite when he says 'I won't go back, never'. I believe him.

'Eddie' is 32, a slight man, soft voiced and well spoken. Like Matt, Eddie has had only one stint in prison but he can still relate its 'ongoing effect'. When we meet in a suburban café, he describes his experience of imprisonment, which was brief but chastening. At the time, he 'had an amphetamine habit, [was] dealing to support that, [and] got caught'. His charges included a 'very low level armed robbery', which – together with the fact he had missed a previous court date – meant that he was refused bail and remanded in prison until his court hearing. Sentenced to 12 months, 9 of which were suspended, he was released after 3 months for 'time served'.

In the 7 years since his release Eddie has stabilised his drug use. He has 'been charged and convicted for things since then but nothing that carries a custodial sentence' and, though still a regular cannabis user, he admits, 'I'd be very reluctant to do anything that did [mean custody] – I wouldn't enjoy the experience'. Eddie says he has 'an anxiety disorder', which makes group situations particularly stressful. Though he 'might have had that before that, I don't know', prison certainly amplified his anxiety. He gets panic attacks now, which he never had before.

Eddie describes the whole experience of his escalating drug use and subsequent imprisonment as 'part of a process of a not very happy adolescence almost turning into a pretty tragic early twenties'. He expresses a sense of defeat in that he might 'otherwise . . . [have] made some use of my education . . . I don't know'. Eddie has little work history and lacks formal training: 'I worked in a book shop when I was in high school but that's the only job prior to that, no real work'.

As well as a theme of intermittence – in work, relationships and patterns in his life – Eddie's story conveys a sense of being reconciled to a future shaped by his past. He describes the stigma of imprisonment:

> When you get out . . . you're still treated like . . . a deviant . . . so, what's that term, deviance amplification . . . that's what prisons do, and that's what . . . being released does.

He reflects upon the impact of having a criminal record as limiting his options for employment: 'Nowadays, it's getting a lot stricter, even on cleaning jobs'. His future is therefore constrained: 'yeah, I could pack boxes for the rest of my life'.

Matt and Eddie were 'first timers', both unlikely to return, their imprisonment associated with a past they no longer identified with. Both seemed intelligent, thoughtful and reflective. What differentiated them appeared to be a sense of hope and possibility for the future. For Matt, with no previous connection to the prison world, his horizons seemed barely shadowed by his prison time. Eddie – whose grandfather and uncles had been in jail – seemed less hopeful, less confident, his aspirations limited by a sense of uncertainty. It seemed that, for Eddie, the prison's shadow loomed larger.

This chapter establishes a conceptual framework for the study, comprising three themes: assemblage, culture and liminality. These ideas are drawn together as a lens through which to 'see into' the post-release experience. They are embedded in the questions at the heart of the study: *How is prison release (and post-release life) constructed? And how do these constructions conflict and cohere?* The purpose of this chapter is to explain how these ideas fit together, and why they work to give voice to the various conceptions and lived experience of prison release. It begins by exploring the notion of assemblage (Deleuze & Guattari, 1987), as developed by DeLanda (2006), and how this may be usefully employed as a way of viewing the post-release terrain as a complex, multilayered social phenomenon comprising varied perspectives and understandings. Assemblage provides a framework within which the lived experience of release and the practice of post-release support work may be conceptualised in terms of their interactions, their connections and collisions.

The second part of the chapter considers culture as way of understanding and explaining how prison culture leaks out into and inflects the post-prison sphere. It begins by tracing the anthropological roots of the culture concept and exploring its use and usefulness as lens and analytical device, specifically as a semiotic-practical approach (Wedeen, 2002), underpinned by Swidler's (1986) 'culture-in-action' model. This lens is applied to culture as an 'emergent product and producer' (Sampson & Bean, 2006: 27) of the carceral assemblage. The construction of masculinity is analysed, illuminating the study's gendered perspective and its focus on maleness as an aspect of the cycle of imprisonment. The third section explores the theme of liminality, which runs through the post-release literature, albeit largely implicitly, as an element of life following release from prison. Liminality is located at the heart of the post-prison experience and is examined in terms of its significant implications for (re)integration. Liminality emerges as a defining characteristic of prisoners' experience of getting out – a state of being in-between, neither inside nor yet fully part of the outside world. Lastly, the chapter attempts to synthesise these three elements, showing how the theoretical links are forged to provide insight into the experience of prison release. For Deleuze, 'a theory is exactly like a box of tools . . . it must be useful' (Deleuze & Foucault, 1977: 208); each theory's usefulness to this study is described below.

Assemblage

The concept of assemblage emerges from the work of Deleuze and Guattari (1987). They elaborate concepts that, though barely amounting to a 'fully-fledged theory' (DeLanda, 2006: 3), are nonetheless the basis for DeLanda's (2006) 'reconstructed theory of assemblages' (p. 4), a useful device for modelling and conceptualising relations between social entities. Assemblage also provides a way to transcend traditional binary views of social reality. Although several approaches succeed in revealing other layers beyond the micro–macro dichotomy, DeLanda (2006) argues that assemblage theory can both frame and reveal connections between ontologically disparate views of the world and various social network-oriented theories. Assemblages can thus contain and convey collisions between realms of conception, meaning and experience. This possibility is explored below.

The assemblage concept

Assemblage[1] has been widely and increasingly accepted as a theoretical concept in the social sciences since first translated from French in the 1980s. But, as Phillips (2006: 109) argues, there is meaning and subtlety lost in the translation. The English word assemblage – designating a collection of things – generally has rather technical connotations, describing, for instance, an archaeological scatter or an artist's rendering of found objects; its 'noun-ness' tends to obscure its verb status and evoke the outcome rather than the process of assembling. And, although the French might similarly talk about the *assemblage* of ingredients in a recipe, to imply, 'blending, collating, gathering and joining' (Phillips, 2006: 108), this word is never used in a philosophical sense, least of all in a Deleuzian lexicon. Deleuze and Guattari's French term *agencement*, however, is nuanced and pregnant with connections to other philosophical concepts, such as Spinoza's 'common notion', and the ideas of 'event', 'sense' and 'becoming', which relate closely to it. Its translation as assemblage risks missing much of this complexity and the capacity of the term to capture paradox. Nonetheless, it behoves closer examination of its philosophical undercurrents.

A 'common notion', for instance, as Phillips (2006: 109) explains, arises:

> when two or more bodies have something in common. . . . When two or more bodies come into contact or otherwise enter into a relationship they form a composition. A *common notion* is the representation of this composition as an independent unity.

And, to co-opt his example of 'a poison and the body poisoned':

> the unity, for instance, of a [prison and the body imprisoned] can be regarded as a state of becoming and an event which is reducible to neither the [prisoner] nor the [prison]. The [prisoner] and the [prison], rather, participate in the event (which is what they have in common).

In exploring such unities in terms of their 'eventness', their sense and their becoming, a Deleuzian perspective encourages an ontological shift towards thinking of 'the real as a process', as Boundas (2005: 191) explains, away from perceiving the fixed nature of things to seeing the dynamic relations between them (Semetsky, 2005). This evokes a view of the significance of process over structure, of the living dynamics of human action over the structure of society (Mentore, 2009). Thus, rather than viewing the prison and penal system as containing and regulating the bodies and movements of individuals tagged 'offenders', 'prisoners', 'parolees' and so on as a rigid reality, the interactions and relations within and between these bodies can be seen as shifting and tangential, inherently contingent. And, rather than trying to represent such a reality by imposing meaning, the attempt is towards an 'assemblage of enunciation', based on 'an AND rather than an INSTEAD OF logic ("instead of" [being] the motto of representation)' (Lecercle, 2002: 54). As Lecercle explains, this logic of assemblage is one of mixture, of conjoining things that:

> can function in various assemblages, which always involve texts, symbols, patterns of behaviour, institutions and objects. . . . And the assemblage does not discriminate between them, does not establish hierarchies, as representation does – causal chains go in every direction, and not only from object to sign.
>
> (2002: 60)

Thus, a process of circular conjunction is implied. Connections are made between, for instance, the way post-release housing is described in policy terms, how its practicalities are perceived and managed by post-release support workers, and how it is experienced by homeless ex-prisoners.

Lecercle (2002) links this logic to the way language works: arranging clauses side by side, without subordination. Thus, a Deleuzian approach invites an analysis of language and symbols that does not privilege hegemony, that gives equal voice to the lived experience of those imprisoned and released. It is Guattari (1979), as Lecercle observes, who offers:

> the beginning of a theory of assemblages, of which he gives a first definition: their main characteristic is that they do not so much 'speak of things' as 'speak among things', '*à même les choses*', in the midst of facts, states of affairs and subjective states.
>
> (Lecercle, 2002: 34)

It is this characteristic of being among, rather than apart from, that Lecercle captures when, in summarising Deleuze's philosophy of language as a list of concepts and their opponents, he describes assemblages as 'neither *subjects* nor *system*' (2002: 255). This transcending of the micro/macro divide may be characterised as 'ontologically "bottom-up" . . . with the assumption that individual persons are the bottom-most level' (DeLanda, 2006: 32). This does not mean an individualist approach that assumes individuals are 'rational actors' making decisions on their own. Rather, in assemblage theory, individuals exist and interact with one another as part of populations. Within these, identities emerge from the interactions of their component parts, whereby this 'emergent subjectivity' is seen as an assemblage in itself (DeLanda, 2006: 33).

The notion of relational networks of connections, rather than hierarchical structures and orders of meaning, is captured in Deleuze and Guattari's (1987) concept of the 'rhizome', which they conceived as a challenge to traditional and habitual ways of thinking and dominant ways of knowing that they characterise as 'arborescent' or 'arboreal'. The tree-like metaphor evokes the vertical, hierarchical arrangement of knowledge and conceptualisation, a closed system of thought rooted in a determining principle shaped by a superior concept from which other concepts stem, decreasing in importance, power, relevance or value, and fixed in terms of their relationship to other concepts. Such thinking, from a Deleuzian perspective, serves to privilege – and cocoon from critique – dominant concepts and ways of seeing (Stagoll, 2005). For example, the criminal justice system embodies an arboreal schema, rooted in the primacy of the law and the capacity of judicial and penal institutions to secure and administer justice. The fixed nature of this hierarchy allows for supposed 'truths' to persist uninterrogated, such as the apparent certainty associated with the use of actuarial tools, which 'maintain a veneer of objectivity and "truthfulness" because of their reliance on and production of numerical calculations' (Maurutto & Hannah-Moffat, 2006: 441).

In contrast, the rhizome 'conceives how every thing and every body – all aspects of concrete, abstract, and virtual entities and activities – can be seen as multiple in their inter-relational movements with other things and bodies' (Colman, 2005: 231). Just as the rhizome offers 'a powerful way of thinking without recourse to analogy or binary constructions' (Colman, 2005: 233), the assemblage concept is useful to this study as it provides a means of transcending the carceral/post-carceral (macro/micro, structure/agency) dichotomy by conceiving instead what Halsey (2007) terms the 'reincarceration assemblage'.

Assemblage in a post-release context

This conception affords a view of the penal system beyond a simple divide between its subjects/objects and its (social, economic and political) architecture and machinery. Instead, a social assemblage is envisioned: an assemblage of bodies and other material components – the labour, buildings, physical and structural elements of prisons and courts – and its expression in forms of language and symbol and various other 'non-linguistic social expressions' (DeLanda, 2006: 13); what Deleuze and Guattari (1987) might refer to as 'machinic assemblages' and 'collective assemblages of enunciation', respectively. The focus is thus shifted away from the individual and the risk inhering in a person's circumstances and behaviour, to the webs of connectivity in which individuals are enmeshed and in which they participate in meaning-making, albeit in conflicting and disparate ways. Conceiving of a reincarceration assemblage affords insight, for example, into Wacquant's (2002: 382) '*carceral-assistential continuum*', whereby the regulation of poverty is effected by the 'intermingling' of social institutions with the prison.

At the heart of Halsey's (2007) reincarceration assemblage sits the notion of 'risky systems of post-release administration', comprising 'programs and procedures which . . . literally assemble the conditions for recidivism and repeat incarceration' (p. 1212). In explaining how reoffending and reimprisonment may be viewed as a '*collective* process', Halsey (2007: 1247) refers (and adds emphasis) to comments by Deleuze in a 1980 interview:[2]

> There are various kinds of assemblages, and various component parts. On the one hand, we *are trying to substitute the idea of assemblage for the idea of behaviour* . . . On the other hand, the analysis of assemblages, broken down into their component parts, opens up the way to a general logic . . . Assemblages are a bunch of lines. But there are all kinds of lines. Some lines are segments, or segmented; some lines get caught in a rut, or disappear into 'black holes'; some are destructive, sketching death; and some lines are vital and creative. These creative and vital lines open up an assemblage, rather than close it down . . . But an assemblage is first and foremost what keeps very heterogeneous elements together.

For Halsey, assemblage allows a focus on difference and heterogeneity in perspective and experience. In describing a collective process, he is thus evoking a multiplicity – a gathering of threads or currents of activity, of what people do, variously yet within the same realm – rather than a mutually constructed phenomenon.

Halsey alerts us to a fundamental aspect of assemblages as comprising a bunch of lines, of which Deleuze and Guattari (1987: 204) describe three kinds: molar lines of 'rigid segmentarity'; molecular lines of 'supple segmentarity'; and lines of flight, which dissect the other two:

> [C]ausing runoffs, as when you drill a hole in a pipe; there is no social system that does not leak from all directions, even if it makes its segments increasingly rigid in order to seal the lines of flight.
>
> (p. 204)

An additional characteristic of an assemblage is its territory, its 'home' (Deleuze & Guattari, 1987: 504), within which it is divided into expression – 'a *semiotic system*, a regime of signs' – and content – 'a *pragmatic system*, actions and passions' (p. 504, original emphasis). These divisions make every assemblage 'simultaneously and inseparably a machinic assemblage [i.e. content] and an assemblage of enunciation [i.e. expression]' (p. 504). Deleuze and Guattari further divide assemblages along axes: the horizontal axis comprises its territoriality, including its two segments of content and expression; the vertical axis is constituted by '*lines of deterritorialisation* that cut across it and carry it away' (p. 504). As if pre-empting calls for clarification, they summarise:

The concrete rules of assemblage thus operate along these two axes: On the one hand, what is the territoriality of the assemblage, what is the regime of signs and the pragmatic system? On the other hand, what are the cutting edges of deterritorialisation, and what abstract machines do they effectuate? The assemblage is tetravalent: (1) content and expression; (2) territoriality and deterritorialisation.

(1987: 505)

To use prison as an example: 'the prison is a form, the 'prison-form'' (Deleuze & Guattari, 1987: 66), easily identifiable by its impenetrable walls, its fortified perimeter, its razor wire. Yet:

This . . . form does not refer back to the word 'prison' but to entirely different words and concepts, such as 'delinquent' and 'delinquency', which express a new way of classifying, stating, translating, and even committing criminal acts. 'Delinquency' is the form of expression in reciprocal presupposition with the form of content 'prison'.

(p. 66)

As Deleuze and Guattari explain, we can neither reduce the content of the prison to a 'thing' nor reduce its expression to single words; rather, 'there are two constantly intersecting multiplicities, "discursive multiplicities" of expression and "nondiscursive multiplicities" of content' (Deleuze & Guattari, 1987: 67). The latter, the machinic aspects, might include: the architecture; the physical cell spaces; the routine and regime of control; the pharmacotherapy dispensaries; work and education spaces; prisoners, officers, psychologists, parole hearings; 'an intermingling of bodies reacting to one another' (p. 88). The former – the collective assemblage of enunciation, 'of acts and statements' (p. 88) – may comprise: laws, judicial rulings, orders and sentences; images from movies, *Chopper* or *Ghosts of the Civil Dead*; the language of the prison, the bodily gestures, tattoos; headlines about killers and rapists, gangsters and hit men; radio talk of dangerous criminals, 'taxpayers' money'; policy talk about 'keeping the community safe from offenders', and so on.

What does it mean to think about these 'intersecting multiplicities'? What sense do they help to make of the reincarceration assemblage? On one hand, the prison may be described as 'a factory of exclusion and of people habituated to their status of the excluded' (Bauman, 1998: 113). Yet, returning to the idea of lines, in pondering our thinking about prison in terms of 'exclusion, enclosure and separation', David Brown (2009: 313) suggests that, if we conceive rather of *connection*, of:

the prison as a sort of railway station, a node or radial point along which lines of force stretch out, not randomly but in highly patterned and structured ways, like railway lines, we may come closer to making sense of why these unseen but nevertheless tangible lines of criminalisation and penality travel to and from certain post codes or geographical locations, penal way stations. . . . Or why it is that 20% of Indigenous children have a parent or carer in prison . . . and what effect this might have on the inter-generational transmission of penal culture.

These 'lines of force' can be seen to constitute the lines of territorialisation that supply and maintain the incarceration assemblage, coalescing and gathering intensity around 'penal way stations'. Thinking in this way, in terms of *connection*, illustrates how penal threads may be assembled to offer new insight into the functioning and effects of the penal machine. The perspective is shifted: the prison is seen as part of a world, not separate from it; a rest stop on a well-travelled road; a familiar place, a home away from home. The idea – albeit counter-intuitive – of the prison as a routinised, domestic space is evoked (Crawley & Crawley, 2008).

Maurutto and Hannah-Moffat (2006) use the concept of assemblage to illustrate inconsistency and mutability in the way risk is variously applied and interpreted. They draw on O'Malley's (2004) conception of risk as 'a fluid, inclusive, heterogeneous array of practices with diverse effects and implications' to consider how 'risk is assembled into complex configurations with other technologies' (in Maurutto & Hannah-Moffat, 2006: 439). Assemblage allows them to explore how risk relates to 'other logics, such as clinical assessment, rehabilitation and welfare practices', enabling them, moreover, 'to counteract the presumption that risk technologies necessarily operate in opposition to rehabilitation or more welfare-based approaches' (2006: 439). By encompassing – indeed inviting – multiplicity and complexity, the idea of assemblage offers a way of circumventing traditional dichotomies that serve to reinforce the myth of coherence, reliability and objectivity underpinning the 'hegemonic dominance' of the risk paradigm (p. 438). Maurutto and Hannah-Moffat instead show how risk is assembled and reassembled with other penal practices to become less actuarially oriented and assume 'more ameliorative, productive and rehabilitative connotations' (p. 439). An example is that of the 'transformative risk subject' (Hannah-Moffat, 2005), 'who is amenable to change via targeted treatment strategies' as a result of merging 'risk with dynamic need factors', which thus renders 'a fluid malleable understanding of risk' (Maurutto & Hannah-Moffat, 2006: 443).

Similarly, the use of assemblage as a theoretical frame allows for a contextual understanding of the experience of released prisoners, in terms of the personal, social, economic, political and cultural barriers they face, and how these dimensions operate in relation to each other, affecting and informing each other. The liminality of the post-release state may be conceived as an assemblage of the symbols and stigma associated with imprisonment, the connections, meanings and interactions arising from and inflected by this experience, and their emergence as at once relational and mutual, yet also the intensely personal, idiosyncratic and heterogeneous ways they are experienced. The relations between the parts of an assemblage are characterised as relations of exteriority, which, unlike in 'organic totalities', implies that a component can be 'detached from it and plugged into a different assemblage in which its interactions are different' (DeLanda, 2006: 10), as Maurutto and Hannah-Moffat's (2006) work exemplifies.

Although an ecological model, such as proposed by Graffam and Shinkfield (2007), also enables an integrated dynamic view of the process of post-release adjustment, it does not allow for subjectivity to surface or for components to be 'plugged into' different assemblages with different relations – how substance use, for instance, may be assembled in various configurations. In addition, assemblage theory takes account of and permits analysis of the surrounding assemblages of prison and post-release policy and administrative systems and the world of post-release support work from the practitioners' perspective. Seeing these interconnected realms as assemblages, rather than as discrete, closed systems, allows the research to piece together and pick apart the components and connections that make up and permeate each assemblage, as well as trace overlapping and underlying assemblages that may remain invisible if viewed through a different lens. It is a way, too, of 'connecting "official discourses of confinement" to the discourse of the confined themselves, a move that is simultaneously theoretical and practical' (Baugh, 2005: 277). Assemblage, in its 'evocation of emergence and heterogeneity' (Marcus & Saka, 2006: 106), is thus both the lens and the task of this book.

Culture

Culture is a word laden with interpretations, implications, connotations. Its limited adoption into the criminological vocabulary reflects the conceptual confusion, definitional diversity and perceived analytic imprecision that 'culture' tends to evoke. Stowell and Byrne point out (2008: 28), for instance, that, although 'culture' is frequently linked causally to prison violence and disorder, it is 'difficult to quantify' owing to the various ways it is 'defined and operationalised' by penal researchers. Though the present study is concerned not with quantifying but with understanding and explaining 'culture', this example nonetheless highlights the term's ambiguity, its notorious multivalence (Garland, 2006). The aim of this section, therefore, is to clarify the meaning of culture in the context of this book and explain how it relates to the concept of assemblage in informing and underpinning the research. It begins with a macro perspective.

The culture concept

A scan of anthropological literature – the discipline from which the concept is drawn – reveals a clear lack of consensus over the meaning and usefulness of the term 'culture'. Indeed, Kroeber and Kluckhohn (1952) catalogue nearly 300 definitions. The concept has been defined, refined, rejected and elaborated since its earliest anthropological formulation by Tylor (1871) as 'that complex whole which includes knowledge, belief, art, morals, law, custom, and any capabilities and habits acquired by man as a member of society' (in Kroeber & Kluckhohn, 1952: 81).[3] This definition, according to Weiss (1973: 1379), has 'been the touchstone for all subsequent considerations of the concept in anthropology', despite the 'dissatisfaction' it engenders.

Williams (1976, 1985) describes culture as 'one of the two or three most complicated words in the English language', owing partly to its complex historical development, in several languages, and mostly to its diverse application and conceptualisation within a wide range of disciplines (in Delaney, 2004: 11). Williams does distinguish, however, three broad meanings: the first relates to the idea of civilisation and its intellectual, spiritual and aesthetic development; the second refers to culture as a way of life peculiar to a social group – its material and practical characteristics, and its signifying and symbolic aspects; the third and narrowest definition encompasses the arts and intellectual pursuits (in Eagleton, 2000: 9–16). It is the essence of the second meaning, the concept of culture as a way of life – the collected ideas and habits learned, shared and transmitted between generations (Linton, 1945, in Haralambos, 1986: 3) – that has been heralded by anthropologists as the flagship of their discipline, notwithstanding ongoing conceptual development, confusion and debate. It is this idea of culture that seeped into other disciplines through the mid to late twentieth century as a nascent theoretical concept and burgeoning analytical approach.

Critics argue, however, that 'culture is essentialized, reified, and overhomogenized' (Brumann, 2004: 199). It is either conceptualised so broadly as to be rendered meaningless, or so narrowly that its theoretical validity is limited; it appears 'torn between an empty universalism and a blind particularism' (Eagleton, 2000: 44). Rational-choice theorists have rejected cultural accounts as 'tautological, untestable, or beside the point' (Wedeen, 2002: 714). Sewell (2004), however, draws an important distinction between the use of the plural form ('cultures'), describing 'concrete and bounded worlds of beliefs and practices', and the singular concept, denoting a 'semiotics of social life' (p. 202). Sewell argues that the elision of these two distinct meanings of culture causes confusion and gives rise to criticism of the culture concept based on the shortcomings inhering in the former interpretation.

For instance, Larmour (2008) refers to three common misuses of culture as a concept: as an 'uncaused cause', as an 'explanation of last resort' and as a 'veto on comparison' (p. 228), which seem to illustrate Sewell's contention and that of Garland (2006), who draws on Sewell's distinction to differentiate culture as an analytic concept from its use as a 'totalizing term' (p. 423). Similarly, Wedeen (2002) describes the latter use of culture as a 'fallback' position to account for the unaccountable, which, she affirms, succeeds only in 'reviving an outmoded and unhelpful understanding of the concept' (p. 714). Wedeen (2002) argues instead for a conceptualisation of culture as 'the practices of meaning-making through which social actors attempt to make their world coherent' (p. 720). Cultural analysis from this perspective involves studying the relations between people's practices and their signifying systems of language and other symbols, an approach characterised as 'semiotic practices' (p. 714).

Culture as semiotic practices

Culture as semiotic practices, Wedeen (2002) contends, operates on two levels: first, referring to 'what language and symbols do – how they are inscribed in concrete actions and how they operate to produce observable . . . effects'; and second, offering a lens, focusing attention on how and why phenomena are invested with meaning (p. 714). Wedeen's cultural analytic framework is clearly tied to Geertz's (1973) concept of culture, which is:

> essentially a semiotic one. Believing with Max Weber, that man is an animal suspended in webs of significance he himself has spun, I take culture to be those webs, and the analysis of it to be therefore not an experimental science in search of law but an interpretive one in search of meaning.
>
> (2002: 5)

More specifically, Geertz defined culture as 'a system of inherited conceptions expressed in symbolic forms by means of which men communicate, perpetu- ate, and develop their knowledge about and attitudes toward life' (1973: 89). Notwithstanding Geertz's shortcomings,[4] his definition is useful for our purposes in that it encapsulates the notion of 'conceptions', and 'knowledge about and atti- tudes toward life', underpinning the idea of semiotic practices as meaning-making processes (Wedeen, 2002).

To go beyond mere description, Wedeen emphasises 'intelligibility' as an analyt- ical criterion, affording the semiotic-practical approach its 'explanatory purchase' (2002: 726). Explanation, after all, as Garland (2006) reminds us, is the primary sociological task. Although conceding that description is important and necessary, Garland urges the cultural analyst to 'show how culture relates to conduct, how specific symbols, values or ideas come to be a motivational force or operational basis for action' (2006: 438). Wedeen's (2002) semiotic-practical approach is use- ful in this explanatory task, as it conceives of the processes of meaning-construction as people's practices and signification operating in a dialectical relationship that allows for conceptual and logical incongruities. The notion of intelligibility implies recognisability by others, insofar as 'instabilities in discourse and in practices make sense only within the signifying operations of a shared conceptual system' (p. 722). This idea varies from 'common knowledge', however, in that language and symbols are observable in practices, rather than assumed. Furthermore, a shared concep- tual system may be less coherent or integrated than a shared episteme and marked instead by variability and inconsistency (Wedeen, 2002).

Thus, culture does not refer to essential values or particular traits isolating one group from another. Rather, a cultural view obliges 'an account of how symbols operate in practice, why meanings generate action, and why actions produce mean- ings, when they do' (Wedeen, 2002: 720). From a Deleuzian perspective, 'the theory of signs is meaningless without the relation between signs and the corre- sponding apprenticeship in practice' (Semetsky, 2005: 243). The apprenticeship (the experience, the doing) in the context of this study involves men's release from prison and the behaviours and actions arising from that experience, not as a simple causal chain, but as an accretion of ways of being in the world, related to and reflect- ing the experience of – and imprints associated with – being removed from the 'outside' community. I thus construe 'culture' here, not as a fixed frame or social entity to be entered into or navigated, but as a multiplicity of meanings, an inter- weaving of semiotic threads; a collectivity of practices, behaviours, experiences and understandings of post-prison life, and the intersection of these with the means by which they are signified, expressed and conveyed. The network of connections within which these elements cohere constitutes the culture this book seeks to map, tracing its contours and whorls, convergences and divagation.

Culture in action

There is no clear criminological lineage for thinking about culture in this way, however. Until very recently, penological research conceived cultural forms narrowly, if at all (Garland, 2006). The growth of 'cultural criminology'[5] embodies a resurgent interest in ethnography, subjectivity, lived experience and the phenomenological, emphasising 'the subjective, affective, embodied, aesthetic, material, performative, textual, symbolic and visual relations of space, as well as recognising that the settings of crime are neither fixed nor inevitable but are relational, improvised, contingent, constructed and contested' (Campbell, 2012, in Hayward, 2012: 450). Yet, O'Brien (2005) argues that cultural criminology under-theorises its concept of culture and thus lacks explanatory or analytical power, indeed that it is political rather than analytical in orientation (also Fenwick, 2004; Young, 2008). Though certainly critical, and plainly political (see Ferrell, Hayward & Young, 2008), cultural criminology shares this study's focus on meaning and lived experience, yet offers few, if any, analytic tools.

Sampson and Bean (2006) contend that, until the late 1980s, three conflicting ideas about crime and culture dominated the literature. The first sees so-called criminal cultures as 'pseudo-cultures', entirely epiphenomenal and, therefore, lacking causal power. The second views culture as an adaptation to structural constraints, transmitted via social learning and role modelling, and mutable according to changing conditions. The third ascribes enduring causal power to subcultures that, once created, take on a life of their own, such as the 'oppositional culture' arising in 'high-poverty neighbourhoods' (p. 19). These traditional cultural approaches comprise a 'culture as values' paradigm that assumes culture to be: *personal*, embedded and operating within each individual; *authentic* and fixed in terms of identity; based on *value-rationality* – an ends/means view of values driving behavioural choices; *consensual* – a set of shared values; and comprising a *worldview* whereby culture and social structure are polarised (Sampson & Bean, 2006: 20–6). As a model for understanding culture's effect on action, however, 'culture as values' is 'misleading' (Swidler, 1986: 273) and can lead to the kind of conceptual confusion of which Garland (2006) and O'Brien (2005) warn.

It was after Swidler (1986) introduced her idea of the 'cultural toolkit', Sampson and Bean (2006) argue, that a 'post-1980s culture-in-action paradigm' (p. 20) emerged, a relational theory of culture differentiated from the 'old' paradigm by its contrasting characteristics. Swidler's 'culture in action' model views culture as a 'toolkit' – a 'repertoire' of habits, skills and styles that shape and guide people's problem-solving and decision-making, and from which they construct 'strategies of action' (Swidler, 1986: 273), where 'strategy' means 'a general way of organising action' rather than a conscious plan (p. 277). Culture is causative in that it 'shapes the capacities from which such strategies of action are constructed' (p. 277). Sampson and Bean (2006: 21–2) characterise 'culture in action' as *intersubjective*, or created between people in social interaction; *performative*, in that identity is performed; and *affective-cognitive*, in that behaviour arises out of the skills and cognitive tools at hand, out of impulse or habit, rather than rational decision-making. Moreover, culture is *relational*, 'the map that people use to position themselves in social space' (p. 24), and *world-making* (as opposed to 'worldview'), which evokes Bourdieu's idea of the social field – a network of relational positions existing and reproduced in/via social action and interaction.

Importantly, in the context of post-prison experience, Swidler distinguishes between how culture affects action in 'settled lives' and 'unsettled lives', in terms of sustaining continuities and constructing new patterns (1986: 278). In 'unsettled lives', Swidler (1986: 279) explains:

> People developing new strategies of action depend on cultural models to learn styles of self, relationship, cooperation, authority, and so forth. . . . Rather than providing the underlying assumptions of an entire way of life, [such cultural models] make explicit demands in a contested cultural arena.

The initial experience of imprisonment and adaptation to prison life may be viewed in this way, as a period during which competing ways of organising behaviours contend for dominance (the prison regime, officers' culture, prisoners' social hierarchies, individual histories and identity), and new strategies of action are constructed from an available repertoire of 'symbols, rituals, stories, and guides to action' (p. 277). In contrast, settled cultures claim 'authority of habit [and] normality', and yet 'constrain action by providing a limited set of resources out of which individuals and groups construct strategies of action' (1986: 281). As Karp (2010) avers, in prison, 'masculinity resources are severely limited' (p. 66). The process of settling into prison life or into a 'prisoner' identity can similarly be seen as constraining future action, owing to what Swidler calls the 'high costs of cultural retooling' (1986: 284) involved in crafting new ways of being, particularly when post-release cultural resources are limited, such as if an ex-prisoner's friends and family share habits, skills and styles oriented towards violence and drug abuse, for example. Thus, Swidler's culture-in-action model can explain how culture influences behavioural choices in prison, as well as ways of being upon release and return to community. Stowell and Byrne (2008) endorse this 'new cultural paradigm' (p. 38).

Wedeen's (2002) semiotic-practical approach clearly draws on Swidler's formulation of the relations between symbol/meaning and action. Such a relational approach understands culture to be:

> an inter-subjective *organizing mechanism* that shapes unfolding social processes and that is constitutive of social structure. From this perspective culture is simultaneously an emergent product and producer of social organization, interaction, and hence structure.
>
> (Sampson & Bean, 2006: 27, original emphasis)

Wedeen's focus on language (symbols) and how it relates to behaviour (practices) is useful because it emphasises the observable. It enables analysis of the relationship between 'narratives of identification and everyday activities' (Wedeen, 2002: 724) that, if left uninterrogated, serve to perpetuate themselves. This works on a micro (prisoner) and macro (societal) level, in what Arrigo and Milovanovic (2009) describe as 'the coproduction of penological reality' (p. 101). They argue that the language and logic that 'essentialise' and reify the prison imprison us all. Examining semiotic practices, as a culture-in-action approach, permits an understanding of how this process unfolds.

Delineated thus far is the use of culture as an analytic tool, one that allows a foregrounding of subjectivity, with an emphasis on the collective (in the sense of the multiple rather than the shared), the social, the relational, and the participatory and performative aspects of meaning-making and practice or action. Through this lens, culture is now considered in terms of ways of being a man and the cultural toolkit on which men draw in negotiating and 'doing' (Jewkes, 2005a) masculinity in prison.

Prison masculinities

As Bernie Matthews, long-time prisoner, career bank robber and latterly journalist and blogger asserts: 'You can take the man out of the prison but you cannot take the prison out of the man' (Matthews, 2008). Though time-worn, Matthews' truism evokes the sense of the imprisonment experience as formative and one that leaves a lasting imprint on a prisoner's sense of self and way of being in the world; it is 'world-making' (Sampson & Bean, 2006). The notion of prison institutionalisation – Clemmer's 'prisonisation' – is thus invoked, and its immutability is implied. In describing his own prison experience, Tim Anderson (1992) refers to the 'positive value in forming and maintaining solidarity amongst the people with whom you live . . . 24 hours a day, for years on end' (pp. 259–60). Highlighting the functional aspect of adopting prison norms and ways of being, Anderson's observation also implies intentionality and a degree of agency at odds with the unconscious absorption of culture that Matthews evokes. Suggested thus are different ways of experiencing, adapting to, and *performing* prison life that permeate and shape the post-release experience.

Central to the performative aspect of prison cultural models is the very notion of maleness. The concept of hegemonic masculinity has infused and informed two decades of research and thinking about men, gender and social hierarchy (Connell & Messerschmidt, 2005), not least in the hyper-male prison setting where its exaggerated manifestation verges on parody (Toch, 1998). Derived from early work by Connell (1982, 1983, 1987; and Carrigan, Connell & Lee, 1985, in Connell & Messerschmidt, 2005: 831), hegemonic masculinity comprises the dominant notion of masculinity in a particular historical context. Conceived as one of multiple masculinities, it was, in its original formulation, 'not assumed to be normal in the statistical sense; only a minority of men might enact it. But it was certainly normative. It embodied the currently most honoured way of being a man' (Connell & Messerschmidt, 2005: 832). If indeed, as Denborough asserts (2001), the prison is 'the most masculine institution in our culture'(p. 73), and as 'hegemonic patterns of masculinity are embedded in specific social environments' (Connell & Messerschmidt, 2005: 839), the concept is useful as a way of understanding the hierarchy of prison masculinities (both hegemonic and subordinated) as 'a pattern of hegemony, not a pattern of simple domination based on force'; a model permitted and sustained by, 'cultural consent, discursive centrality, institutionalisation, and the marginalisation of . . . alternatives' (Connell & Messerschmidt, 2005: 846).

The idea of 'cultural consent' offers a lens, relevant to the present study, through which to analyse prison masculinities in relation to – indeed, as magnified versions of – broader social constructs, because, as Messerschmidt affirms, 'specific forms of masculinity are available, encouraged, and permitted, depending upon one's . . . social situation' (2001: 67). 'Cultural consent' thus underpins the process whereby models of masculinity are sustained and reproduced through performance and interaction. For example, cultural consent for hegemonic models of aggressive competition, emotional suppression and physical prowess inheres in stories and images of military and sporting heroism. These norms, however, when imported into the closed, microcosmic prison environment are hothoused, amplified, exaggerated into extreme models of hypermasculinity marked by physical domination, misogyny, homophobia and the performance of these attributes, through which violence and intimidation become normalised and legitimised (Denborough, 1994; Phillips, 2001; Kupers, 2005; Whitehead, 2005; Evans & Wallace, 2008; Karp, 2010).

At one extreme, Kupers (2005) defines as 'toxic masculinity' the socially destructive aspects of hegemonic masculinity – misogyny, homophobia, excessive greed and violent domination – which, he argues, is a significant barrier to treatment and therapy. Any challenge to the performance of such identity can trigger fierce confrontation and, thus, also contribute to inter-prisoner violence and volatility (Sampson & Bean, 2006: 22). Through the concomitant effects of 'institutionalisation and the marginalisation of alternatives', these patterns of hegemony may be carried by prisoners, either as performative habits, styles and practised skills, or as subtle cultural imprints, in their post-release wake. Conversely, as Connell suggests (1995, 2000), resistance may emerge from 'marginalised masculinities' (Lusher & Robins, 2006: 15), highlighting the precariousness of power exercised solely through violence. As Connell (1995) states, a 'thoroughly legitimate hierarchy would have less need to intimidate' (p. 84). Violence is, thus, a means to exert power, yet also 'a measure of its illegitimacy' (Lusher & Robins, 2006: 15), emphasising its contingency upon the prison microcosm. Within the prison, cultural consent is granted by the inmate code, buttressed by the physical isolation of prisoners from the community, and reinforced by the norms and practices of correctional officers and prison management.

In maintaining authority and compliance, prison officers may tacitly or overtly sanction elements of the inmate code, 'to manipulate prisoners and enforce order' (Sabo, Kuper & London, 2001: 12) by, for instance, orchestrating or ignoring inter-prisoner violence. More benignly, fitness activities that 'provide prisoners with vehicles for self-expression and physical freedom' also render them 'more tractable and compliant', whereby physical exercise becomes 'simultaneously a source of personal liberation and social control' (Sabo, 2001: 65). This paradox may be seen as central to the process of institutionalisation and subsequent diminishing of prisoners' capacity, through their settling into the structures and constraints of prison life.

Upon release from that environment, cultural consent for prison norms is withdrawn, overridden by the community's behavioural norms and gender expectations. To the extent that their prison way of thinking persists, negotiating a path between conflicting normative systems can present uncertainty and confusion for released prisoners. This represents the rupture of cultural continuity and the demands of constructing new strategies of action, or 'cultural retooling' (Swidler, 1986: 284). Crime, however, may involve gendered social practices that 'can provide an alternative resource for accomplishing gender and, therefore, affirming a distinct type of masculinity' (Messerschmidt, 2001: 68; also Jewkes, 2005a: 50). Post-prison cultural consent for prison norms is thus conferred by a continuing culture of criminality, the sustaining continuities that permit culture to endure. 'Discursive centrality' may be seen to operate at a mythic level, in the everyday and in the stories and symbols of prison life in popular representations (Mason, 2006), both of which perpetuate stereotypes of the prison experience. Insofar as prison models of masculinity accord with those 'available, encouraged and permitted' (Messerschmidt, 2001: 67) by the (largely imported US) 'gangster' aesthetic, for example, its trappings can provide – for young men in particular – an accessible and appealing identity (see also Jewkes, 2005a). In this way, hegemonic masculinities embedded in the prison environment – and their associated gender roles – can leak out into the post-release sphere.

Masculinity is increasingly understood as a fluid, emergent construction, rooted in 'perpetual performance' (Phillips, 2001: 13). 'Men cultivate their bodies', Sabo (2001: 65) writes, 'in order to send a variety of messages about the meaning of masculinity to themselves and others', thus performing either 'the credo of hardness' or an ethic of 'self-care'. The public performance of manhood is seen to be a key aspect of its continual reinforcement and reconstitution.[6] In the context of the prison, a setting that intensifies gender dynamics (Jewkes, 2002, 2005a; Kupers, 2005), this continual reconstruction may be seen as an adaptive response to the environment of danger and deprivation (evoking Sykes, 1958), which forces men to refashion their manhood using limited available resources and according to strict rules. Phillips (2001) identifies the 'core cultural strategies' men use to gather 'resources to reconstruct manhood': the social mapping of relationships; being a 'stand-up man'; avoiding social isolation by forming associations; managing reputation by concealing or displaying crime status; and showing a readiness to fight (p. 15). 'The bottom line ... for protecting one's manhood', she concludes, 'seems to be to never let anything be taken away, whether it is sneakers and soup or dignity and manhood' (p. 16). This illustrates how meaning-making manifests in action (Wedeen, 2002) and the causal role of culture in shaping the 'capacities' from which prisoners construct their ways of being (Swidler, 1986). The idea of maleness as a key constituent of gendered prison culture is underscored.

Reflecting on the 'hypermasculine' culture of the prison as part of a broader ethnographic study of constructions of self in four men's prisons in England, Jewkes (2005a) argues that, as prison populations worldwide are predominantly constituted by men, the highly gendered nature of the setting is often treated as incidental by researchers. It is assumed that normal rules of patriarchy do not apply. 'Doing' masculinity, however, may be seen as an adaptation to a prison hierarchy prescribed and underpinned by patriarchal norms. Although prisoners bring with them a set of experiences, beliefs and values, 'the experience of confinement nonetheless unites them, to some degree, in a shared experience of and response to pain and deprivation' (Jewkes, 2005a: 45). Of all the pains of imprisonment (Sykes, 1958), it is arguably the fear for personal safety that characterises prison life, particularly as the 'inmate solidarity' described by early prison researchers (Sykes, 1958; Irwin & Cressey, 1962) has been supplanted by a drugs culture marked by volatile and unstable alliances (Jewkes, 2005a: 46). Nevertheless, 'pressure to fit in with the dominant culture is . . . strong' (Jewkes, 2005a: 50). The most common strategy involves 'wearing a mask' (p. 53), yet inevitably this entails the internal tension between 'coping with conflict, fear and disorientation' and reconciling this with 'the construction and maintenance of a culturally acceptable, masculine identity' (p. 53).

The distinction between private ('backstage') self and public ('frontstage') identity evokes Goffman's (1959) dramaturgical conception of self and highlights the performative aspect of masculinity as key to its ongoing corroboration and reconstitution. The importance of performing a prison persona shows how an individual's way of being is shaped by the demands of available and competing models (Swidler, 1986). The constitutive process whereby gender order is established and maintained involves 'incorporation' as much as 'oppression' of non-hegemonic patterns of masculinity. Indeed, the durability of the latter may represent 'well-crafted responses to race/ethnic marginalisation, physical disability, class inequality, or stigmatised sexuality' (Connell & Messerschmidt, 2005: 848).

Jewkes (2005a) observes prisoners' 'sense of the masculine changing as their sentence proceeds' (p. 57). The hegemonic masculinity can be challenged by alternatives, such as student, artisan or tradesman. A kind of 'psychological one-upmanship' (Cohen & Taylor, 1972) is afforded by other skills or knowledge, such as becoming an 'expert in legal matters and prisoners' rights' (Jewkes, 2005a: 61). This seems to exemplify the cultural processes arising in Swidler's (1986) 'unsettled lives', in which prisoners use cultural models to learn 'styles of self, relationship, [and] cooperation' (p. 279). It suggests that prisoners who resist the dominant models, such as Jewkes's alternative 'experts', are the least 'settled' in terms of acculturation to prison hegemony. Perhaps these men's construction of and investment in an alternative model serves to increase rather than diminish their cultural repertoire.

Jewkes (2005a) notes the importance of prisoners' footwear as an indicator of social standing and pre-prison identity. This highlights the significance of the social embodiment of identity and its interweaving – or, in this case, contrasting – with cultural context (Connell & Messerschmidt, 2005). In the prison context, tattooing is the most obvious manifestation of embodied masculinity and an example of 'the imperative for inmates to fashion a masculine "way of being" . . . as an adaptive stance to the patterns imposed on them by their environment' (Jewkes, 2005a: 59). Inscribing patterns on their own body allows prisoners, in a symbolic way, to subvert or counteract the bodily constraints of imprisonment. The causative role of culture in shaping action is made manifest (Swidler, 1986). Masculinity comprises multiplicity and complexity. There is no 'one way' of being a man in prison, because, as Jewkes points out, hegemonic masculinity 'carries no intrinsic meaning without the subordinated versions against which it is pitched' (2005a: 61). Various cultural models compete and clash in the closed, gendered world of the prison.

Culture and meaning are central concerns of this book: prisoners' adoption (explicitly, deliberately, strategically, consciously) and absorption (inadvertently, subconsciously, as an adaptive response and/or survival mechanism) of the codes and symbols of prison culture, and its inherent maleness, and the extent to which these pervade and colour the post-release experience and shape men's post-prison identity. The iterative impact of serial imprisonment has been discussed in terms of the shadows of post-release homelessness and mortality, which loom larger and with increasing likelihood each time a person is released. Reflecting on the idea of the 'responsible prisoner' and the consequences of 'unnecessarily' removing responsibility from those imprisoned, Pryor (2001: 88) notes:

> The 'revolving door' shows how easily people grow weaker and weaker, their social contract increasingly one-sided, their natural environment one where others take control. They cannot do the time outside, so they do the crime and they become skilled at doing the time inside.

Becoming 'skilled at doing the time inside' underscores Swidler's point that culture is a 'toolkit', that people develop their tools from the resources at hand, and that behaviours arise from these out of habit and exigency (Swidler, 1986; Sampson & Bean, 2006). Pryor hints at the internalisation that this process involves, whereby stripping prisoners of responsibility gradually reduces their capacity for – but also their expectation of – civic inclusion. This is the serial depletion of resources that undermines men's reintegrative capacity (Baldry et al., 2003; Grunseit et al., 2008). Swidler's (1986) concept of diminishing cultural repertoires, constricted by prison life, also reveals the limiting effects of meaning-making processes on the capacity for post-prison 'transformative revival (becoming)' (Arrigo & Milovanovic, 2009: xx). Jewkes (2005b) similarly describes the experience of reception into prison as 'disempowering and infantilising', making the 'entrant . . . feel powerless and stupid on a continuing basis' (p. 373). Implied is a whittling away of a 'responsible self' – a weakening of autonomy, a closing in of conscience, a shrinking of capacity – shadowed by the emergence of a shaky prison-self in response to the experience of being 'a prisoner'.

This form challenges Irwin's (1970) 'convict identity' in its becoming-ness, its being in relation to a former self, its emergence in gaps. In terms of the rein-carceration cycle, this form is embodied in the 'short-termer', who does not quite fit in, and yet who is always coming back. This state of being forever in-between, interstitial, is nebulous: contingent upon interactions and reactions, and ascribed and assumed identity. It is an assemblage comprising (molar) lines of penal reality: risk/needs profiles, parole conditions, Centrelink requirements, criminal records, being an ex-prisoner. These intersect with (molecular) lines of post-release life: resuming old habits, associations and patterns of behaviour, having to make ends meet, pay bills, negotiate relationships. The connections between them are inherently conflicting and unresolved. Some find a pathway through this period of uncertainty by drawing on personal and social resources. Others get stuck, no longer imprisoned, yet unable to find ways of being free. This phenomenon of perpetual transition may be described as one of liminality. The following section examines this notion as characterising post-release experi-ence and shaping post-prison identity.

Liminality

Recent post-release writings (Jewkes, 2005b; Baldry et al., 2006, 2008; Baldry 2009; Healy, 2010) have utilised the notion of post-prison liminality to evoke the disconnected, indeterminate state in which released prisoners typically find them-selves ahead of their hypothetical 'reintegration', or their return to custody. The focus of this research on the lived experience of release, in its sociopolitical con-text, requires a way of understanding and talking about that experience in terms of its social and emotional landscape. Liminality provides a way to conceptualise the state of 'in-betweenness', the subjective experience of lives in transition.

The liminality concept

Jewkes (2005b: 374) describes liminality as inherently transitional, charac-terised by chaos, uncertainty, instability, vulnerability and transformational potential. An anthropological concept, liminality derives from Van Gennep's (1909) early three-part formulation of rites of passage, comprising a pre-liminal phase (separation), a liminal phase (transition) and a post-liminal phase (aggre-gation, incorporation or reintegration). Turner (1967, 1982, 1986) explores and expands Van Gennep's concept of liminality, describing individuals in this tran-sitional state as being 'betwixt and between': neither belonging to the society of which they were previously part, nor yet reincorporated into society; in 'a sort of social limbo' (Turner, 1982: 24). This concept connotes the post-prison experience of exclusion that Clemmer (1940: 300) evokes when he describes as 'next to impossible' the 'happy adjustment' of ex-prisoners.

Thinking about the penal process in terms of rites of passage: (pre-liminal) imprisonment comprises the separation of an offender from society; the (liminal) release–post-release period represents the transition from custody to the community;

and (post-liminal) reintegration is constituted once an 'offender' is able to participate in 'normal life' as a law-abiding citizen. As earlier discussion indicates, however, social constructions of 'offenders', systemic hurdles (such as housing availability) and structural barriers (against employment, for instance) combine to thwart the reintegrative efforts of prisoners released without the social and structural supports required to sustain them. For these men, serially depleted of resources through repeat incarceration, the effects of the penal machine are cumulative and recursive, as explored further below.

Turner, in conceiving liminality as 'a limbo of statuslessness' (1969: 97), argued that, in the process of moving from one status to another, liminality and its opposite (reintegration) 'constitute one another and are mutually indispensable' (Turner, 1969: 97). He saw liminality as 'the generative, creative principle of ritual' (Grimes, 2000: 122). That is, without a state of social exclusion, there is no need for or meaning to reintegration. The liminality inhering in such states generates the need for ritual to allow passage through the 'dangerous zone' (Grimes, 2000: 6) of social limbo and exclusion. Without ritual, Grimes (2000) argues, 'a major life passage', such as imprisonment and return to community, 'can become a yawning abyss, draining off psychic energy, engendering social confusion and twisting the course of the life that follows it' (pp. 5–6). This image evocatively conjures the post-prison experience of being released, yet not free.

Van Gennep (1909) warns that transitional phases 'do not occur without disturbing the life of society and the individual' (p. 13); they are inherently disrupting and unsettling (recalling Swidler's 'unsettled lives'). Danger is implicit in the idea of prisoners' release and return to the community. News headlines such as 'Wife killer back in business' (Rolfe, 29 May 2011) exemplify public disquiet about a man imprisoned for killing his wife being entitled, upon release, to resume company directorship. These examples reveal how states of transition are invested with the fears and anxieties of the wider social group (Douglas, 1966, 1975). Danger is perceived, Douglas (1966) observes, 'simply because transition is neither one state nor the next, it is indefinable. The person who must pass from one to another is himself in danger and emanates danger to others' (p. 119). According to Van Gennep (1909: 13), however, 'rites of passage' function to counter the 'harmful effects' of such states. As Douglas explains: 'The danger is controlled by ritual which precisely separates him from his old status, segregates him for a time and then publicly declares his entry to his new status' (1966: 120). The physical and symbolic aspects of such ritual are equally significant for the initiate and the wider social group. Without ritual to signify inclusion, exclusion can persist.

Sustaining exclusion

The importance of symbolic process – particularly the notion of 'ritual dying and ritual rebirth' (Douglas, 1966: 120) – resonates strongly in the work of advocates of reintegrative ceremony and restorative practice, such as Braithwaite (1989; Braithwaite & Mugford, 1994; Braithwaite & Braithwaite, 2001) and Maruna (2005, 2006; Maruna & LeBel, 2003). Echoing Douglas (1966), Maruna

(2011b) argues that ex-prisoner reintegration cannot be achieved without ritual. An example is provided by Naylor (2011: 79), examining the implications of criminal records for reintegration in Australia, who quotes from 'Jack Charles v The Crown'[7] to highlight differences between Aboriginal and non-aboriginal penal processes:

> Under Blackfella law . . . a period of exile, spear in the leg . . . Exile ends, Wound heals. Better now Jack? Yes, I'm better now Uncle. Warm yourself at the fire old son. . . . And I'd be accepted back in the fold. Whitefella way: the Convict Stain endures, lingers, and your past Shadows, Stalks your present, and Stymies, Jinks your future.

Ritual (in this case, exile and spearing) enables reintegration; its absence, in contrast, generates sustained exclusion and enduring stigma. Or, more precisely, without a rite signifying the third phase – a rite that, in Douglas's words, publicly declares his entry to his new status – the liminal phase persists. This example also highlights the social dimension of the ritual process: though the crime and its punishment are individualised with a 'spear in the leg', once 'exile ends' and the 'wound heals', the offending individual is welcomed back into the group, indeed received *with care*. Such intangible aspects are critical reintegrative elements (Maruna, 2011b).

The social context, which either sustains liminality or fosters reintegration, thus emerges. To initiate reintegration, a way of signifying the 'end of exile' is required. Informally, this might be a family homecoming, return to employment or renewal of a club membership. Formal means include the institutionalised redemption rituals of expunging criminal convictions, such as under France's 'judicial rehabilitation' model (Herzog-Evans, 2011; Maruna, 2011a). The burgeoning 'reentry court' concept in the US also embodies such a process, notwithstanding its paradigmatic framing as 'managerial' (Miller, 2007). Though the concept holds restorative promise, its lack of a sustaining policy narrative threatens to render the reentry court an extension of the penal control mechanism, further solidifying the deficit-focused risk/needs approach to offender management (Maruna & LeBel, 2003). Moreover, the restrictive after-effects of criminal conviction militate against re-entry courts' reintegrative potential. The rise of therapeutic models in Australia (Bartels, 2009), including judicial monitoring, similarly heralds expansion of the control apparatus. Importantly, as Maruna and LeBel (2003) point out, 'the carrot and stick model of reentry fails to assign a meaningful role to the community' (p. 96), a means by which 'moral and social inclusion' (p. 97) may be fostered. This omission amounts to a failure to acknowledge that reintegration is indeed a 'two-way street' (Maruna, 2011a: 106).

Emblematic of this failure is the lack of ritual processes signifying 'rebirth' in the Australian penal landscape. Whereas sentencing and imprisonment symbolise moral and corporeal exile, there is no equivalent at the other end to signify return to community, no 'rite of aggregation' (Douglas, 1966: 121) signalling the resumption of active citizen status. Douglas (1966: 121) observes that the difficulty social workers face in ex-prisoner resettlement 'comes from the attitude of society at large':

> A man who has spent any time 'inside' is put permanently 'outside' the ordinary social system. With no rite of aggregation which can definitively assign him to a new position he remains in the margins, with other people who are similarly credited with unreliability, unteachability, and all the wrong social attitudes.
>
> (p. 121)

Besides 'these common assumptions about ex-prisoners', notable is 'that marginal status produces the same reactions the world over' (Douglas, 1966: 121). Ex-prisoners' marginalisation is equally observable through history, as this colonial account suggests:

> Victoria was not a very hospitable country even for persons of decent reputation, if they had no money and no friends; it was still more inhospitable in the case of persons with a gaol reputation.
>
> (*The Argus*, 1 August 1872, p. 3)

The phenomenon of post-release liminality emerges as neither temporally nor culturally or geographically bound. Without rites to renew social status, ex-prisoners remain forever 'in the margins' – perpetual outsiders, socially excluded.

Vulnerable populations

As Baldry (2009) and her colleagues (2006; Baldry, Dowse, Snoyman et al., 2008) argue, liminality renders socially invisible the most vulnerable, including the imprisoned mentally ill and cognitively impaired. The effects of short yet frequent prison terms on people with MHD and CD manifests as 'serial institutionalisation', which has a particularly destabilising impact on their capacity to maintain housing on their return to the community (Baldry, Dowse, Snoyman et al., 2008: 38). The increased risk of homelessness increases their risk of reimprisonment (as, if charged with an offence, a man without an address is likely to be remanded rather than bailed). These circumstances may be associated with social dislocation and isolation, family breakdown, disruption to and alienation from employment and training opportunities, poverty and increased harmful drug or alcohol use (Baldry et al., 2006).

The recursive nature of this phenomenon is acutely apparent in light of findings that homelessness can aggravate problematic drug use (Bessant et al., 2003, in Kinner, 2006a: 8), and more problematic drug use is predictive of return to custody (Baldry et al., 2003). These conditions can trigger episodes of mental illness, 'in both a causative and consequential sense' (Baldry, Dowse, Snoyman et al., 2008: 39), which can result in behaviours leading to further criminal justice involvement. So the cycle continues, in clear evidence of research suggesting that the post-release impact of incarceration is exacerbated by shorter yet repeated stints of imprisonment (Liebling & Maruna, 2005; Carlton & Segrave, 2009). Baldry (2009) paints a picture of this experience as:

> one of cycling around in a liminal marginalised and fluid community–criminal justice space . . . liminal in that it is both in and between the outside community and . . . prison . . . marginal in that it does not afford access to stable support and services in either place and in fact promotes serial institutionalisation.
>
> (p. 20)

The interpretation by Peacock (2008) of this as a 'third space' is refuted by Baldry (2009: 20), who argues that Peacock depicts 'an autonomous space' and thus misjudges its inherent instability, lack of autonomy and constant state of flux, which is 'negatively dependent upon, created and controlled by interaction amongst human service and criminal justice agencies' (Baldry, 2009: 21). On closer inspection, however, Peacock's (2008) construal of a 'third space' is revealed to mirror Baldry's conceptualisation, as a:

> space that sits between exclusion (as an imprisoned citizen with limited rights) and inclusion (as a full citizen entitled to freely participate in the community). [Its] contours . . . not fixed, they are comprised of multiple layers including practices of surveillance and social control.
>
> (Peacock, 2008: 309)

Further, Peacock describes it as 'neither prison nor the community, but a place that continues to shift between both. A space which is excluded and controlled but is disguised by notions of re-integration' (p. 310). The experience for its inhabitants is of being 'trapped in this third space which ebbs and flows between the prison and the community . . . never fully allow[ing] the person occupying it to emerge and become an included member of the community' (Peacock, 2008: 310). Baldry's (2009) critique seems to hinge on the perceived 'autonomy' of this third space. Yet this belies the main thrust of Peacock's analysis, in which the parallels with Baldry's are clear: both writers emphasise the fluidity, the in-betweenness, the mutability of this state of being both 'in and between' community/criminal justice spaces. It is with pathos that Baldry (2009: 21) observes: 'Persons cycling in this space are invariably searching for safe structured spaces and support that have been lacking in their lives. . . . Appallingly the prison is often the only place that provides that'. This evokes images of the prison as a domestic space where routine prevails (Crawley & Crawley, 2008), and as 'the most prominent, powerful, and "reliable" state institution in the lives of the poor and dispossessed' (Comfort, 2002: 491). It highlights the inherent uncertainty, instability and vulnerability of liminal states of being.

Baldry's (2009) account of the rise in imprisonment of vulnerable groups through the lens of patriarchy and Australian colonial institutionalism is compelling. It resonates with Wacquant's (2002) portrayal of the US's 'unique socio-historical' trend towards diminishing 'social-welfare regulation of poverty . . . through an emerging *carceral-assistential continuum* interlinking and intermingling the practices, categories, and discourses of "workfare" with those of a hypertrophic and hyperactive criminal-justice apparatus' (p. 382, original italics). Western (2008b) similarly observes as 'historically novel' the 'normality of imprisonment for young black men with little schooling' resulting from 'a newly punitive criminal justice policy applied most zealously in poor urban neighbourhoods that offered few legitimate economic opportunities' (p. 8). Wacquant (2002) laments a post-Foucauldian void in US prison sociology, precisely at the time when it is most needed, highlighting the importance of empirical accounts of prisoners' experience and post-prison subjectivities. 'Subjective perceptions are', as Maruna and LeBel (2003: 93) insist, 'crucial in understanding the success or failure of correctional practice'.

Exploring the relationships between American mental health and prison populations, Harcourt (2008) conceptualises incarceration 'through the lens of aggregated institutionalization' (p. 5). He traces 'the continuity of spatial exclusion and confinement . . . from the high rates of mental hospitalization in the mid-1930s to the high rates of imprisonment at the turn of the twenty-first century' (p. 6). The correlation between the deinstitutionalisation of psychiatric patients during the 1960s–1980s and the subsequent rise in imprisonment of people with MHD (Baldry, 2009) may be realistically described as 'transinstitutionalisation' (Gronfein, 1985, in Harcourt, 2008: 19). Just as the eye of Wacquant's 'paternalist penal state' is 'trained primarily on the destitute, the disreputable and the dangerous, and all those who chafe in the lower regions of social space' (2002: 382), Baldry argues that the prison has been repositioned – legislatively and socially – 'to control and accommodate . . . those with serious disadvantage, co-morbidity and dual diagnosis who have no safe place for healing, housing or care' (2009: 28). The effect is to render invisible the most marginalised in the community, their presence – outside imprisonment rates – barely perceptible.

Baldry (2009: 28) refers specifically to the vulnerability of Indigenous women to penal institutionalisation, and thereby to liminal states of being, though her thesis might equally apply to Indigenous men. Levy's (2008) finding that one-fifth of Aboriginal children have a parent/carer in prison attests to the normalisation of imprisonment in some aboriginal communities, amplifying existing social dysfunction (in Brown, 2010: 142). Parenthood itself emerges as a site of liminality when parental roles are disrupted by incarceration and dislocated by community breakdown. In terms of what it means to inhabit such a space, on a structural and individual level, Kelly's (2008) conception of 'living loss' is evocative of a social and emotional landscape marked by grief and loss. Though she examines loss associated with AIDS dementia, her analysis illuminates how the experience of post-prison liminality can manifest, particularly in aboriginal lives still shadowed by the effects of colonial oppression. The lived experience of liminality might also be understood as 'living loss' for non-indigenous imprisoned parents. The term connotes the experience of families as the 'collateral casualties of prison' (Arrigo & Milovanovic, 2009: 40).

Kelly suggests that the burden of inhabiting liminal space arises from it being 'socio-cultural' yet 'simultaneously a medical and psychological space' (2008: 336). She asserts that to be 'in liminality is to be in limbo, on the threshold of between here and there, without socio-cultural classification or a medical diagnosis of where "there" is, will be, or if the ritual subjects ever make it there' (p. 336). The lack of a 'medical diagnosis' may be seen as a metaphor for ex-prisoners' indeterminate status: no longer classified 'prisoner', yet forever shackled by 'ex-prisonerhood', 'reintegration' signifying an uncertain destination. This has particularly stark significance for ex-prisoners with MHD/CD, whose 'criminal' label can overshadow their disability.

Structural invisibility

Liminality is a 'psychological space' in that its inhabitants become pathologised by such defining labels as 'criminal'. Structural constraints, such as offender registers and criminal records, can consign ex-prisoners to perpetual outsider status: 'screened out of legitimate opportunities' (Jacobs, 2006, in Maruna, 2011a: 106), structurally invisible. According to Turner (1967), this structural 'invisibility' has two aspects: 'they are at once no longer classified and not yet classified' (p. 96). In terms of being 'no longer classified', they are represented by symbols of waste, refuse, detritus, symbols 'drawn from the biology of death, decomposition . . . and other physical processes that have a negative tinge' (p. 96). The label 'ex-prisoner' carries such a stigma. Indeed, the categorisation of the 'mentally ill', the 'cognitively impaired', even the 'socially disadvantaged', to some extent resonates with Turner's symbolism associated with damage or demise. The other aspect, being 'not yet classified', in contrast, 'is often expressed in symbols modelled on processes of gestation and parturition'. The key characteristic of both symbolisations is that people in such liminal states 'are neither living nor dead from one aspect, and both living and dead from another. Their condition is one of ambiguity and paradox' (Turner, 1967: 97).

The symbolism associated with growth and (re)birth finds echoes in notions of rehabilitation, reform, reintegration, restoration and redemption. As Polizzi and Arrigo (2009: 124) argue, these words and concepts signify imposed meanings that limit the emergence of their subject. The ambiguity inheres in the 'not yet' aspect of the liminal state, the becomingness, the perpetual 'in-betweenness'. The paradoxical image of being 'neither living nor dead' and 'both living and dead' evokes the social death of which Jewkes (2005b) writes in relation to the experience of a life sentence, which she likens to a terminal illness. People enduring such forms of social exclusion, she writes, 'may experience a permanent liminality in that they are not moving between established boundaries' (Jewkes, 2005b: 376). Kelly[8] (2008: 335) similarly found that, instead of 'a transitional space, liminality (living in a threshold) became a way of life'.

The notion of social death derives from the legal doctrine of civil death that describes 'the status of a person who has been deprived of all civil rights' (Harvard Law Review (HLR), 1937: 968). Although Goffman (1961) described entry into the 'total institution' of prison as a 'civil death' (p. 25), the term resonates in a post-release context with the sense that Turner evokes of being 'living men regarded as dead, dead men returning to life, and the same man considered alive for one purpose but dead for another' (HLR, 1937: 968). In the US, for instance, the 'collateral consequences' of a criminal conviction include ex-prisoners' ineligibility for voting, public housing, many forms of employment, and jury service.[9] In Australia, though less extreme, the restricting effects of criminal records on employment are nevertheless a structural barrier to reintegration that limits ex-prisoners' claim to full citizenship.

Kelly describes a perpetual state; however, conceiving of liminality as 'living in a threshold' also implies its potential as an opening, a doorway to another way of being. From this perspective, liminal states need not be experienced as fixed, but as a 'suspension' or a period of disengagement from a previous way of being, after which a reconstruction of the 'narrative of self' may ensue (Jewkes, 2005b: 375). The liminal state can thus be a phase – a gap – out of which change emerges. Maruna's (2001) 'redemption narratives' are evoked as strategies of resistance and self-determination whereby prisoners create new 'unspoiled' identities to move beyond past or present circumstances (Jewkes, 2005b). Turner's (1986: 42) definition of liminality – 'a fructile chaos, a storehouse of possibilities, not a random assemblage but a striving after new forms and structures, a gestation process' – reinforces the metamorphic imagery, and the notion of emergent subjectivity.

Liminality as a site of becoming

The notion of 'liminoidity', which Turner (1982) distinguishes from liminality, embodies metamorphosis. 'Liminoids' are creative, resistant, change-oriented and critical. They manifest the liminal state's transformational potential (Turner, 1982; Jewkes, 2005b), by challenging, testing and potentially subverting the status quo (St John, 2000). Hence, the liminoid is perceived to be freer than the liminal (Turner, 1982; St John, 2000), and more visible. Ex-prisoner activists embody liminoidity in actively seeking and effecting positive change through their experience of imprisonment. Concealment is one response to stigma and discrimination (Goffman, 1963). Engagement in social and political activism is an alternative: a way of actively reclaiming a more positive identity (LeBel, 2009).

LeBel notes the scarcity of research on ex-prisoner activism, yet notes the growth of US groups comprising former prisoners, giving voice to their experience and striving to influence penal policy. One such group[10] emphasises the importance of language in identity formation. They advocate the use of 'people-first language such as "people currently or formerly incarcerated" instead of dehumanizing language such as "offenders" and "ex-convicts"' (LeBel, 2009: 167–8). United in their view of the penal system as 'unfair, unjust and illegitimate' (p. 169), such groups seek to challenge the status quo by confronting the 'invisible punishments' (Travis, 2002, in LeBel, 2009: 171) that hamper effective reintegration. Such activity, which is clearly liminoid, provides a way of inhabiting liminal social space that is proactive instead of reactive, active rather than passive, promoting resistance rather than submission.

Earlier characterisations of liminality evoke 'a non-place' (Kelly, 2008: 336). Liminoid phenomena actively create their own place, reproducing their own meanings and producing new cultural forms[11] (St John, 2000). In Deleuzian terms, liminoidity comprises lines of flight, cutting across the territorial lines of the post-carceral landscape, deterritorialising in its 'augmentation of capacities' (DeLanda, 2006: 50). A 'line of flight', according to Lorraine (2005: 145), 'is a path of mutation precipitated through the actualisation of connections among bodies that were previously only implicit . . . that release new powers in the capacities of those bodies to act and respond'. Former prisoners – impliedly connected by their common experience of imprisonment – may discover shared conceptions of that experience. This can trigger a collective resistance, 'striving after new forms and structures' (Turner, 1986: 42) out of which the possibility of transformation emerges. Thus, liminality can represent a 'path of mutation', a site of becoming.

Prisoners experience imprisonment in different ways. Some adapt, according to classic accounts of prison life.[12] Some fail to cope, even resist coping (see Liebling, 1992, 1999, in Jewkes, 2005b: 378). Similarly, post-imprisonment liminality – as a state of being, a social space – holds a varying promise of renewal for its inhabitants. For some ex-prisoners, it provides an opportunity to reconstruct self-narratives (Jewkes, 2005b). This implies the importance of autonomy, self-determination, self-respect and resistance in order to survive, 'not as a shadow . . . but as a man' (Bettelheim, 1960: 147). Others remain in transition, no longer 'inside' and not yet wholly free on the 'outside'.

The shadow

The metaphor of the 'shadow' is useful in conceiving the social landscape of liminality, and ex-prisoners' experience of 'unfreedom' (Oppenheim, 1955). Their continued exclusion may be understood, as Garland (2001) suggests, by the construction of offenders as 'alien others' (p. 253). Maruna, Matravers and King (2004), for instance, draw on Freud and Jung to account for public punitiveness in terms of 'shadow projection'. This involves separating parts of the self, deemed abhorrent and intolerable, and then projecting these on to an external object – a scapegoating process comprising the rejection and denial of the unconscious 'shadow' by the conscious ego (Maruna, Matravers & King, 2004). Arrigo and Milovanovic (2009) use the concept of the 'criminological shadow' to develop their 'penal harm' thesis. Polizzi and Arrigo (2009) argue that the prevailing binary construction, the 'us and them' archetype, imprisons the penal subject in a 'cycle of otherness that . . . denies the possibility of transformation' (p. 118). The language and logic sustaining this cycle collectively serve to inhibit human potential (Arrigo & Milovanovic, 2009).

The condition under which such logic arises is a prevailing sense of threat. This gives rise to the process of 'othering', involving:

> The projection of essentialist attributes on another and, by means of this, oneself in order to justify privileges and deference and to stem feelings of

ontological insecurity. It promises fixed lines of orientation in a late modern world of hyper pluralism and disembeddedness; it guarantees structures of superiority and inferiority. . . . Thus the 'normal' is contrasted with the 'deviant' and the law-abiding with the criminal . . . their vice corroborates our virtue.

(Ferrell et al., 2008: 23)

Maruna, Matravers and King (2004) turn to psychoanalytic theory to explain the nature of the shadow projected in terms of shame, guilt/blame, jealousy, sadism and ambivalent sexual morality. Solzhenitsyn (1974: 168) identifies its paradoxical source:

If only there were evil people somewhere insidiously committing evil deeds, and it were necessary only to separate them from the rest of us and destroy them. But the line dividing good and evil cuts through the heart of every human being. And who is willing to destroy a piece of his own heart?

The indivisibility of self and shadow underpins the Jungian call to 'own our own shadow' and thereby accept collective responsibility for human failings (Maruna, Matravers & King, 2004: 294). Community responsibility for ex-prisoner reintegration would then naturally ensue. Emphasising the permanence of stigma, of classifications such as 'ex-prisoner', Douglas (1975) qualifies that, 'rites of passage . . . do not redefine and restore a lost former status or purify from the effect of contamination, but they define entrance to a new status' (p. 56). Neither negating the crime, nor revoking the punishment, rites of aggregation can enable growth, transformation and becoming. They allow a society to forgive, yet not forget (Maruna, 2011a). Without such rites, these possibilities fade, and post-prison shadows linger. The 'shadow' thus characterises both the interior experience and exterior landscape of post-prison liminality.

Assemblage–culture–liminality: A synthesis

The 'toolkit' motif recurring throughout this chapter is a useful way of summing up its purpose: to provide a set of conceptual tools fitting the task of qualitatively mapping the post-release experience, in its broader social context. The study applies these tools with particular aims: to see prison release as comprising multiple perspectives and layers of meaning-making; to conceptualise how these meanings relate to practices and behaviours; and to understand how the intersection of meanings and social action gives rise to and perpetuates a social space characterised by uncertainty and instability. This space contains both risk and promise: the promise of renewal and community integration, and the risk of perpetual exclusion, of being caught in the inexorable orbit of the carceral machine. The resources (personal, social, cultural, economic and structural) available to inhabitants of this post-release space determine their trajectory. To trace the contours of this space, examine how its lines coalesce and clash, and explain the ramifications of these relationships, the conceptual tripod of assemblage, culture and liminality is useful in the following ways.

Assemblage provides a way of modelling and charting the post-release terrain that dislodges dominant ways of seeing and thinking about imprisonment and release. Prison and prisoners are generally located at the base of a superstructure geared towards correction and control and maintained by its accompanying socio-political narrative. Assemblages, however, dissolve binary constructions. They 'combine the abstract materiality of utterances and institutions and the concrete materiality of objects. In them, base and superstructure are irredeemably mixed' (Lecercle, 2002: 185). Assembling the component parts of the post-release domain – its forms of content and expression – around the nub of lived experience enables an interior focus on post-prison subjectivity. The voices of the carceral subject are foregrounded, yet as collective rather than individual subjectivities. Watkins and Swidler (2006) point out the difficulty confounding social scientists who seek to capture collective meanings and the dynamic processes through which they emerge and evolve, yet who rely on methods (such as the interview) tending to produce individualised accounts. This study is less concerned with these dynamic processes as they occur than with the effects observable in actions and behaviour. Its semiotic-practical approach fits this task.

Wedeen's semiotic-practices approach is used as shorthand for an approach focused on the relationship between meaning-making (and its forms of expression) and behaviour or practice – or seeing culture in action (Swidler, 1986). Culture is conceived, not as the 'basis of social solidarity', but as a relational phenomenon, a map that prisoners use to 'position themselves in social space' (Sampson & Bean, 2006: 23–4), a toolkit from which men construct their strategies of action (Swidler, 1986). In fact, culture is an assemblage in itself, territorialised through *'habitual repetition'* together with 'the effects of the *acquisition of new skills'* (DeLanda, 2006: 50, original emphasis) and destabilising earlier cultural norms and identities. Thus, prison habits and skills accompany released prisoners into the community. Conceiving of post-prison culture in this way, as prison culture leaking into the post-prison realm, is a way of challenging 'the paradigmatic construction of incarceration as a linear and causal progression of events characterised as pre-imprisonment, in-prison and post-release' (Carlton & Segrave, 2009: 44). It allows, instead, an understanding of how release from prison can give way to a chaotic swirl of marginalisation and criminalisation, of which imprisonment and reimprisonment are compounding and iterative elements.

Liminality is a conceptual window into the social and emotional space of post-release transition and how its lines are experienced: lines that territorialise and deterritorialise it and lines of flight that allow the possibility of transformation. It is territorialised by the rigid (molar) lines of parole conditions, post-sentence restrictions, pharmacotherapy queues, income support requirements, criminal records, public housing waiting lists and, for some prisoners, the need to conceal where they have been while imprisoned. Deterritorialising are the supple (molecular) lines of homelessness (and 'couch-surfing'), drug use (and 'doctor-shopping'), mixing with the 'wrong crowd', overt police attention and the increased risk of return to custody. Both these domains are characterised by their instability, insecurity, uncertainty and vulnerability: they are inherently liminal spaces. They exist outside, parallel to and beneath the lines along which 'integrated' society flows: having a home and a regular (legal) income; freedom of movement and association; participation in education or meaningful learning; pro-social community engagement; having a political voice. Lines of flight create possibilities for moving beyond liminality: finding a home, somewhere safe and permanent to live; employment and a secure financial future; the support and care of family or significant others; escaping the cycle of addiction; *belonging* to a (law-abiding) community; and hope, simply, a reason to live.

Conceiving of liminality as an element in a ritual process highlights its symbolic function as a transitional stage between prisoners' separation from and return to the community. It makes clear the need for a subsequent (post-liminal) rite to mark the end of the liminal phase and thus signify the subject's 'incorporation' back into society. Without such a process, ex-prisoner reintegration remains 'next to impossible' (Clemmer, 1940: 300). The process of cultural retooling (Swidler, 1986), to enable post-prison integration, relies on resources that ex-prisoners may or may not have access to: individual/inner resources that also require community investment in the form of acceptance, opportunities to rebuild trust, emotional support and material assistance. A society lacking such reintegrative social infrastructure risks consigning whole populations to liminal states of being, with the accompanying risks of social exclusion, serial institutionalisation and entanglement in the lines of force that territorialise the reincarceration assemblage. Liminality provides an important tool for directing attention to the symbolic and material aspects of the experience of release from prison.

Applying the assemblage–culture–liminality lens to the problems seen to characterise ex-prisoner populations – homelessness, unemployment, legal problems, family breakdown, physical and mental ill health, substance abuse and subsequent reoffending – allows a vision of these as elements of a broader social phenomenon, or, more precisely, a set of phenomena connected to, arising from and intensified by the penal/correctional apparatus. For instance, the assemblage–culture–liminality lens allows relationships between released prisoners and programme workers to be seen in the wider context of psychotherapeutic expansion (Rose, 1989). Ex-prisoners' housing options and employment opportunities blocked by structural deficits and constraints can be seen as constitutive elements in circuits of inclusion and exclusion (Rose, 2000), whereby individuals bear the consequences of societal failings and lack of reintegrative social infrastructure. Individualised 'client plans' may be seen as a form of colonial institutionalisation (Baldry, 2009), masking wider social problems, such as the dislocation of Indigenous culture and communities, and failing to address the marginalisation and criminalisation of Indigenous people.

Through this lens, these problems are seen to comprise webs of meaning and practice in which men become entangled and from which they struggle to extricate themselves, rather than individual risk factors to be studied discretely or addressed through programmatic solutions. Assembling these individual and social factors and the relationships between them, seeing them in terms of meanings generated through prisoner interactions that shape men's relationships with people outside prison, and seeing into the experience of being 'betwixt and between' imprisonment and freedom allows a wide-angle view that foregrounds the subjective. It reveals, in equally sharp focus, the background textures (feelings, expressions, attitudes), shapes (constraints, barriers) and forces (expectations, narratives) against which the subjective experience is set. The risky post-release subject is seen as embedded in risky systems of imprisonment and release.

Conclusion

This chapter has explained the concepts of assemblage, culture and liminality in the context of post-prison experience, and how assemblage–culture–liminality fits together as a lens. The chapter thus establishes a conceptual framework that permits analysis of the processes through which collective meanings are made and recursive patterns of behaviour and action emerge. It provides a way to make sense of the experience of inhabiting transitional social space, and the lines of force – and inertia – that sustain it. The study's focus on the multiple and collective, the relational and intersubjective, required a technique for capturing and mapping these aspects of post-prison life. The following chapter explains how phenomenography fulfilled this methodological function, and why phenomenographic methods help to answer the questions central to this book: How is prison release (and post-release life) constructed? And how do these constructions conflict and cohere?

Notes

1 Assemblage is imperfectly translated from Deleuze and Guattari's (1987) term *agence-ment*, a common French word variously used to refer to the act of fixing (or affixing), fitting together or arranging of things – parts of a body or machine, for example – as well as the arrangement itself, such as the fittings or fixtures of a room or building.
2 In Gilles Deleuze, *Two Regimes of Madness: Texts and Interviews 1975–1995*: pp. 177–9 (David Lapouiade ed., Ames Hodges & Mike Taormina trans. 2006).
3 Also Seymour-Smith, 1993: 65; Watson, 1995: 683; Eagleton, 2000: 34; Fischer, 2007: 2.
4 For example, see Ortner, 1999.
5 Ferrell, 1999, 2001; Fenwick, 2004; Hayward & Young, 2004; Kane, 2004; Presdee, 2004; Ferrell, Hayward & Young, 2008.
6 See Herzfeld, 1985, in Phillips, 2001: 14; Messerschmidt, 1993; Jewkes, 2005a.
7 *Jack Charles v The Crown* premiered at the 2010 Melbourne International Arts Festival, a one-man play performed and co-written, with John Romeril, by Koori elder 'Uncle' Jack Charles.
8 Kelly (2008) describes findings of her study of the experience of AIDS dementia.
9 Olivares, Burton & Cullen, 1996; Ewald, 2002; Hirsch et al. 2002; Mukamal & Samuels, 2002–3; Pinard, 2010.
10 The Centre for NuLeadership on Urban Solutions is an activist academic centre, policy think-tank and community organizer based at Medgar Evers College, at the City University of New York. Founded and run by people formerly incarcerated, it is the only one of its kind in the US (www.citizensinc.org/centerfornuleadershiponurban.html).
11 Examples of new cultural forms include the growth in web-based resources associated with reentry, such as http://rethinkingreentry.blogspot.com.au and www.ridgehouse.org
12 Clemmer, 1940; Sykes, 1958; Goffman, 1961; Irwin & Cressey, 1962; Cohen & Taylor, 1972.

5 Phenomenography

'Wayne'

Wayne, aged 43, got out on straight release 3 months ago, having served his first prison sentence. None of his friends or family – he tells me, when we meet at the office of the employment service that is helping him try to find work – has ever been imprisoned. He explains how he ended up in jail after the courts 'ran out of patience' with him:

> I've ... been through court a few times where you might get a slap on the wrist or a fine, and then served a community based order ... and then ... a suspended sentence, I think it was, and then it was just like 'we've run out of patience' ...

His problem is alcohol. He drinks to excess. 'I can't seem to find a happy medium of just having a couple', he admits, adding, 'I'm just sometimes irresponsible when I drink too much'. This has led to several drink-driving charges and an assault, which ultimately meant a longer sentence than he had anticipated: 'I ended up doing yeah 17 months'.

There is a sense of a loss of agency running through Wayne's story. Acknowledging 'it sounds silly', he explains:

> I knew I was in trouble and I was looking at jail anyway, because they had already charged me ... so I knew I was getting a jail term, and then you just had this little mad patch that you're going to jail so then you don't care if you get caught driving unlicensed ... It's like ... you're a walking dead man ... you think 'what else can go wrong?' ... You're almost becoming a prisoner even before you've gone to prison.

In hindsight, he is contrite: 'looking back, on reflection, it's stupid because like you could have run over someone, and then how would I live with that?'. Wayne's explanation gives insight into how people's behaviour can spiral out of control, with prison having little or no deterrent effect in that moment.

Wayne feels that, once inside, even on remand, it is hard to get out: 'You walk in through the side of the court ... in cuffs, in your greens and things like that and say 'not guilty', you haven't got a chance'. Nevertheless, in contrast to other 'guys' whose 'dad was in prison . . . they've just got no hope', for Wayne, prison was a break in his normal life: 'I tried to pretend it was just like . . . you've moved out, and gone . . . somewhere different, like you're in a different place for a year . . . and then you can go back home'

Since his release, he has been living with his parents, which is not ideal: 'I need my own space at 43, if I go out it's like "what time will you be home?" It's like I'm 18 again'. But, as he says, 'I'd rather live with my parents than live at a caravan park or a boarding house . . . it's ideal compared to there'. Getting out, he admits, has been harder than he anticipated: he has struggled to find the motivation to ride his bike, get up early, or look for work; but 'it's been a couple of months now so it's time to move on'.

He is keen 'to find something' – anything really – 'the money is the biggest worry . . . I'm . . . really not that fussed what I do at the moment'. And, though he is concerned about what to tell prospective employers when they ask what he has been doing for the last year and a half, he says he will 'cross that bridge as I come to it', adding, 'it is a worry but it's not going to put me off going to an interview'. Despite acknowledging the practical limitations of a criminal record, and now a prison record too, he seems confident that someone will give him a chance. Perhaps this self-assurance comes from having worked most of his life – 'I've just always felt the need to work just to get some money' – and having a social network, a group of 'mates' he used to play golf with regularly.

Although he doesn't anticipate returning to prison, and never wants to go back, he does concede that, 'once you've been to prison it's very easy to go back there . . . you don't have to do anything that serious and they just say well you're not learning you need more time in prison, let's go'. There was very little 'learning' in prison, however, apart from 'rules' such as borrowing something and not paying it back: 'in prison, that's the big no-no'. Most of the time was spent drinking coffee, smoking cigarettes . . . It really was 'just a waste of time'. And Wayne doesn't strike me as a man who wastes much time.

Phenomenography provided the methodological vehicle for the study, as it allowed the construction and depiction of a qualitative map of what it means to be released from prison. This chapter begins by orienting the research philosophically, outlining its ontological and epistemological bases and its qualitative approach. It then describes phenomenography, why it was used and how it shaped the research questions. The questions, restated here, are followed by a detailed description of the methods, including the sample and data collection and analysis. Lastly, I briefly discuss ethical and access issues.

Philosophical orientation

Philosophical issues, as Scott and Usher argue, 'are *integral* to the research process' because they represent 'what researchers "silently think" about research' (1999: 10). To ignore or discount the significance of these silent thoughts is to diminish the trustworthiness and legitimacy of the investigation (Kvale, 1996).

It implies a privileging of positivist assumptions about truth and objectivity, and of research as an exposition of facts using a set of techniques unimpeded by values or social context (Scott & Usher, 1999). Such an approach clearly belies the situatedness of the researcher and the researched (Denzin & Lincoln, 1994; Scott & Usher, 1999). As a social practice, research is both embodied and embedded and thus demands a reflexivity that begins with an explicit account of its ontological and epistemological premises.

Ontology and epistemology

This study assumes a critical-realist social ontology. From this perspective, 'the world is viewed as multi-faceted and constituted by complex systems' (Ward & Maruna, 2007: 30). Reality contains multitudes, constructed, divergent and inter-related, and the social world is greater than individuals' perceptions of it. This position, distinct from a traditional realist view of reality existing independent of mind, draws on DeLanda's (2006) realist social ontology.[1] As DeLanda points out, social entities would not exist without human minds and so cannot be seen as mind-independent. Rather, social entities, from people to interpersonal networks to institutional organisations to nation-states, are seen as 'conception-independent' (2006: 3), existing outside and beyond the conceptions we have of them. This is not to diminish the value and significance of human conceptions, but to acknowledge that they invest and embroider social reality with layers of meaning – both conflicting and cohering – that provide its depth and texture. This perspective invokes a view of reality grounded in the objective existence of institutional organisations (courts, prisons, parole boards), norms (laws, sentences, court orders) and practices (arrest, imprisonment, release, supervision) forming the context and background to the experience and meaning-making of its human subjects (DeLanda, 2006: 2). The social world is thus real and imagined, its reality coloured by our imaginings.

This book's critical stance is anchored in its assumption of the multiplicity of social entities and the conceptions overlaying them, and its commitment to privileging the voices of the less heard alongside prevailing sociopolitical thinking. In Deleuzian terms, a rhizomatic schema supplants an arboreal one (Deleuze & Guattari, 1987). Traditional hierarchies of knowledge are dismantled and reassembled. The associated epistemological basis is constructionist – presuming that reality is socially constructed by its human participants – and subjectivist in that the researcher (the observer, the knower) and the subject (the observed, the known) interact to create and share understandings.[2] The tension arising from the apparent duality between researcher and subject is resolved through a Deleuzian lens, whereby, as Boundas explains (2005: 2268), 'subjectivity is not given; it is always under construction'. Constructionism, Crotty (1998) argues, focuses on the social dimension of meaning, whereas constructivism emphasises the unique experience of the individual, thereby allowing such accounts to be cocooned from potential criticism. Crotty's version evokes the more literal sense of 'construction' – 'of building or assembling from parts' – that is often ignored by constructivists in favour of its metaphorical meaning (Hacking, 1999, in DeLanda, 2006: 3). Constructionism is thus seen to interlock with culture and assemblage. For my purposes, Crotty's distinction is a useful one.

Qualitative research as bricolage

This study's qualitative mode of enquiry implies its interpretive perspective. In keeping with Deleuze's idea of a conceptual toolkit, the image of the qualitative researcher as a *bricoleur* is apt. *Bricolage* describes the 'piecing together' of research strategies and methods, deliberately and pragmatically, in a way that will most aptly and precisely address the questions at the heart of an investigation (Denzin and Lincoln, 1994). The notion of *bricolage* enables and validates the development of a methodology by adapting and combining methods to suit particular research aims. In this case, using phenomenography to qualitatively map men's post-release experience, and applying the assemblage–culture–liminality lens to see into that experience.

The interpretivist focus on the construction of meaning in ordinary experience is anchored in the study's broadly phenomenological approach, in the 'general non-philosophical sense' of phenomenology as understanding social phenomena from the subjects' perspective, describing the world as subjects experience it, and 'the assumption that the important reality is what people perceive it to be' (Kvale, 1996: 52). Taylor and Bogdan (1996) use the term phenomenological interchangeably with interpretivist to denote the concern with understanding social actors' perspective. In fact, this book's orientation might more aptly be labelled 'phenomenal', as its methodological scaffold is a *phenomenographic* one, wholly distinct from its ('philosophical') phenomenological forebear.

A phenomenographic approach

What is phenomenography?

In the 1970s, a Gothenburg University team researched student learning using a qualitative methodology later labelled 'phenomenography'[3] by Ference Marton (1981). This approach was directed towards 'description, analysis and understanding of experiences' (Marton, 1981: 180), its most distinctive feature being its focus on *conceptions*. Phenomenography developed as an empirical, pragmatic approach without any clear philosophical or conceptual basis. Epistemological grounding was sought retrospectively, drawing on Husserlian phenomenology and Gestalt psychology.[4] Marton's use of the phenomenological tradition as the rootstock of phenomenography highlights similarities between the two approaches in terms of their subject matter and relational, content-oriented and experiential characteristics. The phenomenological concern with 'bracketing' or suspending preconceptions is seen as critical in phenomenographic research and lends credibility to its commitment to understanding and describing lived experience (Richardson, 1999; Ashworth & Lucas, 2000).

Despite its similarities with phenomenology, and notwithstanding the suspicions of some critics[5] that the two approaches are essentially the same, phenomenography claims certain foci as its own, including its 'second-order' perspective (Marton, 1981; Webb, 1997). Whereas a 'first-order' perspective leads to descriptions and statements about the world, a 'second-order' perspective is oriented towards people's ideas about and experience of the world, a distinction between reality and perception of reality not afforded by phenomenology (Marton, 1981). Further, whereas phenomenology investigates the 'pre-reflective level of consciousness', phenomenography aims to describe the 'conceptual and the experiential', 'that which is lived', as well as 'what is culturally learned' and 'ways of relating ourselves to the world around us' (Marton, 1981: 181). Phenomenography seeks to characterise the 'collective mind' (Marton, 1981).

Phenomenography relies chiefly on interviews to gather data (Green, 2005), emphasising techniques that aim to 'elicit underlying meanings and intentional attitudes towards the phenomenon being investigated' (Akerlind, 2005: 65). Beginning with a set of questions to establish the focus, the phenomenographer uses probing questions to flesh out responses and explore examples. However, phenomenographers 'are not interested in the details of the example per se, but in using them as a *medium* for exploring the way in which the interviewee is thinking about or experiencing the phenomenon' (Akerlind, 2005: 65). The methods, though grounded in individual understandings, thus enable a focus on collective human experience.

Marton (1986: 31) has defined phenomenography as 'a research method adapted for mapping the qualitatively different ways in which people experience, conceptualise, perceive, and understand various aspects of, and phenomena in, the world around them'. Significantly, it is assumed that there exist a limited number of qualitatively different ways of experiencing a phenomenon.[6] In mapping 'person–world relationships' in relation to a particular phenomenon, phenomenography seeks to characterise different conceptions, or ways of experiencing, in terms of 'categories of description', which are then related to each other in a form designated an 'outcome space' (Hasselgren & Beach, 1997). Its aim is thus 'to describe the *key aspects of the variation* of the collective experience of a phenomenon rather than the richness of individual experiences' (Trigwell, 2006: 368–9, original emphasis). Phenomenographic analysis is an inductive process involving both discovery and construction, in that themes emerge from the interview transcripts and are constructed through iterative analysis (Mann, Dall'Alba & Radcliffe, 2007). This involves drawing meaning out of the data and allowing categories to emerge to assemble a set of discrete, yet interrelated, aspects of the phenomenon.

The absence of a consensus method spurred several emergent phenomenographers[7] to propose some useful guidelines. Barnard, McCosker and Gerber (1999: 222–3) suggest three rules to guide both the interview and analysis phase: epoché or bracketing of presuppositions; description focus, rather than explanation focus; and 'horizontalisation', whereby all description and experience are ascribed equal value. Ashworth and Lucas (2000) emphasise the importance of 'bracketing' and careful listening: 'It is the research participant's experience which should be revealed, not the researcher's expectations' (p. 298), highlighting the need to attend to participants' meanings with empathic understanding in order to faithfully represent them. 'Conceptions', or ways of experiencing and understanding, are the units of analysis in phenomenography (Marton & Pong, 2005). As Säljö (1997) points out, ways of experiencing are only available through discursive accounts; hence, the specific forms of language used by participants are the basis for analysis (Svensson, 1997; Patrick, 2000). Rather than beginning with a set of predetermined categories into which data segments are slotted (Bowden, 2000), the phenomenographic approach seeks to capture conceptions via people's 'utterances' (Hasselgren & Beach, 1997: 194).

Svensson (1997) allows that, although conceptions are most accessible through language, they may be expressed in various ways. Participants' meanings and conceptions are identified and summarised in categories of description, which represent 'a reduction of data to a limited and pregnant form', yet 'as close to data as possible' (Svensson, 1997: 167). The categories that surface through iterative readings of the data transcripts thus remain anchored in the 'expressed content' of participants, to which the language used is subordinate (Svensson, 1997: 170; Barnard et al., 1999). Indeed, thinking and meaning may be expressed directly through the body (Hwang & Roth, 2011, in De Freitas, 2013: 289–90). Nonetheless, where particular language conveys specific meaning, the participants' words serve to ground the interpretation within the categories of description. Ways of experiencing and perceiving the phenomenon of prison release – articulated verbally and in symbolic and embodied forms of communication – were gleaned from interview data using the phenomenographic method.

Why choose phenomenography?

Social scientists seeking to gather collective meanings and explore social processes face a dilemma when they rely on individualised methods such as interviewing (Watkins & Swidler, 2006). Phenomenography circumvents this problem. The strength of phenomenographic analysis is its capacity 'to create a landscape view that encompasses diverse perspectives . . . while simultaneously highlighting the relationship among these variations' (Daly, Adams & Bodner, 2012: 193). This 'landscape view' distinguishes phenomenography from analyses focused primarily on thematic similarities or individual experience. Though phenomenographic results cannot be generalised, 'the range of variation in the sample is expected to reflect the range of variation in the population' (Daly et al., 2012: 194). It is this focus on difference that characterises the research.

Phenomenography's subjectivist and relational view, implied in its focus on conceptions and the assumption of knowledge as 'meaning in a social and cultural context' (Svensson, 1997: 163), clearly aligns it with the concept of collectivity – and the idea of assembling threads, themes and contours of meaning – underpinning this study. The task is to assemble and qualitatively map the post-release experience. The object is the relationship between the phenomenon of prison release and the individual released, to reveal 'the (often taken-for-granted) foundations for human ways of acting within and perceiving the world' (Abrahamsson et al., 2005: 368). Assemblage provides a framework within which the perspective of post-release support workers and the lived experience of release from prison may be viewed and understood in terms of their interrelatedness, the connections and tensions between them. In modelling the phenomenon of prison release as a semiotic space, assemblage allows a view from within and beneath the conventional 'arboreal' representation of the penal/post-release system, to conceive the 'rhizomatic' networks of meaning and activity by which it is constituted. The cultural lens shapes the field of enquiry around the assembled threads of meaning, directing the focus of analysis to the areas of intersection – where perspectives collide, where meanings clash – and the implications for practice and behaviour arising from these points. Phenomenography is the methodological vehicle enabling the construction, depiction and analysis of this qualitative map.

Research questions

The theoretical perspective outlined above orients the research philosophically and shapes its concerns into questions:

How is men's prison release (and post-release life) constructed?
And how do these constructions conflict and cohere?

A series of related questions arise, shaped by the concepts of assemblage, culture and liminality and the phenomenographic focus:

• What are the qualitatively different ways men experience release from prison?
• How is post-release support conceived and experienced?
• How does culture flow from and feed into the reincarceration assemblage?
• How is post-release liminality experienced? What are its interior and exterior dimensions, and how do these facilitate or impede community (re)integration?

Methods

Rationale for the sample

The research sample comprised men released from prison, in Victoria, and post-release support workers. The rationale for including workers was twofold. First, workers provided a way of gaining access to ex-prisoners, a difficult-to-reach population. Establishing a rapport with people already known and trusted by released prisoners enabled this access. Second, workers have an intimate understanding and knowledge of what it means for men to be released from prison. This knowledge provided a broader view of the post-release world – its sociopolitical features as well as the characteristics of its subjects – and context for the lived experience. Workers were able to give a 'first-order' explanation of post-release issues from a practice-oriented perspective, as well as 'second-order' account of their ideas, understandings and experience of post-prison life (Marton, 1981; Webb, 1997). Thus, collective meanings of release and post-release experience could be assembled to examine their points of intersection and divergence.

Selection of the sample

Using a purposive sampling approach (Neuman, 1997), participants were recruited through the post-release service agencies comprising the Link Out consortium. Additional contacts were made with WISE Employment and with two independent (church-based) post-release support workers involved in the Five8 programme. The sample was indicative, if not statistically representative, of the range of post-release services available in Victoria. Purposive sampling fitted the study's focus on gaining in-depth understanding of a particular, difficult-to-reach group (released prisoners) and its emphasis on qualitatively rich data. In anticipation of the difficulties gaining access to willing ex-prisoner participants, I employed opportunistic and snowball sampling strategies.

The size of the sample was based on a number of factors. Phenomenologically oriented studies typically select a small sample based on the guiding principle that participants must have lived experience, which they are able to articulate, of the phenomenon under investigation (Polit & Beck, 2005). Another issue is the quality of data and the amount of useful material provided by participants (Morse, 2000). My interviewing experience helped to establish rapport, build trust with participants and thus yield meaningful data. The size of a purposive sample is generally determined according to the concept of saturation – the point at which no new categories emerge from the data – which has been found often to occur within twelve interviews (Guest, Bunce & Johnson, 2006). The scope of the research also determined sample size, in that, the broader the scope, the longer it takes to reach saturation (Morse, 2000).

The initial research plan was based on a sample of thirty: fifteen ex-prisoners and fifteen post-release workers. This plan was confounded by access issues.[8] It was difficult to establish contact with ex-prisoners to interview, particularly those not engaged with post-release programmes. After conducting interviews with fourteen workers, efforts were focused on finding released prisoners willing to participate in the research, through programmes and via word of mouth. Ultimately, twelve ex-prisoners were interviewed. The sample size was therefore reduced from thirty to twenty-six, approximating equal numbers across the two groups while still satisfying the 'saturation' criterion.

I encountered no obstacles in selecting the worker sample. There were enough Link Out workers alone to meet the sampling criteria, though some diversity was achieved by sampling across programmes and organisations. I initiated this process through contact with the Link Out programme manager and then attended a coordinators' meeting to outline the research project and its aims. Data collection commenced with interviews with Link Out and Konnect workers at ACSO and the Brosnan Centre. The first ex-prisoner interview took place 2 months after the initial Link Out meeting, after a worker forwarded the details of a client ('Scott') interested in participating in an interview. Referrals trickled in over months, via workers, through word of mouth and after I posted flyers promoting the research in local employment services. One ex-prisoner, referred via word of mouth, talked about a programme called Five8. Grounded in restorative principles, Five8 stood out as less dogmatic and more reintegrative than other church-based programmes, adding a new element to the post-release landscape that seemed important to capture. I subsequently interviewed the programme founders.

The research sample

The final sample comprised twelve men who had experienced release from adult prison in Victoria[9] and fourteen post-release support workers/professionals in the field. To protect confidentiality and ensure anonymity, each interview participant was assigned a code: either 'RP' (released prisoner) or 'SW' (support worker), preceding a numeric tag relating to the total number of interviews conducted, from 01 to 26. These codes are used for the workers throughout the book; however, I have used aliases for the men. Methodologically speaking, individualising experience was a 'no-no', to use Wayne's expression, but I wanted the men's stories to anchor the text in a way that brought them to life for the reader. Giving them names was part of this. The workers I interviewed were not asked about their story in the same way. I felt that giving them names would over-personalise them and distract from the men whose experience of release is the focus of the work. Hence, they remain coded.

The workers

The fourteen workers consisted of case managers, intake and assessment staff, a team leader and programme managers, within Link Out, Konnect and WISE Employment's Ex-offender Program, as well as the couple, both with extensive experience supporting prisoners, who founded Five8. The worker sample comprised nine men and five women, aged from their mid 20s to late 50s. In terms of their training, eight held social work or related degrees, two held a diploma in welfare work, two had studied criminology, and two had drug and alcohol training. These qualifications were combined with broad experience in prison education, human services, case management and disability fields. Two of the men interviewed as workers had also served prison sentences and, although it was more than two decades ago, they were also able to draw on their own experience of release.

At the time, Link Out comprised four agencies delivering pre-and post-release support to adult men exiting prison in Victoria. Konnect was the equivalent programme for Indigenous men and women. WISE Employment's Ex-offender Program, unique in Victoria, offered post-release support focused on employment, similarly based on an individualised case management model. Caseloads varied from around eight (Konnect), between ten and fifteen (Link Out), and up to sixty clients per worker (WISE). Meeting individually with participants, generally on a fortnightly basis, Link Out/Konnect workers agreed that, for this degree of intensive support, up to eight was 'ideal' (SW09).

In contrast, Five8 grew out of a Christian church-based community and largely comprised volunteers. Modelled on the Canadian Circles of Support and Accountability (COSA) approach to offender reintegration, Five8 aimed to build a 'micro-community' of four to six people (including other ex-prisoners) around the ex-prisoner 'core member'. The approach involved 'building a solid foundation of friendship and . . . mutual trust' and regularly 'gathering for a "Circle" meeting . . . to reflect upon, and create strategies for, the issues affecting the . . . Core Member' (Five8, 2011). Intensive and practical in focus, it promoted honest and emotional exchange: 'saying the difficult things in the safe context of a Circle meeting . . . in the spirit of friendship and love' (Five8, 2011), most importantly, as a group. Still developing at the time of the interviews, Five8 was about to celebrate its first participant's 12 months out of prison.

The ex-prisoners

The men's ages ranged from 23 to 43. All were Australian, all English-speakers. In terms of ethnocultural background, one identified as Aboriginal, one as Persian and one as Italian; the other nine men claimed Anglo-Celtic ancestry. Five had been involved with child protection (three had been State Wards), four of whom had also had contact with youth justice, three having been in custody as a young person, one in secure welfare from the age of 8. Another, raised by his grandparents, had a juvenile record. In terms of family criminality or imprisonment, five reported that family members had been imprisoned – mothers, a father, stepfather, sister, uncles and grandfathers. In terms of their support network, six reported stable and supportive relationships with at least one family member, though only two included both parents (with whom they were living).

Five reported unstable family relationships; one reported few family relationships, but a strong friendship network. Three reported a relationship with one parent; five stated one parent was unknown to them or long deceased. Two reported a relationship with a step-parent, though these were relationships fraught with tension and/or conflict. Two had been raised by close family members. Two others reported deeply entrenched criminality in their family; 'Glen's' family provided a strong, supportive network, despite having only one 'legit' member. Five men had ex-wives with whom they had children; one had regular contact and weekly involvement with his children, the other four reported conflict with their former partners over custody and access to the children. The other seven men were single and childless, though 'Scott' reported a fond relationship with his sister's children.

Four of the men had been imprisoned only once: 'Matt' and 'Dale' for first-time offences; 'Wayne', after progressing through court sanctions ranging from a fine, to a community-based order, to a suspended sentence – in his words, the courts had 'run out of patience'; 'Eddie' had been imprisoned on remand, owing to the seriousness of his drug offences, which included an armed-robbery component. The other eight men had been imprisoned repeatedly: the youngest participant ('Tom'), twice; 'Ben', five times during a 5-year 'bad cycle'; others reported numerous periods of imprisonment, indeed more of their adult years spent in jail than out.

Although dependency on drugs and alcohol featured prominently among the men, three reported no problematic drug use at all, and 'Glen' considered his heavy drinking incidental to his offending. Four others smoked cannabis regularly, yet did not link this to their offending. For three men, alcohol was the most significant factor associated with their offending. Four men were on methadone: two to treat heroin addiction, one was still struggling to manage his heroin habit, and one reported poly-drug use (including amphetamines, methamphetamine and benzodiazepines). Two said they were prescribed methadone in prison for anxiety and pain relief.

The extent of the men's criminality varied: 'John' reported having grown up in a criminal family and organised-crime network; at times, his role had been to deliberately be arrested and jailed in order to carry out tasks associated with illegal activity in prison. 'Glen' described strong ties to a motorcycle club and a close family within which crime was normalised. Two men had never had any prior criminal involvement; each was sentenced to a long term of imprisonment for a serious crime. 'Matt' was involved in a crime of kidnapping and extortion, though he maintained no one was physically hurt. 'Dale' was involved in a 'tragic accident' that resulted in the deaths of two people, for which he was charged with arson causing death. They served 7 and 6-and-a-half years, respectively. The shortest time served within the sample was by 'Eddie', who was imprisoned on remand for 3 months. 'Rob' had also served several periods on remand until his last release, nearly 2 years ago, and 'Paul' was most recently imprisoned on remand, though in the preceding 2 years he had served a sentence of just under 2 years. The other eight men's last sentences ranged from 12 months to just under 2 years, with an average time served of 14 months.

In terms of engagement with targeted post-release support, four of the men received none, and eight were engaged with programmes: three with Link Out, four with WISE Employment's Ex-offender Program, and one with Five8. The pattern among Link Out participants reflected their 'high-risk' designation: all had served multiple periods of imprisonment, reported past involvement with juvenile justice and child protection, reported family criminality, lacked social support and were variously drug-dependent. A pattern similarly emerged among WISE Employment programme participants, who reported no history with juvenile justice or criminality in their family, and who had the social support of at least one key person; they had each served at least 17 months under sentence. These patterns loosely reflect the eligibility criteria of the programmes in terms of risk of reoffending and job readiness, respectively. The men's stories, and to some extent the idiom in which they were expressed, flesh out this background information.

Data collection

Data were gathered using face-to-face, semi-structured interviews. With partici-pants' permission, interviews were recorded using a small digital voice-recorder. Observational notes supplemented the recorded material, with signifiers such as expression, tone, body language, gesture, stance, demeanour and physi-cal appearance. 'Culture can be most easily "read" in texts, images and rituals but it is also embedded in non-discursive, non-ceremonial practices – such as . . . bodily postures, habitual behaviour and specific performances' (Garland, 2006: 427); hence, my eyes and ears were sensitive to these elements as well. Probing and open-ended questions were used to explore participants' experi-ences, understandings and expectations of life after release from prison. The key characteristic of phenomenographic data collection is its 'explorative' nature, whereby the researcher focuses on expressed conceptions of phenomena and seeks to explore interviewees' meaning (Svensson, 1997). Questions to ex-prisoners were directed towards discovering how the stigma of imprisonment was experienced, pre-release thoughts and expectations of release, past and current experiences of release, familiarity with and expectations of post-release support, and how 'success' was construed.

Interviews with released prisoners

The interviews with ex-prisoners took place in a range of settings: eight took place in public cafés (one at a licensed hotel); three were conducted at an employ-ment or support agency; and one was held in a boarding house. The length of the interviews ranged from 30 minutes to 3 hours, with an average time of 1 hour 30 minutes. Before commencing the interviews, I reinforced the men's voluntary participation, confidentiality, anonymity and conditions around any discussion of illegal activities. Interviews proceeded roughly according to the schedule, with some exchanges more structured than others, depending on the men's response to my initial invitation to tell 'a bit of a story about how you ended up in jail'.

The men's stories unfolded during these interviews. Some are more detailed than others, reflecting a range of factors. The extent to which personal histories were revealed was dependent upon the trust and rapport established between us, listener and speaker. My questions, and my responses to the men's replies, shaped the conversation that a single interview permitted. Each individual's nature and inclination (or capacity) to divulge personal information and/or reflect on his inner world determined his responses. The setting potentially influenced the nature of the exchange too: interviews conducted at an agency familiar to the interviewee from previous appointments may have been slightly more formal or constrained that those held in the 'neutral', more informal set-ting of a café. Nonetheless – and reflecting the self-selection of the sample, whereby only men interested in relating their experiences did so – the men spoke openly about their experiences of imprisonment and release and the life stories in which those experiences were embedded.

Interviews with post-release support workers

Fourteen workers were interviewed. The average interview length was 1 hour 10 minutes. Each was recorded with the participant's permission, with voluntary participation and confidentiality assured. Initial questions gathered general information about the worker's role, background and experience. Ensuing questions were aimed at capturing workers' conceptions and understandings of their role and practices and how these link to outcomes for ex-prisoners. The interviews proceeded mostly according to a prepared schedule, though respondents' volubility varied, and some questions elicited more wide-ranging responses than others.

The questions that yielded the most expansive responses were: 'What are the most difficult issues you face in post-release support work?', and those about 'successful' post-release outcomes: 'How do *you* define "success" in relation to your clients' outcomes?', 'What factors need to be present to ensure "success"?', and 'What are the main obstacles to "success"?'. Although my own casework experience meant that some of the workers' responses were foreseeable, my last question – 'Is there something you'd describe as a culture among professionals in your field, the realm of post-release support? If so, how would you characterise it?' – yielded the least anticipated responses, as they reflected aspects of particular programmes and organisations.

Data analysis

The analysis entailed a twofold process: data from interviews with post-release support workers comprised a description of the post-release experience and its landscape from a practice-oriented perspective; ex-prisoners' lived experience of release constituted a 'second-order' perspective (Marton, 1981). Interviews were transcribed verbatim, with care taken to capture meanings expressed in the participants' words and use of language, as well as in the gaps – the spaces between words, the pauses to think, the meanings expressed in intonation and sentence structure – with the aim of 'accurately reflecting the emotions and emphases of the participant' (Ashworth & Lucas, 2000: 304). The initial phase of analysis entailed careful reading of each transcript, listening again to the recorded interviews and identifying themes, which were grouped under broad headings. Emergent themes were identified in early analysis of interview transcripts, using colour codes to represent different conceptions. Themes were traced through iterative reading of the data.

The worker interview data were organised around emergent themes about workers' conceptions of the post-release domain, the support role and the released subject. The ex-prisoner data were initially arranged under headings relating to phases of men's experience: in prison, release, post-release support, post-release liminality, risk of return, and reintegration. These broad themes allowed the mass of data to be broken down into manageable parts, within which emergent patterns, commonalities and discrepancies could be discerned. As the unit of phenomenographic analysis may be described as 'ways of making sense'

(Abrahamsson et al., 2005: 368) – the object of study comprising both 'how something is talked about and possible ways of experiencing' (p. 368) – care was taken to sift through the meanings expressed in interviews to glean variations in thinking and experience. These layers of analysis revealed outcome spaces comprising different categories of description.

From the worker data, categories of ways in which the ex-prisoner support role is conceived and experienced were pooled into three areas of meaning: conceiving the subject of post-release support, understanding prisoners' release, and the post-release support role. The outcome space for the lived experience of release comprised three broad categories of description: getting out, being out and staying out; each category comprised sub-themes emerging from the ex-prisoners' interview material. Each category was ordered according to the density of a conception – in terms of its number of appearances or references to it – and the intensity of its expression: the extent to which the meaning was contained in the interview content. Patterns in the interview data emerged visually, in the number and density of references to particular conceptions, indicative of commonality in collective experience and understanding. The order in which the categories are discussed reflects the logic and flow of the participants' collective experience of prison release and the post-release realm, rather than any order of significance.

Each emerging outcome space thus comprises, not so much a hierarchy of meaning or importance, as a set of overlapping realms of understanding, constituting a phenomenographic portrayal from which the whole sense of the experience and context of release and post-release support work might be gleaned. Though the initial motivation for the research was to hear the voices of men inhabiting an invisible social space, phenomenographic analysis demands that individual voices and stories be subsumed within the larger focus on ways of experiencing a phenomenon: in this case, men's release from prison. For the purposes of this book, however, it seemed more important to foreground the stories by interweaving them through the text.

Ethical issues

There are important ethical issues to consider when doing research with ex-prisoners, given the institutionalisation and disadvantage characteristic of this group and their potential impact on their interactions with the researcher (Willis, 2005). Assuring the confidentiality of participants' responses is critical in establishing trust, as is a guarantee of anonymity. These were ensured via de-identifying codes/aliases. All prospective participants received plain language statements and consent forms to explain the study and inform their consent to participate, taking into account varying levels of literacy. Importantly, interviews with ex-prisoners emphasised that the research was concerned with their post-release experience and not their offending or their experiences in prison. The issue of compensation for research participation raised ethical concerns that were resolved with agency consultation and support, according to university ethics guidelines.[10] Each ex-prisoner who participated in an interview was given a AU$20 supermarket voucher.

Access issues

I have outlined issues associated with attempting to gain access to a hidden group such as released prisoners. Without direct personal contact, access is only readily available to men via their programme participation or engagement with agencies and services. Access to clients of these services is rightly guarded by ethics protocols. Skilful measures emphasising flexibility, tenacity and respect – for programme exigencies and personal privacy – were required to locate, make contact and meet with participants to conduct interviews. Many leads proved fruitless. Ultimately, a strategy of persistence and openness, and a demonstrated willingness to meet people on their terms bore the fruit of twelve men's experiences of release from prison.

Conclusion

This chapter has outlined the philosophical and methodological foundations of the research and explained why and how phenomenography has been applied to the study. A critical-realist social ontology and constructionist epistemology underpin its focus on the subjective, the relational, and the multiplicities of experience and perception that comprise social reality in a post-prison context. Phenomenography is shown to provide useful tools for qualitatively mapping this phenomenon. The methodology is linked to the assemblage–culture–liminality framework, and it is this intersection that gives rise to and shapes the research questions: *How is men's prison release (and post-release life) constructed? And how do these constructions conflict and cohere?* The questions reflect the study's focus on the qualitatively different ways of experiencing and making sense of the post-release phenomenon from the perspective of support workers and ex-prisoners. The final categories and themes that emerged out of the process of iterative reading and analysis of the interview material are described in the next two chapters. As the experience of imprisonment and release logically precedes that of post-release support, Chapter 6 presents the men's experience of release, and then Chapter 7 depicts the workers' perspective.

Notes

1 An aspect of this realist social ontology differentiating it from pure social realism is its rejection of essentialism. As critics of a realist approach may argue, assuming social entities have a mind-independent identity implies that essences exist that define that identity. However, as assemblages are characterised by parts in synthetic and emergent relationship, rather than a seamless whole, and their synthesis can be explained by historical processes, an ontological commitment to essences is avoided (DeLanda, 2006: 4, 26).
2 Guba & Lincoln, 1981; Denzin & Lincoln, 1994; Taylor & Bogdan, 1998; Scott & Usher, 1999.
3 Phenomenography derives from the Greek *phainomenon* (appearance) and *graphein* (description; Hasselgren & Beach, 1997).
4 See Hasselgren & Beach, 1997; Svensson, 1997; Webb, 1997; Richardson, 1999.
5 See Richardson, 1999.
6 Hasselgren & Beach, 1997; Säljö, 1997; Bowden, 2000; Trigwell, 2006.

7 Hasselgren & Beach, 1997; Barnard et al. 1999; Ashworth & Lucas, 2000; Patrick, 2000; Marton & Pong, 2005.
8 A constraint arose from my initial decision not to apply for Victorian Department of Justice ethics approval. Unforeseen was the departmental condition that no Link Out/ Konnect clients be interviewed if they were on parole. As a large proportion of Link Out/Konnect clients were parolees, this significantly limited the pool of potential research participants.
9 The men had mostly been released within the preceding year, though one had been released 5 years earlier. They had been imprisoned for a range of different offences, under sentence and on remand, in various prisons across Victoria.
10 The University of Melbourne's Human Research Ethics Committee granted ethics approval for the research.

6   Lived experience of release

'Nick'

Nick is 30 and has been in and out of jail for most of his life, released about seven times from adult prison and 'about ten from juvenile' detention. He was locked up in secure welfare from the age of 8, owing to his mother's and stepfather's heroin addiction, and 'all because I wanted to run away and go to my parents'. His step-father died of a heroin overdose when Nick was 12. Around this time, Nick's own heroin use began and 'it just spiralled from there', as he explains:

> I got sexually assaulted when I was really young . . . and . . . the way I deal with it is I go out and steal something and that makes me feel better about myself cos I know that I got away with it, and then the remorse and guilt kicks in and then I get worser [*sic*] and then I go and do it again to make myself feel better and it just goes and goes, and then I put myself in jail 'cos I feel better [than] where I am, you know, it's better there. It's not the way to go, you know?

Recently Nick 'got stabbed' in jail, and 'because of that I just don't want to go back, it really scared me you know'. His reiteration that it was 'all over a female, you know?' provides a glimpse of the overblown and proprietorial type of masculinity that prevails in men's prisons. Nevertheless, this fear is impetus for him to stay out and the sense that, 'if I don't make it now that's it for me . . . It doesn't get any easier . . .'.

Nick speaks about his last release as a change for him, as he completed parole for the first time ever. He had invested great hope in securing a transitional house, from which he could apply for more permanent public housing, as he recounts:

> I was really happy . . . cos I thought I was going to this place, and I told me mum, everyone was rapt . . . I was excited to see me family, knowing that I had a place.

Yet the promised house was given to someone else – 'an older person and he's very sick' – and Nick's Link Out worker took him instead to a boarding house, which was so squalid that he 'broke down crying in that room', his dashed hopes overwhelming him:

> It was a boarding house, it was just – mate I was going back to jail if I'd stayed there – lucky my auntie said 'no you can't, I'll give you a month at my house'.

His aunt – 'she's straight as anything . . . she's got her own restaurant' – let him stay with her for a month. After that he went to live with his second stepfather, which caused 'drama', however, as he has bipolar disorder and 'really tried to make things hard' for Nick. Nick thus hints at two sides of his world: the auntie living the 'straight' life, but with whom he doesn't quite fit, and the volatile and exploitative stepfather, who is separated from but still 'bags' Nick's mother, who is still his 'mum' despite her own instability: 'she's very neurotic . . . she's hard to get along with'.

Recently, through his stepfather's neighbour, Nick met Eddie, who said he could move into his place. This has been good, except that Eddie 'smokes choof' and drinks a bit, which makes it hard to avoid the lifestyle and the people Nick's trying to stay away from:

> they're all on drugs or crooks . . . and I know when I meet up with them I'm just gonna do the wrong thing . . . it's just hard . . . I got no friends that are normal.

Besides his aunt, his Link Out worker and Eddie, Nick is socially isolated. His one constant companion is his dog. He declares, with a sense of loneliness and solidarity, 'I'm just with me dog now', as though this represents turning his back on 'all I've known for all this time', though it is with reluctance, almost embarrassment, that he adds, 'he's like my best friend', implying a canine companion's value perhaps unequal to human company. As evidence of their close bond, he points to the dog's rump where the hair is thinner:

> See . . . that light bit? It's separation stress – he's only starting to grow it back . . . I was away for nearly eighteen months, nineteen months – and he's just chewed it and chewed it and chewed it . . . I took him to the [animal hospital] and . . . it's stress, he just loses it and he bites on it . . . when I go. Yeah, we're pretty close.

Nick sustained serious back injuries in a motorbike accident, 5 years ago, which means that he is on a disability pension, unable to work. He also suffers from anxiety – 'moderate anxiety in jail but high anxiety on the outside'. This explains why 'coping' is a priority when I ask him what 'reintegration' means to him:

> Coping, being normal again, doing the right thing, getting a house . . . being able to be, just sitting here like this [having coffee] . . .

We've been sitting in a small shopping-centre café for more than an hour, Nick drinking his cappuccino, when I realise how significant this 'normal' interaction must be. I wonder what Nick means by 'being normal again', when it sounds as though he's never really had a 'normal' life to begin with.

This chapter presents a phenomenography – a qualitative map – of men's lived experience of release from prison. The themes that emerged from my interviews with the twelve men are grouped in categories that reflect three phases: getting out, being out and staying out. Each depicts the diversity of experience, the heterogeneity of being an ex-prisoner. Quotes anchor the themes in participants' own words and meanings. The lived experiences of the ex-prisoner interviewees intersect to varying degrees with the perspectives of the workers interviewed. Eight of the men were engaged with specialist post-release support: three with Link Out, four with WISE and one with Five8; four received no support. As specific, tailored post-release support is available to only a proportion of men released from prison, it follows that the experience of these latter four more closely represents that of the majority of men released in Victoria.

Some themes featured more prominently than others: having 'somewhere to go', finding 'a decent job' and having support, finding stability emerged as the most significant aspects of the men's post-release experience. The density (frequency of expression) of a theme across the group, however, belies other thematic intensities. That is, the themes with the least prominence among the men, 'prison ingrained in me' and 'stuck in prison world', were nevertheless intense in content. These themes encapsulate ways of experiencing 'being out' that profoundly shaped men's lives and post-prison identity. This range of intensity in men's experience is explored below.

Getting out

The experience of release – of getting out – is conceived in different ways, from which five categories of description emerge: 'gate fever', 'culture shock', 'just another day', having 'somewhere to go', and 'nowhere to go'. 'Gate fever' tends to coincide with men knowing when they are getting out, such as having a set parole date, the expression used to evoke the excitement, anticipation, anxiety and sense of the surreal associated with getting out. 'Culture shock' similarly connects with the disorientation prisoners feel upon leaving one world and entering another. A contrasting conception of getting out as 'just another day' (Glen) reveals a sense of predictability: suggesting that it has been planned and rehearsed to such an extent that its eventuality is met with almost perfunctory indifference; or denoting cyclic experience of imprisonment and release within which the inevitability of return gives rise to apathy. Another cause for men's anxiety and uncertainty relates to housing insecurity, even for those who have somewhere to go, but especially for those with nowhere to go. In addition to these material challenges are the psychological difficulties in adjusting to post-release life.

'Gate fever'

'Gate fever' is experienced as intense anticipation, ranging from dread to euphoria. Matt recounts anticipating his imminent release: 'I was really anxious just to get out, they call it gate fever. . . . I just knew that it's all over now, it's finished'. He conveys his sense of the time having finally arrived when he could turn his back on his years in prison, and the crime that lead him there: 'I did something stupid which I took account for and did my time. I wanted to move on from that'. This anticipation manifests variously: from longing – 'I was aching for it' (Dale) – to excitement and jubilation; to anxiety, fear, even depression – 'others are depressed, a lot of them. It's sad but it's reality' (Matt). The men's excitement is expressed in varying degrees of intensity: 'My whole mind was buzzing; I was really happy and couldn't sleep' (Matt); it was 'like winning Tattslotto' (Dale). For those who have previously experienced release, there is the added dimension of familiarity, as Nick conveys: 'It's one of the best feelings you could ever have, you know, when you get your freedom . . . like when you were a little kid waiting to open your presents at Christmas time'. Even Glen admits, 'you always look forward to getting out', whereas, for Eddie, it was more 'just relief I was getting out'.

Matt celebrated his impending return home by giving away 'everything in my room'. The night before his release: 'we had a party and . . . everyone wished me good luck'. His excitement was palpable:

> That whole night I couldn't sleep. I woke up about five in the morning, had a shower; just sat there waiting until the time hit, and when I went to the front when they process your property and stuff, they said, 'Where's this? Where's that?' I said, 'I don't know. I lost it, threw it away,' and that delayed me for like half an hour.

Though excited, Matt concedes he was also 'really anxious when I left, and my mum came and picked me up and I went home'. His 'leaves', though, 'took the edge off' that anxiety. His first 'escorted leave' – 'I went home for the day' – he describes how his parents had sold the house he lived in 'before I got locked up':

> I hadn't seen my new home. So to me everything was new. . . . I remember seeing the house, my mum opened the door and she just started shaking and crying and she couldn't control herself. She wouldn't let me go for like ten minutes. I suppose that took the edge off the first time.

Although Matt was 'excited to get out of jail', he described other men who:

> didn't want to get out or were scared to get out. . . . [People] getting out to nothing . . . [who]'ve got nothing to look forward to . . . guys [that] have been in and out of institutions since they were twelve, so that's all they know.

Dale observes, 'for a lot of them, getting out is the prison sentence', by which he invokes the struggles many face post-release. Although all the men interviewed expressed their desire to get out, anxiety was nevertheless a shared experience: 'I was a bit worried and anxious' (Tom); Eddie was 'anxious . . . [about] everything probably, social anxiety'. Scott and John recount anxiety building as release day loomed, John recalling prior experiences of getting out: 'I was always failing. Within a week . . . I'd have a full-on heroin habit again'. John describes the intensity of his 'anxiety and fear':

> Coming up to release . . . I started to really shut off from prison life . . . it was really, really hard for me and I was talking a lot on the phone to my Five8s. . . . I was really fearful of using again, really fearful of my old crew getting in touch with me again and forcing me to do things that I really didn't want to do, because that happened last time.

For John, release represented venturing back into a dangerous world, within which his role was cemented and from which it was difficult to extract himself. As he explains:

> I'd spent a lot of time negotiating with certain identities to secure freedom from that life, to cut the cord, and knowing the things I knew it was very, very dangerous for me . . . so I'd spent a lot of time negotiating and talking and putting my case forward. In the end people accepted what I was doing and trusted me and . . . they could accept 'this is what he wants to do'. And now I play the role, if anyone else wants to take this path they're able to. I'm the 'go to' person for that.

John thus had to craft a new role, a new identity, to separate himself from his old life. The fear of venturing into that new life, leaving a familiar world behind, was immense.

'Culture shock'

Notwithstanding his determination and desire to change his life, John experienced 'culture shock' upon getting out, which he tries to impart: 'Imagine yourself being in jail. That's what it feels like for me to be on the outside now. It's just so foreign. It's culture shock'. The collective experience of getting out is of sudden arrival in an alien place, a jolting strangeness and disbelief. John's experience was 'really, really hard' and persistent: 'it took me months just for it to sink in that I was actually free and on my way to a normal life'. John conveys a sense of resurfacing in an unfamiliar world in the days and weeks after getting out:

> I used to sit in the backyard and dawn would come and just watch the sun come up . . . just sit there in amazement and just watch the birds flying in and out and animals and cats and people walk[ing] past.

This evokes the collective conception of release as 'really surreal, a surreal experience' (Ben), 'a weird feeling' (Nick). Matt portrays feeling odd:

After my sixth leave I was dropped off at the train station with a pack of $100 and . . . 'we'll meet you back here tonight at 9 o'clock'. Jumped on the train, went to the city, went home, had dinner with my family, went out. It was really weird. . . . I was . . . just giggling to myself looking around . . . everyone was probably thinking, 'what's his problem?'.

Despite the unconditional support of Matt's family's, who were 'very welcoming in every way', he admits feeling 'weird' – 'like a stranger within your own family'. And more generally, too, 'it felt real strange', for Tom, whose 'body just took like two weeks to adjust to the environment again'. Compared with, 'in prison [where] there's no noise, no traffic and everyone's walking, there's no buses and cars and toots and traffic lights' (Wayne), 'walking through the city . . . [was] . . . a little bit agoraphobic' (Eddie). Agreeing that, 'so many more people around . . . was a bit of a culture shock', Dale also expresses men's common conception – particularly after a long sentence – of the world outside being changed:

Everything's on steroids now . . . everyone's got iPods, iPhones . . . It wasn't around seven years ago. Camera phones . . . weren't here . . . people all connected in the way that they are now, so everything is sort of souped up.'

He expresses a sense of having fallen behind: 'I used to be ahead with computers . . . and suddenly I'm like eehehhh – what do I do?'. This recalls the notion of lost time and 'a lot of adjusting to do' (John). The men experienced 'culture shock' as strangeness, feeling foreign, removed. For other men, who apparently make little adjustment between prison life and life outside, release day is 'just another day'.

'Just another day'

There is a lot of talk among prisoners about how it feels to be released: 'everyone would say, "something is going to hit you"' (Matt); 'you won't sleep' (Glen). Yet some men's experience belies these predictions, as Matt describes:

When I went on my first leave . . . it was just like another day. . . I'm thinking something is going to hit me, something is going to happen, but it was just another day.'

Glen, too, confesses, 'the screws had to come and wake me up. . . . They're all going, "oh, you won't sleep, you won't sleep" and I was asleep before most of them anyway – I was comfortable'. Indeed, Glen alludes to the expectation of return to custody, the revolving door that prison officers often reportedly convey: 'I was . . . put on a train and . . . the screw who dropped me off, he goes, "so when am I picking you up again?"'

Many men evoke the sense of being unceremoniously 'dumped': 'I was dumped at the train station' (Glen); 'there's the front door . . . there's your train ticket, see you later' (Wayne); 'bang, bang, there you go' (Eddie). Implied is an expectation of a more exhaustive exit process, to absorb the impact of release from one environment into another. Otherwise, release is portrayed as a straight-forward administrative procedure: 'You get told by the parole board, processed and your friend picks you up and it's just very straightforward. You just take everything that has sort of accumulated in prison and off you go' (Dale). Glen depicts it as routine, humdrum, a non-event:

> It was about four o'clock, four thirty when they come and grab me, then you gotta go through your property and sign paperwork, then you sit in your cell until they're ready to drop you off at the train station. . . . You get an EBT[1] card and your 'roll-through' – they'll give ya two hundred of that in cash, I think, then a cheque . . . You've gotta buy your own train ticket . . . Just another day.

Glen's jaded account suggests an emotional hardening, dulling his response to an event he admits 'always look[ing] forward to', his seeming indifference signify-ing regularity and a degree of inevitability characterising his multiple experience of imprisonment.

Similarly, there is a sense of familiarity and repetition underlying Scott's account of his experience of straight release:

> I found out . . . the day before . . . the screws come to my cell and said 'pack your shit, you're going home tomorrow'. And then another time I got a let-ter and it said you're getting released tomorrow. . . . This time . . . the chief calls me into the office and goes, 'have you heard yet?' and I go 'what?' – 'you're going home tomorrow', and I go 'what? Bullshit!', and he goes, 'you're going home, pack your shit'.

Notable is the irony of the officer telling Scott he's 'going home', when, in fact, he has never previously had a home to go to. Having nowhere to go foreshadows reim-prisonment for many men: 'that's why they end up back in jail' (Scott). Yet, even having 'somewhere to go' is revealed as varying in its stability and permanence.

'Somewhere to go'

Eddie 'was lucky with housing' – 'my brother was kind enough to help me out'. Indeed, the 'first-timers' interviewed all had somewhere to go: 'my mum came and picked me up and I went home' (Matt); 'I had a place to stay and my friend picked me up' (Dale); and Wayne was able to move in with his parents, which is 'not ideal' but preferable to 'a caravan or a boarding house'. Others similarly relied on relatives and friends for support: John 'moved in with one of my friends from Five8'. Glen had a strong family network to return to, in a familiar region; he has since moved in with an old friend, now his de facto partner, sharing her place: 'a commission house, so the rent's cheaper'. These men's experience is characterised by an impression of security, a sense of having a home, somewhere they can either remain or use as a stepping stone to further independence. For Eddie, for instance, 'working and [being] in a relationship' later enabled him to find his own place.

Ben returned to his mother's house and a relationship that is fraught, yet without which 'I'd be stuffed', as he explains:

> Every time I get out I have to go back to my mum's and me and her clash . . . as soon as I . . . have one bad day, she's on my case and I have a big blow-up. I mean a couple of times, before, I was doing well when I got out and we had a fight and I went to a boarding house . . . [But] in the boarding house I couldn't have my kids . . . I had to go and pick them up and take them to the park.

Besides the tenuousness of having somewhere to go, Ben's experience illustrates the problems associated with a lack of available housing, and the limitations of post-release assistance in prison, even for men facing homelessness:

> I had an 18-month sentence, I thought give them plenty of notice and they could help me with housing and when I get out, if I just had that basis of seeing my kids and somewhere to see them . . . [But] they just basically got me a hotel room. I was . . . telling them I had absolutely nowhere to go – I did have my mother's, but I was telling them I had nowhere – and still all they did was get me a hotel, for the first two days I was out.

As a result, Ben felt hopeless: 'I was really trying to do the right thing but . . . life was just crap. It just felt impossible'. Following his latest release, after an argument with his mother, he moved in with a neighbour/friend, who is 'a bit mentally ill and . . . he can't do a lot and his house is pretty horrible'. Nevertheless, determined to have his 'own place somewhere', Ben spent 'five days scrubbing everything and had my kids there on the weekend and it was good, better than my mum's'. Ben's experience attests to the importance for 'a bloke who's getting out to have their own place somewhere, somewhere where you can work, because no-one ['with a brain'] wants to go back to jail'.

Nick was 'rapt . . . really happy', believing prior to his last release that he had secured, through Link Out, 'a transitional house, and from there I could get on segment one'.[2] The arrangement foundered, however; his Link Out worker took him instead from jail to a boarding house so dirty and squalid that he 'broke down crying'. As he maintains, 'I was going back to jail if I'd stayed there – lucky my auntie said "no you can't, I'll give you a month at my house".' After staying with his aunt, he went to live with his stepfather, though, when this became untenable, he moved in with Eddie, whom he met via a neighbour. As emerges in Nick's story, the support of family is conditional: contingent upon the nature of relationships and past interactions and behaviour.

Rob describes, for instance, that, apart from one sister, 'my whole family disowned me', to the extent that, 'because of what I've been accused of . . . my own mother can't trust me in a kitchen with a knife when I used to cook for them all, all the time'. Nevertheless, he was 'kind of lucky' once, in that:

> I had friends that had houses . . . so I slept in a school next to my mate's parents' house, and he'd bring me breakfast and lunch and dinner and stuff. And then his parents moved . . . and my mate said 'oh, there's a spare room now, you might as well move in'. So I was only on the streets for about three months before I got a house. But it wasn't my house. So when he moved I had to move too.

The basis of Rob's conception of having somewhere to go is inherently transitory, unstable, at the whim of circumstance – 'a house' that 'wasn't my house' characterising his experience.

Family support saved Scott from homelessness this time: his sister's offer of her couch to sleep on for 3 months while he completed intensive parole meant that for 'the first time I've had somewhere to go' upon release. Since then, with Link Out support, he was able to secure 'a little studio apartment – I've got me own bathroom and shower and kitchenette' – in a boarding house, as 'a two month thing', after which:

> I was supposed to go back to court on the 20th of this month or something to prolong the lease or something but I didn't go, but I think I didn't have to go, I think it's alright . . . I think, I hope.

The vagueness with which he describes this arrangement denotes a conception of someone else being in charge, his unsure 'I think, I hope' implying a diminished capacity for responsibility, to which – through 17 years of repeat imprisonment – he has become accustomed. Underpinning these latter men's conception of having somewhere to go, then, is a sense of impermanence, of moving from one mooring to another, a future coloured by uncertainty.

'Nowhere to go'

Scott's past experience is characterised by having 'nowhere to go' – a cycle of homelessness, drug abuse and reimprisonment – as he describes:

> In a five year period I was out, like, two days, and then five days, because I had nowhere to go; so I just got out, got stoned off my head and then done a burg, got pinched, and then gone back to jail for like another year or two; got out, nowhere to live again, got off my head, done another burg, got pinched, and done another year or two.

This pattern disqualified him for parole. Instead, 'straight release' means, 'no support, nothing . . . it's out the door, bad luck, "oh, you've got nowhere to live? Oh, here y'are, we'll give you three days in a hotel"'. This systemic response is seen to exacerbate rather than alleviate the problem, perpetuate rather than interrupt the cycle. It testifies to the perception of prison housing assistance as 'a joke' (Ben), 'a farce' (Wayne). The 'set aside' system, which is 'supposed to help you out', Matt suggests is useless: '$1200 I walked out with. Imagine if I didn't have any support, nothing. What would $1200 do?'. Men on short sentences or remand would receive much less, and nowhere near enough to secure housing:

> These days if you walk out to nothing, you've got no home, no clothing, nothing, what's $2000 going to do for you? Seriously, it sounds like a lot of money. . . . How much is your bond for a basic one bedroom apartment, $2000?

Rob evokes the experience of remand, release and cyclic homelessness:

> On the streets, I just knock about until I find somewhere to live. It's been easier the last couple of times because I haven't had an animal. Now I've got a dog. . . . And since I've had him I was on the street purposely. . . . [M]y social workers . . . were saying 'if you get rid of the dog we can get you a house'. But I wouldn't give him up. So I spent eight months longer on the streets until they found somewhere I could have a dog.

Without the dog, he could 'go straight to a homeless boarding shelter . . . where they give you workers that help you find accommodation. Whereas . . . you can't take the dog inside . . . [or] on a tram, you know?'. Nevertheless, with the help of a housing service, he is living in a boarding house with ex-prisoners, various 'weird' people and his dog, though 'not for much longer because the house is for sale', reiterating the sense of impermanence shaping his experience.

Rob believes, 'it should be mandatory . . . to have a house to go to . . . because you're so used to sleeping inside, when you're released, it's a shock to the system to go straight on the streets', highlighting the need for post-release housing for all prisoners. Perceiving prison housing assistance as futile, however, Scott concludes, 'you're better off getting out – like every time I've got out I've been homeless', the implication of which is: 'you're better off . . . homeless'. This is almost expressed as a half thought, 'you're better off getting out', put together with the realisation, 'every time I've got out I've been homeless', as if underpinning this experience is familiarity, a path that he has walked and survived. Intimated is a sense of dominion over this fate, as if being homeless represents freedom and provides a sense of identity – 'I am homeless' – a way of delineating his world that makes sense and that is preferable to being stuck in an administrative 'letterbox' (Scott). Rob relates the experience of his 'two best friends', who:

> come out of jail and they don't want housing . . . It's too hard to pay rent and live. . . . [So] they live on the streets and then they get emergency accommodation through winter and then go back out on the street again . . . that's how they live.

Rob's and Scott's experience typifies that of some men, cycling in and out of jail with nowhere to go in between. As Matt evokes, 'they get out, a month, two months, they're back in because they find it hard. And a lot of people don't have the basic social skills, they struggle with it'. Nick also fits this category, his assessment – 'my problem was no accommodation' – suggesting that reducing a lifetime's trouble to a single problem renders it bearable. The paradox of freedom manifests in men leaving the relative comfort and security of the prison environment to meet the uncertainty and precariousness of temporary housing or homelessness.

Being out

The sense of 'not quite fitting in, not quite being accepted, not quite belonging' (SW22) is a strong theme underlying the men's experience of being out, one that they had not anticipated. This section expands upon the following themes: 'the psychological aftermath'; prison being 'ingrained in me'; loneliness; 'fitting in'; being 'stuck in prison world'; 'same old shit' – using drugs, being broke; and the struggle to find 'a decent job'.

'The psychological aftermath'

Dale recounts, 'I expected to hit the ground running and have no problem and resume life . . . I didn't expect a few of the troughs that I fell into'; he had 'three panic attacks within four months of being out', and then, at 'the six month point . . . my biggest crash . . . that was hard, dealing with the psychological aftermath of it'. Dale identifies an aspect of this 'aftermath' as the return of feelings of guilt, suppressed during his imprisonment, as he explains:

> In prison you've got a safety net, that is you are actually doing a sentence so you are being punished for what you did, so emotionally you can [cope] . . . But when you get out . . . it comes back . . . that safety net and the emotional barrier between you and dealing with the guilt is removed.

For some men, imprisonment's psychological aftermath arises from family breakdown. As Paul relates of his 6-year-old daughter, 'I haven't been able to spend a birthday with her . . . I've never been able to live with her as a father. . . . Not knowing what's happening to her has been the hardest thing'. For Ben, too, the most significant effect of imprisonment has been 'losing my family. If I didn't go to jail we'd still be together'. He evokes the desolation and despair of finding himself alone following his release:

> When I got out she was in Queensland, with my kids, with him. And I got home and all the kids' toys and everything everywhere and, yeah, no friends, nowhere to go, nothing to do, just sit here and get drunk and start going downhill quick.

Ben implies a sense of shock at finding his family gone – 'I was used to being a family' – suggesting his anticipation of returning to what he had left. This suggests the cocooning effect of imprisonment – on both prisoners and their outside relationships – which tends to magnify the psychological aftermath following a prisoner's return to their world in the community. As Rob avers, 'the hardest thing [is] . . . reuniting yourself with your family . . . the emotions of not being able to see my children, not being able to talk to my family, people not understanding'. The men's sense of abandonment, rejection and loneliness is explored below.

One way of dealing with the psychological aftermath is to focus on the positive effects of the experience of imprisonment. John, for instance, describes 'the edge': a heightened 'understanding and awareness . . . [an] ability to read people'; being 'one step ahead of a person always'; 'it's a habit I've got from being a criminal'. John describes this habit of hypervigilance learnt in prison as life-saving: 'I've been in situations, very, very dangerous and I have to assess quickly is it safe, is it a safe situation? . . . I can't tell you how many times it's saved my life'. Rather than the anxiety implied by such situations, however, John also attributes 'a peace and calmness and . . . an element of truth' to this 'edge'. Dale similarly describes one 'good effect' of his imprisonment as being 'a bit more evolved' through observing 'different types of people . . . [and] certain behaviours . . . I read situations really well. . . . [I'm] tuned into everything that is going on . . . you really do have awareness of people and behaviour'. Dealing with the effects of imprisonment and the shock of getting out thus emerges as closely tied to men's pre-prison personality and ways of coping, and their sense of who they are.

Prison 'ingrained in me'

Adapting to prison life clearly involves the forging of a prison identity and the destabilising of men's pre-prison identity, their social place. Although different prison-selves manifest – arising from individual circumstances, causes and conditions – a common thread links their emergence into post-prison light: the sense of not fitting in, of feeling different. This is conceived by workers as relating to the length of time spent in prison, and yet the men's pre-prison sense of self appears to shape the degree to which their prison identity becomes 'ingrained' (Scott). Scott, for example, has a clearly demarcated prison identity and describes the choosing and crafting of implements his prison role entails:

> I prefer . . . [to] snap open a razor blade and melt the blades into a toothbrush, shave the toothbrush bit off and melt the blades into it, melt about three or four blades in, all different ways, so no matter which way you get them . . . it will open up in two spots so it's harder for 'em to sew back together, and leaves a bigger scar, and you get 'em straight down the face and that way everyday they look in the mirror they know that it was you who done it.

Scott conveys a sense of asserting his prison identity through his attack strategy, as though, by leaving his mark on his victim, so 'they know it was you who done it', his reputation of being 'a bit fucked in the head', and hence not to be messed with, is underscored.

Notwithstanding the matter-of-fact way Scott relates this experience, implying its normality, he also recognises that – although functional in prison – such behaviour is dysfunctional and unacceptable outside: 'that's the type of thing that I bring outside with me, and then I've gotta try and not be like that out here, you know?'. He describes how being 'like that' is 'just ingrained in me now', implying that violence is an expectation: 'everywhere I go I've usually got an icepick and a box cutter on me, just in case'. Violence is an automatic response: 'it's like . . . over twenty bucks the other day I was gonna go to my mate's place and kick his front door in, with three other people, and . . . just *wreck* him over twenty bucks, man, you know?'. His sense of dismay at being 'like that' is palpable. Scott gives another example of the implications of being 'like that', describing how his 'best mate got set up' after he robbed a wealthy, mafia-connected fruiterer: 'he was just like me . . . just a heroin addict just doing what he needs to, to get his heroin, you know, robbed the wrong [man] and . . . got set up and got [killed]'. Scott's conception of 'just a heroin addict' evokes another prison identity framed in terms of necessity, as 'just doing what he needs to' implies. This gives insight into how being a drug user is conceived as an occupation, defined by 'the ritual, the scoring, going to the dealers and mulling up, doing it' (Scott). It reveals how a drug user identity can shape and anchor men's lives, in the sense, for example, of resignation or hopelessness, manifest in men's thinking 'how can I change?' (SW06).

The men interviewed attest to the universality of 'Ox' as prison tobacco,[3] and how it identifies people as having been inside. As well as its strength – 'it'd be milder smoking tree bark . . . and gum leaves, god it nearly knocked me out!' (Wayne) – and, hence, its addictive quality, cigarette smoking represents a punctuating rhythm in the daily routine of prison life, a physical and psychological habit that – through frequent repetition – becomes entrenched. As Wayne recounts:

> I tried to stop smoking when I was in there and I gave that up for a month, and that was just torture, because that's all you've got in there is coffee and cigarettes . . . [*Are you still smoking?*] Yes, guess what, I'm smoking this stupid pouch [of] White Ox, yeah, that's what I did when I got paid, I bought two pouches of that, and I bought a couple of papers and four train tickets.

Implying it is one of his daily necessities – along with newspapers and train tickets – Wayne links smoking Ox to prisoner ways of being that, despite 'trying to move away from that' and admitting 'cringing', are a hard habit to break:

> on the outside . . . all these people smoking Super Mild, Ultra Mild, and they go to prison and everyone's making these [thin 'roll-your-owns' with Ox] . . . you can get [other brands] . . . [but they] say if you have this it's stronger, and you get used to it, and you don't want another cigarette as

quickly. I said Christ I don't need a cigarette for six hours after that one! I said I'd be in an iron lung before I have one of these again! . . . Yeah I don't have to buy Ox, I don't know why I keep buying it, I think just out of habit.

Though Wayne shielded himself from the absorption of prison mores or the development of a prison identity through his sense of passing through, of never belonging in prison, he nevertheless took on the habit of smoking Ox, without really being aware of how or why. Ways of being in prison can thus permeate thinking and inhabit prisoners' bodies, ingrained through repetition.

Loneliness

Just as smoking and drug-using can anchor men's identity, the social dimension of prison habits can similarly infuse prisoners' sense of self and belonging. The experience of displacement following release from an environment of regulated activity and constant company is marked by loneliness and the need for human connection. Loneliness is exacerbated by the experience and meaning of friendship in prison. For prisoners, 'so-called friends' (Matt) or 'associates' are people they share tobacco with, people with whom they have a functioning relationship of some kind. Scott describes people in prison knowing his name, calling out a familiar 'Hey!'. Ben, though 'not a real social person', expresses the familiarity of knowing people in jail, which Glen echoes: 'I know more people inside than I do outside nowadays'. Nick expresses his loneliness and lack of 'straight' friends most poignantly: 'I haven't got *any* friends, I'm just with me dog now . . . he's like my best friend'.

Dale concedes, 'one of the biggest things about getting out is the loneliness'. He was 'fortunate' to maintain a strong support network. He nevertheless describes a feeling of social isolation, in contrast to the constant activity of prison life:

> Even though you've still got your circle of friends . . . they've got their own lives . . . you visit them once every now and then, but in prison it's like this [at a city café] . . . every day and things are going on. There's a confounding sort of loneliness in that that's not there anymore, and that becomes really difficult. You've lost your network of friends in that sense.

Ben evokes a similar sense: 'it changes when you get out, all those lives and you separate. It's hard to fit each other in. You used to sit there 24/7 together and then all of a sudden – yeah. . . . ' Trailing off, Ben implies the contrast between the constant activity in prison and the social isolation he now experiences. He hints, too, at the abruptness of the transition. Ben has tended to isolate himself, 'to withdraw and guard', which, though observed as an effect of incarceration, is 'an issue' Ben has had his 'whole life'. Indeed, he admits, 'I was already like that. It's hard for me to distinguish whether [jail's] made me worse'.

In contrast, Dale finds a way to replicate the physical company missing from day-to-day life on the outside: 'I've slotted in and I hang around . . . in the city [with] . . . people that hang around in the park and drink . . . not all deros, younger people', though he admits, 'it's a temporary thing' that has functioned as an interim integrative measure; now 'I've got the full-time work . . . it's not going to be hard for me'. His previous experience of having a 'scene', work, a strong friendship network, and his driving desire to regain these things underpin Dale's conviction. Dealing with the effects of imprisonment thus emerges as closely tied to men's personal resources and their need and desire to fit in with other people.

'Fitting in'

The men variously conceive of 'fitting in': as belonging in the prison world, to varying degrees; identifying and being identified with other ex-prisoners, and yet wanting to escape this world; and not feeling part of the prison world, and yet struggling to fit in with the wider community. Prison life is characterised by its social dimension: having 'so-called friends' (Matt) is a significant part of the sense of belonging in prison, of having an identity, knowing where you fit in. As Dale observes, 'a lot of people go back to prison because they are something there – even though they're *not* – they can be something in there, and they have their little crews'. This understanding is set against being a 'nobody' on the outside: 'when they get out, they've got nothing . . . and they'll do something to get back in' (Dale). This is the experience of the dispossessed outsider, such as a man Paul describes, for whom:

> Jail . . . was where he lived. He [told me] . . . 'this is where my friends are, I don't know anybody outside, I don't trust anybody outside. I come to jail and people know me, I can integrate, I can be myself'.

Yet the social aspect of imprisonment also reflects the extent to which prison life is incorporated into some men's regular experience, as Glen relates: 'I have me crew inside, and I got me crew outside'. Similarly, Ben – who tends to 'isolate' – 'know[s]a hundred more people in jail than what I know outside'.

Scott evokes a similar experience: in prison he fits in, 'I know nearly everyone', yet he confesses:

> You have to turn into a different person out here . . . if you want to fit in with normal people, and if I want to go back and stay with my druggie friends I can stay . . . like that, but if I want to go fit in with normal people I have to change everything, you know what I mean? It's like trying to become a different person, and it . . . feels like it's not who I am.

For John – as 'everything I know is in there' – 'fitting in' is his greatest post-release fear, even 9 months later:

> There's still a lot of adjusting to do . . . especially in social situations. I get really nervous in some situations. Anything to do with normal life and normal situations I have real difficulty in communicating and having a conversation . . . I sort of shut down.

For others, 'running into' people from jail can make it difficult to escape that world, as Matt admits: 'I don't catch public transport anymore . . . because I'm guaranteed to run into someone'. Yet, even though 'nobody really wants to be hanging out with them sort of people, unless you're a career criminal' (Rob), it can be difficult to avoid other ex-prisoners, as Rob describes:

> You see them outside jail, they recognise you straight away. If you don't acknowledge it and say 'hey, how're you going' they can either get shitty, or think you've got a grudge against them, [or] you just befriended them in jail so you could get looked after . . . I don't want to hang with them, but everywhere I go they are. And . . . most people coming out of jail are on methadone . . . so just lining up to get my methadone there could be ten people in the line that I know from jail.

Rob thus portrays the way prison dynamics can inflect social relations on the outside, cementing ties through the common experience of imprisonment and reinforcing ex-prisoners' sense of not fitting in with the wider world.

Even for released prisoners who felt 'no belonging in there' (Dale), the experience of dislocation from pre-prison life nevertheless manifests as a sense of not fitting in. Dale describes, 'when I got out, I was left like "sceneless" . . . it was like "where do I slot in? What do I do? How do I slot in?"'. One of the hardest things about adjusting to prison life, for Dale, was losing his sense of belonging in a post-prison world, which he articulates:

> I didn't belong anywhere . . . I would go to a nightclub and I would feel like an observer and not a participant – you know, it's a nightclub anyway – but I felt really outside of everything . . . everywhere I went . . . I didn't feel part of society, and it was a really *grotty* feeling; it was really . . . pronounced.

Dale's experience of feeling 'outside of everything' contrasts to his life before prison, when he had 'always been involved in a scene around people', though far removed from prison 'types'. He therefore construes his imprisonment and subsequent sense of isolation as being 'twice removed': removed from society, yet also from his social milieu. The latter experience exacerbated the former.

'Stuck in prison world'

These conceptions of fitting in are underpinned by a sense of flux or unsettledness, of being part of a process, as John suggests, of 'adjusting'. In contrast, Dale conjures the notion of being trapped when he describes trying to get out of a 'vile' prison – housing 'child sex offenders, and . . . some really creepy people' – as 'like being stuck to a fly [strip] . . . like, "get me out of here!"'. This image of being 'stuck', glued, unable to free oneself is one way men conceive of their post-release freedom: being 'stuck' in a prison world, as if shackled to a past unable to be shaken off; 'no matter how hard I try you can't get away from it' (Rob). Indeed, Rob relates his recurring dream:

> trying to escape from prison because I'm innocent and no-one will listen to me . . . It's like I'm stuck in prison world. And once I do get out I always get caught and taken back. . . . I just get a little taste of freedom and then they catch me. It's a horrible dream.

The recurrence of the dream invokes the cyclic aspect of being 'stuck in prison world', manifest in Rob's everyday reality:

> mixing, living and hanging with jailbirds, yeah. You can't get away from them. Once you've met them and know them, if you dodge them they go, 'what are you fuckin' dodging me for?' . . . And if you don't dodge them you get mixed up in their shit.

Ben suggests a similar conflict, deciding 'I don't want to do this no more', yet finding 'you're stuck in certain circumstances, you just fall straight back into it. You think you get away with it again and you never wanted to go the first time'. Evoked again is a cycle of reimprisonment characterised by inexorability. Ben infers men's lack of control over their fate, reinforced by their reliance on prison structures and routine, which diminishes their decision-making capacity. For example, as Ben relates, 'half the [jail] population get into the gym and . . . blokes . . . train for two years, every day . . . then get out and just drop it'. Losing their determination also diminishes hope, a factor further entrenching 'prison world'.

Another aspect of being 'stuck in prison world' is having 'a jail head', meaning 'you have to be harder . . . stronger . . . more secure, more tight than the rest of the population . . . everything is shielded off' (Paul). This obduracy – the rigid thinking observed by workers (in Chapter 7) – serves to solidify the experience of being 'stuck'. As Paul explains, 'it becomes a tool . . . once you deal with it . . . it fits your personality, it becomes a strength instead of a weakness'. Moreover, it's 'driven into' prisoners (Paul), implying a process of habituation through pressure and coercion, its indelibility ensured by virtue of its emphasis on closing and hardening, as Scott's acknowledgment – 'it's just ingrained in me now' – suggests.

Concomitant with the accretion of prison ways and thinking is the experience of prisoners cocooned from the realities of life outside. Scott reveals the sort of hopes men nurture while in prison: 'I had a diary and I wrote down things . . . like buy my nephew a go-cart . . . [and] take him to [an amusement park] . . . things I wanted to do with my family'. Yet these things, upon release, emerge as impracticable and naïve: 'I get out and no one wants to do those things'. This example evokes the unrealistic expectations that workers' commonly observe, the imaginings by which prisoners remain caught in familiar cycles, as Scott relates:

> I sort of imagined it to be a lot better than it really is . . . like the first day you get out it's like, 'oh man, it's grouse!' But then the second day it's like, 'well, what are we gonna do man?' . . . you know, same old shit.

Scott's 'same old shit' centres on drug use, being broke, needing money for more drugs.

'Same old shit' – using drugs, being broke

For eight of the twelve men interviewed, drugs are a constant in their lives: four rely on methadone to manage heroin addiction or pain; four smoke cannabis regularly. Ben, for instance, admits 'I've got a marijuana issue'. For Tom, 'the drug use is still a bit of a problem, smoking marijuana and drinking, but I don't drink as much, I just smoke, a lot'. Scott, Rob and Nick are poly-drug users, although Nick insists, 'I've stayed off all the drugs' since his release, apart from methadone, which he was prescribed in prison, as he explains:

> When I had the motorbike accident they wouldn't leave me on morphine in jail 'cos people divert [it] . . . so they put me on methadone 'cos it's a pain killer, so I've been on that and I'm really trying to get off it . . . I've been off heroin for 5 years now . . . But me back, I couldn't handle the pain.

Owing to the 'horrible' (Rob) effects of methadone – 'it's wrecking me teeth' (Scott), for example – the men are all keen to 'get off it', though Rob is, 'not allowed until I finish my corrections order and then I can drop off it as quick as I want'.

Scott has incorporated his methadone use into his propensity for getting 'wrecked' – injecting it to induce a 'heroin stone' – signifying the extent to which 'drugs have been such a big part of my life', indeed, shaping his past post-release experience into a drug-fuelled cycle of imprisonment:

> When I get out . . . I'll go and see my family, first day I get out, and then I usually say . . . 'listen, I'm just going to see a few friends', and . . . for a couple of days . . . I'll go and binge . . . just party, and get wrecked to celebrate. . . . it's just like a merry-go-round . . . I'm out now for six months, in six months I might be back in, and in six months I might be back out . . . it's like I'm on a merry-go-round.

Scott connotes a sense of methadone as a friend, a stabiliser, when he describes how he made a choice to avoid jail 'friends': 'I've avoided two people the other day I'm pretty good friends with . . . I would've followed them like a sheep, so I thought fuck it, just go home and chill out, I've got my methadone'. Scott's decision – 'it was like, "do I or don't I?"' – hinged on having an alternative to following his friends 'like a sheep'. At that point, having somewhere to 'go home and chill out' and having 'my methadone' represented that alternative.

Rob similarly conceives of drug-using as a way to manage his 'problems' and 'stress'– 'I've been using ice . . . to try and make myself feel better . . . it makes me feel . . . happy' – and as a locus of decision-making: 'if I smoke lots of marijuana I don't dream, but it's too expensive so I prefer to have the dream than be broke'. This contrasts with earlier conceptions of the compulsion of drug use, reflecting the difference between heroin addiction and dependence upon drugs such as ice or cannabis.

Implied are the conceptions of different drugs' functions and the decision-making involved in men's self-medication: as Ben relates, 'I use drugs but it's not a social thing or a party thing, it's more a self-medication thing for me'. Drugs offer a way of coping with emotional turmoil or simply an enjoyable experience. As Paul recounts, of a drug treatment programme in prison:

> [One] bloke said, 'I just like drugs.' A lot of other blokes say 'we don't want to be dependent on drugs, we don't want to have to use drugs every day, but we don't mind drugs' . . . being able to have a smoke or a drink or a tablet . . . [is] the thing that they'd be looking for.

Men's drug use is revealed to entail a degree of lifestyle choice, locating them incidentally within the bounds of criminality, as Ben conveys: 'I've got a lot of strange issues . . . I don't think I'm a bad drug addict, criminal, just emotional crap'. Using is a way of dealing with 'stress', pain, boredom and 'emotional crap'. For most of the men, being a drug user does not necessarily mean being a 'crim'.

Although being a 'crim' implies an illegal income, the men interviewed characterise being out as having no money. Yet, as Rob suggests above, his recurring 'horrible dream' is more tolerable than being 'broke'. As he explains, apart from family alienation, the hardest thing about being out is:

> adapting to spending money properly . . . You get so used to living off nothing, that when you come back out into the real world, and you don't get your sugar and that for free, it's like 'fuck, I've gotta buy everything'. You know, you've gotta pay for power, water . . . it's . . . so much harder to live.

Significantly, prison is conceived as 'easy' in contrast to some men's experience of freedom and their perception of the outside world as complex and challenging, or simply frustrating and bothersome compared with the familiarity of life behind bars, as Glen's sarcasm suggests: 'I got a partner and kids anyway so that's a jail sentence of its own'. Glen confesses frankly, though, 'sometimes you feel you're better off inside than you are outside, especially when parole break your balls, and Centrelink, and all the bills, and all the pressure, you think . . . I'm better off in prison!'. This conception confirms workers' notion of prison as a haven, release from which represents far greater difficulty than spending time in relative comfort, security and stability.

The post-release reality of being broke is the antithesis of pre-release dreams of freedom, as Scott conveys:

When you get out, you think the sun's gonna shine every day, and you're gonna have a thousand dollars in your pocket every day, and everything's gonna be good and, you know, you're gonna be able to buy whatever you want. But you gotta pay bills and methadone, medication, and you find out you've got no money to live and . . . you're doing things like this [interview] to get a twenty dollar food voucher, just so I'm not going out committing violence.

Evoked is the precariousness of post-release life for men like Scott: trying to manage his addiction, suppress his prison habits and cultivate a pro-social way of being, while balancing on the edge of poverty, the prospect of homelessness and return to prison lurking in the shadows.

'A decent job'

At the root of having 'no money' is unemployment, which, for many prisoners, stems from lacking the foundation of education, skills, experience. These things are also the basis of men's self-concept. When identity is framed by criminality, it can be difficult to imagine an alternative. For instance, John feared, 'what would my life be without the crime, the excitement and the drama and the friends?'. Scott recalls 'the old days':

I'd sit at the pokies all day selling heroin and I'd be . . . making that much money I'd be putting hundreds through the machines and I'd have five machines going, and I'd be going to the toilet to have a shot and [people'd] be ringing me and it's just like exciting, . . . an exciting life.

Now, Scott concedes, 'I can't picture myself doing any sort of work except being some sort of labourer . . . but with epilepsy and hep C . . .' His poor physical health is a barrier to meaningful or long-term workforce participation. Nick, 'on the pension 'cos of me back', is similarly excluded. Addiction – with its attendant mental health disorders such as anxiety and depression – is also conceived as a health problem that precludes the commitment required to work, as Rob implies when he describes himself and other methadone users as 'on their way to getting better', recovery a precondition for any possible employment. Prisoners' sense of being outside 'normal' society – arising from being 'stuck in prison world' – can undermine their confidence and impede their employability. As Paul observes, 'there's quite a few things that, even though prisoners want to be able to do it, they either don't feel comfortable doing it because it's been driven into them to have a jail head', or they lack the necessary skills or training. Indeed, although Glen is able to use his pre-prison trade qualification to make a living, he completed counselling training in prison, yet laments, 'it's qualifications that I've got that I can't use outside 'cos you don't pass the police check'.

Having a record is a significant impediment to employment, as Eddie – for whom 'work's been intermittent' – conveys: 'if you have to tick that box . . . it's getting a lot stricter, even on cleaning jobs'. A criminal record affects 'your hopes or plans' and shapes post-prison horizons, as Matt explains: 'I've got a record now . . . I can't become a cop or I can't work for government. It's realistic; you've got to be realistic with those things. So you have to work around that'. Paul is similarly pragmatic about his future: 'I've got a Year 8 pass and I've got criminal convictions. I can't become a doctor or . . . a vet. I'd never be able to work with precursor chemicals that people can make drugs with'. Nevertheless, Paul is aiming to complete a fitness course and build a career as a personal trainer. Ben, also hopeful of finding work, has found the specialised assistance of WISE Employment's Ex-offender Program helpful:

> If it wasn't for that, I wouldn't know how I was going to go about, I'd have to eventually wait for word, friend of a friend or something like that because I'd have no hope of going through a normal job network, trying to get work and my history.

As Ben suggests, generalist employment agencies can hinder employment prospects by not understanding the particular issues ex-prisoners face, or, as Glen observes, 'as soon as they know you've been inside they just look down their nose and ignore you, you know'. Another way of experiencing this is 'being labelled' by potential employers. As John explains of a former manager:

> [He] said to me, 'look, the harsh reality is that when something goes missing from work . . . you're going to be the first suspect' and that was it. I started looking for a new job.

John is forthright: 'This is who I am. I'm an ex-criminal, I'm a drug addict', acknowledging that some people 'can't get past . . . my past. . . . Some people can deal with it, some people can't'.

In contrast, neither Matt nor Dale encountered trouble in securing ongoing employment since their release – Dale in a call centre, and Matt supervising a team of twenty-seven people – despite anticipating some difficulty. Whereas Dale concedes, 'the stigma of having been in jail . . . doesn't seem to have affected me yet', Matt admits thinking, 'what would happen if these guys find out I've been to prison?'. Wayne, keen, though yet to find work, exemplifies this common apprehension:

> The biggest thing I'm worried about if I go to an interview – and I haven't worked since 2008 . . . since I went to prison – [is] 'what have you been doing in that time?' And if it comes out 'have you got a police record?' I've got to say 'yeah', [then] 'have you been to prison?' I don't know what to say.

Wayne manifests flexibility and a preparedness to 'work around' this problem, however, by planning to 'tell a white lie'. These men, imprisoned once and never identifying with the prison world, demonstrate a confidence in their abilities that those more entrenched in prison life might lack – John, for instance, initially relied on the support of his Five8s to find work – and a capacity to put their prison sentence behind them that appears to mitigate the problem of having a record.

Staying out

The shadow of the prison emerges as a key element of the men's post-release experience, shaping their hope and belief and capacity for staying out. Paul, for instance, evokes the sense of the prison looming on the periphery of some men's vision, inferring that 'reintegration' entails 'losing that'. As he explains, 'when you first get out . . . [it's] like, 'am I a prisoner still', or 'do they know I'm a crim?' . . . then no longer having that [sense of] "jail's just there, or just there".' He implies that, while men retain a sense of prison being just around the corner, they remain on the threshold of the community, unable to be integrated. This sense abides for men on parole or with court orders or cases looming. For example, Paul is 'facing court' and, though neither the solicitor nor the police officer think 'there's much chance of conviction', he concedes, 'I just have to wait'. It is this indeterminate state of waiting that perpetuates a sense of being in limbo, of being released but not yet free. For Ben, the shadow has lifted: 'now I'm off parole I definitely don't expect to go back'.

The men's resolve to stay out of prison begins with intention and expectation. Ben sees prisoners' intention reflected in their physical discipline: 'half the population get into the gym and they turn into fitness fanatics, and the other half turn into fat slobs . . . and they're the ones talking about making money and taking more drugs' (Ben). Positive intentions representing a genuine desire to change are thus physically embodied. Wanting and expecting to stay out are conceptions the men variously expressed, their capacity to realise this aspiration appearing to hinge on their perception of the risk of reimprisonment and, in avoiding that risk, having the support they need to imagine, realise and sustain their life in the community. Indeed, Ben's humble intention – to 'start from where I am, so far back' – appears most realistic in its expectation of success. Four themes encompass the men's experience of freedom in terms of their resolve and capacity to stay out: 'the family thing'; having support, finding stability; wanting 'a normal life'; and leaving prison behind.

'The family thing'

Motivation to stay out arises from a range of sources, yet primarily when the desire to avoid the pains of imprisonment and release overrides any tolerable aspects of prison life, recalling the extent to which some men perceive they are 'better off inside'. As Ben concedes, 'at the end of the day, jail's pretty simple these days . . . but it's the family thing', in that, 'I miss them and they miss me and we're used to seeing each other'. For Ben, despite prison having been 'good for me in a way', far more powerful in motivating him to stay out is the unbearable pain he and his children endure 'every time' he is jailed:

going through pain and missing me and [me] worrying more about them . . . because they can't stand it. Every time I've gone in I've [got] a letter from the ex saying 'when I've told the kids, this is how they reacted', and I'm like sitting in jail and I can't – you know you love your kids as much as you do and you cause them that sort of pain, well it's unbearable. And . . . you're just helpless . . . all I could do is sit there and think about 'I'm not going to put them through it again'. So I just have to remember that.

That realisation serves to sustain Ben's resolve to avoid reimprisonment. Moreover, being able to fulfil the role of father to his children underpins his desire to 'to get a bit further on that what I am, I want my own place and a car and a job basically, just what everyone else has got'. Also driving this desire is disillusionment with prison and its aftermath: being 'sick of living like a piece of shit' (Ben); 'sick of living like a crumb with no money' (Scott). Thus, the men's resolve to stay out is expressed as a confluence of these two flows: being sick of prison and a desire for a life beyond prison.

Having a plan for the future embodies the men's sense of hope that a life beyond prison is possible. For Ben, prior to getting out, the thought of having to manage the 'challenges of life . . . getting a job, getting up of a morning, public transport until I can have enough money or whatever to get a car and to get a licence and to get a house' was fraught with anxiety. Yet his relationship with his children buoyed his resolve – 'that's the only thing really that makes me try' – as did his resentment at being told 'what to do' by prison authorities, by parole officers, by his mother:

> When you see your kids you've got your mum telling you what to do . . . it's unbearable. I've got a really good relationship with my kids and I've got to have someone standing over me telling me, like trying to rule my relationship with them.

Although he confesses, 'I'm a bit slack. I don't make them eat their vegetables and I let them stay up a bit late and I don't make them put their pyjamas on', he also defends his approach to fathering: 'that's how I am . . . And they brush their teeth and you know, I see them once a week and I've been in jail and people expect me to [do things their way]'. Now that he has 'a stable environment', sharing a neighbour's house, where he 'spent like five days scrubbing everything' in preparation for having his children, he feels confident in his ability to stay out of prison, sustained by visualising his daughters: 'I was cleaning that bloody house, [thinking] this is for the kids so they can come over and stay with me'. This thinking also enables him to manage long-term social anxiety:

> I'm really worrying about starting [work] . . . and I want it really bad but I'm sort of facing my issues . . . [about] mixing with other people and worrying about what other people think of me . . . that's something I grew up with . . . and jail probably made it worse.

Resolute that, 'I won't be having a drink or a smoke', Ben is focusing on the thought, this is 'for my kids, they're getting older now and it's just something I just know I've just got to do it and I've got to grin and bear it and get through it'. Glen relates his comparable experience of times, 'when I've come close' to violence or law-breaking, 'but then I've thought of the kids, and going back, and it's just not worth it anymore'.

Scott expresses similar motivation for managing his drug use, his niece and nephew being:

> The main two reasons I'm out – them and my mum and my sister – if it wasn't for them I wouldn't [care]. . . whether I was dead or alive . . . I'd just go and use as much heroin or whatever I could find, it wouldn't really worry me.

His family are the only thing in his life worth living for, the only thing that interrupts his desire to get 'wrecked'. They are the drivers underpinning his newly honed resolve: 'I'm seeing a doctor and I'm trying to get on [a] program to try and get rid of the hep C . . . if I find out I'm on it . . . I'll put in 100% effort to stay clean'. Age is catching up with Scott too, as he reflects:

> When I was younger it was all about me, but now that I'm getting older and I've got me bubbas, and people are dying around me . . . it puts things into perspective – I don't wanna die man, and leave me bubbas with no uncle.

Even Glen, for whom prison life presents little challenge, evokes 'the family thing' in ruing time lost through imprisonment:

> All the stuff you've missed out on over the years, like I've got kids I've never seen, my eldest . . . I haven't seen her in a long while 'cos she'd more or less give up on me ever coming back, I've spent most of her life in [prison].

The motivating effect of fatherhood appears strongest when there is an active relationship between father and children. Glen shares his love of motorbikes and camping with his 9-year-old son, for instance, and Ben's 'got a really good relationship' with his daughters. In contrast, Paul and Rob feel the pain of being separated from their family more than they perceive their children suffering emotionally from not having them around. Their desire to be fathers to their children is constrained by their lack of contact. The potency of the 'family thing' is, for them, diluted by distance.

Having support, finding stability

For many of the men, family provided critical post-release support that enabled them to stay out of prison. For Scott, it was the first time he had somewhere to go, a place to live, when his sister allowed him to stay for 3 months while he completed intensive parole. Nick's aunt and Ben's mother similarly provided

somewhere to go that meant these men were not homeless, as they had been following previous experiences of release. Glen, too, relied on the support of his
mother and extended family for somewhere to live, before moving in with his
de facto partner. For the first-timers, the support of family and friends was also
critical: Dale's strong friendship network meant he had someone to live with,
Matt and Wayne returned to their families, and Eddie was assisted by his brother.
Indeed, strong family relationships sustained these men through their sentence as
well as post-release, as Matt suggests: 'I was fortunate enough to have my family
and friends out there that supported me in every way possible'.

Tom highlights the importance of having support from the perspective of having very little besides his Link Out worker. Indeed, the agency has become his
proxy family. He appears to seek stability through his relationships with workers by mirroring their support role, implying the significance of opportunities to
help others walking a similar road. He talks about telling other young people he
has met, since his release, that, '"jail's a place you don't wanna really go to, it's
not good" . . . Some actually have listened to me . . . some people I've notice it
does sink into 'em and they realise no mucking up'. When asked, '*Do you think
that would've helped you, if someone had said that to you?*', he admits: 'yeah
I would've listened, but I should've known anyway 'cos my uncles have been
in jail, so. . . [I] found out the hard way'. He is thus telling his story of being
imprisoned in the past tense. Despite his youth and lack of social support beyond
his workers, he is narrating his own success, reading from the script of the transformed client. Whether he has the capacity to sustain this success is unclear.

Rob has also lacked family support or prosocial influences in his life, which
perhaps explains why he has formed an attachment to his pharmacist:

> He's like a drug counsellor . . . he's changed my whole life I think. When
> I first met him I was probably a one out of ten, whereas most of his clients
> are now like eights and nine out of ten, on their way to getting better. And
> now he reckons I'm an eight or a nine, from being a one.

He hints at a familial, almost parent–child relationship when he admits, 'there's still
stuff that I don't let him know . . . that if he knew he'd be devastated. . . . [about
my] stress and drug use'. This lack of disclosure conceals the real risk of his
return to prison arising from his drug use. The support of Rob's pharmacist and
the stability of being 'an eight or nine' is undermined, his potential for staying out
diminished by his drug habits.

Family support can be fraught with its own risks and problems. Ben's emotional
clashes with his mother meant he struggled to find stability while having to rely on
her for somewhere to live. Similarly, Paul's negative relationship with his mother
meant he relied on the support of his grandparents, becoming homeless after his
relationship with his grandfather soured. Nick's parents exemplify the type of relationships that can militate against the positive aspects of having support. Whereas
Nick's aunt provided a temporary solution to his post-release homelessness, his
mother and stepfather had destabilising effects. As Nick describes:

> The hardest thing was I had to live in a house with my stepfather . . . I don't want his headache mate, you know? . . . It's really hard with him . . . I wanna get out of there, I wanna live my own life you know?

Nick highlights how positive intentions may be physically embodied when, in jail, 'you've been so clean and . . . you just feel invincible you know, you're so confident [and] healthy . . . I train and I box, and when you train like that you're very on the ball you know?'. Yet these can be stymied by fraught family relationships and structural barriers such as having 'no housing when I get out of jail'.

The support of peers – even criminal peers – emerged as significant in enabling men to stay out of prison. For men deeply embedded in a criminal milieu, for instance, this desire and their intention to forge a post-criminal identity must be communicated and accepted by their peers, as Glen, having 'cut ties with pretty much everyone', hints: 'they know I've gotta do it, I ain't getting any younger'. John, too, relates the importance of being released from criminal obligations: 'in the end people accepted what I was doing and trusted me . . . I'd paid my dues and they knew what I was made of, so they could accept this is what he wants to do'. This highlights the importance of tacit support and understanding in validating men's decisions. The symbolic endorsement of peers is seen as licensing their career change, as it were.

Glen and John evidently found support to sustain this change in alternative relationships: Glen with his de facto partner and children; John with his Five8s, who 'were totally behind me'. These function as alternatives to earlier criminal ties, in that they embody a new identity: 'I'm a parent' (Glen); 'I'm an ex-criminal' (John). Whereas the material and social support of non-criminal peers is clearly critical for those men with a non-criminal identity to resume their pre-prison life, for John, his Five8s provided a safe haven in the lonely and unfamiliar non-criminal world. This time, knowing 'exactly what my problems were going to be from experience', staying out meant organising 'proper accommodation where I was going to be safe'. Having support enabled him to find post-release stability for the first time.

Underlying men's conceptions of stability is the ongoing risk of going back to prison. As Ben explains, 'I can't take no more risks because it isn't worth the risk, one risk . . . really when you've got kids'. Similarly, Glen describes the 'couple of [times] when I've come close, but . . . it's just not worth it anymore'. For these men, the risk of returning to custody hinges on everyday decisions and their negotiation of day-to-day relationships and interactions. For Glen, it means 'not getting on a bike' (motorcycle) despite its temptation and convenience; because he has lost his licence, being charged with 'driving while disqualified' would give a magistrate little choice but to return him to prison. Impending matters to be heard by various courts at some unspecified time in the future throw shadows over everyday experiences of freedom. This perpetual sense of risk, of uncertainty, of not knowing characterises some of the men's post-release experience and shapes their conceptions of being other than a 'normal' person.

'A normal life'

Being a 'normal' person, a functioning, participating member of law-abiding society, represents reintegration into the community following release from prison. Reintegration is conceived variously among the men: as a distant goal, as a state they are approaching or as a different reality entirely. As Rob observes, for instance, 'you're not really a member of society if you're on the streets, you know?'. Homelessness, for him, defines his excluded status. Similarly, John explains, 'I don't see it as re-integration because I wasn't integrated to begin with'. From his perspective, 're-integration was going back to my previous lifestyle'; becoming 'integrated' meant having 'to learn a whole new way of life, how to live life all over again. It's like going to another country and learning the language and learning the dos and don'ts'. As Matt conveys, the possibility of reintegration for many prisoners is thus 'very limited':

> Let's be realistic . . . In practice, there's not much support out there, and the support that is there is very limited in what they can do, because they have this mentality . . . if you've got a record, that's it, you're brushed with [that] the rest of your life, it's the end for you, so this is the only thing you have. And that's what they tend to believe. They have no belief, no goals . . . [only] hopelessness.

In contrast, the notion of reintegration embodies Ben's aspiration to live a 'normal life': 'I want my own place and a car and a job, basically, just what everyone else has got'. Scott similarly expresses a desire 'just make my own way in life and try and do everything that every other normal person does'. He evokes an idealised version of a reality in which he will 'settle down and have a family and a house, two cars and two and a half kids . . . and a dog, you know?'. I asked, *'How will you know if you are integrated?'* His reply – 'I think I will just feel it and not have the urge to want to use drugs' – implies that his entrenched drug habits are the main obstacle to achieving the dream. He adds, 'I'm on the waiting list to see if I get on the disability support pension', hinting that this prospect holds the promise of an identity that might sustain him in the outside world, as though becoming a 'disability pensioner' offers an alternative identity to that of 'drug user', because, as Scott confesses, 'I can't see myself doing anything [else]'.

Nick also yearns for a new identity: 'I'm just over it, just over knowing them people . . . I just want to live normal'. Yet, like Scott, Nick has never experienced the 'normal life' to which he aspires. As for John, it means learning 'a whole new way of life'. In contrast, Dale describes his own sense of reintegration as 'finding your place again', whereby he evokes the sense of having been integrated and eventually returning to that state. Though he admits to experiencing a transitional phase of 'that feeling of not belonging . . . feeling sort of not part of the whole thing', that phase 'subsided after probably six months, five to six months . . . that's completely gone now'. For Dale, notwithstanding his involvement in the city's street life, the critical ingredient was having a strong network of non-criminal friends:

> Whether the park had happened or not, as in the city sort of scene that I have got involved in, it is good to have friends you know on a daily basis that I can call or that call me.

The strongest indicator for Dale is that: 'I have almost forgotten that I was in there, it almost doesn't exist, as if it didn't happen. I don't ever think about it'.

Dale thus highlights the difference between men who belong to a criminal milieu and those with a non-criminal history and identity. The difference emerges as knowing 'what needs to be done', as Paul puts it, 'which a lot of crims don't. They're not happy with their life, but they don't see anything else'. Furthermore, he concedes, 'leaving the criminal mindset behind is probably the hardest thing'. John explains the criminal mindset as limiting many prisoners' desire for a 'normal' life, to integrate into 'normal' society:

> A lot of prisoners reject society, they have huge issues with society and normal people, straight people, they have resentments and jealousies. They don't want to be a part of that because that's everything they've been taught to hate the man, the rich banker, the system. And they've been taught to fight that their whole life . . . They've been functioning their whole lives against the grain . . . A lot of them think that they're betraying everything that they believe in by cooperating with society, by cooperating with the system.

Though John defines integration as 'simply being able to function in the world in harmony', which 'doesn't mean you have to give up your beliefs', he candidly relates the fragility of those beliefs and the fear shared by many men at the thought of 'being a normal person':

> I was terrified. What would my life be without the crime, the excitement and the drama and the friends? . . . Who was going to be my friend? Who was going to be my confidante? Who was going to be my support? Would I be able to get along with people in society, normal people? Would I always be looked at as, 'he used to be a prisoner and a drug addict'?

Paul echoes this theme in imagining a point at which 'nobody looks at you as a prisoner anymore and you don't look at everybody looking at you as a prisoner'. He evokes the interactive aspect of social identity: the relationship between an individual's self-concept and the mirror of society. Paul also suggests broader community responsibility for integrating ex-prisoners, which involves them 'being listened to . . . being able to settle things'. This requires active community understanding and engagement with ex-prisoners – 'being able to help en masse, everybody who can' (Paul) – though this 'depends on the prisoner being able to integrate as well' (Paul), by 'cooperating with society . . . with the system' (John).

Leaving prison behind

The desire to leave a criminal life behind emerges as the critical driver for men to move towards law-abidance and broader societal integration, a 'normal life'. This desire, to manifest, must exceed the desire to continue a life of crime. But, for men for whom crime has been normalised, '[who]'ve been functioning their whole lives against the grain' (John), this transition to an acceptance of 'normal' society's values and norms represents a total transformation in identity. Leaving prison behind encompasses two extremes of experience: One is the repeat offender, for whom leaving prison behind requires some effort and ongoing support and commitment. This comprises those inhabiting criminal worlds (John, Glen) and those brought up 'in the system' (Scott, Tom, Nick). At the other extreme are the men who are just passing through, for whom imprisonment was a 'one off' (Matt, Dale, Wayne, Eddie).

For men for whom crime has been their career, income and social world, leaving prison behind means forging a new path towards a new, non-criminal identity. The data suggest that age and fatherhood are twin catalysts, as it was men in their 40s (John and Glen), with children, who were motivated to leave their prison lives and criminal careers behind them. Realising this intention involves cutting ties to the criminal world. John achieved this by extricating himself from underworld obligations through careful negotiations; Glen, by withdrawing socially from his motorcycle club, where guns and drugs were normalised, and avoiding 'the club-house' or riding his motorbike on the road (for which he would face certain reimprisonment). Maintaining this commitment, however, requires support, company and alternative activities to engage in. John found this in Five8 and Narcotics Anonymous, whose regular meetings provided a sense of purpose and structure. Glen, with the social support of his de facto partner and their children, had to 'change [his] lifestyle totally around', pursuing non-criminal pastimes – motorbike riding, sailing, camping – and doing 'work from home . . . making a bit of money'. These things were able to sustain the men's resolve.

The men above relied on their criminal colleagues to respect their decision to leave that world. The strong sense of family and belonging in the criminal world provided a platform that enabled them to leave it behind, a 'jumping-off point'. Other men, whose formative years were shaped by institutionalisation and state control over their lives, seem to lack that sense of connection to a criminal community and, therefore, lack a 'place' – a position within a criminal hierarchy or organisation – to leave. Their criminal ties are built on drug deals and opportunity: doing burgs, getting money, chasing drugs. Their criminality is pervasive and diffuse, less a career than a habit, a cycle in which they become enmeshed. Although they also expressed the hope of leaving prison behind, their experience is of being caught in 'the system' (Scott, Nick, to a lesser extent Tom), graduation from juvenile detention to adult prison precluding opportunities to develop the skills and supports needed to sustain a life beyond custodial settings.

For these men, prison has been the most significant shaping force in their lives – their identity, self-concept and experience of the world – moving beyond which requires sources of human, social and cultural capital – the ongoing support, company and alternative activity that the men above found. With no 'straight friends' (Scott, Nick), however, their social network is limited to individual family members' temporary, provisional support and their Link Out workers. Tom 'do[es]n't 'really associate with much people . . . any more, 'cos all they do is get you into trouble'. Nick's 'best friend' is his dog. Where, then, do they learn how to have 'normal' conversation? How do they build a bank of 'normal' experiences – 'schooling and stuff, normal stuff' (Nick) – upon which to draw? Their lack of education, work skills or history combine with physical and mental ill health to limit their possibilities for breaking out of the circuits of social and economic exclusion they inhabit. Though they hope to 'find a girl' (Nick), 'settle down' (Scott) and 'live normal' (Nick), their possibilities are limited. Their aspirations to leave prison behind are circumscribed by 'the system' whose subject they have been throughout their lives, and whose orders, programmes, assessments and waiting lists for housing, income and/or disability support continue.

In contrast to the experience of men who feel a sense of belonging in a criminal world, or who were raised 'in the system', 'first-time' prisoners Matt, Dale, Wayne and Eddie locate their experience of being imprisoned firmly in the past. Even Tom, who had served time in juvenile detention, talked about being locked up as an adult as though it were behind him. Matt's experience of release signifies his leaving prison behind: his connections to the prison world, the relationships and roles he forged within it, were symbolically severed by his 'giving everything away' the night before his release. His actions flouted prison rules: 'everything . . . I had I gave away, which you're not supposed to do, you're supposed to take all your property with you'. The importance of this symbolic act, however, is clear in his account of forfeiting precious time in order to leave on his terms: 'when I went to the front where they process your property and stuff, they said, "Where's this? Where's that?" I said, "I don't know. I lost it, threw it away", and that delayed me for like half an hour'. Matt also ritually cut social ties: 'that night before I left, everyone, half the prison – it was only 120 people, so half the prison was in my unit – we had a party and so everyone wished me good luck'. The next day, 'my mum came and picked me up and I went home'.

The first-timers had a home – friends, family – and a past to which they could return – a history of work, non-criminal activities. Their criminality was associated with a narrow slice of their life, their persona, their experience: drink-driving (Wayne), involvement with co-offender workmates (Matt) or a terrible accident (Dale). The non-criminal part of these men was bigger, overshadowing the prison experience. These men's capacity to work provided a key reentry point, a site of potential reintegration. More important, though, was their sense of not being 'criminals', of their crime being 'a one-off' (Matt), which meant that, once released, they could return to lives in which crime and prison did not feature. For Eddie, his ongoing cannabis use and sharing a house with an ex-prisoner was an ostensible link to prison world. Rather than these elements, however, it was his lack of work history and skills, and having a criminal record that meant unemployment had to some extent become a site of socio-economic exclusion.

This experience suggests the enduring effects of imprisonment on men's confidence, capacity and sense of self-worth that can shadow post-prison lives.

What about the men (Paul, Rob and Ben) for whom leaving prison behind was not expressed directly? These men aspired to a 'normal life', yet were pragmatic about their experience of imprisonment as having shaped their futures and their horizons. Nevertheless, hope glimmered in each man's account of his prospects of staying out, particularly for those who were active fathers (Ben and, to a lesser extent, Paul). These men expressed hope of finding a job, finding stability, being able to be a father to their kids, 'getting better' (Rob), and thereby implicitly leaving prison behind.

Conclusion

This phenomenography of the lived experience of release illuminates the fears, anxieties, hopes and expectations associated with getting out, being out and staying out of prison. To the extent that prison becomes a home – a place of stability, familiarity and security – men's experience of release is marked by instability and uncertainty. Whereas, in prison, responsibility is curtailed by rules and routine, post-release life is overwhelming in its demands and complexity. For all the men, the three most prominent themes in their post-release accounts were having 'somewhere to go', finding a 'decent job' and having support, finding stability. The difference between getting out and having 'somewhere' or 'nowhere to go' was conveyed starkly, particularly by those without an address to return to and/or who specifically identified being homeless as part of their social identity.

The different experiences of being out were marked by a sense of being 'other' than 'normal' society and carrying prison baggage that persisted to varying degrees. For some, fitting in and overcoming loneliness were part of a gradual process. Others found themselves caught in webs of connectivity with other ex-prisoners and displaying patterns of behaviour and thinking that reinforced those connections, despite their desire to escape them. Some men's drug use and addiction appeared to perpetuate poverty and their sense of 'unfreedom', the irony being that they used drugs to try and alleviate the anxiety and distress associated with day-to-day living. 'Being broke' was also the result of unemployment and men's struggle to find work, impeded by criminal records and the stigma of imprisonment. The importance of finding work to be able to stay out of prison or to simply 'get back on their feet' was common throughout the data. Staying out also demanded that men have support – family, friends or workers – to be able to sustain a life outside. The 'family thing' emerged as critical for motivating, inspiring and enabling men to put prison behind them. Children, in particular, provided a strong impetus for men to maintain their intention to stay out and pursue a 'normal life'. Finding stability in the form of a house, a job and emotional control over their lives meant that men could either rebuild a 'normal' life or begin to craft a new lifestyle, a non-criminal identity that would allow them to leave prison behind.

Notes

1 An EBT card is the Electronic Benefits Transfer card provided by Centrelink to prisoners upon their release.
2 Segment one refers to the Office of Housing's priority housing list.
3 Smoking was permitted in Victorian prisons until a state-wide ban came into force on 1 July 2015.

7   Post-release support perspectives

'Ben'

I meet 'Ben' at an outer suburban shopping centre near where he lives. He explains his polite reserve as we sit down to do the interview: 'I'm very anti-social'. No taller than average, his relaxed clothing shields a neat frame, yet belies a certain tenseness. I notice a thin rat's tail at the back of his hair and wonder if it holds any particular meaning in his world. When I ask him to tell me about how he ended up in prison, he thinks for a moment, then says simply, 'boredom, stress, alcohol'. He elaborates later: 'I've had a lot of emotional shit happen and just being drunk, I just do stupid things . . . I'm a bit hectic'.

'Ben' is 36, a father of three children. He has a son with an 'ex-ex' girlfriend with whom he has no contact. But he is very involved with his two daughters – who are aged 7 and 9 – seeing them every weekend. He lived with them, and their mother, until the girls were 2 and 4. He confesses sadly that he has missed 4 years out of the last 6 and he has resolved not to miss any more: 'It isn't worth the risk'.

Ben was 24 when he first went to prison, and he has been jailed four times since then. This time, he has been out for just over 4 weeks – he finished the last month of a 2-year parole last week. He talks about the capricious decision-making involved in such circumstances, conceding that, although parole has 'been helpful . . . it depends on the parole officer':

> Some of them have a hard line approach, which probably some people need, but with me, I didn't really need it, and . . . I sort of get my back up too. . . . I missed a couple of appointments. It was sort of a comedy of errors. It was just there'd been a few things happening and one parole officer that didn't have any tolerance, she's gone 'boom', you know? . . . I went in two days after that and I asked to see her and she refused to see me. And next thing I know the coppers are at my door and took me to jail for another three months.

This 'you can comply or I give you some tough love' approach reminds Ben of his mum. His mother is a drug and alcohol worker with whom he has 'problems' – she's 'full on' – yet on whom he relies, and without whom, he says, 'I'd be stuffed'. He was living with his mother briefly following his release, but, after this relationship became unsustainable, he moved in with a neighbour whom he has known for years. He can have his children here at weekends, which is the most important thing. He defines his future – and his motivation to stay out of jail – in terms of being a father to his daughters.

Ben doesn't view himself as a criminal, attributing his drug use to 'emotional crap', as he explains: 'I've got a lot of strange issues. I've had bulimia'. He describes himself as 'an extremist': from binge eating and 'doing weights' to substance abuse and social avoidance. He says that smoking marijuana, 'self-medicating, having a couple of drinks' help him manage these issues. However, reflecting on the 'unbearable' pain that he and his daughters go through when he's locked up, he has resolved:

> I won't be having a drink or a smoke. . . . [It's] for my kids, they're getting older now and it's just something . . . I've just got to do . . . I've got to grin and bear it and get through it.

Ben admits that, 'jail has been good for me in a way' – in that he's 'been off drugs and living a healthy life' – 'but in another way it's devastated me and it's sort of set me back'. He's focused on trying to 'get the emotional shit together' and is feeling more confident in this respect: 'I'm over my ex and all that, I'm all content with how that sits now so yeah . . .'. All he needs now is to get a job, but he confesses he's 'really scared':

> I want it really bad but I'm sort of facing my issues . . . being with other people and mixing with other people and worrying about what other people think of me. . . . I know after a few days I'll get along with people, I always do, I always have this before something, but once I'm there, yeah, yeah.

I think he'll get there.

This chapter presents a phenomenography of post-release support, portraying the different ways in which practitioners conceptualise their role and experience the practical aspects of working with released prisoners. The 'outcome space' comprises different three 'categories of description' that emerged from interviews with workers: conceiving the subject, understanding prisoners' release and the post-release support role. Consistent with the phenomenographic logic, the focus is on areas of difference rather than commonality. Variation is emphasised in an attempt to cast new light on an old problem: men's struggle returning to the community following release from prison. The most notable area of divergence in the data is in how the subjects of post-release support are conceived: as 'clients' or 'ex-prisoners'. The latter shows consensus within workers' conceptions. From a phenomenographic perspective, this finding is less significant in that it reveals little about the different ways in which prisoners' release is understood by workers. It is important here, though, because it provides a contrasting perspective to ex-prisoners' own conceptions about the post-release experience.

Conceiving the subject

The starting point for a portrayal of how post-release support is conceptualised by its practitioners is how they conceive of their subject: Who is he? How is he defined, constructed, characterised? How is his experience understood? These conceptions shape how the role is carried out and thus have implications for prisoners' post-release outcomes. The data reveal that individuals at the receiving end of post-release support are variously conceived as 'clients', 'ex-prisoners' and, to a lesser extent, 'ex-offenders'. Even when seen as men, as individual human beings, they are nevertheless thought of as part of a group marked by their various, often multiple, experiences of imprisonment.

'Clients'

WISE Employment and Link Out workers refer to their 'client group': a population with 'complex needs' and entrenched problems, prisoners deemed 'high risk' in terms of their likelihood of reimprisonment. These are men who have been released several times previously, who have breached parole conditions and/or had parole revoked in the past, who have 'burnt bridges with family [or other] meaningful relationships' (SW01), and who lack any 'kind of stable relationship with others' (SW01). Workers concur most are struggling with alcohol or drug addiction. Many have 'major literacy problems, major mental health problems, and/or an acquired brain injury' (SW12). They are likely to be homeless or 'couch-surfing' (SW01, SW09, SW12, SW14), living in temporary or unstable accommodation. Family breakdown, conflict with ex-partners and access to children are 'huge' issues (SW14). And, despite having 'positive intentions' upon release, many men lack 'the skills and support to back that up when they get into the community' (SW02); they are 'really, really isolated' (SW14), they are 'dis-abled' (SW12), 'dis-habilitated' (SW22). These factors, combined, make reoffending/reimprisonment inevitable.

Konnect workers additionally refer to cultural factors that differentiate their Indigenous client group. The 'notion of professional capacities' means less than personal and community connections (SW10): 'how you fit into the world and into the Aboriginal community . . . that's really important to them. And without that there's . . . a real barrier to really working with them in a meaningful way' (SW10). This requires 'greater personal disclosure' and flexibility in workers being 'not so governed by working hours' (SW10). Although these clients are characterised as 'very disconnected from you . . . you're just like any other screw [prison officer] or social worker', particular barriers arising from being 'a white guy' (SW10) – especially for older men, 'when so many have been . . . removed by white social workers in the past' (SW10) – 'and being young as well' (SW10). SW12 affirms, 'being senior aged in our community has got some weight'. These circumstances heighten the need for awareness and understanding of Aboriginal ways: 'little things like knowing stuff about what their totem might be or knowing the handshake that their local area use . . . that kind of thing . . . allows them to kind of open up' (SW10).

In addition to the difficulties faced by the wider client group, 'family issues and custody issues with children' are notable among Aboriginal clients (SW10). SW12 hints at the recursive nature of these problems:

> They go from one couch to another couch, to another, particularly the males. They may not be formally homeless but they are. They're staying with relatives in overcrowded circumstances, sleeping on couches, often sleeping in houses where they bring their crises with them, and suddenly the whole house is in crisis.

The idea of problems attaching to individuals – who 'bring their crises with them' – gives insight into the way the prison and its shadow can leach into households, and thus communities, inflecting those relationships and interactions. Problems such as drug and alcohol abuse tend to pervade families, so that released prisoners:

> get sucked back in because it's what they know and it's who they know and it's their community. And the only way to disconnect from that is to disconnect completely from their community . . . [This is not] appropriate in Aboriginal culture . . . because there's responsibilities and there's funerals and there's family things to be part of [and] that is all so many of these guys have.
>
> (SW10)

Moreover, these men 'feel less easily integrated into mainstream communities anyway, [which] . . . drives them towards the same communities [and] . . . the same issues' (SW10). SW10 observes, 'The guys . . . that have been successful are the ones that have had to make very strong conscious decisions to disconnect from their communities a lot and they've often found that really quite difficult'. 'Because', SW12 explains:

> particularly in our culture, it's very, very difficult to refuse relatives. It's almost like you can get struck off from being black. And we have that. . . . You can be struck off if you don't cooperate or collude.

So, although ex-prisoners share common post-release needs, Indigenous clients confront particular relational issues stemming from culturally nuanced kinship obligations and a living history of colonial oppression. As SW12 notes, many 'come from families which have had issues with the criminal justice system and the world at large ever since colonisation'. The Indigenous subject of post-release support, then, is conceived primarily as an Aboriginal person who, by virtue of his cultural identification and experience, is part of a social group with particular vulnerability to the issues faced by ex-prisoners more generally.

Within the broader 'cohort of clients' (SW13), two distinct characterisations emerge in the workers' conceptions: released prisoners as manipulative, yet vulnerable. In prison, the skill of manipulation is perceived as 'a survival thing' (SW13); prisoners 'learn . . . how to manipulate, how to con, how to self-protect' (SW22). This ability is honed through time spent absorbing the skills and habits of other prisoners, to the extent that it becomes the default way of relating to others. As SW05 observes, 'it's not malicious, it's often pointless the things they get you to do', highlighting how this pattern of prisoner behaviour, reinforced through reiteration and some small yield of power in the prison hierarchy, persists post-release, despite having little currency in the outside world.

Workers associate this habit of manipulation with clients' acculturation to prison ways and to having things provided for free, so that any kind of help or support service is 'there to be screwed over, we are there to be manipulated' (SW22). The 'client' categorisation is both ascribed and assumed as part of an ex-prisoner identity, manifest in a 'user' mentality that lacks any sense of reciprocity or exchange. Knowing 'everything that's out there' (SW22) is perceived as a source of pride: 'pride in knowing how to get through the system . . . in getting resources or just getting by . . . Pride in being able to screw over a couple of agencies and get something extra' (SW01). This pride includes a sense of satisfaction of getting something from 'the system', in retaliation for the injustice of being locked up and for 'being treated unjustly . . . it's about "they've taken away my dignity . . . my rights"' (SW23). A sense of entitlement is apparent: 'people owe me this because this happened to me' (SW14).

An element of self-importance is discernible: 'what's in it for me; what can I get out of that?' (SW14); 'it's all about me in prison and what can I get . . . and that can come out in the community as well, it's all about me, I shouldn't have to wait' (SW04). This attitude frequently manifests in prisoners volunteering for Link Out solely to secure housing, and disengaging from the programme when none is available. Interestingly, from SW06's perspective, 'the Vietnamese prisoner [is] very different, they don't think about the provider, the supplier . . . the Aussie prisoner – they know [where] to get a free lunch'. Implied are cultural variations on ideas of dignity and pride, associated with different subgroups within the prison population. For 'Vietnamese people', for instance – 'they think they lose face, they scared of the people in the community' (SW06) – social honour is a more significant motivator than getting 'a free lunch'.

The conception of ex-prisoners as manipulative suggests workers' inherent cynicism and distrust of the men they work with. In fact, this belies a strong sense of empathy with and loyalty to their clients, whom they also conceive as vulnerable. This second characterisation, of prisoners as 'very vulnerable people' (SW12), takes into account the 'complex, difficult backgrounds' (SW02) of many men, 'damaged' by 'traumatic' histories (SW13). These men are seen as 'disadvantaged and voiceless' (SW09), treated unfairly and without compassion by an unforgiving society. Workers tend to take an 'eco-systemic' view (SW12), seeing 'it's as much about health and homelessness as it is about justice because you're dealing with people whose mental illness and social marginalisation manifest in offending' (SW12). Rather than the pessimistic outlook suggested above, the workers convey a shared optimism and desire to advocate for these men. SW08 evinces this common pragmatism about Link Out/Konnect clients:

> We are working with the most hopeless, most likely to reoffend, most likely to screw up. This is a bloody hard group and by the time people are getting locked up in adult custody they have generally burnt all their bridges anyway, there are not many . . . Glenn Wheatleys[1] out there, in for a bit of white collar fraud and coming out to perfectly good models on the outside with their mortgages covered, there are not many of them, you know. We're dealing with some really chaotic people, and if we're not dealing with the really chaotic ones then we're not doing our jobs.

This work is conceived as inherently challenging and difficult, yet worthwhile; indeed, an essential public service.

'Ex-prisoners'

Another conception of the subject of post-release support arises from workers' own experience of imprisonment. Two of the workers revealed having been prisoners themselves, an experience that has shaped them and their work with ex-prisoners. As SW06 (imprisoned in Vietnam for 7 years) relates:

> I understand because I was in prison . . . I understand. . . . You . . . remember your parents, your friends, your neighbour, your dog, your house, everything. Your baby's smell, your children's smell, everything . . . And I understand. Nobody say[s] with me, 'I'm proud because I was in jail', sorry . . . you can find somebody else to say it [to], don't say with me. I understand you. . . . If you think like that you'll never change. . . . Young or old – if you don't change, you don't change.

SW06 thus evokes the universality of the experience of being 'locked up', his intolerance of men who attach any pride to that experience, and his belief in the possibility of reclaiming freedom post-release. Moving beyond imprisonment, however, demands the rejection of prisoner values and ways of being. As long as prison life is conceived as remotely positive or desirable, or the prison world is extolled, ex-prisoners remain imprisoned in that world.

SW22, imprisoned for 5 years as a young man, likens the post-release experience to that of returning war veterans, in that:

> Anyone who's ever been to prison . . . is permanently affected and damaged by that experience . . . you are traumatised. There's pain, there's scars, there's fears and there's the sense, which even I've got until this day, of not quite fitting in, not quite being accepted, not quite belonging. Feeling different . . . that's just something that you have to learn to live with, and some of us live with it better than others . . . It's who I am and having shared

the experience of imprisonment I know the damage it does and I know how important it is to try and help people to redeem themselves and give them an opportunity . . . It's not a job for me, it's my life.

Both men draw from their experience of imprisonment a strong sense of empathy, which drives their commitment to their work and shapes their conception of the ex-prisoner: as like himself, capable of change, yet who, without support and understanding, risks further marginalisation, even permanent social exclusion. A deep-rooted belief in every person's claim to the 'full rights of citizenship' (SW22) is manifest. At the heart of both men's perspective is the notion that change must begin within the individual, with intention and belief in the possibility of change. Whereas SW06 sees taking on an affirmative prisoner identity – feeling 'proud because I was in jail' – as obstructing post-release adjustment and change, SW22 hints that this may in part constitute how prisoners are 'permanently affected and damaged' by their carceral experience, nonetheless implying the potential for redemption.

This empathic approach is restricted by the designation of the ex-prisoner as 'client' in a bureaucratically framed programme, such as Link Out. The label symbolises the professional distance embodied in the worker–client relationship, as discussed below. Cultural factors may mitigate or offset this constraint, however, such as the Vietnamese tradition of evoking kinship to symbolise trust and connection. As SW06 (who works with Indo-Chinese clients) describes:

We all call each other like family . . . most of my clients call me uncle . . . I say [to] them all the time, if I treat you like a brother – my young brother, my nephew – depends on you, if you treat me like the uncle, like a brother, fine, if you treat me like a worker, I will treat you like a client . . . [For] example, you tell me the truth, this means you believe me, and then I try to solve anything you want. If you treat me like a worker it means you hide something and you try to get from me something – sorry – I treat you like a worker, and the difference is if I have a look at my watch, 5 o'clock, I stop.

Embedded in this approach is an awareness of the importance of family in providing long-term support. Conceiving of his ex-prisoner client as a 'relative' (SW06) engenders the level of trust required for the client himself to believe he can become drug free, for instance. It also gives SW06 permission to engage with the ex-prisoner's family to enable them to support their son/brother/husband/ nephew. Whereas 'some workers . . . don't think about the family', it represents a crucial reintegrative base to SW06, who explains: 'if you are a train, [it's] easier to go more than a car . . . even a four wheel drive!' – meaning the interdependence of collective resources surpasses individual effort or capacity. SW01 also hints at this understanding when she remarks, 'there's only so much support they can get from a case manager. It really depends on who else is in their life'.

For SW22, the term 'client' is emblematic of the culture of 'the professional helper', limited in its capacity for anything beyond a 'superficial' human connection:

> It's like a neutral term. It's a non-offensive term, but it's also an invisible term. It makes you invisible as if you are not a person. At least as an ex-prisoner . . . I know what I am and don't dress it up.

As suggested above, 'client' implies a user of a service, exemplifying the individual responsibility ascribed to an 'offender' for his behaviour, yet belying the social context and construction of his actions and interactions. The designation 'client' neutralises – indeed renders invisible – the need for reciprocal social transactions that allow the ex-prisoner to participate in community life. It thus forms part of the othering process whereby ex-prisoners experience stigmatisation and social exclusion.

Human beings, as SW22 insists:

> need dignity, you need belonging. You need to contribute. You need to just do the ordinary day-to-day things that people do that give them life and these relationships must be life-giving and you can't do that when you are a professional.

SW22 argues that, if professionals – who understand the issues facing released prisoners and who care about their clients – are unable, owing to their professional constraints, to 'have a relationship, a friendship with [them] . . . to actually engage them personally' (SW22), then how can ordinary people be expected to include and embrace ex-prisoners in the community, when they have no understanding of the cultural chasm dividing them? His mission, therefore:

> is about educating the community, raising awareness of the issues, because . . . fear usually occurs because of ignorance. . . . It's about society getting to the point where we [see ex-prisoners] are human beings with issues, and our society, which helped to create them, must take some responsibility to help to reintegrate them.

This undertaking is buttressed by SW22's Christian faith – emphasising compassion, community and social justice – which enabled and has sustained his own post-prison integration.

Conceptions of the subject of post-release support include 'ex-offenders', though this is used incidentally rather than to specifically describe programme participants. A more generic term, it evokes the language of the correctional domain to describe people who have moved beyond offending to become 'ex-offenders' or reformed criminals, implying a unilinear track to desistance. It is an ideal destination, yet one that belies the journey, as SW22, 'an ex-offender', explains:

> Not re-offending is a long-term, sometimes a life-long process and it may take you another two, three, five, ten years before you get to the point where you never re-offend and you are fully sort of socialised. So it's a process.

'Ex-offender' rings hollow and meaningless in the context of this process and the post-prison struggle towards this end. In contrast, 'ex-prisoner' invokes the unequivocal status of someone who has experienced imprisonment and inevitably carries the imprint of that experience on his psyche. As SW22 argues, 'I prefer ex-prisoner because at least you know what you are'. Paradoxically, it is the professionally cloaked case manager, wearing the badge of 'helper' yet constrained by ethical and personal boundaries, whose role appears ill defined against the ex-prisoner archetype: 'they are blunt and honest and in your face and . . . generally speaking, they call a spade a spade . . . and you know where you stand with them. That's stuff we need to learn about' (SW22).

Understanding prisoners' release

Two conceptions take shape in workers' understandings of men's release from prison: these are framed as the paradox of freedom, and the prison thinking that leaks into post-prison life. The paradox of freedom is that prisoners leave the safety and security of prison life and return to instability and uncertainty; simultaneously, their capacity for integration is diminished by their experience of imprisonment. Prison thinking reflects the values and meanings that prisoners adopt and absorb while in prison and then bring with them into the community. This shapes ex-prisoners' post-release behaviour, their expectations of freedom and of fitting in to 'normal' life.

The paradox of freedom

Workers see men getting out of jail as moving from one world into another; this experience arouses prisoners' fear and anxiety, as well as anticipation and excitement. Making the transition from prisoner to freedom entails having 'something to go back to' (SW22) – family, community, a job – which many prisoners lack. Hence, 'for most of them, getting out, it's fear of the unknown' (SW22; also SW13), 'what they're going to face, and what the world is going to be like' (SW10). SW22 speaks from experience – and conveys workers' common understanding – when he describes release from prison as 'a paradox':

> On the one hand you want to get out so badly, you know, you live and dream it, but the reality of it scares you and guys will say 'I'm shit scared. I can't wait to get out, but I'm shit scared'. Why? Because of the unknown, because it's a big world out there and prison is a microcosm, it's a cocoon and as we all know it's an institution and you are institutionalised by the fact that you survive in an institution. So . . . there's a lot of fear, a lot of anxiety.

Even for men who 'know they're getting out in two weeks and they've got somewhere to go . . . it's excitement, but there's a lot of anxiety still' (SW10). Workers concur that many prisoners' trepidation around their release and transition to freedom is based on past experience of being released back into lives marked by dysfunction and instability; of having nothing and no one to go back to; of leaving the security and predictability of prison life to navigate the difficult waters of life in the community. SW12 sums up, 'the relationship the person was pinning all their hopes on, she's moved on and suddenly he's back to the reality of being isolated, alone'. And the 'easy' familiarity of prison underscores the contrast with life outside:

> Prisons are comfortable and modern and there's things going on and you're a prisoner and you're one of the boys and the next minute you're nothing in a world of nothing and miles from anywhere with no money in your pocket because you're paying $10 [for] a pack of cigarettes.

The only men observed to lack the fear and anxiety commonly associated with release are 'those who've been in for a shorter period' (SW13) or 'white collar offenders ... who have something to go back to' (SW22), though this is countered by SW10's observation, above, and the ex-prisoner interview data, which suggest that men with a life to return to still experience anxiety.

More widely across the data, the experience of imprisonment is seen as cocooning prisoners from the practicalities of the outside world, allowing a proliferation of unfounded hopes and aspirations. The other emotional extreme – anticipation and excitement about their release – is thus experienced as 'euphoria, they're all excited, they're released, they're free, that's all they have got in their head' (SW14). This is enhanced by a degree of mental clarity while in prison, as, 'they're not drinking ... [and] they're usually using drugs to a lesser extent. And that gives them a chance to think and to reflect on their life and to really take stock of what it is' (SW10). There is plenty of time to dream, 'time to reflect on things' (SW01):

> In prison, you've got nothing much to do, and you're thinking of all your good plans and you're feeling good about yourself. . . . People can be reasonably clear in prison because ... they're full of hope.
>
> (SW12)

The euphoria of release is founded on unrealistic expectations and a forgetting of the pressures of reality, yet 'there's a sense of hope ... that often changes when the pressures kick in' (SW01); 'when they get out ... they hit the wall' (SW12). Hence, it is short-lived – 'it becomes clouded very quickly' (SW12) – and inevitably unsustainable:

> It's usually only a week or two and it starts going down. Yes, it's only that first week, first and second week, they've got that euphoria. And then they still hold onto a fair bit of hope, you know, for the first month at least.
>
> (SW14)

The initial euphoria, moreover, is tinged with a restless frustration, a naïve impatience:

> This is how they talk, 'fuck it this time, you know, I'm sick of fucking prison and I fucking hate it and, you know, I'm gonna fucking, you know, I'm gonna do this' – and they go through all the things that we'll put in a case plan – 'you know, I'm gonna do this' or 'I'm gonna do that', you know, blah blah blah.
>
> (SW09)

This illustrates the apparently adolescent expectancy of many prisoners, not used to having to wait for things: 'it's very instant gratification' (SW14); 'they all want material stuff now, you know? So they want the best job, they want a great car, they want the best clothes, a chick . . . and before six months it's all going to fit into place' (SW23). Prisoners' unrealistic expectations also manifest in their unwillingness to accept help, their assertion of being 'able to do it on my own' (SW14). SW14 describes a man who 'decided "I'll be all right. I'll get a good job on my own". It's that euphoria . . . [that] often happens'. After 3 months, 'he started to go downhill, and started to go into depression, he was just starting to use again'. When asked why he didn't seek help, 'he said "I don't know, I really thought I would get a job on my own"'. The initial confidence, bolstered by the excitement of release, quickly diminishes with the realisation that 'getting a job' is not so easy.

This example contains a collective experience: cocooned within the confines of the controlled and easily navigable prison environment, where futures are mapped out, possibilities are imagined and resolve is honed, men are buoyed by the thought of freedom. Yet their imagined horizons are uninterrupted by financial pressures, familial tensions, the day-to-day difficulties of navigating public transport, finding work or finding drugs: 'they are isolated from their world and their environment, and they're not using as often or using as much' (SW10); 'jails tend to be a kind of safety net' (SW12). Their aspirations soon collapse as these elements converge. Their determination fades, they 'go downhill, and . . . into depression' (SW14), which provides a footing for old habits and addictions to resurface.

The paradox of freedom emerges, then, in the notion of prison as 'a haven' (SW12), a refuge from an outside life 'of constant stress' (SW12). As SW04 sums up:

> It is easier in prison than in the community. You don't have to pay bills . . . and you do have friends that you see every day . . . they may be associates . . . but they're still there. You're getting a meal, you have a gym you can work out at.

In contrast, life outside is fraught with everyday challenges, 'things like' (SW04):

> I'm going to have to get to Centrelink, I've got to go to parole, I've got to pay my bills, I've got to pay my rent, I've got to deal with my partner or my ex-partner, then I've got my children, then I'm battling anxiety, depression, whether I want to use drugs or not, I've got no licence, catching public transport.

These things add up to 'a whole heap of issues for them to get through the day' (SW04). This conception recognises that, 'the community is a very difficult place to live. It's very demanding, and you have to be very highly functioning to be able to work in it' (SW12). Many ex-prisoners, lacking sociocultural and personal resources, have 'got to work a lot harder at it' (SW04).

Rather than seeing imprisonment as harmful and brutalising (SW22, SW23), SW12 argues that prison provides an escape or respite from 'the big challenges [that] are in the community', and that 'jails can turn people around. They're clean and they're supportive' (SW12). Although SW09 conceives of prison as a 'detrimental negative community', she contends that, 'it works . . . because everyone knows where their place is'. SW04 concurs: 'You know where you stand in a prison'. Spaces are contained, routines are enforced, and necessities are provided. Prisoners 'know how prison works' (SW09). It is predictable and familiar. SW13 even ascribes familial connotations to prison life, emphasising the security its 'rules and instructions' prescribe at a domestic level:

> 'All right, time to get up. Time to have breakfast. Time to go to exercise. Time to do this' . . . So the prison is almost like a parent, a parent they never had, and they say they hate it . . . and a lot of the times, they do. But at the same time, if you could get your sex and drugs, it would be a fantastic place to live.

This conception of prison as 'a fantastic place to live' – a home – not only accentuates the anxiety of prisoners being released from this haven, but also illuminates key ingredients in the process of institutionalisation and 'prison acculturation' (SW12): an environment marked by control, security, routine and familiarity. Living in an institution means that, 'invariably you become dependent' (SW22); 'decision-making has been taken away from you for so long [that] it affects your psyche profoundly' (SW23); prisoners 'learn not to be able to do anything for themselves' (SW01). This means, particularly for 'long-termers', that 'everything they know . . . just comes unstuck when they get out' (SW09). As SW01 observes, 'it's really hard for them to have to direct themselves . . . to get up in the morning, to just function in everyday life.'

Living in this 'haven' has the dual effect of weakening prisoners' connections to outside resources – housing, relationships, employment and community ties – and diminishing their inner personal resources – confidence, decision-making capacity, social skills, for instance. As SW09 describes: 'They're paranoid, they've got no confidence; they've got no control'. This 'lack of control' over their dominion manifests thus: 'They've got sweet FA ['fuck all'] money, they could be going to [transitional housing] or a rooming house, you know, crisis accommodation, [or] back to their mum's that they haven't seen for three years' (SW09). SW05 gives another example of diminished capacity, which he frames in terms of a lack of 'foresight to avoid the crisis in the first place'. One man, for example:

> knew his accommodation was unstable and he wasn't welcome where he was but he couldn't or wouldn't take the steps necessary to address it. He lived

just down the road from [a housing support agency] . . . [but] he just didn't do it until I got the phone call, 'I got kicked out a couple nights ago'.

This example further elucidates the fear and apprehension prisoners associate with release, when they are seen as stepping from a place of safety into a world of everyday obstacles and demands they are ill-equipped to meet.

The paradox of freedom also manifests in men's alienation and estrangement from, and sense of not belonging in, the wider community, of 'not quite fitting in, not quite being accepted, not quite belonging' (SW22). 'Not quite' hints at an ostensible acceptance – the promise of redemption, of having 'done your time' – which is belied by the lived experience of release. As SW22 explains, there is a tension between an abstract notion of prisoners being 'rehabilitated' and their experience of 'being stigmatised by society, told you are a prisoner, knowing you are a prisoner'; not wanting anyone to know they were imprisoned, 'getting out and never feeling that you are one of them' (SW22). He knew, for instance, of 'a guy who did twelve and a half years, got out, got into business, did really well, got married, has got two teenage kids, neither his wife nor his kids know nothing about his past'. He is too 'afraid' to talk about it (SW22).

For SW22, being an ex-prisoner 'is who you are and if you deny who you are, then really you are kind of living a lie'. Yet behind this logic is the reality that prisoners become practised in pretence, adept at concealment, skilled in perform-ing a role. People, through imprisonment, become familiar with inhabiting an identity as, 'in prison, you are a prisoner, you know who you are. It's reinforced every day . . . your identity is set clear. Then you step out of prison into the free world and honestly you don't know who you are' (SW22); 'you're nothing in a world of nothing' (SW12); you 'don't have a place' (SW09). Evoked are the distress and disorientation associated with release into a society where the only certainty is that, 'you know that you are not accepted' (SW22). In this inhospita-ble environment, concealment is adopted mechanically, unconsciously, a safety mechanism.

In addition, the perceived hypocrisy of societal expectation upon the post-release subject gives rise to confusion and disillusionment:

> You are expected to suddenly be this honest person who's upfront, who's transparent . . . [yet] they confront a society which itself is full of double-standards, contradictions, con artists, employers who rip them off. . . . They look at that and they think 'hang on, I'm the crook, and they want me to become like what?'.

(SW22)

The paradox of freedom, then, comprises the convergence of impediments imposed by societal constraints and demands, and internal factors, including the way prison thinking seeps into and permeates post-prison life. This connects to workers' conception of the psychological baggage prisoners carry with them that shapes the experience of release.

Prison thinking

A significant challenge to prisoner integration arises from having to 'undo a whole lot of the prison thinking . . . that you can trust no one' (SW23). In addition, 'a lot of mistrust of the system and authority' – particularly among people who have 'done a lot of time' (SW01) – is projected on to workers. Workers can represent 'the system', because prisoners typically 'don't have any power in determining what happens in that relationship' (SW01), with prison officers, for example. SW01 sums up the 'biggest' challenge of working with ex-prisoners as 'this kind of dog-eat-dog world [mentality], "I have to look after myself and I'm not going to let anyone in", a constant sense of struggle that often gets them into trouble in the community'.

The 'struggle' arises from 'never [having] been able to navigate through the system before' (SW01), which generates a sense of powerlessness and subjection. Also, becoming acclimatised to 'a really ultra-masculine environment where proving how powerful you are is [the] more important thing . . . "someone's wronged me, so I have to go out and stand up for myself; otherwise someone is going to get me"' (SW01). The dominant mode of being in prison is perceived as self-preservation, the 'survival' instinct (SW09, SW13, SW14, SW22), engendering 'the inability to be vulnerable and . . . the inability to trust' (SW10). This impinges on every relationship and, hence, on prisoners' capacity to experience freedom. As SW12 observes, prisoners' 'problem . . . is they're institutionalised in a particular cultural way and many are not able to adjust and re-acculturate themselves'.

Equally valued alongside the skills/habits of manipulation, 'conning', and self-protection (SW22) – paradoxically – are the ideals of honour and respect. These frequently manifest in norms of violence, domination and retribution, as the notion that 'someone's wronged me' implies. SW22 admires the 'staunchness of the prisoner to defend his friend to death', conceding that such thinking is 'counterproductive . . . when you get out' (SW22); it 'gets them into trouble' (SW01). Connected to the earlier point, about prisoners struggling in a post-prison environment, 'trouble' manifests in degrees: for instance, grown men learning how to manage their impulses and emotions, to manage anxiety and to feel safe without the need to carry weapons (SW02). At the other extreme are certain prisoners, 'ring leaders', thriving in the prison setting because 'they're the bullies and they get so much power and they're given so much attention . . . people do what they say and people get out of their way' (SW10). The disruption of these men's identity, entrenched in prison culture, can be difficult to accept when they get out:

> It's the complete opposite because they're an offender . . . they've been convicted of something and they can't get a job and they can't do anything. Nobody knows who they are and there's no power. They often find that really disturbing and they try to get themselves back in prison just so they can have that power and that controlled environment all over again.
>
> (SW10)

Notwithstanding this extreme archetype, adapting to prison life clearly involves the forging of a prison identity – 'you're a prisoner and you're one of the boys' (SW12) – and the destabilising of men's pre-prison identity. Although different prison-selves manifest – arising from individual circumstances, causes and conditions – a common thread links their emergence into post-prison light: 'when they get out . . . they lose whatever sense of self they had . . . which can cause that out-of-control spiral' (SW09). This is conceived as largely relating to the length of time spent in prison: 'when it gets into two, three years, it becomes a little more freaky for them' (SW13). Some men are bewildered, 'traumatised' (SW22), unable to reconcile their experience of imprisonment with their pre-prison self: they 'need that opportunity to debrief, "what happened to me and how do I deal with that out here?" And many are lost, they are really lost, they drift' (SW22).

Many display what SW22 identifies as a 'male trait . . . more pronounced with ex-prisoners . . . the deep-seated underlying . . . anger that can flare in different ways and which must be managed in the community'. Combined with habituation to the culture of violence and intimidation that marks the prison environment, this anger can underscore men's sense of alienation from the wider community, where such behaviours are contained and sanitised – for instance, in sporting or corporate settings. SW23 notes that an incident of 'road rage' can become a matter of 'they've taken away my rights'. This thinking is indicative of common traits observed by workers: immaturity, impatience, rigid attitudes and 'closed thinking' (SW13), particularly among younger men whose prison identity is developing, who are growing into their prison skin: 'they want to tell me all about their crime and what they've done and how much time they've done in the "boob" [jail]' (SW09), exemplifying the kind of pride SW06 eschewed.

These traits can be seen as symptomatic of prisoners' institutionalisation. Moreover, 'a lot of them know the language', some even announcing to their worker, 'I am really institutionalised', as if that has been adopted as part of their identity (SW01). Having 'a worker' is part of this institutionalised self and enables a delimitation of the extent of a person's need: for instance, 'sometimes, depending on who they're speaking to, [they'll say] "this is my housing worker" [as if to say] I don't have any issues, I'm just homeless' (SW01). SW01 suggests 'that kind of language has seeped into what they think is important', as though co-opting the language of 'support agencies' affords ex-prisoners a degree of involvement or complicity in their fate, a sense of dominion in otherwise aimless and chaotic lives. Or, as if limiting their problems to a single one – 'most of my issues are because I don't have permanent accommodation' (SW12) – allows them to cope with an otherwise insuperable mass of difficulty.

'Drug user' identities can similarly shape or anchor men's lives: with a sense of resignation or hopelessness – 'how can I change?' (SW06), or through belonging to a group with a shared focus and a common language, doing 'burgs . . . to get the money to get the supply . . . the little group that'll do that together' (SW14); or, by engendering a sense of control, as SW13 explains:

they all believe they are in control of their drug use, and they get to this point where they're starting to feel out of control, so they put their hand up and say, 'detox – I need to go there'. They are not saying it's because they want to stop – they are saying '[I] want to get back in control of my drug use'.

Often, a hiatus in drug use – caused by imprisonment, as 'it's quite hard to get drugs in prison despite what people say' (SW13) – can serve to reinforce the impression of being in control, although, as SW13 contends, 'the biggest problem with drugs in prison is smoking tobacco', an addiction strongly tied to prison life.[2] Smoking a particular brand of tobacco is indicative of how prison habits persist, post-release, as symbols of a prison-inflected identity:

> They'll roll cigarettes like they are still in prison, like pencil thin. They will smoke a particular brand of tobacco called White Ox that everyone smokes that has ever been in jail . . . they all smoke the one type of tobacco.
>
> (SW08)

Cigarette smoking represents a punctuating rhythm in the daily routine of prison life, a physical and psychological habit that – through frequent repetition – becomes entrenched. Just as prison tattoos inscribe the skin, ways of being in prison can thus permeate thinking and inhabit prisoners' bodies, as SW08 describes:

> When the guys come out of prison and they meet up here . . . they will often pace up and down in their little basketball yard at the back, have you ever seen men in a prison walking up and down just doing laps? They will go this way, and then they turn right, and then go back and then turn left and go that way, and you see them pacing like that, and they won't even know they're doing it. . . . They'll pace up and down; they'll dress like they are still in prison. They'll carry themselves like they're still in prison.

Evoked is a robotic return to the way physical space is navigated and traversed in prison, as though its spatial patterns are, like a tobacco habit, ingrained through repetition.

Paradoxically, despite the institutionalised thinking and diminished decision-making that imprisonment engenders, prisoners are also encountered as fiercely independent and wary of accepting help, such as SW14's client convinced of being 'able to do it on my own'. These characteristics are perceived as arising out of mistrust and an adaptive aversion to showing vulnerability. They signify the immaturity and rigid thinking of many men who mask their fear and trepidation of the world around them with a superficial independence. Challenging such thinking, and replacing it with more functional attributes, entails a slow process of stripping away of prison accretions: 'a gradual re-acculturation and a de-acculturation from the prison scene' (SW12).

SW12 observes that, over 20 years of experience around prisons, 'prison culture's changed a lot . . . it's not the sort of man's tough-it-all sort of world as it used to be'; 'prisons [and] prisoners vary a lot'. He even contends, 'There is no such thing as a prison culture'. Rather, prisons are 'very variable, multi-faceted places', marked by difference and producing different degrees of institution-alisation and prison acculturation. At one extreme are the rigid gender models characterising some male prisons, where 'doing those small petty things like cooking, and cleaning, and keeping your house is really below you' (SW01). In one prison, for instance, there are men with 'very seriously entrenched behaviours around being a "warrior" or "real guy". . . . They do very badly in the community, and that's why they're locked up in maximum security' (SW12). This is 'the hard end', which gives rise to common conceptions of prison culture: 'it comes from television, it comes from movies', but, SW12 argues, 'it doesn't really relate to prisons as I know them'.

One common conception is of men 'who have been in contact with the jus-tice system ever since they were children' (SW12), who are particularly prone to display thinking distorted by their experience. A skewed notion of pride, for instance, is evinced in different ways: many 'won't wear second-hand clothes' (SW05, also SW06). Some men express their pride at never having burgled any-one's house, despite their patent tendency to violence. A burglar might proudly claim never to have hurt anyone, despite his many thieving exploits (SW05). A 'code' is discernible, that 'it's okay to rip off big business or . . . do burglaries on big shops and things like that, but it's not okay to do minor burglaries, like stealing from someone on the street' (SW01).

Oppositional thinking is observed, with some men expressing their resolve to stay out of prison in terms of the justice system as an abstract adversary: 'people say . . . "I'm not going to let the bastards" . . . there's tenacity and determination' (SW23). In SW12's experience, some Aboriginal men:

> see being an offender . . . as a way of fighting this huge juggernaut . . . it's kind of a Robin Hood attitude . . . and being in jail . . . a firm part of Aboriginal culture today, a part of your identity, a part of becoming a man, part of being a number one fella, a stand-up guy who's staunch.
>
> (SW12)

Most, however, have been put 'at risk of being an offender rather than them choosing to be an offender' (SW12). A sense emerges of men attempting to stake a claim over their individual manhood in the face of pervasive social, economic and political powerlessness, yet, ultimately and ironically, cementing their disen-franchisement and marginalisation.

Many ex-prisoners are conceived as regular guys, with whom 'you're kind of friends' (SW12). For these men, the post-prison baggage they carry is less dramatic, less noticeable than that of the men at the 'hard end', yet equally alienating and disorienting in terms of their post-prison identity: Who are they? Where do they fit in? Many ex-prisoner 'clients do like to use the word friend-ship' (SW01) in relation to workers – 'a lot of them want you to be their mate' (SW09) – to enlist an ally amid the 'constant sense of struggle' (SW01) shaping their lives. 'Old mates' (SW09) often refer to partners in crime – 'non-prosocial friends' (SW13) – people to avoid in order to avoid reoffending and reimprisonment, yet also people to whom a sense of 'allegiance' (SW13) persists, through a shared history:

> They can fall back into the groove when they spot someone who has just come out, or someone they haven't seen for a while. They become very comfortable with that group, unless they really are desperately trying to stay away from it . . . [but] that's easier said than done because they come out and they're lonely.
>
> (SW13)

Falling 'back into the groove' and feeling 'very comfortable' evoke the sense of strong habits and social ties from which men find it difficult to extricate themselves: for instance, when 'you've got someone in your ear saying, "let's go and do a hit and we'll buy up big and we'll start selling this and we'll earn two grand a week" and they think well, yeah' (SW09). Mateship in a prison context is more about familiarity than trust, and a 'shallow sort of loyalty', as SW09 explains:

> They know at the end of the day, in the back of their minds, if shit goes down, they're not . . . people they can depend on. . . . It's that shallow sort of loyalty that 'you don't dog your mates', and prisons are full of people who dog their mates.

In this way, acculturation to prison mores and prison thinking is seen as diminishing prisoners' capacity and inclination to trust, making 'de-acculturation' (SW12) even more challenging.

The post-release support role

This chapter is about the difficulty of providing post-prison support. The following shows how workers struggle to observe professional boundaries while providing genuine support, such as articulated in the Brosnan Centre's philosophy of 'a friendship model' (SW08). Two very different conceptions of the post-release support role emerge in the data: professional worker and volunteer 'Five8'. These reflect two distinct modes of post-release intervention. One is the programme model, delineating the professional role of the specialist caseworker to whom clients are referred. The Five8 model is built on a relational approach, where prisoners join via personal connection and recommendation: 'we identify people who really want to change . . . [who've] been recommended by people we trust and know' (SW23). The community emphasis distinguishes Five8. Whereas other programmes recognise a social support network as a resource to develop or harness, it is Five8's grounding principle and basis for action.

In the programme model, there is a clear separation between worker and client, professional helper and subject helped. In contrast, the Five8 approach aims to break down differences between the individuals involved. It recognises and seeks to reconcile cultural disparity between the newly released prisoner and his Five8s: 'it's almost like a "them and us" . . . They are two different cultures . . . the hardest thing is merging those two cultures so that we are on the same level' (SW23). Rather than accentuating the separation, the focus is on uniting, integrating, bringing together. Five8 actively seeks to engage ex-prisoners in the micro-community-building process. This model of support is a social process rather than a single relationship: individuals 'are not alone in this . . . the responsibility is shared' (SW23). The conceptions of 'caseworker' and 'Five8' thus contain differences in what they do and how they do it, yet share a motivation to help. These differences between the two models are now explored in terms of categories unfolding in the data: boundaries, friendship, trust and power.

Boundaries

Professional boundaries frame the role of the programme worker. The 'case manager' title underscores the specialised role of the worker in relation to their clients, even though, as SW01 admits, 'they would never call me case manager because you don't manage them'. This remark evokes the tension between the apparent precision of the term 'case manager' – with its administrative and bureaucratic aspects – and the individual responsiveness and flexibility that the role demands. Indeed, 'case management' appears an attempt to corral, mask, even negate the elements of trust and empathy at the heart of the support relationship. The 'case manager' is assigned a 'case' (a job, a task, a problem) to 'manage' (direct, supervise, control). Yet, this professional designation neuters the individual in their ability to generate or foster new life, in terms of post-release recovery or reintegration. In work 'so stringently based on professional boundaries', SW23 observes, 'people have to . . . put aside their heart for their job security'. The case manager's capacity to meet the human need for connection, to be able to engage and support ex-prisoners, is ostensibly neutralised by the way her/his role is framed.

How relevant, though, is this framing to the doing of the work? The data suggest workers' strong sense of autonomy and independence in relation to their clients; of being guided, yet not constrained, by programme structures or protocols. SW09, for instance, relates how her commitment to providing 'consistent' support for her clients can override her strict observance of programme rules or professional advice:

> I actually got a phone call last night at 9 o'clock . . . I'm a sucker like that . . . [if you] ring me and said 'I've been locked up, can you come and see me', I'd say no, I can't, but I will talk to you for an hour if you're feeling that down about it, stressed or whatever. But I wouldn't go out until the next day, in working hours.

Her reasoning is that the men

> we work with, they've never had continuous support . . . between the hours of 5 pm and 9 pm, which can be some of the most crisis times of the night, they've got no one, nothing. And if I can talk someone down of a night time . . .

Implying the difference may be one of life and death, SW09 thus feels vindicated in her decision-making, conceding lightly, 'I'll probably lose my job for that though', acknowledging that, from a professional perspective, she has transgressed the boundaries of her role. SW09's example implies how the term 'professional relationship' is eschewed by Link Out workers, such as SW01:

> When working with ex-offenders, I don't think it works very well when you have those clear cut lines. It's more of a supporting role. Clients do like to use the word friendship, which is too much on the other end.

She thus hints at balancing extremes of 'professional' and 'friendship', which she develops further as 'having clear cut boundaries, however not a really distinct line to keep it a little bit more informal in the relationship' (SW01), as SW05 concurs:

> It's really important to draw that line in the sand when they start asking you about your personal life, your family, where you live and things like that. I mean you do have to give a little of yourself up but you have to keep it professional; you have to draw that line.

It is telling that workers conceive of boundaries in terms of 'lines', evoking a visual sense of demarcation between them and their clients, perhaps to define what seems indefinable.

Beyond its broad guidelines – 'you create a support plan, you identify goals together and then you work on them' (SW01) – an inherent ambiguity and a lack of definition surface throughout workers' conceptions of their role, which is shaped by its discretionary application to individual circumstances. Indeed, there appears more clarity about what the role is not, than what it is. In reiterating to clients, 'I'm not your mate. I can't do what I can do for you if we're mates. That's not how it works . . . No, no, no, we're not mates', for instance, SW09 establishes a neutral platform for support. This neutrality gives workers the capacity to be flexible, to tailor their way of working to meet individual needs, and to adjust the boundaries of the relationship as it develops, and as trust grows. As SW09 explains, 'there's a lot of room for [being] laid back, sort of chilled out, but I think if you go down that path you get into trouble if you don't have the . . . consistent boundaries from day one'. SW23 contrasts her Five8 experience with past situations:

> [Of] supporting someone getting out of prison and we've been alone in it, and the anxiety that that entails . . . they ring at all hours of the night and they are spinning out . . . it's incredibly intense and I don't ever want to do that again.

Clearly, boundaries are needed around a one-on-one post-release support relationship.

Friendship

The Brosnan Centre espouses a particular 'friendship' model of support based on Father John Brosnan's maxim: 'Three things are needed by people upon their release from prison: a place to live that is decent; a job that they can handle; and friendship, and the hardest to provide is friendship'. Friendship between workers and clients is founded on ambiguity and potential misinterpretation: 'what we would sort of call a friendship model, it can't be friendship because it's defined by the fact of incarceration' (SW08). SW08 concedes that, 'once someone has been out for a while lines can get a little bit blurred' (SW08). The blurring implies, 'you don't want to be too formal because they will start being formal back' (SW05), yet this can mean 'clients do forget that it is a professional relationship', and dependency can arise. As SW05 relates:

> One client repeatedly would ask me to go out for dinner, come round, hang out, go to the beach, those type of things . . . I have to say, 'look, 'I'm sorry, I'm just a worker and you're a client' . . . that can be shattering for them sometimes. I had another guy cry when I was telling him I was closing off the programme.

SW23 observes of programme workers: 'When they are taking on the job, they are not taking on a personal relationship', which emerges as the key differ-ence between the two models. The Five8 experiment suggests that it is not the 'fact of incarceration' that means the relationship 'can't be friendship' (SW08), but the constraints of the professional relationship. In contrast, Five8s are 'not bound by that stuff' (SW23). Perhaps the difficulty arises out of the uncertainty about what this relationship entails, and what friendship variously means. SW22 reiterates Father Brosnan's counsel: 'prisoners need . . . a friend, or friends, community', and explains that Five8 'provide[s] the community, the friend'. The relationships engendered through the Five8 process are 'real friendship' (SW23):

> The depth of relationship that we have is not even ordinary friendship . . . it goes beyond [that] . . . it's just brought us to this place where he sees us as family, and I think he's a little shit, but I love him so much . . . I really do.

What enables this degree of intensity in the relationship is that, 'we are not alone in this . . . the responsibility is shared' (SW23). The 'micro community' functions as a microcosm of social relations, diffusing the reliance on a single relationship.

As SW08 suggests, the longer someone is out of prison, the more time is spent in building trust and replacing prison habits with more pro-social ways and thinking. This is a gradual process, as SW22 describes of a Five8 participant:

'he's been around people so much it's almost like he's been saturated with their thinking, their behaviour and like osmosis, he's kind of absorbed it . . . he's around us so he's becoming more like [his Five8] mentors' (SW23). Similarly, programme workers are 'role models' (SW04), modelling pro-social ways of relating to others as a way of demonstrating a type of friendship:

> Some [ex-prisoners] don't have friends . . . or family members that aren't drug users, so having somebody that you can contact who's not your CCO [Community Corrections Officer] . . . they see it as a contact that they've got in the community that is safe and secure, that's not going to be judgmental, that's going to be there to assist them.
>
> (SW04)

The key elements of the professional 'friendship' are thus: being safe, non-judgemental and there to assist. This does not imply a shared conception of the meaning of friendship, which can be unequal, as SW08 acknowledges:

> Former clients . . . they'll call me a friend and I'm uncomfortable saying 'yes, we are' but I won't say 'no, we're not' so . . . I change the subject . . . I don't say, 'well I'm actually your ex-worker and we're not friends and we will never be friends, but we can be something in the middle of friendship and professional' . . . that is the fence you are sitting on a lot.

Despite the 'fine line' between formality and 'attachment' (SW05), a commitment to considering the men's needs and well-being remains. Workers behave as 'friends ought to . . . in a perfect world' (SW08). By modelling this ideal, clients 'start to understand that there are people around that are prepared to give them a chance' (SW13); as SW09 intuits, 'they really feel someone cares and that's a nice feeling that they're not used to'. SW09 highlights the unfamiliarity of trusting relationships for some men, particularly those who have spent years 'in the system'. SW23 recounts a Five8 participant who, 'after a relapse', expressed his amazement that, 'people didn't just kiss me off, you know? They didn't just say "Go, that's it. It's all over, finished. We don't want anything to do with you anymore". He said, "you were still there"'. For the first time, he had 'something to come back to' (SW22). Through such experience, trust starts to grow.

Trust

Trust is the bedrock of the support relationship, built through 'just hanging in there, hanging in there' (SW22). It is the foundation of working 'to habilitate them . . . to create a pro-social community' (SW22). From SW12's perspective: 'you really need to have that kind of relationship with the person where you're not going to dump them because they've stuffed up'. He qualifies, however:

That doesn't mean you're a walkover, because I've had guys who've been really incredibly arrogant like, 'What are you doing for me?' And I say, 'Nothing' . . . It's like expecting us to deliver a winning Tattslotto ticket. It's not going to happen.

(SW12)

This example illustrates the way boundaries and expectations are established early on in the relationship. Importantly, in building a trusting relationship, workers 'have to demonstrate to them that we're genuine. We can't just say we're genuine – they wait for the scores to come on the board by the actions we take, and how we do that' (SW13). For Konnect workers, their relationship with their clients is shaped by Aboriginal cultural understandings: 'we're Kooris and we're Indigenous workers. It's . . . very personal' (SW12). However, this 'doesn't mean that just because you've got Indigenous descent that you have a good rapport with the client' (SW12); crucially, 'you have to be a functioning caseworker. They'll soon suss you out if you don't deliver' (SW12). Constancy is emphasised and modelled as a critical element of any support relationship, as is 'consistency . . . being honest, straight' (SW13).

Establishing rapport is conceived in terms of 'engagement' (SW14) and the first steps towards building a relationship. Link Out and Konnect include 3 months pre-release for the purposes of 'having a good rapport by the time they get out' (SW01). SW10 explains the importance of that initial rapport, as, 'when they're actually released, engagement is often very different from when they're inside . . . it usually dissipates quite a lot'. The things that buttress this rapport vary: from wearing particular status-invested footwear – 'it's an immediate rapport with clients . . . if I wear my trainers' (SW05) to truthfulness and advocacy, and, arising from these things, acceptance and caring, and:

Openness . . . transparency on my behalf . . . not hiding anything and . . . if I say I'm going to do something, I'm going to do it. So to follow through . . . is really important. Or staying true to your word . . . And advocate. They feel so empowered by you when you advocate for them. They're like, 'someone gives a shit'.

(SW09)

In the Five8 model, being truthful manifests as an important part of the mutual 'process of learning to be honest with one another', which is 'all we demand' of participants: 'we just say, "all we want is for you to be honest with us and we will stick by you", although they all "had to learn that that is a huge process"' (SW23). SW23 elaborates on the challenge of learning to trust and be honest with one another:

Like [one ex-prisoner] was making claims that we were all ganging up on him . . . and to some extent we were talking behind his back because we were baffled, you know? We didn't know how to deal with someone who was using drugs and saying they weren't. So it was a real lesson for us in how to be really, really honest, but also really listen to him to undo a whole lot of the prison thinking, which was that you can trust no one.

Other conceptions of mutual learning emerge, as SW14 describes, of WISE Employment's ex-offender programme:

You can't put a homeless person straight into a job because where are they going to go home and have a shower? It's not going to happen, so they're not going to keep their job. . . . Someone who is on a very high dose of metha-done or morphine . . . they're not going to be able to work machinery. So, all these factors we had to really learn to work with the client one on one.

The learning emerges through 'engagement' with clients (SW14), which involves winning their trust, knowing their language, understanding their issues, such as:

[If] they're on . . . [an] intensive court order, if they're on parole . . . Because if we set them up for failure there, they're going to go straight back to jail . . . if they breach parole, and a lot of job services just don't take this into account.

(SW14)

Having this basic practical awareness is crucial because, as SW14 observes:

They are not communicators. They are not going to . . . disclose something unless they already know that you understand where they're at and what they're talking about. . . . Other job services . . . have a lot of problems with this client group . . . because they don't know their language . . . and the issues they're facing.

SW14 sees mutual learning as the challenge and enjoyment in engaging with clients, conceding: 'I've learned more from them than what I have from any education'.

Power

SW14's insight about communication and disclosure implies complex power dynamics underpinning the support relationship. First, few men exiting prison have 'any healthy, positive starting blocks' (SW09); 'your average offender, your stereotypical crim, is a person who is dysfunctional, who is disadvantaged' (SW22). They are 'dis-abled' (SW12), 'dis-habilitated' (SW22). SW22 contrasts their experience to that of 'someone who has a family, who has a job to go, who had education, just that alone sets [him] apart', and indeed his own experience: 'I came out of prison . . . I was equipped with an education that . . . empowered me to do a whole host of things'. Dysfunction and disadvantage are seen as inherently disempowering. The 'strengths-based' approach to post-release support 'means basically empowering them, getting them involved in the process of their own future and their own decision-making' (SW22). Yet, the empowering process needs also to account for the impact of imprisonment and release, of entering and leaving different worlds, where different power structures apply. As SW22 observes:

> When we are in his world he has the power and he can dictate and he doesn't have to come out on a visit, or if he's not happy . . . they can get up and walk back in. But out here we have the power and a lot of ex-prisoners . . . are really conscious of that.

Delineation between 'professional' and 'client' is seen to generate 'condescension' (SW22, SW23). As Five8 proponents argue, involving ex-prisoners in the support process 'negates some of that condescension' (SW23) and counteracts some of the power imbalance inherent in support relationships. Yet, neither claims to fully engender equality between participants and clients and supports and workers: 'even in . . . Five8, there's not equality because you are coming from a completely different world. . . . We are the ones who have the power because he's now in our world' (SW22). In the world outside prison, power is negotiated largely through verbal exchange. And, although the requirement for reciprocal effort is common to post-release models, Five8 emphasises the mutual aspect of that exchange: 'one thing we impart to the ex-prisoner . . . is that you are helping [Five8 volunteers] too to understand your world. And that's an important dynamic, and that's where . . . equality . . . comes in . . . it's a mutual thing' (SW22), as many volunteers 'are extremely naïve . . . they are in a process of learning too' (SW22). This is compared with programme workers' knowledge and understanding of prisons and post-prison issues gained through professional training and experience. Power imbalance inheres less in the nature of the human interaction than in the parameters enclosing that interaction: professional boundaries, for example.

Facilitating power is conceived as a crucial element in the support relationship, and sometimes a tricky balancing act. Although the casework approach is 'to work collaboratively with someone on an agreed set of goals' (SW08), this can involve a degree of directiveness, as SW08 explains:

> Quite often the case manager needs to push the harder stuff towards the client and the participant will shy away from that stuff so it's about identifying the right time to deal with the issues, in what order, and those sorts of things.

SW02 relates the trap of being like a 'mother figure', by which he means, 'making the appointments and doing everything for the client rather than supporting the client . . . to establish themselves in the community, themselves'. In a similar vein, SW13 says:

You've got to weigh up, are you 'over-nurturing' . . . when maybe they should be tested to try and fend for themselves? It's that balance all the time and . . . sometimes you get it right . . .

Highlighted is the dependence that can develop in prison, through deresponsibilising processes, and the paradox of the 'empowerment' project with men adept at manipulation and exploiting opportunities.

Power is negotiated at every turn: by 'clearly enunciating what you can provide and what you can't provide' (SW03); 'you have to be very upfront about what you can deliver' (SW12); 'being clear . . . about what you can do and what you can't do for them' (SW13). For instance, 'we can help them with release clothes so they don't have to go visit their family in prison greens or whatever. But [we can't] take them to Ralph Lauren and get them jeans and Polo shirts' (SW09). Setting boundaries entails 'managing expectations' ex-prisoners have 'for us to do things for them' (SW02). They can be demanding: 'fellas say . . . "when are you going to get us a phone? And . . . I need some new threads, and . . . I need some new kicks [shoes]"' (SW09). SW09 explains:

> I think some of them have this real sort of expectation that we'll get them a house and we'll get them nice shoes and, you know, we'll buy them food and we'll take them out for lunch . . . and I think by setting those boundaries in the beginning, by saying this is a twelve month intensive thing that we can help you with, they sort of start to see.

Boundaries encompass an intangible 'line in the sand' (SW05). This intangibility enables flexibility and discretion, which can serve to distance clients with difficult behaviours or unreasonable expectations: 'Some guys it's really easy, I have got [a] . . . client who's quite aggressive and I find it really easy to be "a worker" with him . . . he is quite unpleasant' (SW05). Here is another difference between models: Five8 selects its participants. Link Out and Konnect do not choose their clients, as SW12 explains: 'the door's always open . . . I can't just pick the ones I like'. The push and pull of power play is revealed here, the extent to which the workers' management of their clients, their demands and their relationships with them is under constant challenge. These are not docile bodies but a 'bloody hard group' (SW08). Only occasionally is a client rejected: 'very rarely do we knock people back . . . [except] where their rudeness and their arrogance and their unreal demands are just such that they're really not wanting to engage with us into some kind of partnership' (SW12).

Generally, though, the support relationship is marked by 'trust, appreciation, [and] unconditional regard' (SW12). Universally, the workers express their genuine care for and interest and belief in the men with whom they work. They are driven to form these relationships by a strong sense of understanding and empathy. And they are acutely aware of their own human frailty, 'their own baggage. . . . You need one eye on yourself as well as the client' (SW12); you need to 'know where you are in your life to help them in theirs' (SW09). What surfaces is an unflagging pragmatism: 'In the end, all we can do is facilitate . . . to find out what are they wanting from us, or what are they wanting for them and what are they going to do to get there' (SW13). Workers' realism abounds: 'there's no magic bullet' (SW13). Supporting ex-prisoners towards (re)integration is a gradual, 'long-term' process (SW22).

Men 'staying out of prison for a few months rather than a few days' (SW01) is a significant achievement and to be celebrated. For some men, 'not using drugs for six weeks instead of one when they get out is a huge victory' or 'seeing their kids twice instead of not at all' (SW10). SW03 hints that a 'history of success' is an important element in ex-prisoners' path to (re)integration, without which they have nothing to build on. People's horizons are delimited by their experience of the world, which then shapes their expectations of future experience. 'Success' is conceived as a step-by-step process, rather than in binary terms of success or failure. SW10's use of the term 'victory' evokes the sense of battle that some ex-prisoners face, which is in sharp contrast to the way 'success' is construed in ordinary terms, for people living a 'normal life'. A success, such as completing parole or surviving relapse, painted as a 'victory' implies the other side of it as defeat: 'for many people it is' a battle (SW10).

Ex-prisoners' power to bring about change in their lives and be (re)integrated in the community is constrained by the need for belonging and acceptance. One man's experience is illustrative: 'he's in the community, he's not using, he has relatively stable accommodation, but he doesn't feel like he belongs . . . he feels he doesn't fit into the community as well as he does in prison' (SW02). This example gives insight into a problem to which SW10 alludes above, that reintegration – 'where you never reoffend and you are fully . . . socialised' (SW22) – may not be a realistic goal for some men whose experience of life is wholly shaped by their experience of imprisonment. The crucial importance of community and belonging for human well-being is underscored, which is at the heart of the Five8 model, and yet programme workers are not equipped to provide it.

Conclusion

This phenomenography of post-release support work has revealed qualitatively different ways in which men's release is understood by those supporting their post-prison transition. Two distinct conceptions emerge: 'clients' and 'ex-prisoners'. These largely, yet not wholly, intersect with the two modes of post-release intervention manifest in the data: the 'programme' approach and the Five8 model. Although the motivation to help is shared by all workers, significant differences emerge in the way the post-release support role is conceived and performed. Programme workers imply some appreciation of intangible goals, such as giving clients 'a sense of self and a sense of meaning and worth' (SW09), and yet the programmes are instrumental in their approach and the successes they measure. Five8, in contrast, is explicit in its recognition that the transition to freedom and the power to change hinge on a man's self-concept and identity, and that these are shaped in the crucible of social interaction. Adapting to post-prison life is seen to entail either reconstructing a pre-prison identity, or constructing a post-prison identity, that allows a degree of participation and integration into the broader social world. This means transformation from a prisoner mentality to an ex-prisoner way of thinking; a drug user becoming an ex-user or non-user; homeless to having a home; being 'institutionalised' to becoming 'integrated' or free. Thus, the notion of *being* is contrasted to *becoming*, a gradual process of flourishing to which Five8s appear more attuned.

Notes

1 Glenn Wheatley is an Australian former musician and entertainment industry figure who, in 2007, was convicted and sentenced for tax evasion, for which he served 15 months in prison.
2 This was prior to Victorian prisons becoming smoke free as of 1 July 2015.

8   Home, identity, connection

'John' and 'Glen'

John and Glen had lived lives of crime. John was 'trained into it' from a young age, his 'whole family was into crime'. Glen also grew up in a criminal milieu, 'knocking around' bikie clubs 'ever since [he] was a young kid'. Both spent years in prison. Now aged in their 40s, with children who barely knew them, they wanted to leave prison life behind.

'John' is 42, of Italian ancestry, whose compact frame belies a tightly coiled energy and an intensity of awareness marked by sharp-eyed acuity. These traits may reflect what he describes as 'the edge', a capacity for reading people and situations, honed through his years in prison. More than that, however, John's experience epitomises the notion of being 'trained into' crime:

> When I was a kid, I was taught everything about crime and drugs and money . . . everything about the criminal world, when I was very, very young, pretty much conditioned to take that sort of lifestyle on. My whole family was into crime . . . so for me . . . it was just normal.

Moreover, he was 'very, very good at it', which meant he was made 'a protégé type criminal and trained really specifically . . . [in] the world beneath the world, beneath the world, and for a long time I didn't get caught and felt very safe'. However, he 'ended up with a heroin habit and . . . that's when I started really taking risks and doing foolish things and getting caught for them'. From then, his criminal path diverged, in a way that illustrates the integration of the prison world into the broader criminal world: 'I started being used to do jobs in jail so I was actually meaning to get caught to go into jail to deliver information and to do certain tasks'. John thus became embedded in the prison world: 'for the last eleven and a half years I've spent about nine of those in jail. It's almost become like a lifestyle. . . . All my friends are in there. Everything I know is in there'.

His desire and determination to leave that life behind have faltered in the past. This time, he feared the same thing happening again: '[I was] fearful of my old crew getting in touch with me again and forcing me to do things that I really didn't want to do, because that happened last time'. And he worried that he would be confounded by loneliness and seduced by heroin, as he describes:

I'd come out and I'd just have no one, nothing to do and I'd go nuts, I'd go stir crazy. I'd be able to maintain it for a month or whatever, but sure enough after a few months or a year or whatever, it just got too lonely and too boring. I'd look for company and female companionship and I'd go back to that life to find friendship and somebody to talk to and something to do and sure enough I'd become involved in it again and end up using again and the snowball effect takes place. . . . Before I know it I'm in jail again.

But his resolve is stronger now, now he has the support of Five8. And he attends regular meetings at NA, which gives him a sense of purpose and routine. He's been out for a year, the longest time in over a decade, which he attributes to his involvement with Five8 and the unwavering support and sense of belonging this has given him. He describes his experience of freedom and entering into the non-criminal world as a slow and gradual process of getting used to a whole new way of life and way of being. Being a 'spiritual seeker' gives him a philosophical perspective on his experience, emphasising acceptance and growth, rather than regret and shame. His first granddaughter is just about to turn 1, and he speaks of a new-found sense of responsibility. Nevertheless, he laments a lost life: what he could have been, done and become if he hadn't lived a life of crime. As I walk away from John, after 3 hours of talking, I too am struck by a sense of immense potential having been wasted.

'Glen' is turning 42, a stocky man sporting well-worn tattoos on his arms. We meet in a shopping-centre café, near where he lives. His wary demeanour softens slightly as we talk, over the next hour. Glen lives with his de facto partner, whom he has known for years. She has a son, aged 10, with whom he has an active involvement. He also has children he never sees, including his eldest daughter, aged 23, who lives and works interstate. He has not seen her 'in a long while, 'cos she'd more or less given up on me ever coming back, I've spent most of her life in [jail]'. She has telephoned him 'a couple of times', yet he places the possibility of further contact firmly on her side: 'if she wants to see me, she knows where I am'. This logic seems to typify Glen's fairly rigid thinking style.

He lives in the coastal community where he grew up, among people for whom law-breaking is normalised, yet a strong sense of justice prevails. Among his family, he can think of only one 'legit' member, a cousin. His family is close: his mother, his auntie and another cousin all live nearby; he sees his dogs, two 'Staffies' that live at his auntie's house, every day.

Glen has an extensive criminal history, associated with the motorcycle clubs he has 'been knocking around . . . ever since [he] was a young kid'. It is particularly 'the clubs' from which he has had to distance himself since his release, in order to reduce his likelihood of rearrest and return to prison; as he concedes, 'I start mucking round at the clubs, I'll get back on a bike and start riding on the road again, and that's enough to put me back in jail'. In his world, prison is part of the landscape: his birthday next week will be his 'second birthday out of prison in sixteen years'.

To stay out of jail, he has had to 'change me way of thinking and me lifestyle', including reducing his alcohol intake, helped by his 'missus restricting me drinking at night'. He admits he has to 'try and not let things get to [him]', and, while 'there's been a couple of issues when I've come close', he has 'thought of the kids, and going back, and it's just not worth it anymore'. For Glen – who 'ain't getting any younger' – his age and his children are motivators to stay out for good this time.

Notwithstanding a familiarity with guns and a propensity for violence that place him outside the pro-social norms of the wider community, Glen participates in 'normal' life: he has a small catamaran and enjoys sailing and kayaking with 'a mate'; he 'had a ball' helping out at his son's school swimming programme; and he relaxes by sitting in the backyard having a 'few beers' with his partner, or with 'mates'. Yet his greatest passion is motorbikes – building, fixing and riding them – as well as camping, which he does with friends and family.

After he got out, the job he had lined up in prison fell through: 'they've gone really quiet at the moment . . . there's no work there'. A boilermaker by trade, Glen can always make money welding and fixing things from home – cars, motorbikes, trailers, lawnmowers and brush cutters. Yet, since his release, it's been a struggle:

> Just all the bills rolling in at once, the car playing up, trying to find money – we're used to working and earning two, three grand a week, now we're getting $460 a fortnight, I don't know how people live on it . . . [My partner's] in a commission house so the rent's cheaper . . . she gets her money and then my money. We do it, it's still a struggle though.

He resents having to rely on income support and having to attend appointments, complaining: 'I'm sick of Centrelink harassing me, they harass me, parole harass me, I don't get many free days!'. He thus alludes to a sense of being corralled by administrative impediments to his freedom. I get the feeling that, if Glen were a younger man, he would not tolerate such impediments, which perhaps explains why jail has been such a familiar landscape.

The data reveal commonalities in how post-prison life is experienced and understood. The significance of having 'somewhere to go', 'a decent job' and the support of trusted friends or family, strongly expressed by the men and identified by the workers, clearly echoes Father Brosnan's mantra about the three things ex-prisoners need: a home, a job and a friend. Throughout the post-release literature, correlational research has noted the link between housing stability, employment, social support and reduced recidivism. The convergence in the findings confirms the importance of these domains. But, this book would offer little if it were simply to reproduce these well-established aspects of the post-prison experience. Attention turns instead to what its conceptual tools can uncover. In this chapter, the assemblage–culture–liminality lens is applied to the layers of meaning contained in Chapters 6 and 7. Three assemblages emerge as key elements of the post-prison experience, characterised by significant variation: home, identity and connection.

Now to briefly recap the main features of the three concepts shaping the analysis, beginning with assemblage theory: assemblages are networks of connections between interacting component parts. They are characterised by relations of exteriority, meaning that the identity of their parts is not constituted by their relations, so that parts may be unplugged from one assemblage and plugged into another, different assemblage. Further, assemblages are defined along two axes: (1) the stabilising lines of territorialisation, together with the destabilising lines of deterritorialisation, which cut across and carry it away; and (2) the pragmatic, material aspects of content at one end, and the expressive, discursive, signifying components at the other (Deleuze & Guattari, 1987; DeLanda, 2006).

The concept of culture applied in this book may be summarised as follows: culture as an analytic concept is differentiated from its 'totalising' form (Garland, 2006), as in 'prison culture'. Culture as semiotic practices (Wedeen, 2002) directs attention to meaning-making in practice, how actions are invested with meaning, and why meanings produce effects in behaviour, which builds on Swidler's (1986) 'culture-in-action' model. Swidler views culture as a 'toolkit' – a repertoire of habits, styles and skills that shape decision-making and govern action. Men's behaviour is guided and constrained by the cultural resources available to them, which are constituted by the meaning-making processes and practices in which they participate.

Liminality draws on rites-of-passage theory[1] to characterise the post-release state as one of social limbo, 'betwixt and between' release and reintegration. Liminality constitutes a psychosocial space outside, parallel to and beneath the lines of 'integrated' society. For its cyclic and most vulnerable inhabitants – the repeatedly imprisoned, the mentally ill or cognitively impaired, the drug addicted and homeless (Baldry et al., 2006; Baldry, Dowse et al., 2008; Peacock, 2008; Baldry, 2009) – this space is experienced as chronic exclusion. Liminality has a symbolic function too, as a transitional stage in a ritual process, enabling emergence into a new status of 'formerly imprisoned person'. These concepts of assemblage, culture and liminality shape the analysis that follows.

Home

As the post-release literature suggests, stable accommodation is the most critical factor influencing outcomes for released prisoners. The men and the workers confirmed that having 'somewhere' or 'nowhere' to go shaped men's experience of getting out, being out and staying out of prison, and that limited housing options constrained workers' capacity to help released prisoners stay out of jail. Men reported being released with a voucher for three nights in a motel as an interim solution to having nowhere to go. Squalid boarding houses shared with other ex-prisoners, drug users and the mentally unstable are frequently the only accommodation available. The dream of securing a transitional unit for 12 months is realised by very few, as there are just over 100 units, and Link Out alone services more than 500 clients each year. If this were simply a problem of housing supply, it would be relatively straightforward to ameliorate: if housing were provided for all released prisoners, none would be homeless. But 'home' is not simply a matter of having a roof over one's head: it is more than the security of a lease; more than the safety of a locked door. Home is a refuge, a place of belonging.

One key aspect of the problem for some men leaving prison is that prison is where they feel at home. For men who have experienced serial imprisonment, a sense of belonging arises from being known by and knowing more people on the inside than on the outside. This is partly indicative of the serial depletion of resources that Baldry and her colleagues (2003) describe, and that Grunseit et al. (2008) confirm. However, this may be seen equally as a loss of connection to the outside community and a solidification of connection to the community of men similarly flowing in and out and through the penal system. Becoming part of this flow engenders a strong sense of association, perhaps reflected in the use of the term 'associate' to describe affiliations among prisoners. The men and the workers suggest men's sense of being bonded to other prisoners solely, yet ineluctably, through the common experience of imprisonment. This link manifests variously, from men recognising other ex-prisoners in the street to 'mixing, living, and hanging with jailbirds' (Rob), and lacking additional social resources to be able to extricate themselves from the social obligations embedded in 'prison world'.

Thus, prison mores are seen to leak out into the post-release sphere, shadowing the everyday experience of men ostensibly released, yet 'stuck in prison world'. From a culture-in-action perspective, in prison, men position themselves in relation to others along lines of trust/distrust and allegiance. These positions are established and expressed through association and avoidance, roles that are performed and thus communicated. This performative aspect of prison culture apparently becomes habitual behaviour that is continued post-release and serves to maintain the social ties between prisoners, despite men's efforts to sever or 'dodge' them. As Rob explains, 'if you don't dodge them you get mixed up in their shit', suggesting the process ('getting mixed up in') of accretion of these associations in the outside world. The cultural retooling to enable these men to escape these connections involves, in effect, relearning how to be in the world. This demands a significant cultural investment from outside the individual that is unavailable to most men ensconced in imprisonment cycles, as explored below. In this way, men are drawn into a possibly uncomfortable, yet pervasive, sense of belonging with/connection to other prisoners.

In addition to, and emphasising, this phenomenon are the effects of imprisonment seen to characterise men's thinking and habituation, which Haney (2003) describes as 'normal adaptations' prisoners make in response to the 'abnormal conditions of prison life' (p. 38), evoking Clemmer's (1940) prisonisation thesis and the diminishing of men's cultural resources it implies. The adaptations Haney (2003: 40–6) identifies clearly resonate throughout the data: dependence on prison routines and regimes; the hypervigilance construed as 'the edge' (John); the lack of trust and suspicion men develop, their emotional hardening and containment, social isolation and withdrawal, adoption of prison norms of violence and domination, reduced self-esteem and post-traumatic stress reactions. The reduced sense of self-worth and feelings of being 'other' than, different to and apart from 'normal' society manifests as the paranoia released prisoners commonly report. These effects – notwithstanding their varying degrees, as the data show – nevertheless impinge on post-release life and relationships, most markedly when other stressors are present and compounded by social and economic disadvantage and marginalisation, as Haney (2003) described.

These psychological responses to the experience of imprisonment exemplify how culture is both producer and product of the carceral assemblage. Men's acculturation to prison routines, from Ben's gym regime to Rob getting his sugar for free, combined with the perceived pressures of everyday living – having to pay bills, keep appointments, travel distances on public transport – make outside life seem far more challenging than life in prison. This is the paradox of freedom that the workers so clearly articulate and the men variously convey. This means, for many, prison is a haven from life in the community: a safe, predictable, familiar environment that thus feels more like home than their outside home, as SW13's analogy between prison and 'a parent' suggests. Post-release life seems precarious in contrast to the stability and security of prison life. The pains of imprisonment (Sykes, 1958) thus manifest as the pains of release (Arrigo & Milovanovic, 2009), which are associated, for some and in different ways, with going 'home'.

One way of experiencing and conceptualising going home is release itself: being told 'you're going home, pack your shit' (Scott); the packing of belongings, the unlocking of doors, being let out; getting into a car or a train carriage and leaving the prison behind. The moment of freedom is brought into sharp relief by the heightened sensations associated with release: anticipation, anxiety, elation, dread. These are felt in the body, in the pit of the stomach and coursing adrenalin. The contrast between confinement and freedom is sharpened by the hyperreality of men's dreaming in the nights and days leading up to their release: the plans devised and hopes nurtured in the hours spent cocooned in pre-release chatter; men in conversation with themselves and with each other. There is plenty of time for talk in prison. These lines of talk become lines of flight, imagined, yet soon curtailed by the realisation that going 'home' is fraught with danger and uncertainty: returning to relationships patterned by conflict and emotional demands; the financial pressure of making ends meet; the lure of old habits, old 'mates'; couch-surfing or 'knocking about' on the streets. The euphoria of release is short-lived: to this, the men and workers attest. Going home is experienced as a dream in itself, and one from which men are abruptly awakened when they find themselves with nowhere to go, or with three nights in a motel room. Somehow, by adding a layer of temporariness, an additional transit zone, the latter seems to magnify the precariousness of release to homelessness.

The administration and allocation of housing stock constitute the molar lines of the post-release housing assemblage, the lines that territorialise its terrain and circumscribe men's experience of being homeless. Homelessness is a way of being that becomes familiar the more it is experienced. This familiarity holds a greater degree of comfort than depending on a housing worker's promise of accommodation that may never be fulfilled. Both the familiarity of having nowhere to go and the promise of housing are lines that territorialise the 'home' assemblage.

These molecular lines, supple compared with the rigid lines of administrative bureaucracy, are nonetheless repetitive, habitual and iterative. These lines describe the experience of uncertainty, instability and perpetual waiting. Inherently liminal, being homeless thus connects with the 'identity' assemblage (explored below), marked by lines of possibility – the promise of a waiting list, the dream of having a 'home' – weighed down by the reality of a bed here, a floor to sleep on there.

Being on a waiting list engenders a sense of anticipation sustained by hope. Hope is the line of flight that sustains the intention of some men to stay out of jail. It is the hook on which their imagined possibilities hang, yet also the snag on which their plans disintegrate. For some men, conflating into one problem all the difficulties they encounter in their post-prison interactions – both social and structural, from personal to societal – appears a way of managing and containing things that seem beyond their control. When homelessness or lack of housing is conceived as 'the problem', it becomes the locus of men's hope and, accordingly, the reason why their hopes are dashed, their expectations of freedom founder and their intentions falter. Investing all hope in one thing means not having to think about or address other problems. Relying on a worker to solve problems, such as 'housing', engenders an abrogation of responsibility to which the cultural tools men acquire in prison are well adapted; they are men habituated to having someone else do things for them. Thus, hope is seen as a sustaining force, yet also a line leading to and constituting a liminal psychosocial space.

Just as culture-in-action can be seen as causative, as producer and product of the carceral assemblage, so too can liminality. The meanings, signs and symbols – the '*semiotic system*' – and the '*pragmatic system*, actions and passions' (Deleuze & Guattari, 1987: 504) – comprise the 'territoriality of the assemblage' (p. 505). In terms of liminality, the exterior components of the experience of going home and of being homeless engender anticipation and uncertainty, the risk of disappointment, failure and defeat. These comprise: housing waiting lists and priority 'segments'; looming family court matters and criminal cases; Centrelink appointments and 'mutual obligations'; correctional orders to be completed; parole conditions to be met. Assembled, these constitute a social terrain of in-betweenness, neither here nor there; the landscape of men, neither locked up, nor yet entirely free. As Tom's investment of hope and expectation and reliance upon his 'housing worker' exemplifies, men may participate in a dynamic that situates them as 'clients' in relation to 'professionals' responsible for securing accommodation for them. Yet the reality of limited housing stock means this relationship hinges on structural uncertainty that renders it provisional, unresolved and therefore inherently liminal. Nick's experience of being 'housed' in a squalid room in a boarding house attests to this precariousness and the sense of defeat it can engender. Such meanings and symbols territorialise the 'home' assemblage.

The data show that the recurring experience of disappointment and defeat has the effect of deflating men's hopes, frustrating their intentions and progressively reducing their expectations of success. Once again evoking the serial depletion of resources (Baldry et al., 2003), this also signifies the internalisation of a liminal state of being. Men become accustomed to never quite getting there, so that 'liminality (living in a threshold) [becomes] a way of life' (Kelly, 2008: 335). In contrast to the euphoria of release, the emotional landscape of this state appears characterised by despondency, despair and hopelessness. The bleakness of the liminal landscape and its inherent instability can induce a forgetting, whereby men recall the structure and safety of the prison world and yearn for the familiarity and security it provides.

In contrast to the accumulated disappointment and despair experienced post-release, prison represents the setting with which emotional connections and feelings of elation are associated, albeit in relation to getting out. The experience of emotional intensity linked to the prison world contrasts sharply with the post-prison experience of men 'having to battle every time they turn around, battle and battle and battle' (Paul). The positive aspects of being locked up – constant company, having everything provided for you, knowing where you stand – serve to reinforce the isolation, loneliness and not knowing how to fit in, in the outside world. For these reasons, and stabilised by these symbolic meanings, prison can feel like home.

Another meaning of home is 'other': the ideal of a safe, stable place to live and sustain a life outside prison as somehow belonging to the experience of others; 'normal' people perceived as subscribing to a different set of norms and values. Nick hints at this when he describes his aunt as belonging to a different world – 'she's straight' – one in which his place is only fleeting, temporary. For such men with no prior experience of this 'other' ('straight', 'normal') home, it remains an ideal: a dream held with little hope of being realised. This way of experiencing is in sharp contrast to the experience of men for whom prison held no sense of belonging, men (such as Matt, Dale, Wayne) just passing through, for whom 'home' means the haven to which they return following their release. Going home means having a pre-prison life to resume, albeit gradually: family, friends, a sense of familiarity and belonging; a life associated with places, spaces, people and patterns deeply engraved in memory and upon which the imprint of imprisonment leaves a mere shadow. For these men, home means the support and stability they left behind and to which they now return.

A 'home' is clearly one of the most important things people need upon their release from prison, but it is much more than 'a place to live that is decent'.[2] The key element in the experience of post-release housing is the need for stability, security and belonging, which is critical in either intensifying or lessening the experience of liminality. For men whose need for stability, security and belonging is accommodated in the prison setting, release is experienced as uncertain, unstable and chaotic. Their precariousness is magnified by symbolic and physical gestures, such as 'three nights in a motel room'. Without stable accommodation, men's ability to parent, to engage with services (parole conditions, mental health or drug treatment, and so on), to seek or find work is destabilised. Having to rely on housing assistance makes them vulnerable to a lack of dominion and to recurring disappointment and defeat. The interaction of these factors deepens the experience of liminality, of being no longer a prisoner and not quite a citizen. Where the need for stability, security and belonging is met outside the prison, in having somewhere to go and finding a space of one's own, the ex-prisoner's liminal status can begin to recede. These differences in men's experience of home, or being home*less*, interact in important ways with their sense of belonging in prison and the ways in which a prison identity develops internally and manifests outwardly. These variations are now explored.

Identity

The idea that a prisoner becomes an ex-prisoner once he walks out through the prison gates to freedom is belied by the data, and by wider conceptions of desistance as 'a process . . . not an event' (McNeill et al., 2005: 30). Indeed, this process of becoming may take a lifetime, as Maruna (2001) suggests and John and SW22 attest. As the data show, the embodied experience of release and the mental and psychological awakening to being no longer imprisoned are not experienced in the same way. Just as imprisonment is experienced differently, so is release. Applying the assemblage–culture–liminality lens illuminates the processes of being and becoming associated with this multiplicity of experience. This part of the analysis comprises four assemblages: being an ex-prisoner, being a drug user, being unemployed and being a father. These are explored in turn.

Being an ex-prisoner

Being an ex-prisoner begins with the experience of being imprisoned and released. Prison assemblages are territorialised physically and symbolically: their human parts designated, marked and classified by sentences to imprisonment, bail applications denied, orders for remand to custody, risk/need assessments; bodies contained by barred windows, locked doors and gates, the walled and bounded spaces of cells, prisoner transport vehicles, prison yards and buildings. Behaviour is governed and controlled by penal temporal and spatial regimes. Prisoners become acculturated to (SW12) and dependent upon the rigid strictures of prison life in the process of institutionalisation. Prisoner identities emerge through the interaction between internal 'subpersonal components' (DeLanda, 2006: 32, 52), and men expressing what Goffman (1967: 1) describes as 'the external signs of orientation and involvement – states of mind and body'. Yet, unlike Goffman's (1967) shifting social entity, 'created by arrivals and killed by departures' (p. 2), prison assemblages are maintained and fed, their signs reiterated, through the looping cycles of arrival and departure that characterise the prison world.

The men and workers talk about elements of prison language and culture, for example, that seep through the prison system via these human flows. These elements are assemblages in themselves, each emerging from the interaction among its parts – words, signs, symbols, tattoos, individual prisoners, prisoner groupings, particular prisons – and each subsequently able to affect the other parts (DeLanda, 2006). Whereas prisons contain bounded, localised, high-density assemblages, territorialised by the prison form described above, post-prison assemblages are by nature dispersed and low density, deterritorialised by the physical release of men from prison. Their lines continue nonetheless. Being an ex-prisoner is shadowed by parts of the prison assemblage that are not contained by concrete walls and steel bars: the expressive, non-material components that are nevertheless capable of constraining and enabling its human components; evidence that 'you can take the man out of the prison, but you cannot take the prison out of the man' (Matthews, 2008).

Ex-prisoner assemblages are territorialised by the reach of the correctional arm. The 'pragmatic system' (Deleuze & Guattari, 1987: 504) of parole appointments, conditions requiring attendance at drug and alcohol clinics, and methadone queues serve to maintain the lines and territory of post-prison assemblages, as the men attest. Contiguous to the virtual space of public housing waiting lists and welfare-to-work regimes, boarding houses marked by squalor and instability constitute physical spaces where ex-prisoners gather. These places become nodes of post-prison activity, continuity and performance; places where prison selves are carried as hand-luggage. Thus, prisoner assemblages are re-territorialised, their cultural resources, norms and tools reissued and reinforced. But, what of the variation between men's differing sense of (post-)prison identity and of being and becoming an ex-prisoner?

There are embodied ways of being an ex-prisoner, a set of habits and acculturations that manifest in physicality: a man's walk, his posture; his way of observing those around him without looking at them; the rolling of a cigarette, the brand of tobacco he carries, as the data reveal. The theme 'prison ingrained in me', for instance, reveals men's conception of their behaviour and aspects of their identity as shaped by and infused with prison culture (habits, styles, skills). Scott's account of his adoption of prison norms of violence and retribution show how the repertoire of skills and habits learnt through his imprisonment constrains the capacities from which he constructs his strategies of action (Swidler, 1986) in a post-prison setting. Glen similarly evokes having to restrain his inclination towards violence by considering 'the risk' and it 'not being worth it', thus drawing on a wider set of resources in constructing a new way of being, as explored below. At the other extreme, a subtle aspect of prison culture is embedded in Wayne's continued smoking of White Ox since his release.

These extremes illustrate variations in ex-prisoner ways of being: Scott's toothbrush and razor-blade weaponry symbolises his absorption of prison norms of pre-emptive and retributive violence. His prisoner identity, donned as protective armour and then reinforced through repeated performance, has congealed around him like a carapace. Notwithstanding his regret at being 'like that', Scott attests to prison being 'ingrained' in him physically and psychologically, so that his prison identity inhabits his whole being; he cannot imagine being any other way. Having spent most of his adult life behind bars, his identity has been forged in the crucible of prison culture. In contrast, men such as Matt, Dale or Wayne, who were imprisoned once and maintained a strong sense of not belonging there, leave with imprints perceptible only to the experienced eye, such as the tobacco they carry.

Smoking 'Ox' is nonetheless a badge worn by ex-prisoners and signifies a habit ingrained in the body and in thinking. The function of this habit emerges through Sampson and Bean's (2006) characterisation of Swidler's (1986) 'culture in action': It is intersubjective, in that it is created through social interaction. It is performative, in that, as a ritual performed, it expresses and reiterates its social function with every performance, punctuating the daily routine and thus structuring the passing of time. It is affective-cognitive, in that it arises out of impulse, association and habit rather than rational decision-making. It is relational in terms of being a tool men use to position themselves in relation to other prisoners, to cement alliances and avert conflict. It is world-making, in that it locates the individual prisoner within the social network of the prison and reproduces this position each time tobacco is bought or exchanged, a cigarette is rolled or smoked. The rules and codes around tobacco can be seen to reflect broader prison norms and values, such as borrowing something and not paying it back: 'in prison, that's the big no-no' (Wayne).

The subtle imprint of a tobacco habit can be seen to carry within it the deeper lines of ways of being in prison that remain etched in a man's psyche and become part of his identity. Although the implications of a 'toxic' prison identity are clear, recalling Kupers' (2005) toxic masculinity, what impact might the smoking of a particular brand of tobacco have on a man's integrative capacity or risk of reimprisonment? What are the implications of these subtle layers of identity for a man's sense of being and becoming? As noted, there are embodied ways of being an ex-prisoner, which persist after release. These are the shadows that ex-prisoners perceive and recognise in each other: words, expressions, gestures, clothes, particular styles of footwear. The significance of men's footwear signifying identity, as Jewkes (2005a) notes, is revealed in the data: 'it's a real status thing . . . they all wear similar types of trainers . . . [and] they have to be particular brands and models' (SW05). These are the signs, symbols and meanings associated with prison life. As long as these shadows persist, men's memory of having been imprisoned inhabits their bodies, their thinking and, therefore, their sense of self. This explains ex-prisoners' shame and fear of discovery, their sense of not fitting in, of not quite belonging, that thread through the men's and workers' accounts. These outward signs and symbols may also signify the persistence of a liminal state, of stasis rather than transition, of being rather than becoming, of which Arrigo and Milovanovic (2009) warn.

These lines of expression are territorialising in that, through the process of repetition, they stabilise the assemblage of being an ex-prisoner: every time an ex-prisoner rolls a cigarette with 'Ox', or is recognised by an ex-prisoner in the street, this process occurs. A personal identity is stabilised to the extent that 'habitual or routine associations are constantly maintained' (DeLanda, 2006: 50), and may be destabilised by the 'augmentation of capacities' or 'the acquisition of new skills' (p. 50), through cultural retooling (Swidler, 1986). However, ex-prisoner identities are also subject to the territorialising forces of external forms of expression and content that are constantly reiterated and reinforced. These include having a criminal record and having employment possibilities curtailed, or not being issued a passport. Being an ex-prisoner is thus, not only experienced internally, but reaffirmed externally in a way that constrains the transformative potential of post-release liminal states (Turner, 1982; Jewkes, 2005b) and delimits ex-prisoners 'becoming' what they '*could be*' (Arrigo & Milovanovic, 2009: 151, original emphasis).

The inner dimensions of being an ex-prisoner encompass, to varying degrees, the sense of uncertainty and risk associated with being known to police and being caught for something, particularly for men engaging in illicit drug use or activity for which they could be arrested and reimprisoned. Men with a history of repeat imprisonment thus inhabit a liminal space between prison and the community (Baldry et al., 2006; Baldry, Dowse et al., 2008; Baldry, 2009), the 'third space' to which Peacock (2008) refers, where they are neither locked up nor wholly free. This space is characterised by the perceived inevitability of reimprisonment, related resignedly yet pragmatically, and indicative of the extent to which being an ex-prisoner suffuses and inflects the identity of its inhabitants. Rob, waiting 'until they find something else to lock me up for', palpably conveys his resignation to this fate. This resignation explains why men are inclined to continue using illicit drugs to cope with their predicament. The key element in the experience of being an ex-prisoner seems to be the extent to which men's self-concept intersects with, and is mirrored or reinforced by, their interactions with others. Being a drug user is similarly a self-identity and a socio-legal-normative designation.

Being a drug user

Being a drug user – when plugged into an assemblage comprising lines of criminal law, criminal records, drug courts and treatment programmes – is seen as transgressive behaviour that generates an increased risk of arrest and reimprisonment. Yet, the same term can express a multiplicity of meanings: the self-medication function of substances such as ice ('to feel happy') or Valium ('for my anxiety'); the stabilising familiarity of methadone; the enjoyment of smoking 'a few cones' or drinking 'a few cans', signifying the normalisation of drug use and even a man's sense of being in control of this aspect of his identity. Thus, between assemblages, 'a relation may change without the terms changing' (Deleuze, 2002, in DeLanda, 2006: 11). The drug using remains the same; the meaning and framing of it vary.

A drug-user identity is territorialised through habitual repetition and through the acquisition of skills associated with using: the knowledge acquired through involvement and participation in the drug world, seeking out, buying, sharing, ritualising, experimenting, mixing and enjoying the use of various forms of stimulant and sedative; the connections to other users ('druggie mates'); and the activities associated with stealing to get money (burglary, robbery, mugging, thieving): being 'a heroin addict just doing what he needs to, to get his heroin' (Scott). Underlying the multiplicities of being a drug user, directly or indirectly expressed, is the manifest need or desire to escape pain, fear, boredom or despair. And, although drug use functions to numb these feelings in the short term, it also has the effect of amplifying rather than diminishing their causes. In this way, drug use produces and perpetuates liminality. Its framing as transgressive – legally and socially – locates users outside the law. Its stigma diminishes social bonds through perceptions of danger and mistrust, and limits users' access to health and medical care. These are the external lines of liminality. Internally, too, a space of being 'neither here nor there' is maintained by the physical and psychological nature of addiction and craving: perpetually going up or coming down. The search for the plateau of satiation is driven by the memory of craving's fleeting cessation.

Anxiety is a particular line constituting and recursively stabilising the drug-user assemblage. A mental phenomenon, anxiety is also embodied, its physical sensations associated with physiological responses to stressors. Dependency on any addictive substance naturally gives rise to anxiety as an element of the withdrawal phenomenon, and the craving for more of the substance, and yet this particular stressor did not feature in the men's accounts. Rather, men talked about their anxiety as a chronic symptom arising from or intensified through their experience of imprisonment, which accords with Haney's (2003) account of the psychological effects of incarceration. They talked about their drug or alcohol use as a way of managing or coping with their anxiety, yet without attributing any causal link to their long-term use. The men conceived their anxiety as a chronic condition, a disability that they managed, albeit largely through illicit drug use, yet that also constrained their freedom in terms of employment or training prospects. Thus, the men decentred their drug and alcohol use as 'the problem', instead placing anxiety squarely at its centre, one over which they assumed no sense of control or responsibility. This cycle was conceived in conflicting terms by workers, whose conceptions shed a different light.

Workers' conceptions challenged men's account of their drug and alcohol problems and thus destabilise the 'being a drug user' assemblage. Workers saw men's use of drugs to manage or cope with difficult or uncomfortable feelings or situations as part of a broader lack of skills and capacities associated with the social and economic disadvantage of ex-prisoner populations. This disadvantage can be explained in part by the constraints on their cultural resources caused by their experience of poverty, lack of education, family breakdown and various forms of abuse and trauma, and exacerbated by their acculturation to criminal and prison norms, styles, skills and habits, and the social connections forged through imprisonment. Workers also perceived men's superficial sense of dominion over their drug use, manifest in talk such as 'detox – I need to go there' – as SW13 explains, not 'because they want to stop – they are saying "[I] want to get back in control of my drug use"'. This evokes a similar sense of identity as being homeless, as described above. A sense of being moving parts in a larger system, territorialised by workers, programmes, services, other users, ex-users, and being as familiar with this territory as with the knowledge, habits and patterns of thinking and behaviour it assumes.

The repetition inhering in drug habits and dependency has built into it its own territorialising force: every hit, every instance of 'getting on the gear', is shadowed by the push and pull of craving, an undertow experienced in the blood, flesh and follicles, driving muscle and bone. These physical aspects felt in the body are resolved through further use of the satiating substance. The habits and skills – the cultural repertoire of drug use – are also reiterated through continued use, though in a way that feeds the pervading sense of loss from which men are seeking escape. This is implied when men talk about their shame and concealment of their ongoing drug use, or their disillusionment with 'druggie mates'. Again, these expressive components of the drug-user assemblage serve to produce and perpetuate a sense of being outside the 'straight' world, on the edge of the law, and therefore in a liminal state of in-betweenness.

The issue of men feeling in control of drug use emerges throughout the data, perhaps as an antidote to the inherent uncertainty and instability of liminality. Workers, experienced in the reality of addiction, treatment and relapse, note with scepticism men's claims of being 'in control'. Among the men, a sense of resignation is apparent, most strongly expressed in relation to methadone, which none of them chooses to take, yet upon which their daily functioning depends. Indeed, methadone treatment might be conceived as an assemblage in itself, so strong are its lines of territorialisation: its legality; its provision by prescription; its dispensing, often by a trusted professional, at a local pharmacy – the clean brightness of this physical location somehow intensifying the legitimacy of its supply; its addictive nature and relief of physical symptoms and pain; its incorporation into poly-drug use; the familiarity among users; and the extent to which these aspects serve to stabilise the 'methadone-user' identity.

So, what are the 'cutting edges of deterritorialisation' (Deleuze & Guattari, 1987: 505) that cut across these lines? They are the end of parole or a correctional order requiring methadone treatment, the gradual reduction of the prescribed dose and eventually 'getting off' methadone altogether. The latter being expressed as an ideal, a future hope, signifies the control this pharmacotherapeutic regime wields over men, entrenching them in relations of dependence, as perpetual clients, patients or service users. Rob's 'being an eight or nine' – symbolising his possibility of recovery or rehabilitation or 'getting better' – exemplifies this line, this aspiration to freedom. Yet, beyond this line is an unknown, a stepping off into a void, as this component is connected to lines territorialising other assemblages: being homeless, being an ex-prisoner, being unemployed, being a father, and lacking social support or connection to community. For some men (such as Rob), the connections within and between these assemblages are the lines that constitute the broader reincarceration assemblage (Halsey, 2007), the web in which they are caught. Thus, the only line of hope and possibility of freedom that cuts across and deterritorialises a drug-user assemblage – the thought of 'getting better' – can be the same line that serves to territorialise it, reiterating and delimiting its cultural repertoire and constituting its inherent liminality. Central to the experience of being a drug user, then, is the interaction between its functional aspects and its addictive and criminalising aspects, which produces a state of liminality, inside yet outside the bounds of law-abiding society. From this interaction arises the risk of reimprisonment, which amplifies the experience of liminality.

Being unemployed

The men similarly experienced being unemployed as a liminal space, comprising lines of exclusion, immobility and disengagement. Men conveyed an implicit sense of powerlessness, of being becalmed, and a lack of dominion or capacity to change their circumstances due to unemployment. This powerlessness manifests as pragmatism and resignation, as the following signifies: 'I've got a Year 8 pass and I've got criminal convictions. I can't become a doctor' (Paul). Having a record, compounded by people's knowledge of their having been in prison, gave men a sense of otherness, of being 'different'. This manifests as perceived inferiority – 'as soon as they know you've been inside they just look down their nose and ignore you' (Glen) – and feelings of insecurity and fear: 'someone's going to ask and say, "You've got a record, get out"' (Matt). A further signifying element of this assemblage is the loss of confidence and self-esteem. Any sense of self-worth not already diminished through imprisonment (Haney, 2003) is further depleted by the powerlessness associated with the limited opportunities for men with criminal records – education, skills and training (or their lack) notwithstanding. These are the practical, real-world aspects of post-prison unemployment.

Less frequently expressed in the data was Rob's fatefulness, verging on melodrama: 'I can't guarantee a boss that I'll live long enough to work for them'. His haplessness, lacing a bitter reality with irony – 'some jobs I can't work in anymore because I don't like people telling me what to do after a year and a half of it [in prison]' – expresses the institutionalised, inflexible thinking that workers observed. This acculturated cognition reveals the extent to which, for men 'stuck in prison world', cultural resources are limited to those at hand, and prison mores are reproduced on the outside. Prison thinking generates lines that territorialise the liminal space associated with being unemployed: men's claims of being unemployable, unable to do certain things because of the experience of imprisonment, imply the 'dis-ability' to which SW12 alluded. When conceived as disability or inability, this space closes in around men, foreshortening their horizons and diminishing hopes for the future. 'Being unemployed' and 'being an ex-prisoner' are thus seen as connected and overlapping components in the broader carceral assemblage.

Another line of liminality comprises the material aspects of men having outstanding 'legal issues' (civil and criminal cases) and being known to police, issues perceived as shadows 'hanging over their heads' associated with their criminal records and relationships in conflict. This sense of insecurity, imminent threat and risk of reimprisonment, together with the feeling of being in limbo it engenders, means men feel unable to commit to a job, as Rob indicates: 'I told myself I won't work again until I beat this case. It's too head-fucking'. The lines stabilising the carceral assemblage – a criminal record, being on parole, police attention, criminal associates and behaviour including drug use, disrupted and dysfunctional relationships outside prison – militate against men's capacity for employment and create the structural and social barriers to integration. These lines thus inscribe post-prison circuits of exclusion (Rose, 2000).

The lines and patterns of these circuits not only impede men's potential rehabilitation, they constitute their *dis*-habilitation. Workers conceive men's diminished capacity as a state of dis-ability from which severe marginalisation ensues, because 'they don't function well' (SW12). They are 'dis-abled' (SW12), 'dis-habilitated' (SW22). To deterritorialise the 'reincarceration assemblage' in which these men are entangled, they first need to be 'habilitated' (SW22). Yet, grounding and connecting this to other post-prison assemblages are lines of disability, tangibly represented in the physical and mental health problems that constitute many of the men's post-release morbidity: depression, anxiety, cognitive impairment, epilepsy and hepatitis C; hospitalisation associated with drug use; and injury and trauma arising from incidents with police or in prison. Some conditions are caused or exacerbated by imprisonment; some involve prescribed medication, such as methadone and benzodiazepines. For Scott, Rob and Nick, for example, these aspects of their ill health constrain their capacity to work, limit their possibilities and curtail their experience of freedom. Being on a disability pension, moreover, constitutes a recursive loop of social and economic exclusion.

Intersecting and carrying away the lines of liminality, though, are lines of flight in the form of generative opportunities conceived by the men, signifying both the creative potential arising from the post-prison experience and the social structural barriers to that creativity, which stifle men's reintegrative possibilities. These barriers are perceived as unfair and irrational. Employment is a clear pathway to social integration and economic participation, and yet the skills men acquire in prison have limited use on the outside. For instance, some of the men were 'peer educators', mentors to other prisoners, and completed training and counselling programmes equipping them with skills to fulfil that role. As Glen explains, however, 'it's qualifications that I've got that I can't use outside 'cos you don't pass the police check'. This inability to transfer skills learnt in prison means that rehabilitation efforts become lines that 'get caught in a rut, or disappear into "black holes"' (Deleuze, 1980, in Halsey, 2007: 1247) beyond prison walls. This renders supposed rehabilitation programmes meaningless – 'a joke' (Glen) – simply another management tool, a way to pass prison time. Significantly, these lines that promise creativity and signify transformative potential become opportunities wasted, with Five8 a notable exception, as discussed below. Several men expressed the possibility of using the experience of imprisonment to help other men getting out, such as 'a mob set up, that's just run by ex-crims that can . . . try and point other crims in the right direction' (Glen). Such expressions of empathic concern represent opportunities for generativity that presage rehabilitative potential.[3]

The cultural aspects of prison life include the sense of 'doing what needs to be done', which usually translates into behaviour arising from threat or conflict within the prisoner hierarchy, as conveyed in stories of violence and retribution. Also embedded in prison codes is the fierce desire to preserve honour and protect the innocent from injustice, a powerful motivator for some men to offer help to those they perceive as willing to receive it. Significantly, this aspect features in the accounts of the two workers who had experienced imprisonment themselves (SW06 and SW22). This represents an important intersection of worker–ex-prisoner experience; of post-prison meaning and action; of lines of flight that transect and transcend professional–client boundaries. The apparent kindness of prisoners (Burnett & Maruna, 2006) suggests an unseen and therefore under-utilised potential for usefulness among men released from prison to help each other stay out of prison. Such a strengths-based perspective sees men as assets to be utilised in the community, 'rather than merely liabilities to be supervised'[4] (Travis, 2000: 7).

The 'post-release problem' of unemployment evokes the disadvantage characterising a significant proportion of prisoners, lacking education, skills and work experience. Yet, the problem with this conception is twofold. First, it ignores social-structural barriers to employment, such as criminal record checking and employers' misconceptions about 'offenders', and the role of the community in integrating ex-prisoners. Second, it fails to account for the heterogeneity of post-prison experience. Several of the men were struggling with self-perceptions of unemployability, mirrored by their experience of long-term unemployment. Some have 'never had a job . . . no experience at being job ready or . . . punctuality' (SW13). Others – Matt and Dale, for instance – despite initial misgivings, found work relatively easily. This can be seen as largely owing to pre-prison resources on which they were able to draw in the form of strong social support and non-criminal identity. This contrasted with the embodied expression of being an ex-prisoner, a drug user or a 'crim', to which other men attested, verbally and physically. Though all those interviewed expressed a desire to work or at least do something constructive with their time, the men and workers all spoke of others who had 'no intention' of 'going straight', men who had every intention to 'run amok' and who would, therefore, inevitably return to custody before long. These divergent currents territorialise the 'being unemployed' assemblage. Although the reintegrative promise of ongoing work was universally acknowledged in the data – a line of flight promising hope – also revealed were the social perceptions of ex-prisoners as homogeneous, risky, not-to-be-trusted, which block men's integrative potential.

Can this potential be fully realised within the confines of programmatic post-release solutions? Do the parameters of deficit-based, risk-focused supervisory regimes or goal-oriented desistance-planning models enable human flourishing? Arrigo and Milovanovic (2009) argue not: their transdesistance concept evokes an alternative vision of the 'subject-in-process', a conception of men becoming other than they are, within 'relational contexts' (p. 134), rather than on their own, as the singular 'offender', the individual risk-bearer. The implications for post-release support are clear: workers unwittingly participate in the reiteration and reduction of men's 'identities to singularities, imaging [him] as nothing more or other than a client/offender indistinguishable from all others . . . [thus] rending the becoming self inaccessible, unrecognizable, and unspeakable' (Arrigo & Milovanovic, 2009: 151). Without opportunity for authentic human engagement and interaction and the personal investment that professional–client dynamics preclude, as the data suggest, ex-prisoners' capacity to shake off the stigma of being an 'offender' is forever constrained.

Men's designation as 'customers' or 'clients', by virtue of their engagement with Centrelink and employment services, temporarily overrides their 'ex-offender' or 'ex-prisoner' status, at least until such labels register on a computer screen. The possibility of engaging in an equal transaction between service provider and customer is withdrawn as quickly as it is presented. These are the administrative lines of the post-carceral assemblage that limit freedom. On a human level, men experienced as a lack of dominion the liminal status produced by being 'an offender', never 'quite fitting in' (SW22), implicit in that 'people look down their noses at you' (Glen). The social construction of identity, solidified in language and labels such as 'offender', yet concealed by others such as 'customer' or 'client', serves to contain and define men as perpetual problems, released yet imprisoned by their past. Such constructions belie the porosity or flexibility of social states, and men's capacity to move within and between them. Where, then, lies the possibility of reintegration? Getting a job, being employed, being useful, allows men to move beyond being a client to being a producer or provider, the inherent creativity of which constitutes the process of *becoming*.

Central to the experience of post-prison unemployment is men's self-identity as employable or unemployable, and the hope or despondency this gives rise to, and the way these factors interact with the experience of having a criminal record and its limitations on their future. This interaction seems to hinge on the nature and extent of men's inner and outer resources, enabled or constrained by their pre-prison capacities and experiences. Enclosing this experience are the stigma of imprisonment and accompanying community perceptions of ex-prisoners, which limit opportunities for reintegration and perpetuate social and economic exclusion. These factors highlight the importance of post-liminal ritual (formal or informal) that can alleviate or close down the experience of liminality.

Being a father

Being a father can signify creativity, generativity, possibility and growth. Yet it is an identity destabilised, deterritorialised, ruptured by the experience of imprisonment. Its lines of connection, familiarity and confidence are dragged down a 'black hole' (Deleuze, 1980, in Halsey, 2007: 1247) by the physical separation and emotional constriction that imprisonment effects. The image of a black hole evokes the chasm, the dark space of shame and loss felt by men whose actions have separated them from their children and sunk a well of pain, as some of the men variously evoke, echoing Walker's (2010) findings. The cultural resources available to fathers in prison, via parenting and relationship programmes, are offset by the physical and psychological constraints of the prison setting, which diminish a prisoner's capacity to feel like a father to his children. This sense of powerlessness, observed by Rosenberg (2009), is reinforced by men's sense of their children's lives proceeding without them, which undermines parenting confidence and capacity. Such deterritorialising effects of prison life and prison culture make fathering beyond bars difficult.

Prisoners' 'hangover identities' (Rosenberg, 2009), revealed in the data, exemplify the prisonisation processes that can diminish men's capacity to father and connect with their children post-release. These identities may be internalised, via men's own lack of confidence and reduced habituation to being a parent, or ascribed externally by other family members judging men's parenting capacity as diminished, unreliable or inherently flawed by virtue of their crimi-nality. Nevertheless, being a father emerges as an important site of identity and difference in the men's experience, and in their motivation and capacity to stay out of jail.[5] The pain and powerlessness some prisoners, such as Ben, feel being separated from their family may also steel men's resolve to make things better, to desist from crime and provide a more stable life for their children (Brown & O'Sullivan, 2013). This seems particularly so for older men (Vinson & Tehan, 2001), as the data suggest: John and Glen, for instance, are both men in their 40s, motivated to leave crime behind for the sake of their children.

Fatherhood consists of lines that constitute post-prison identity to varying degrees. One line that is both territorialising and deterritorialising is the father in conflict, engaged in family court battles and waging war against enforced separa-tion; the man desperate for involvement in his children's lives, perhaps to make up for faulty fathering lines in his own. Paul, for example, has a history of fam-ily instability and childhood offending and lacks pro-social supports, and yet his self-identity as a father and his focus on his children's well-being have apparently inoculated him against the punishing or damaging effects of imprisonment, and underpins his desire to find 'stability'. Other lines constitute failure and absence, again seen to arise in lives characterised by family breakdown, neglect and crimi-nality. Men such as Rob have children too, and yet, as their paternal role has been diminished by circumstance and capacity, fatherhood does not appear to have the same sustaining effect. Moreover, as a repeat remand prisoner, Rob has had little opportunity to engage in programmes or rehabilitative opportunities in prison to enhance his capabilities or expand his cultural resources. These lines are broken, 'destructive, sketching death' (Deleuze, 1980, in Halsey, 2007: 1247) for any meaningful fathering role.

Other lines stabilising this assemblage are constituted by the reintegrative attempts of men, such as Ben, whose efforts are wholly underpinned by his com-mitment to being a father to his children. Though several studies[6] confirm the role of family in sustaining men's reintegration, fewer acknowledge the impor-tance of the fathering function as a potentially ripe reintegrative site. Workers describe men disheartened by custody battles and their children's lives proceed-ing without them, who nevertheless seek counselling to address their emotional problems: 'being locked up, it has forced him to review his life' (SW13). Other men are motivated by their children to take action 'in the right direction' (SW13), to demonstrate their commitment to changing.

The data suggest the critical role of active fathering in shaping post-prison iden-tities leaning towards change and transformation, and leaving prison behind; as well as the force of lines that destabilise being a father, showing how a component in one assemblage has different relations in another. This different perspective highlights the 'becomingness' inhering in being a father, arising perhaps out of its dynamic set of relationships with developing children and, hence, the chang-ing nature of the role. It appears that, when the territorialising lines of being a father act as an anchor, whereby this identity is stabilised through opportunities for repetition, and although post-release liminality may persist in many ways, it can become transformative, a site of becoming, of metamorphosis (Turner, 1986; Maruna, 2001; Jewkes, 2005b), of emergent subjectivity (DeLanda, 2006). Being a father can thus be characterised as liminoid (Turner, 1982) rather than liminal: creative and active, rather than static and passive.

Being a father can cut across lines territorialising 'client' identities. As mentioned above, being a 'client' evokes the 'empowerment' paradigm underpinning many programmatic approaches to transformation and behavioural change that engender a 'situated and finite being' as their subject and thereby limit 'becoming, evolving and transforming' (Arrigo & Milovanovic, 2009: 141). According to this argument, men can become locked into fixed molar identities, such as offender or recovering subject (p. 142). Fatherhood emerges as lines of flight, 'vital and creative' (Deleuze, 1980, in Halsey, 2007: 1247), deterritorialising the molar identities that stabilise the in-betweenness of being an offender, an ex-prisoner. 'These creative and vital lines open up an assemblage, rather than close it down' (Deleuze, 1980, in Halsey, 2007: 1247), and thus become liminoid in their effects, enabling men's cultural retooling via their investment in the lives of others. This focus on their children as a motivating force invokes the power of generativity in enabling and sustaining post-prison change, as Glen's involvement in his son's school beach programme exemplifies – an opportunity for 'normal' community participation, as a 'father', not an 'offender' or 'ex-prisoner'. Being a father thus leads to connection, to possibilities for community participation, acceptance and integration.

These components of identity each centre on the ways in which men's self-concept interacts with the identity ascribed by others and associated with their behaviour or experience. These interactions can lock men into identities, such as 'ex-prisoner' or 'drug user' or 'client', that operate to solidify their liminal status and the experience of being other, outside the 'normal'. Release from this state requires connection to a community in which they can participate.

Connection

The 'connection' assemblage is constituted by internal and external lines of identity, emanating from inside and arising outside the prison. These lines comprise men's varying conception and experience of being connected to other people: having social support and finding stability through that connection, a sense of being moored; or, conversely, of being unmoored, disconnected, 'other' than 'normal', 'straight' society. Between men with the common experience of imprisonment, the lines of connection vary. Some are subtle, faint pencil lines, testament to a fading past. Others are more enduring, reinforced through familiarity and shared experiences, deeply inscribing the present with webs of connectivity that shape and delineate identity. These lines are reissued in methadone queues and Centrelink offices, boarding houses and street corners, places where ex-prisoners gather and prison continuities are sustained. These storylines feed the connections that sustain men's exclusion from non-prisoner society. They mark out ex-prisoner territory as social, cultural and physical 'zones of exclusion' existing 'outside the circuits of inclusion – in "marginalized" space' (Rose, 2000: 331).

The most vulnerable inhabitants of these spaces are men such as Rob, with mental health disorders and/or cognitive impairments, whose often low-level, drug-related offending means short-term cyclic reimprisonment (Baldry, Dowse et al., 2008; Baldry, 2009), frequently through their self-medicating drug use. Thus criminalised, ex-prisoners who are drug-using, unemployed and homeless are deemed risky, albeit they are entangled in lines that mean their day-to-day activities and interactions heighten their susceptibility to police attention, arrest, bail refusal, remand and thus reimprisonment. The criminalisation of their activity ensnares these men in 'an array of micro-circuits, micro-cultures of non-citizens, failed citizens, anti-citizens . . . either attached to no moral community or to a community of anti-morality' (Rose, 2000: 331). Thus, the connections forged in prison manifest as intensities, nodes of activity, microcircuits that constitute the broader post-carceral assemblage.

John evokes a 'micro-culture' of 'failed citizens' when he describes his repeated efforts at drug rehabilitation: 'I was always failing. Within a week of me being released I'd have a full-on heroin habit again'. Despite his knowing who to ask for help and 'a lot of services', the pull and gratification of addiction were stronger than the desire to desist. His account of how good intentions slip and falter is revealing:

> I've had times when I was released and I had all the good intentions and felt serious in myself, felt good about it, very resolute and . . . I'd come out and I'd just have no one, nothing to do and I'd go nuts, I'd go stir crazy. I'd be able to maintain it for a month or whatever, but sure enough after a few months or a year or whatever, it just got too lonely and too boring. I'd look for company and female companionship and I'd go back to that life to find friendship and somebody to talk to and something to do and sure enough I'd become involved in it again and end up using again and the snowball effect takes place. . . . Before I know it I'm in jail again.

John's connection to 'that life', the community of drug users, law-breakers, is symbolic of both failure and function. His heroin habit perpetuated a cycle of crime and imprisonment. Yet, heroin functioned as an antidote to loneliness and boredom: *friendship and somebody to talk to and something to do.* In contrast to the challenges of sustaining good intentions, alone, heroin provided a set of patterns, activities and interactions that were familiar and effortless – 'scoring' and 'shooting up', a set of skills and habits well honed through repetition. Accompanying and augmenting the biochemical processes of addiction, these aspects made leaving heroin behind almost unbearable. Desistance demanded the difficult task of cultural retooling (Swidler, 1986); addiction was a well-worn glove, easy to slip into. Heroin thus inscribed a deep line of liminality, territorialising the reincarceration assemblage in which John was enmeshed.

Rose's description of the excluded as 'non-citizens, failed citizens, anti-citizens' (2000: 331) evokes Turner's (1967) symbolism associated with damage and decay that characterises the 'structural invisibility' of people in liminal states, such as John, who are 'at once no longer classified and not yet classified' (p. 96). Though no longer officially classified 'prisoner', they are nevertheless represented by 'symbols [of] . . . decomposition, catabolism, and other physical processes that have a negative tinge'. The terms 'junkie' and 'smackhead' used to describe heroin addicts evoke such symbols. Their being 'not yet classified' is expressed in terms symbolising growth and birth, which resonates with the language of drug rehabilitation, recovery and reform. Central to these symbolic characterisations is that men 'are neither living nor dead from one aspect, and both living and dead from another. Their condition is one of ambiguity and para- dox' (Turner, 1967: 97). The ambiguity inheres in the 'not yet' aspect of this liminal state, the becomingness, the perpetual 'in-betweenness'. 'Junkies' are not accepted as members of the community and are, therefore, socially 'dead' (Jewkes, 2005b), structurally invisible (Turner, 1967). When engaged in rehabili- tative efforts, they are 'recovering' – 'clients . . . on their way to getting better' (Rob) – but still not there yet. Addicts slipping back and forth between treatment and relapse thus inhabit a liminal social and cognitive space, a threshold that can become a way of life (Kelly, 2008).

For recovering addicts, whose relapses are increasingly infrequent, this thresh- old can become liminoid (Turner, 1982): a platform for transformation, a way of inhabiting liminal space that is active rather than passive, promoting resist- ance rather than submission. John's embracing of NA meetings as a source of structure, purpose and community exemplifies this change-oriented state of limi- noidity. The NA community comprises people sharing the common experience of addiction and thus functions as a community of 'others', people in the commu- nity yet outside mainstream society. Like prison, collectively and recursively, NA reproduces its own meanings and produces new cultural forms (St John, 2000). It enables the process of cultural retooling (Swidler, 1986) through which members develop new skills, habits, identities, and stories of success as well as failure. In this way, NA creates lines of flight that cut across the territorial lines of heroin addiction and its connections to the carceral assemblage, deterritorialising both in its 'augmentation of capacities' (DeLanda, 2006: 50).

This capacity-building function serves to counteract ex-prisoners' serial depletion of resources (Baldry et al., 2003; Grunseit et al., 2008). The capacity of individual liminoids participating in NA is only augmented, their transfor- mation enabled, however, through the collective experience of the group, their 'path of mutation precipitated through the actualisation of connections among bodies . . . that release new powers in the capacities of those bodies to act and respond', according to Lorraine (2005: 145), describing a 'line of flight'. Thus, the liminal state of being addicts or ex-prisoners, when channelled into collec- tive effort, represents a site of becoming, of metamorphosis. This is apparently what many of the men envisioned as a reintegration project when they spoke of 'crims' helping 'other crims' (Glen), an approach evoking Turner's conception of liminality as a rite of passage, an important phase of becoming – indeed, 'the gen- erative, creative principle of ritual' (Grimes, 2000: 122). Liminality and the social exclusion it engenders are part of the experience of imprisonment, but they also give meaning to the notion of reintegration: liminality and reintegration 'constitute one another and are mutually indispensable' (Turner, 1969: 97). A 'limbo of statuslessness' (Turner, 1969: 97) is vital because it generates the need for ritual to allow passage through the 'dangerous zone' (Grimes, 2000: 6) of imprisonment and post-prison exclusion (Van Gennep, 1909; Douglas, 1966). Disconnection brings forth reconnection; social death allows for rebirth.

The 'amazing passion to help other people' that SW23 observes in men who 'have [had] a chance to go straight . . . [to] begin afresh' signifies the generativity of ritual such as Five8 entails. The commitment to 'caring for self, other and future' (Halsey & Harris, 2011: 74) that Five8 engenders also fosters 'a cognitive restructuring towards responsibility' (Burnett & Maruna, 2006: 85). This is a process of cultural retooling, 'undo[ing] a whole lot of the prison thinking' (SW23) and replacing it with pro-social cognition. As Toch (2000a) points out, this process echoes cognitive skills training offered in prison programmes but, importantly, includes opportunities to apply 'cog[nitive] skills in practice', in the 'community where the problems exist, where research and their own histories show they are likely to mess up' (SW22). Such training without such opportunities is meaningless, 'a joke' (Glen). The conception of prison services and programmes as 'a joke' implies the men's sense of a bigger schema, a game in which they are pawns, set up to fail. This is implied in the perception of 'a society which itself is full of double-standards, contradictions, con artists, employers who rip them off' (SW22), which emphasises men's sense of being in a social limbo (Turner, 1967, 1982), perpetually caught between having been released, yet not experiencing freedom, not feeling accepted or 'reintegrated'.

Ex-prisoners' reintegrative efforts, without reciprocation, are doomed to fail, to perpetuate the lines from which they are trying to escape. The best rehabilitative intentions are laid waste by a community unwilling to accept them. In terms of connection between ex-prisoners and the wider community, a discrepancy emerged in men's conception of 'otherness'. The literature describes perceptions of criminals as 'alien others' (Garland, 2001), the othered 'criminological shadow' (Arrigo & Milovanovic, 2009), whereby 'the 'normal' is contrasted with the 'deviant' and the 'law-abiding with the criminal' (Ferrell et al., 2008: 23). Citizens and prisoners are conceived as 'different in kind rather than in degree' (Toch, 2000b: 1). Although the men's experience of not 'fitting in' reflected this sense of difference, many also conveyed a strong sense of 'normal' as 'other', as removed from their experience, turning the notion on its head. This highlights the need to take into account the subjective experience of the formerly imprisoned and the perspectives of the socially excluded.

Genuine reintegration in the form of community trust and acceptance demands an exchange on equal terms, recognising the otherness in each other, or 'commonality' (Toch, 2000b). As SW22 concludes, from his own experience and that of many men he has known, 'success is about making that connection, that exchange'; accepting someone who can say: 'This is who I am. I'm an ex-criminal, I'm a drug addict.

It doesn't define who I am as a person' (John); recognising that, between normal and 'other', 'there's no difference. They're just people having a difficult time' (John). The recognition of commonality lies in harnessing ex-prisoners' desire for accept-ance, for 'fitting in', and conceiving 'overlapping goals or interests [that can] allow for bridging or relatedness' (Toch, 2000b: 1). 'All that is required', to manifest this commonality and achieve reintegration, according to Toch (2000b: 1), 'is to sus-pend the accentuation of differences'. Facilitating this process, however, to 'meet in a way that is mutually productive . . . on common ground' (SW22), requires ritual.

Without reintegrative ritual, as Grimes (2000: 5-6) argues, imprisonment 'can become a yawning abyss, draining off psychic energy, engendering social confu-sion and twisting the course of the life that follows it'. This 'abyss' and its 'social confusion' characterise states of liminality that persist as zones of exclusion (Rose, 2000), emanating risk and danger (Douglas, 1966). Danger is perceived, according to Douglas (1966: 119), 'simply because transition is neither one state nor the next, it is indefinable'. Yet, as Van Gennep (1909) and Douglas (1966) insist, ritual controls the danger by allowing the transformation of the danger-bearer and publicly declaring 'his entry to his new status' (Douglas, 1966: 120). The role of community is, therefore, central in the reintegrative process, to disrupt and forestall the danger emanating from such risky zones, and to interrupt the circuits of exclusion that perpetuate them. Paul's conception of reintegration as 'getting stability in the community so nobody looks at you as a prisoner anymore and you don't look at everybody looking at you as a prisoner' evokes the inter-active aspect of social identity: the relationship between a man's self-concept and the mirror of society (Maruna, LeBel, Mitchell et al., 2004). Also invoked is the broader community responsibility for integrating ex-prisoners, through active understanding and engagement with ex-prisoners, suggesting that reintegration is indeed a 'two-way street' (Maruna, 2011a: 106).

The role of community and connection is most apparent in the example of Five8. John attests to the transforming and enabling power of this model of sup-port, and how a 'micro-community' can model and 'seed' a wider community. As Father Brosnan warned, the hardest thing to give ex-prisoners is friendship; Five8 'provide[s] the community, the friend' (SW22). Many of these men are 'difficult': 'problem clients', the 'hard cases' to which programme workers refer. By committing to providing friendship to ex-prisoners, Five8 provides a set of cultural resources that may otherwise be beyond these men's reach. Five8 also creates proxy connections that allow men to escape 'prison world' (Rob), lines of flight that enable new ways of being and learning new skills and styles to replace prison ways and habits.

The process of cultural retooling (Swidler, 1986) requires mentors, friends who can guide the emerging one in the ways of being a law-abiding, pro-social citizen. Without friends or family to fulfil this role, how or where might ex-prisoners find such guides? As one ex-prisoner expressed to SW23: 'all I want to know is, am I going in the right direction? I need to bounce that off someone because I don't know'. This is the problem on which Five8 was founded and the rationale for the building of 'micro-communities' around individual ex-prisoners, because, as the data reveal, 'there's only so much support' (SW01) one person can provide. To effect real or lasting change, ex-prisoners require social support that extends beyond a case manager or an individual helper: programmes that 'don't provide the social support network . . . [are] going to fail' (SW22). Rather than a programme or systemic failure, however, it is ex-prisoners who are deemed failures: 'failed citizens, anti-citizens . . . attached to no moral community or to a community of anti-morality' (Rose, 2000: 331). But, how can men attach to a 'moral community' that refuses to include them?

The process of inclusion demands ritual to signify ex-prisoners being 'accepted back in the fold' (Uncle Jack Charles, 2010, in Naylor, 2011: 79). Communities provide the sites and sources of ritual whereby a liminal phase is rendered a rite of passage, a state of transition from being an ex-prisoner to becoming an *ex*-prisoner. Lines of ritual territorialise the Five8 process of building 'micro-communities' of support: the 'circle' structure of meetings, their weekly schedule. These are the physical embodiments of principles of openness, mutuality and trust, and of the participants' commitment to the 'core member's' reintegration: 'we are there next Tuesday . . . we are committed to him' (SW23). Other forms of ritual may be equally effective. The routinised, semi-formalised group ritual underpinning Five8's approach contrasts sharply with the informal, ad hoc rituals in which other men found themselves engaging, as a means of turning a state of post-prison upheaval and disorientation into a phase of transition to readiness: to work, to father, to find stability. Ben's hours spent cleaning his house for his children to come and stay, for instance, signified this ritualised transition. Dale's 'hanging out in the park' was a way to emulate the aspects of prison life that he was struggling to replace in the outside world: 'the company and the activity'; a way to deal with the 'confounding sort of loneliness' (Dale) experienced post-release.

Ritual can function to render liminality an active, liminoid rite of passage, and yet it is contingent upon the presence of sociocultural resources: Dale's wider network of pro-social friends; Ben's children and the family relationships (however fraught) that enabled his access and capacity to actively father his daughters. Where these connections and resources are missing, ritual can equally territorialise the lines of exclusion manifest in methadone queues and boarding houses, as Rob's experience attests. Estranged from his family, socially isolated and mistrustful, 'because of prison', Rob's yearning for ritualised acceptance emerges in his relationship with his pharmacist. He attributes responsibility for 'saving' him:

he's changed my whole life, I think. When I first met him I was probably a one. Out of saving, you know, I was probably a one out of ten. . . . And now he reckons I'm an eight or a nine, from being a one.

There is ritual underpinning Rob's account of 'getting better', in the enumeration of graduated steps in his recovery. He evokes an elusive destination symbolised by the number ten, but being not quite there, 'not yet classified' (Turner, 1967). Rob thus inhabits a nether space between prison and the community, a social limbo (Turner, 1982), characterised by chaos, uncertainty, instability, vulnerability (Jewkes, 2005b) and waiting. Rendering that liminality *liminoid* requires resources. Men's inner resources rely on outer resources, connections to non-criminal communities, to be able to realise reintegrative possibilities: to find purpose, to find and sustain employment, to pursue legal activity and avoid reimprisonment. The crucial facets of connection are understanding and acceptance, which can facilitate integration through shared experience, reciprocity and genuine exchange.

Conclusion

This chapter has analysed the phenomenographic findings of the preceding two chapters through the assemblage–culture–liminality lens. The assemblages of home, identity and connection hold the 'very heterogeneous elements' of post-prison experience together (Deleuze, 1980, in Halsey, 2007: 1247) and reveal the ways in which imprisonment shapes and inflects men's post-release experience of liminality, of being no longer a prisoner, yet not quite 'free'. The key element in ex-prisoners' need for a 'home' is the need for stability, security and belonging. The components of post-prison identity extend from the interaction between men's self-concept and the social identity associated with their behaviour or experience: 'ex-prisoner', 'drug user', having 'a record', 'client' or 'father'. Each designation is a critical site for liminality to intensify or abate, either to cement a state of marginalisation and exclusion or provide a way to transcend liminal status. Being a father, in particular, seems to hold the promise of liminoidity through its generative possibilities. Other forms of connection provide a way to transform liminality: connecting with recovering addicts in NA meetings, connecting with a community of 'street people', connecting with other ex-prisoners in a support role. The critical elements of these connections are understanding and acceptance, which foster reciprocity and exchange.

This analysis has revealed aspects of the post-prison experience that accord with other studies, and yet tend not to feature prominently in the wider literature. Research has confirmed Father Brosnan's maxim, that 'three things are needed by people upon their release from prison: a place to live that is decent; a job that they can handle; and friendship, and the hardest to provide is friendship'. But, correlational and experiential accounts do not explain how the broad domains of housing, work and social support connect with the subjective experience of ex-prisoners, or how these interactions operate. Without understanding of these interrelational aspects, effective work with ex-prisoners is always constrained: in terms of providing resources and connecting with ex-prisoners in meaningful ways, and developing policy that reflects genuine understanding of, and conceives effective solutions to, post-release problems.

Notes

1 Van Gennep, 1909; Douglas, 1966; Turner, 1967.
2 To remind the reader, Father John Brosnan, former Pentridge prison chaplain, famously said, 'Three things are needed by people upon their release from prison: a place to live that is decent; a job that they can handle; and friendship, and the hardest to provide is friendship'.
3 Toch, 2000a; Maruna, LeBel & Lanier, 2004; McNeill et al., 2005; McNeill & Maruna, 2007; Healy & O'Donnell, 2008; Halsey & Harris, 2011.
4 Also cited in Burnett & Maruna, 2006: 84.
5 See, for example, Healy et al., 2000; Vinson & Tehan, 2001.
6 Mills & Codd, 2008; Rosenberg, 2009; Tomkin, 2009; Walker, 2010; Lösel, 2012.

9   Being and becoming

'Dale'

'Dale', aged 34, was released 12 months ago after serving 6-and-a-half years in prison. We meet in a city café where the street life hums around us. This, I will soon learn, is an atmosphere in which Dale feels comfortable.

Thoughtful and articulate, Dale is a slight man whose gentle disposition belies a perceptive wit and a quick tongue. Of all the men I have interviewed, Dale seems the most accidental prisoner. His crime – 'a tragic accident' – was the result of a sequence of reprisals arising from a rift in his relationship with a former house-mate; these culminated in a fire that led, ultimately, to her death and the death of the person with whom she was sleeping. For this crime, Dale was sentenced to 10 years' imprisonment. As he says, however: 'I have a life sentence. I've killed two people; I have to wear that for life. That is a life sentence in itself'.

The year since his release 'has been a struggle', and adjusting to post-release life has been a psychological 'rollercoaster'. He experienced 'three panic attacks within four months of being out'. He speaks of the guilt associated with his offence returning to haunt him. Once the prison walls were no longer around him, the 'safety net and emotional barrier between you and dealing with the guilt is removed', whereas, in prison, 'actually doing a sentence . . . you are being punished for what you did, so emotionally you can [cope]'.

A sociable person, Dale has friends who supported him throughout his time in jail, writing and visiting regularly: 'that's what kept me sane, I think'. Although he enjoys his own company, he also craves having 'people around'. He is 'fortunate' to have a circle of friends, yet, since getting out, he has found that, 'they've got their own lives' and he admits to experiencing a 'confounding sort of loneliness' after leaving prison, where days are marked by the rhythms of constant human activity.

Before going to prison, he strongly identified with a 'gay scene' within which he felt a sense of belonging – of fitting in – that he now feels he has lost: he has been left 'sceneless'. To cope with this sense of loss, he has recently 'slotted in' and found company with 'people that hang around in the park and drink – not all deros [derelicts], younger people', among whom he has assumed the role and status of 'peacemaker'. He is ambivalent about this solution, however, stressing that, 'it is a temporary thing', which will pass now that he has secured full-time work.

He has concerns, moreover, about his health – 'I don't want to be drinking every day because it is very dangerous to your body' – and his self-image:

> I don't want to be doing that . . . by the time I'm 35 . . . because it's a bit tragic coming into the city and hanging around with people that are between 15 and 25 . . . it's just tragic. You're like 34 and even though it's fun . . . it's pretty much mirroring what it was like being in prison.

Abandoned by his mother when he was 6, Dale lived with his grandmother and then with foster families until he was made a Ward of the State at 11. At 15, he ran away, moving to Queensland at the age of 16 and returning to Victoria 6 months later to have his wardship revoked. Diagnosed with borderline personality disorder as a youth, he believes he has grown out of the behavioural tendencies that, when he was a young man, led to his suicidal ideations, self-harming and sabotaging 'whatever was dear' to him.

His early experiences afforded him a degree of resilience evident in his account of coping with imprisonment. He was able to reflect on his time spent as a Ward of the State, for instance, and how 'when it was over . . . it was like a click of the fingers. But when you're going through it, it's long'. He describes, too, viewing the prison world as a participant-observer:

> Every now and then I'd sort of take a step back, take a breath and sort of imagine I was just teleported there and watch it from fresh eyes again – you know, like 'oh wow' – to try and get that fascinating – 'look around you' – 'no one gets to see it from this side', like if you weren't imprisoned you'd want to be able to sit there . . . invisible, have a look. . . . I'm a bit of an anthropologist, I love people and watching different people and listening to people's stories and that and so it was kind of fascinating in that sense.

He thus conveys a sense of feeling removed from the prison world, of identifying, not as a prisoner, but as someone passing through. Indeed, he likens himself to a character in the film *The Shawshank Redemption*, who 'walks through the prison yard as if he's got an invisible raincoat to protect him'.

Dale appears to have a deep well of resources – both inner and outer – that enabled him to cope with the experience of being a prisoner. Nevertheless, he speaks of a profound psychological trauma associated, not only with the offence for which he was imprisoned, but also with the experience of being released from prison. Dale's 'confounding sort of loneliness' seems to sum up what it feels like to return to a society following penal exile – a singular aloneness that prison walls mask and contain. Perhaps becoming an ex-prisoner means finding a way to belong – in Dale's case – all over again.

Why do so many men still return to prison? This book opened with this question. The answer it posits is that prison shadows the lives of released prisoners in ways that linger, and extricating themselves relies on the acceptance and support of others. It cannot be achieved alone. Yet alone many ex-prisoners find themselves: disoriented, alienated, homeless, friendless, unemployed, seemingly unemployable. These isolating factors make life in the community difficult to sustain and make reincarceration, for some, inevitable. The research on which this book is based shows that seeing into the post-release experience by using analytical tools that foreground the subjective experience of ex-prisoners, in the context of post-release practice, illuminates the processes whereby prison shadows persist, both in the lives of men released and the communities to which they return. In this final chapter, I sum up the main findings and draw on specific examples to show how the assemblage–culture–liminality lens can deepen our understanding of these processes. In doing so, I return briefly to the research questions.

The main findings

The study's theoretical lens, combining three concepts drawn from distinct areas of the literature, has provided insights that previous post-release studies have left implicit or unacknowledged. These understandings build on the work of Halsey (2006, 2007) and Arrigo and Milovanovic (2009), who use Deleuze and Guattari's (1987) assemblage concept to evoke the web of interconnecting lines giving rise to the imprisonment–release–reimprisonment cycle. Culture is widely understood in the context of prison norms, inmate codes and the effects of prisonisation (Clemmer, 1940; Haney, 2003). This aspect of prison culture is uncontested. A culture-in-action semiotic-practices perspective, uniquely applied in this research, has allowed insight into how meanings inflect and generate behaviours, how behaviour produces meaning, and how these recursive processes perpetuate prison ways of being that, in part, constitute the post-prison terrain. Liminality encapsulates the precariousness of this terrain and provides a window into how ex-prisoners' social and economic exclusion is sustained.

The relationship between meaning and behaviour is evidenced in the way the symbolic aspects of prison life, which lose their meaning outside the social context of the prison, nevertheless persist. Smoking a particular tobacco is an example: the punctuating rhythm of rolling and smoking cigarettes, to pass time; alliances forged through smoking rituals; the rules of currency and trade in tobacco, which mean that borrowing anything is 'the big no-no' (Wayne). As Wayne's experience shows, these meanings are ingrained in bodies and habituated thinking. Underlying the apparent connections forged through tobacco rituals are the deep currents of distrust that characterise prison interactions and affect post-prison relationships, making it hard for men to trust and to seek or accept help. This explains the mask of bravado and indifference that prisoners become adept at wearing.

Similarly ingrained are prison norms of violent retribution and pre-emption, which shape men's actions and reactions in the community when threats are perceived in the same way as they are in prison. These norms can override the shallow loyalty of prison 'mateship', as when Scott describes his intention to go and 'wreck' a 'friend' who owed him $20. Even the way men walk, talk and hold their bodies is inscribed with prison ways of being and of navigating physical space.

The men and workers evoke physical postures and patterned behaviours that evidence this prison 'hangover': 'They'll pace up and down; they'll dress like they are still in prison. They'll carry themselves like they're still in prison' (SW08). When viewed in culture-in-action terms, these physical embodiments signal the persistence of prison thinking and the shadows of prison culture.

Similarly, recursiveness arises throughout ex-prisoners' post-release experience, exemplified in the way men return to domestic settings and relationships fraught with conflict, drug and alcohol abuse, and criminality. An iterative loop is embedded in expectations that men will resume pre-prison offending lifestyles, as if uninterrupted. Imprisonment functions as merely a respite from the chaos of everyday life. The pull of cultural demands and kinship obligations is particularly strong and difficult to elude for Indigenous men, who must negotiate the risk of losing their cultural identity. This explains why imprisonment becomes part of that identity, for some. Recursive patterns are evident in the connections between ex-prisoners who recognise each other on the street, on the train, in pharmacotherapy queues, at Centrelink offices and parole appointments, and drug 'rehab'. These connections, based on little else besides the experience of imprisonment or addiction, can nevertheless be difficult for men to eschew. Without a sense of belonging to an alternative community, and having an alternative identity, these connections tend to dominate men's social interactions. The recursive aspect of this phenomenon is its reiteration of men's social identity as 'ex-prisoners' or 'addicts', impliedly 'failed citizens' (Rose, 2000: 331).

Boarding houses, frequently the only accommodation option for released prisoners, are physical sites of recursive meanings and behaviours: doing deals, doing drugs and smoking 'Ox'; reissuing prison associations, alliances and enmities; reproducing prison codes of keeping 'tight' and 'hard' and looking after yourself; pre-empting violence with violence. The squalor of many boarding houses underscores men's sense of being outside 'normal' society, 'failed citizens', marginalised and unworthy. Depression, anxiety and despair intensify under such conditions. Although the setting mirrors prison social life in some ways, it lacks the structure, orderliness and regime of the prison by which men are contained and controlled. The mundane, domestic nature of prison life underscores its familiarity. This is the paradox of freedom, that men fear release from this haven into the unknown. Though ostensibly freed, the experience of living in a boarding house, surrounded by other ex-prisoners, drug users and the mentally ill, is one of instability, uncertainty and vulnerability. Staying in a boarding house means 'going back to jail' (Nick). It is a transit zone, inherently liminal.

The experience of liminality is evidenced in men's experience of being a drug user: using illicit or illegally obtained substances; 'self-medicating'; involvement in familiar routines, rituals and interactions with other users; celebrating release by getting 'wrecked'; generating, satisfying and generating craving in a recursive loop. Legally prescribed drugs also mark out liminal spaces. Methadone queues reinforce the status of ex-prisoners as correctional subjects, contained within and by imposed conditions that determine how much of the dispensed substance they depend on, and for how long, to be 'cured' of their addiction. These conditions create further dependencies: on the drug, the identity, the routine, the dispenser.

The role of the pharmacist is ambiguous in this circumstance: an authority figure exercising control through their dispensing of the 'treatment', outside the penal apparatus yet still (when court-ordered) operating within its bounds. Rob implies both dependency and dominion in this relationship, relying on the support yet deciding what to disclose or conceal. Perhaps this explains the centrality of Rob's pharmacist in his life, as a source of structure and routine that nonetheless allows him some sense of control. The client–worker dyad underpinning this relationship is an example of the mutually reinforcing dynamic through which ex-prisoners' status is recurrently constituted as emergent, in recovery, in process; approaching an elusive destination of 'getting better'. When this process is solely and entirely reliant on one person, its potential is stymied, as 'there's only so much support they can get from a case manager' (SW01), an individual helper.

A significant site of liminality is the state of being unemployed. When men rely on the assistance of employment consultants, there is the similar potential for client–worker dependency. However, this relationship contains many more possibilities than simply the promise of 'getting better'. For men whose futures are foreshortened by lifelong institutionalisation, men such as Scott or Nick, who 'can't do anything', the disability pension offers a route to an alternative identity and amelioration of the liminal status of being no longer imprisoned yet not quite a citizen. For men with some experience of working, within the practical constraints of a criminal record, there are hope and expectation of employment. This renders the experience of liminality active and creative, rather than passive and inert. Seeing the problem of unemployment in terms of liminality explains how and why a job holds such reintegrative potential. It creates an identity ('worker'), which can diminish the sense of being 'no longer classified' (prisoner, penal subject) and 'not yet classified' (citizen, productive member of society; Turner, 1967), a way out of the 'structural invisibility' of being first and foremost an ex-prisoner. The riskiness of that label, however, does not dissipate. As John's experience with his employer shows, employment does not automatically mean (re)integration. Understanding and acceptance are required for integration to occur.

Liminality as a rite of passage highlights the role of community in fostering post-liminal reintegrative processes. This aspect is demonstrated by Dale's 'hanging in the park', or John's active participation in NA meetings with other recovering addicts. Both 'communities' are outside mainstream society, and yet function to transform the experience of liminality by offering understanding and acceptance. Importantly, they provide men the opportunity to participate in a community beyond the prison. The ritualised aspect is equally significant. Five8 demonstrates the role of a 'micro-community' in mentoring and modelling thinking, behaviour and modes of interaction for the 'core member'.

Embedded in the micro-community model is the assumption and practice of 'cognitive restructuring' (Burnett & Maruna, 2006), which involves, not only fostering of hope and a future focus, but also a shift in the ex-prisoner's identity, from outsider to a valued member of the community. The sense of belonging that this membership engenders meets the human need for connection, through which trust begins to grow, as the Five8s demonstrate. Connection to community is required to sustain hope, intention and possibility, to enable becoming. The ritual aspect is key to the abatement of an ex-prisoner's liminal status and its transformation into an active state of becoming. The twin notions of being and becoming emerge as critical to the idea of *(re)*integration (contingent upon initial *integration*).

The different ways in which release and post-release life are constructed, and how these constructions conflict and cohere, are revealed throughout the discussion. In summing up the main findings, I turn now to address the remaining research questions:

What are the qualitatively different ways men experience release from prison?

The findings show that men experience release from prison in qualitatively different ways that overlap with the ways in which they experience imprisonment: as a one-off event, an aberration, inconsistent with their self-concept as a man and essentially a decent person; or as a familiar and stabilising environment, within which men derive security from knowing where they stand, knowing the rules, in contrast to chaotic lives shadowed by the risk of reimprisonment. Another experience of prison and release is as a non-event, the normalised consequence of criminal choices. The key element in the experience of being an ex-prisoner appears to be the extent to which men's self-concept intersects with, and is mirrored or reinforced by, their interactions with others. There is a societal expectation of prisoners' rehabilitation and reform once they have been 'through the system', with its 'correctional' and behaviour-changing programmes. For men already equipped with cultural resources enabling them to 'make the best of something' (Matt), prison's rehabilitative opportunities are useful, if only to pass the time constructively. For men lacking sociocultural resources or resistant to law-abiding norms, however, learning 'cognitive skills' in prison does not necessarily equip or persuade them to *apply* them, to think or act differently, out in the world. For men, this makes prison programmes seem futile. For communities, reoffending augments the perception of ex-prisoners' 'failure'. The common theme is *failure*.

How is post-release support conceived and experienced?

Post-release support is conceived and experienced in different ways. Housing is constructed as the most pressing issue for men leaving prison: having somewhere to go, 'a place that is decent'. The key aspect of the experience of post-release housing is the need for stability, security and belonging. These are crucial to counteract the experience of liminality. The post-release housing problem is conceived as finding stability, somewhere 'decent', but it is not understood in terms of the implications of stability: security and belonging. Hence, a man can be 'housed' in a flat or a unit, which they think is 'going to change their lives' (SW03), but, without a sense of security or belonging, 'they are just . . . back to square one' (SW03). The analysis has revealed the housing problem to comprise a multiplicity of factors deeply connected with men's self-identity and with the social resources available to them. Unless the interrelationship of these factors is understood, and taken into account, post-release support can have a limited impact in assisting reintegration.

Similarly, responses to men's drug and alcohol issues, experienced by the majority of 'clients', commonly entail intervention in the form of treatment, referral to 'rehab' or 'detox', or drug counselling. Yet, post-release support that does not acknowledge the critical interaction between the functional aspects of drug use and its addictive and criminalising aspects will inevitably fall short of achieving long-term integrative goals. As SW06's approach suggests, men first have to 'want to change', then be supported to sustain that intention, which involves 'just hanging in there, hanging in there' (SW22). Implied is the constancy and consistency that eventually give rise to trust and belief: 'If they believe in me they can change, that is my experience' (SW06). Given the difficulty realising these larger goals, and meeting deeper human needs, post-release 'successes' are measured in 'small baby steps' (SW02), on a long, gradual path towards 'habilitation', 'getting better' and, ultimately, (re)integration. The key site of difference emerges in how Five8s conceive and experience post-release support, in contrast to a case-management approach. Five8 recognises and explicitly engages with the human need for connection, understanding and acceptance. Professional boundaries constrain most workers' ability to engage with their clients at this level of human connection and genuine friendship. SW06 is a notable exception.

How does culture flow from and feed into the reincarceration assemblage?

The reincarceration assemblage comprises lines radiating from the prison, out into the community and back again, in iterative loops. The recursive processes by which men are ensnared in these lines arise from identities forged within prison culture. These prison habits, skills, styles and ways of being provide men with the toolkit from which they construct their ways of being and acting in the community. Replacing these tools with more pro-social strategies demands either the difficult process of cultural retooling or the reliance on pre-existing resources undiminished by prisonisation processes. Each of these possibilities requires the support of an understanding and accepting community. Such resources are beyond the reach of men brought up in the system, such as Scott and Nick. These men's 'ex-prisoner' identities have congealed around the 'dis-habilitation' that their experience of institutionalisation and imprisonment has engendered. In this way, the prison culture is seen as both product and producer of the reincarceration assemblage.

How is post-release liminality experienced? What are its interior and exterior dimensions, and how do these facilitate or impede community (re)integration?

Liminality is experienced as not quite fitting in, not belonging, no longer a prisoner, but not entirely free either. It manifests in the internal feelings of hopelessness, incapacity, loneliness, alienation, exclusion: 'I'm not really worthy, not worth it' (Scott); 'I can't do anything', 'I haven't got *any* friends' (Nick); 'I don't trust many people anymore' (Rob); 'I didn't feel part of society . . . that feeling of not belonging' (Dale). When these feelings manifest in actions and experiences, such as drug use or living on the streets, they become externalised, as Rob suggests: 'you're not really a member of society if you're on the streets, you know?'. When these external lines become entrenched in a man's social identity, he is perceived as a 'failure', an 'anti-citizen', emanating risk and danger to the rest of the community. These perceptions undermine people's willingness to try to understand the experience of being an ex-prisoner, which impedes opportunities for human connection and acceptance. These opportunities, when they do arise, can transform liminal states into liminoid phases of transition, engagement and integration into a community of others. The importance of understanding the experience of liminality, and recognising its function as a transitional and potentially transformational phase, is thus made clear.

The implications of the findings

In uncovering how prison release is constructed, and how meanings and constructions differ and converge, this book reveals a view of post-release life from the inside. The issues men face following release from prison, when seen from this perspective, are not just the result of individual failings or problems. The findings reveal that the lines and flows of the carceral assemblage inscribe men's past, shape their present and constrain or enable their future. The implications are twofold. For ex-prisoners, the need for stability, security and belonging shows the 'housing' problem to be about much more than a place to live, and to surpass the simple binary construct of housing/homelessness. Prison identities inflect and suffuse post-prison identity, both internally, in men's self-concept, and externally, via ascribed labels such as ex-prisoner, drug user or client. The interaction between these aspects of identity is critical in either the accretion or erosion of liminality, and in men's orientation to hope or despair. This orientation is largely influenced by the nature and degree of connection to other people, by whom men feel accepted and understood. Connection, understanding and acceptance are key ingredients of post-prison (re)integration.

For communities, the implications are significant. The expectation that ex-prisoners will become reformed, law-abiding citizens is entirely contingent upon a community available and willing to accept them. And, as the factors above illustrate, ex-prisoners carry heavy baggage, shadows left by the experience of imprisonment that persist, creating a sense of apprehension and fear, or – in Mary Douglas's (1966) terms – danger and contamination associated with the transitional state of leaving prison and returning to the community. To resolve this uneasiness and bring this liminal state to a close require communities to understand ex-prisoners' experience as part of broader human experience, to de-accentuate the differences and find commonality (Toch, 2000b). Without taking this step, communities will continue to bear the brunt of penal harms, manifest in ex-prisoners' ongoing social and economic exclusion and marginalisation, which intensify their risk of reoffending and reimprisonment.

The strengths and limitations of the research

I have drawn concepts from discrete areas of the post-release literature. Bringing together these three critical perspectives allows us to 'see into' the post-release problem, to visualise its constituent lines and forces, and to imagine ways in which these may be interrupted, their effects attenuated. Culture-in-action approaches show how men's post-prison behaviours manifest and reproduce prison meanings. This and the function and experience of liminality – of being no longer a prisoner and not quite a citizen – are elements in the post-release grid to which previous studies have alluded, yet with which few have truly engaged. This study's methodology has opened up a window on an otherwise perplexing phenomenon: how and why men struggle to escape the carceral orbit.

A further strength of this research lies in its respectful listening to the voices of men often invisible and unheard, and its emphasis on the subjective experiences and understandings of both ex-prisoners and workers in the field. The twenty-six interviews yielded an unanticipated depth and richness of information. The openness of the men, together with their ability to articulate their experiences of release and their post-prison struggles, was surprising. The men who self-selected to participate in the research were evidently inclined to tell their story, yet this did not guarantee the candour with which they related and reflected on their experience. The female–male (researcher–participant) dynamic proved advantageous, possibly in that a lack of perceived threat allowed a degree of trust to develop quickly. Because my only agenda was to listen and hear their stories, the men apparently felt safe to share them.

This was a small study in a wide field. This is all it purports to be. The focus on one Australian state and the sample of twelve ex-prisoners and fourteen post-release support workers limit the generalisability of the findings. The constraint on interviewing men currently under sentence – including on parole – reduced the scope of post-release experience on which to draw, in some respects. The practical realities of gaining access to prisoners once they are released, especially those not engaged with programmes, meant reliance on word-of-mouth self-selection, which limited the sample and, hence, the data. I anticipated potential problems, being a female researcher studying men's experience of a peculiarly male institution – thinking that perhaps I would struggle to win men's trust and confidence. This issue was tempered, however, by approaching the research with openness, respect and a genuine desire to understand, which engendered trust. The interviews nevertheless carry the imprint of the researcher–participant interaction, which inevitably shaped the data and its analysis. This is a methodological constraint arising in qualitative research, particularly where there is a single researcher. You, the reader, must be the judge of the authenticity and trustworthiness of this account.

Where to from here?

This book has practical applications in terms of how post-release support is conceived and delivered. The findings of the research highlight the importance of post-release support and the need for a continuum of care to extend beyond the prison and into the community, particularly for prisoners on straight release. Transitional housing is shown to be inadequate, relative to the number of prisoners released without accommodation, and boarding houses are revealed as particularly criminogenic. Unless immediate housing needs can be met, post-release efforts are fruitless, signalling only a temporary release from prison. Further research on the housing needs of ex-prisoners is needed to support post-release work. This research must reflect meaningful analyses of the problem, however, to support effective intervention.

There are practical applications for how post-release support programmes engage with ex-prisoners and conceive of their human needs, such as in terms of *being* and *becoming*, which tend to exceed the boundaries of individualised case-management approaches. Though challenging to implement, Five8's 'micro-community' is shown to have greater capacity to model 'pro-social' interactions, communicate behavioural norms and expectations, and thereby foster (re)integration. From ex-prisoners' perspective, supported by previous work on the reintegrative power of generativity, the most effective post-release support involves other ex-prisoners. This is an important finding to consider in developing models of support and identifying best-practice principles.

Understanding post-prison liminality can help to inform effective transitional support work, by exploring and recognising the sorts of practice that function symbolically and practically to bring the post-prison liminal phase to a close. These may include intensely personal practices, such as Ben's cleaning his house for his children or Dale 'hanging in the park' to bridge his transition back into the wider community. Identifying and acknowledging such practices as positive reintegrative steps, in the context of relationship-based support, can provide a way to gradually build men's hope and confidence towards 'a sense of meaning and worth' (SW09) and, ultimately, becoming other than a prisoner. Reintegrative practices might also be embodied at the social, structural and legal level: generating opportunities for 'crims' to help 'other crims'; promoting access to employment through specialist service provision and business partnerships; different forms of judicial rehabilitation – reentry courts or expunging criminal records – for instance. A liminality-informed perspective thus shifts the focus of reintegration to its all-important community context.

More broadly, this book highlights the need for the criminogenic characteristics of the prison to feature in debate and discussion of imprisonment as a crime prevention strategy. This book adds to the literature that shows that, while investment (political and fiscal) in penal expansion continues, so do the harms that prison perpetuates. Prison is not only socially and economically detrimental, it is ineffective in bringing about the goals of rehabilitation, reintegration and reduced recidivism. It doesn't work. Prison *does* work to reproduce the harms that perpetuate offending: social and economic marginalisation; mental illness; homelessness and housing insecurity; exaggerated models of masculinity; substance abuse and addiction; family disruption and trauma; intergenerational violence and criminality; and punitive, retributive norms. To address these issues, as a society, we need to address the role and function of the prison. Research that highlights the harms to prisoners, families and communities can allow more effective rehabilitative and integrative possibilities to be explored. It can weigh against punitive political tides and challenge increasing investment in this most costly form of punishment.

In conclusion . . .

This book begins with the sense that something is missing from dominant conceptualisations of the 'post-release problem'. Individualist, risk-based accounts deflect attention from the essential ingredient of post-prison integration: a community to be integrated into, or, as it was conceived more than a century ago, 'the assistance . . . and patronage of a society' (*The Argus*, 1872: 3). Without a community available and willing to accept ex-prisoners' (re)entry and (re) integration, post-release problems persist. These problems arise from and are exacerbated by ex-prisoners' social exclusion, which can only be remedied by forms and practices of inclusion that promote and embody ex-prisoners' rights to citizenship. Rather than conceiving post-release problems in terms of individual risk, this book reveals the post-prison terrain to be inherently risky. Risk arises at the intersection of societal expectations and individuals' responses to the pains of release. Society expects that prisons will reform 'offenders' and equip them with skills they need to function effectively and productively in the community. This expectation fails to account for the effects of imprisonment and the disorientating effects of release.

Risk inheres in the ways in which prison-selves emerge and react with their post-prison social environments. These elements of risk feed into and flow from the experience of liminality, which characterises men's status in three key domains: home, identity, connection. For example, some men feel 'at home' in prison in ways that are difficult to replicate outside, and the needs for stability, security and belonging are human needs that go beyond 'housing needs'. The layers of identity embedded in being an ex-prisoner, being a drug user, being unemployed and being a father contain various lines of possibility and constraint. Opportunities for acceptance, trust and generativity, accompanied and symbolised by ritual, allow these sites of *being* to manifest as sites of *becoming*: liminoid, creative, active, resistant. Without such opportunities, these identities can persist as liminal states of in-betweenness, immobility, exclusion. These sites of risk and exclusion constitute nodes in the broader carceral assemblage. The heart of this assemblage, pumping the blood that maintains its lines and flows, is the prison: producing and reproducing, in part, the social harm it purports to remedy.

References

Abrahamsson, A., Springett, J., Karlsson, L. & Ottosson, T (2005). 'Making sense of the challenge of smoking cessation during pregnancy: A phenomenographic approach.' *Health Education Research*, 20(3): pp. 367–78.

ABS, see Australian Bureau of Statistics.

Adult Parole Board. (2009). Adult Parole Board of Victoria 2008–2009 Annual Report, Department of Justice, Victoria.

Adult Parole Board. (2012). Adult Parole Board of Victoria 2011–2012 Annual Report, Department of Justice, Victoria.

AIHW, see Australian Institute of Health and Welfare.

Akerlind, G. (2005). 'Learning about phenomenography: Interviewing, data analysis and the qualitative research paradigm', in J.A. Bowden & P. Green (eds), *Doing Developmental Phenomenography*. Melbourne: RMIT University Press, pp. 63–73.

Anderson, T. (1992). *Take Two: The Criminal Justice System Revisited.* Sydney: Bantam.

Andrews, D.A. & Bonta, J. (1998). *The Psychology of Criminal Conduct*. Cincinnati, OH: Anderson.

Andrews, D.A., Zinger, I., Hoge, R.D., Bonta, J., Gendreau, P. & Cullen, F.T. (1990). 'Does correctional treatment work? A clinically relevant and psychologically informed meta-analysis.' *Criminology*, 28(3): pp. 369–405.

Andrews, J.Y. & Kinner, S.A. (2012). 'Understanding drug-related mortality in released prisoners: A review of national coronial records.' *BMC Public Health*, 12: pp. 270–83.

APB, see Adult Parole Board.

Armstrong, D. (2004). 'A risky business? Research, policy, governmentality and youth offending.' *Youth Justice*, 4(2): pp. 100–16.

Armstrong, D. (2006). 'Becoming criminal: The cultural politics of risk.' *International Journal of Inclusive Education*, 10(2): pp. 265–78.

Arrigo, B.A. & Milovanovic, D. (2009). *Revolution in Penology: Rethinking the Society of Captives*. Lanham, MD: Rowman & Littlefield.

Ashworth, P. & Lucas, U. (2000). 'Achieving empathy and engagement: A practical approach to the design, conduct and reporting of phenomenographic research.' *Studies in Higher Education*, 25(3): pp. 295–308.

Aubrey, R. & Hough, M. (1997). *Assessing Offenders' Needs: Assessment Scales for the Probation Service*. London: Home Office.

Australian Bureau of Statistics. (2008). Prisoners in Australia, cat. no. 4517.0. Canberra: ABS,.

Australian Bureau of Statistics. (2010). Prisoners in Australia, cat. no. 4517.0. Canberra: ABS.

Australian Bureau of Statistics. (2012). Prisoners in Australia, cat. no. 4517.0. , Canberra: ABS.

Australian Institute of Criminology (AIC). (2008). 'Homelessness, drug use and offending', Crime Facts Info No.168. Canberra: Australian Institute of Criminology.

Australian Institute of Health and Welfare. (2010). The Health of Australia's Prisoners 2009, cat. no. PHE 123, Canberra: AIHW.

Awofeso, N. (2004). 'Prison argot and penal discipline.' *Journal of Mundane Behaviour*, 5(1), viewed 17 January 2009 at: http://mundanebehaviour.org/issues/v5n1/awof eso5-1.htm

Baldry, E. (2007). Throughcare: Making the Policy a Reality. Paper presented to the Reintegration Puzzle Conference: Fitting the Pieces Together, Sydney, 7–8 May.

Baldry, E. (2009). 'Prisons and vulnerable persons: Institutions and patriarchy', in M. Segrave (ed.), *Australia and New Zealand Critical Criminology Conference 2009: Conference Proceedings*. Victoria: Monash University, School of Political and Social Inquiry, pp. 18–30.

Baldry, E., Dowse, L., Snoyman, P., Clarence, M. & Webster, I. (2008). 'A critical perspective on mental health disorders and cognitive disability in the criminal justice system', in C. Cunneen & M. Salter (eds), *Proceedings of the Australia and New Zealand Critical Criminology Conference 2008*. Sydney: UNSW, Crime and Justice Research Network.

Baldry, E., Dowse, L. & Clarence, M. (2010). Pathways to Prison for Mentally Ill and Cognitively Impaired Offenders. Background paper, presented to the NSW District Court Annual Conference, Sydney.

Baldry, E., McDonnell, D., Maplestone, P. & Peeters, M. (2002). Ex-Prisoners and Accommodation: What Bearing Do Different Forms of Housing Have on Social Integration of Ex-Prisoners? Paper presented to the Housing, Crime and Stronger Communities Conference, Australian Institute of Criminology and the Australian Housing and Urban Research Institute, Melbourne, 6–7 May.

Baldry, E., McDonnell, D., Maplestone, P. & Peeters, M. (2003). 'Ex-prisoners and accommodation: What bearing do different forms of housing have on social reintegration? Final report. Melbourne: AHURI.

Baldry, E., McDonnell, D., Maplestone, P. & Peeters, M. (2006). 'Ex-prisoners, accommodation and the state: Post-release in Australia.' *Australian & New Zealand Journal of Criminology*, 39(1): pp. 20–33.

Baldry, E., Ruddock, J. & Taylor, J. (2008). Aboriginal Women with Dependent Children Leaving Prison Project: Needs Analysis Report, commissioned by the Western Sydney Strategic Plan against Homelessness, Homelessness NSW.

Ball, D., Weisberg, R. & Dansky, K. (2008). 'The first 72 hours of re-entry: Seizing the moment of release.' The Stanford Executive Sessions on Sentencing and Corrections, Stanford Criminal Justice Centre, California.

Barnard, A., McCosker, H. & Gerber, R. (1999). 'Phenomenography: A qualitative research approach for exploring understanding in health care.' *Journal of Qualitative Health Research*, 9(2):pp. 212–26.

Bartels, L. (2009). 'Challenges in mainstreaming specialty courts.' *Trends & Issues in Crime and Criminal Justice*, no. 383. Canberra: Australian Institute of Criminology.

Bartholomew, T., Patton, S., Balkin, S. & Stock, L. (2004). Final Report of the Implementation of Victoria's Pilot Transitional Housing Management–Corrections Housing Pathways Initiative (THM–CHPI).

Baugh, B. (2005). 'Theory', in A. Parr (ed.), *The Deleuze Dictionary*. Edinburgh: Edinburgh University Press, pp. 276–8.

Bauman, Z. (1998). *Globalization: The Human Consequences*. New York: Columbia University Press.

Beck, U. (1992). *Risk Society: Towards a New Modernity*. London: Sage.

Belcher, J. & Al Yaman, F. (2007). Prisoner Health in Australia: Contemporary Information Collection and a Way Forward. Canberra: Australian Institute of Health and Welfare.

Bettelheim, B. (1960). *The Informed Heart: Autonomy in a Mass Age*. Glencoe, IL: The Free Press.

Biles, D., Harding, R. & Walker, J. (1999). 'The deaths of offenders serving community correction orders.' *Trends & Issues in Crime and Criminal Justice*, no. 107. Canberra: Australian Institute of Criminology.

Binswanger, I.A., Stern, M.F., Deyo, R.A., Heagerty, P.J., Cheadle, A., Elmore, J.G. & Koepsell, T.D. (2007). 'Release from prison – A high risk of death for former inmates.' *New England Journal of Medicine*, 356: pp. 157–65.

Bird, S.M. & Hutchison, S.J. (2003). 'Male drugs-related deaths in the fortnight after release from prison: Scotland, 1996–99.' *Addiction*, 98(2): pp. 185–90.

Borzycki, M. (2005). Interventions for Prisoners Returning to the Community. Canberra: Australian Government Attorney-General's Department.

Boundas, C. (2005). In A. Parr, (ed.), *The Deleuze Dictionary*. Edinburgh: Edinburgh University Press, pp. 191–3; 268–70.

Bowden, J.A. (2000). 'Experience of phenomenographic research: A personal account', in J.A. Bowden & E. Walsh (eds), *Phenomenography*. Melbourne: RMIT University Press, pp. 47–61.

Braithwaite, J. (1989). *Crime, Shame and Reintegration*. Cambridge, UK: Cambridge University Press.

Braithwaite, J. & Braithwaite, V. (2001). 'Part one', in E. Ahmed, N. Harris, J. Braithwaite & V. Braithwaite (eds), *Shame Management through Reintegration*. Cambridge, UK: University of Cambridge Press: pp. 3–69.

Braithwaite J. & Mugford, S. (1994). 'Conditions of successful reintegration ceremonies: Dealing with juvenile offenders.' *British Journal of Criminology*, 34: pp. 139–71.

Brown, C.P. & O'Sullivan, K. (2013). 'Somebody's mum, somebody's dad: Parents as offenders and offenders as parents in New South Wales.' *Australasian Journal of Correctional Staff Development*, Brush Farm Corrective Services Academy, Corrective Services NSW.

Brown, D. (2009). 'Strolling the coastline: Criminology in everyday life: through "landscape" from gaol to "badlands".' *Law Text Culture*, 13(1): pp. 311–38.

Brown, D. (2010). 'The limited benefit of prison in controlling crime.' *Current Issues in Criminal Justice*, 22(1): pp. 137–48.

Brown, M. (2005). 'Corrections', in D. Chappell & P. Wilson (eds), *Issues in Australian Crime and Criminal Justice*. Sydney: LexisNexis Butterworths, pp. 101–38.

Brown, M. & Ross, S. (2010a). 'Mentoring, social capital and desistance: A study of women released from prison.' *Australian & New Zealand Journal of Criminology*, 43(1): pp. 31–50.

Brown, M. & Ross, S. (2010b). 'Assisting and supporting women released from prison: Is mentoring the answer?'. *Current Issues in Criminal Justice*, 22(2): pp. 217–32.

Brumann, C. (2004). 'Comment on James P. Boggs "The Culture Concept as Theory, in Context", p. 202.' *Current Anthropology*, 45(2): p. 199.

Burnett, R. (2007). The Personal Touch in Ex-Offender Reintegration. Paper presented to the Third Annual Conference on 'The Reintegration Puzzle: Fitting the Pieces Together', hosted by Deakin University, Sydney, 7–8 May.

Burnett, R. & Maruna, S. (2004). 'So "prison works", does it? The criminal careers of 130 men released from prison under Home Secretary, Michael Howard.' *The Howard Journal*, 43(4): pp. 390–404.

Burnett, R. & Maruna, S. (2006). 'The kindness of prisoners: Strengths-based resettlement in theory and in action.' *Criminology & Criminal Justice*, 6(1): pp. 83–106.

Butler, T. & Allnutt, S. (2003). Mental Illness among New South Wales Prisoners. Sydney: NSW Corrections Health Service.

Butler, T., Levy, M., Dolan, K. & Kaldor, J. (2003). 'Drug use and its correlates in an Australian prisoner population.' *Addiction Research and Theory*, 11(2): pp. 89–101.

Butler, T. & Milner, L. (2003). The 2001 Inmate Health Survey. Sydney: NSW Corrections Health Service.

Carcach, C. & Grant, A. (1999). 'Imprisonment in Australia: Trends in prison populations & imprisonment rates 1982–1998.' *Trends & Issues in Crime and Criminal Justice*, no. 130. Canberra: Australian Institute of Criminology.

Cardozo-Freeman, I. & Delorme, E.P. (1984). *The Joint: Language and Culture in a Maximum Security Prison*. Springfield, IL: Charles C. Thomas.

Carlen, P. (2005). 'Imprisonment and the penal body politic: The cancer of disciplinary governance', in A. Liebling & S. Maruna, (eds), *The Effects of Imprisonment*. Cullompton, UK: Willan, pp. 421–41.

Carlton, B. & Segrave, M. (2009). 'Surviving outside: Bearing witness to women's post-release experiences of survival and death', in M. Segrave (ed.), *Australia and New Zealand Critical Criminology Conference 2009: Conference Proceedings*. Victoria: Monash University, School of Political and Social Inquiry, pp. 41–50.

Centrelink. (2010). Newstart Allowance payment rates. Available at: www.centrelink. gov.au

CEPT, see Commission on English Prisons Today.

Clemmer, D. (1940). *The Prison Community*. Boston, MA: Christopher.

Cohen, S. & Taylor, L. (1972). *Psychological Survival: The Experience of Long-Term Imprisonment*. Harmondsworth, UK: Penguin.

Colman, F.J. (2005). 'Rhizome', in A. Parr, (ed.), *The Deleuze Dictionary*. Edinburgh: Edinburgh University Press, pp. 231–3.

Combessie, P. (1998). 'The 'sensitive perimeter' of the prison: A key to understanding the durability of the penal institution', in V. Ruggiero, I. Taylor & N. South, (eds), *The New European Criminology: Crime and Social Order in Europe*. London & New York: Routledge: pp. 125–35.

Combessie, P. (2002). 'Marking the carceral boundary: Penal stigma in the long shadow of the prison', *Ethnography*, 3(4): pp. 535–55.

Comfort, M.L. (2002). 'Papa's house: The prison as domestic and social satellite', *Ethnography*, 3(4): pp. 467–99.

Commission on English Prisons Today. (2009). Do Better, Do Less: The Report on English Prisons Today, The Howard League for Penal Reform: London.

Connell, R.W. (1982). 'Class, patriarchy, and Sartre's theory of practice.' *Theory & Society*, 11: pp. 305–20.

Connell, R.W. (1983). *Which Way Is Up? Essays on Sex, Class and Culture*. Sydney, Australia: Allen & Unwin.

Connell, R.W. (1987). *Gender and Power*. Sydney, Australia: Allen & Unwin.

Connell, R.W. (1995). *Masculinities*. Sydney: Allen & Unwin.

Connell, R.W. (2000). *The Men and the Boys*. Sydney: Allen & Unwin.

Connell, R.W. & Messerschmidt, J.W. (2005). 'Hegemonic masculinity: Rethinking the concept.' *Gender & Society*, 19(6): pp. 829–59.

Cook, S. & Davies, S. (2000). Dying Outside: Women, Imprisonment and Post-Release Mortality. Paper presented to the Women in Corrections: Staff and Clients Conference, Adelaide, 31 Oct–1 Nov.

Corrections Victoria. (2009a). Statistical Profile of the Victorian Prison System 2004–05 to 2008–09. Melbourne: Department of Justice, Victoria.

Corrections Victoria. (2011). Statistical Profile of the Victorian Prison System 2006–07 to 2010–11. Melbourne: Department of Justice, Victoria.

Crawley, E. & Crawley, P. (2008). 'Culture, performance and disorder: The communicative quality of prison violence', in J. Byrne, D. Hummer & F. Taxman, (eds), *The Culture of Prison Violence*. Boston, MA: Pearson, pp. 123–36.

Crotty, M. (1998). *The Foundations of Social Research: Meaning and Perspective in the Research Process*. Sydney: Allen & Unwin.

Cunningham, A. (2001). 'Forgotten families: The impacts of imprisonment.' Australian Institute of Family Studies, *Family Matters*, 59: pp. 35–8.

Daly, S.R., Adams, R.S. & Bodner, G.M. (2012). 'What does it mean to design? A qualitative investigation of design professional's experiences.' *Journal of Engineering Education*, 101(2): pp. 187–219.

Day, A., Howells, K. & Rickwood, D. (2003). The Victorian Juvenile Justice Rehabilitation Review. Melbourne: Department of Human Services, Victoria.

De Freitas, E. (2013). 'What were you thinking? A Deleuzian/Guatarrian analysis of communication in the mathematics classroom.' *Educational Philosophy & Theory*, 45(3): pp. 287–300.

DeLanda, M. (2006). *A New Philosophy of Society: Assemblage Theory and Social Complexity*. London: Continuum.

Delaney, C. (2004). *Investigating Culture: An Experiential Introduction to Anthropology*. Oxford, UK: Blackwell.

Deleuze, G. & Foucault, M. (1977). 'Intellectuals and Power', in M. Foucault, *Language, Counter-Memory, Practice: Selected Essays and Interviews*, transl. D.F. Bouchard (ed.) & S. Simon. Ithaca, NY: Cornell University Press.

Deleuze, G. & Guattari, F. (1987). *A Thousand Plateaus*, transl. B. Massumi. Minnesota, MN: University of Minneapolis Press.

Deloitte, see Deloitte Consulting.

Deloitte Consulting. (2003). Victorian Prisoner Health Study. Report to the Department of Justice, Corrections Victoria. Melbourne: Department of Justice, Victoria.

Denborough, D. (1994). 'Inside/outside.' *XY Men Sex Politics*, 4(3): pp. 10–12.

Denborough, D. (2001). 'Grappling with issues of privilege: A male prison worker's perspective', in D.F. Sabo, T.A. Kupers & W.J. London (eds), *Prison Masculinities*. Philadelphia, PA: Temple University Press: pp. 73–7.

Denzin, N. & Lincoln, Y.S. (1994). *Handbook of Qualitative Research*. California: Sage Publications.

Department of Justice. (2009) Annual Report 2008–091. Melbourne: Department of Justice, Victoria.

Dhami, M.K., Mandel, D.R., Loewenstein, G. & Ayton, P. (2006). 'Prisoners' positive illusions of their post-release success.' *Law & Human Behaviour*, 30: pp. 631–47.

Donohue, E. & Moore, D. (2009). 'When is an offender not an offender? Power, the client and shifting penal subjectivities.' *Punishment & Society*, 11(3): pp. 319–36.

Douglas, M. (1966). *Purity and Danger: An Analysis of Concepts of Pollution and Taboo*. London: Routledge & Kegan Paul. Reprinted (2002) London & New York: Routledge Classics.

Douglas, M. (1975). *Implicit Meanings: Essays in Anthropology*. London: Routledge & Kegan Paul.

Dowse, L., Baldry, E. & Snoyman, P. (2009). 'Disabling criminology: Conceptualizing the intersections of critical disability studies and critical criminology for people with mental health and cognitive disabilities in the criminal justice system.' *Australian Journal of Human Rights*, 15(1): pp. 29–46.

Eagleton, T. (2000). *The Idea of Culture*. Oxford, UK: Blackwell.

Easteal, P. (1992). 'Women and crime: Imprisonment issues.' *Trends & Issues in Crime and Criminal Justice*, no. 35. AIC: Canberra.

Easteal, P. (2001). 'Women in Australian prisons: The cycle of abuse and dysfunctional environments.' *The Prison Journal*, 81(1): pp. 87–112.

Einat, T. & Einat, H. (2000). 'Inmate argot as an expression of prison subculture: The Israeli case.' *The Prison Journal*, 80(3): pp. 309–325.

Evans, T. & Wallace, P. (2008). 'A prison within a prison? The masculinity narratives of male prisoners.' *Men & Masculinities*, 10(4): pp. 484–507.

Ewald, A.C. (2002). '"Civil death": The ideological paradox of criminal disenfranchisement law in the United States.' *Wisconsin Law Review*, pp. 1045–132.

Farrall, S. (2002). *Rethinking what Works with Offenders: Probation, Social Context, and Desistance from Crime*. Cullompton, UK: Willan.

Farrall, S. (2004). 'Social capital and offender reintegration: Making probation desistance focused', in S. Maruna & R. Immarigeon (eds), *After Crime and Punishment: Pathways to Offender Reintegration*. Cullompton, UK: Willan.

Farrall, S. & Calverley, A. (2006). *Understanding Desistance from Crime*. Maidenhead, UK: Open University Press.

Farrall, S., Sharpe, G., Hunter, B. & Calverley, A. (2011). 'Theorizing structural and individual-level processes in desistance and persistence: Outlining an integrated perspective.' *Australian & New Zealand Journal of Criminology*, 44(2): 218–34.

Feeley, M.F. & Simon, J. (1992). 'The new penology: Notes on the emerging strategy of corrections and its implications.' *Criminology*, 30(4): pp. 449–74.

Fenwick, M. (2004). 'New directions in cultural criminology.' *Theoretical Criminology*, 8(3); pp. 377–86.

Ferrell, J. (1999). 'Cultural criminology.' *Annual Review of Sociology*, 25: pp. 395–418.

Ferrell, J. (2001). *Tearing Down the Streets: Adventures in Urban Anarchy*. New York: Palgrave.

Ferrell, J., Hayward, K. and Young, J. (2008). *Cultural Criminology*. London: Sage.

Fischer, M.J.M. (2007). 'Culture and cultural analysis as experimental systems.' *Cultural Anthropology*, 22(1): pp. 1–65.

Five8. (2011). 'Circle of support, sure, but why the accountability?', 6 May. [Blog]: five8australia.wordpress.com

Foster, T.W. (1982). '"Mushfaking": A compensatory behaviour of prisoners.' *Journal of Social Psychology*, 117(1): p. 115–25.

Foucault, M. (1979). *Discipline and Punish: The Birth of the Prison*. Harmondsworth, UK: Penguin.

Fox, A., Khan, L., Briggs, D., Rees-Jones, N., Thompson, Z. & Owens, J. (2005). Throughcare and Aftercare: Approaches and Promising Practice in Service Delivery for Clients Released from Prison or Leaving Residential Rehabilitation. Home Office Online Report 01/05. UK: Research development and Statistics Directorate, Home Office, London.

Garland, D. (2001). *The Culture of Control: Crime and Social Order in Contemporary Society*. Oxford, UK: Oxford University Press.

Garland, D. (2006). 'Concepts of culture in the sociology of punishment.' *Theoretical Criminology*, 10(4): pp. 419–47.

Garside, R. (2009). Risky People or Risky Societies? Rethinking Interventions for Young Adults in Transition. Transition to Adulthood, Report no. 1. London: Centre for Crime and Justice Studies.

Geertz, C. (1973). *The Interpretation of Cultures: Selected Essays*. New York: Basic.

Gelb, K. (2007). Recidivism of Sex Offenders: Research Paper. Victoria: Sentencing Advisory Council.

Gendreau, P., Little, T. & Goggin, C. (1996). 'A meta-analysis of the predictors of adult offender recidivism: What works!' *Criminology*, 34(4): pp. 575–609.

Giddens, A. (1999). 'Risk and responsibility.' *The Modern Law Review*, 62(1): pp. 1–11.

Gideon, L. (2009). 'What shall I do now? Released offenders' expectations for supervision upon release.' *International Journal of Offender Therapy & Comparative Criminology*, 53(10): pp. 43–56.

Gilles, M., Swingler, E., Craven, C. & Larson, A. (2008). 'Prison health and public health responses at a regional prison in Western Australia.' *Australian & New Zealand Journal of Public Health*, 32(6): pp. 549–53.

Glaser, W. & Deane, K. (1999). 'Normalisation in an abnormal world: A study of prisoners with an intellectual disability.' *International Journal of Offender Therapy & Comparative Criminology*, 43(3): pp. 338–56.

Goffman, E. (1959). *The Presentation of Self in Everyday Life*. New York: Anchor.

Goffman, E. (1961). *Asylums: Essays on the Social Situation of Mental Patients and Other Inmates*. Harmondsworth, UK: Penguin.

Goffman, E. (1963). *Stigma: Notes on the Management of Spoiled Identity*. Englewood Cliffs, NJ: Prentice-Hall.

Goffman, E. (1967). *Interaction Ritual: Essays on Face-to-Face Behaviour*. Harmondsworth, UK: Penguin.

Gowan, T. (2002). 'The nexus: Homelessness and incarceration in two American cities.' *Ethnography*, 3(4): pp. 500–34.

Graffam, J. & Shinkfield, A. (2007). The Relationship between Emotional State and Other Variables Influencing Successful Reintegration of Ex-Prisoners, Report to the Criminology Research Council. Victoria: Deakin University, School of Psychology.

Graham, A. (2003). 'Post-prison mortality: unnatural death among people released from Victorian prisons between January 1990 and December 1999.' *Australia and New Zealand Journal of Criminology*, 36(1): 94–108.

Gray, P. (2005). 'The politics of risk and young offenders' experiences of social exclusion and restorative justice.' *British Journal of Criminology*, 45: pp. 938–57.

Green, P. (2005). 'A rigorous journey into phenomenography: From a naturalistic inquirer viewpoint', in J.A. Bowden & P. Green (eds), *Doing Developmental Phenomenography*. Melbourne: RMIT University Press, pp. 32–46.

Grimes, R.L. (2000). *Deeply into the Bone: Re-inventing Rites of Passage*. Berkeley & Los Angeles, CA: University of California Press.

Grunseit, A., Forell, S. & McCarron, E. (2008). *Taking Justice into Custody: The Legal Needs of Prisoners*. Sydney: Law and Justice Foundation of NSW.

Guba, E.G. & Lincoln, Y.S. (1981). *Effective Evaluation: improving the usefulness of evaluation results through responsive and naturalistic approaches*. San Francisco: Jossey-Bass Publishers.

Guest, G., Bunce, A. & Johnson, L. (2006). 'How many interviews are enough? An experiment with data saturation and variability.' *Field Methods*, 18: pp. 59–82.

Haermeyer, A. (2001). In '$80.8 million to break the cycle of re-offending', State Budget 2001, press release from the Minister for Corrections and the Attorney General, 15 May.

Halsey, M. (2006). 'Negotiating conditional release.' *Punishment & Society*, 8(2): pp. 147–81.

Halsey, M. (2007). 'Assembling recidivism: The promise and contingencies of post-release life.' *Journal of Criminal Law & Criminology*, 97(4): pp. 1209–60.

Halsey, M. (2010). 'Imprisonment and prisoner re-entry in Australia.' *Dialectical Anthropology*, 34(4): pp. 545–54.

Halsey, M. & Harris, V. (2011). 'Prisoner futures: Sensing the signs of generativity.' *Australian & New Zealand Journal of Criminology*, 44(1): pp. 74–93.

Haney, C. (2003). 'The psychological impact of incarceration: Implications for postprison adjustment', in J. Travis & M. Waul (eds), *Prisoners Once Removed: The Impact of Incarceration and Reentry on Children, Families, and Communities*. Washington, DC: The Urban Institute Press, pp. 33–66.

Haney, C. (2005). 'The contextual revolution in psychology and the question of prison effects', in A. Liebling & S. Maruna (eds), *The Effects of Imprisonment*. Cullompton, UK: Willan, pp. 66–93.

Hannah-Moffat, K. (2005). 'Criminogenic needs and the transformative risk subject: Hybridizations of risk/need in penality.' *Punishment & Society*, 7(1): pp. 29–51.

Hannon, T. (2006). Children: Unintended Victims of Legal Process: A Review of Policies and Legislation Affecting Children with Incarcerated Parents. Discussion paper prepared by Flat Out Inc. and Victorian Association for the Care and Resettlement of Offenders (VACRO), Melbourne.

Haralambos, M. (1986). *Sociology Themes and Perspectives*. London: Bell and Hyman.

Harcourt, B. (2008). 'Rethinking the carceral through an institutional lens: On prisons and asylums in the United States.' *Champ pénal/Penal Field*, vol. V. Available at: http://champpenal.revues.org/7561

Harcourt, B. (2011). 'An institutionalization effect: The impact of mental hospitalization and imprisonment on homicide in the United States, 1934–2001.' *Journal of Legal Studies*, 40(1): pp. 39–83.

Hartley, C. & Baraka, E. (2007). 'Nothing more than chicken feed: The inadequacy of Centrelink's crisis payment for released prisoners and people fleeing domestic violence.' Sydney: Homeless Persons' Legal Service and the Public Interest Advocacy Centre.

Harvard Law Review. (1937). 'Civil death statutes. Medieval fiction in a modern world.' *Harvard Law Review*, 50(6): pp. 968–77.

Hasselgren, B. & Beach, D. (1997). 'Phenomenography – a "good-for-nothing brother" of phenomenology? Outline of an analysis.' *Higher Education Research & Development*, 16(2): 191–202.

Hayward, K.J. (2012). 'Five spaces of cultural criminology.' *British Journal of Criminology*, 52(3): pp. 441–62.

Hayward, K.J. & Young, J. (2004). 'Cultural criminology: Some notes on the script.' *Theoretical Criminology*, 8(3); pp. 259–73.

Healy, D. (2010). *The Dynamics of Desistance: Charting Pathways through Change*. Cullompton, UK: Willan.

Healy, D. & O'Donnell, I. (2008). 'Calling time on crime: Motivation, generativity and agency in Irish probationers.' *Probation Journal*, 55(1): pp. 25–38.

Healy, K., Foley, D. & Walsh, K. (2000). Parents in Prison and Their Families: Everyone's Business and No-one's Concern. Brisbane: Catholic Prisons Ministry.

Hedderman, C. (2007). 'Rediscovering resettlement: Narrowing the gap between policy rhetoric and practice reality', in A. Hucklesby & L. Hagley-Dickinson (eds), *Prisoner Resettlement: Policy and Practice.* Cullompton, UK: Willan: pp. 9–25.

Hellard, M.E., Aitken, C.K., & Hocking, J.S. (2007). 'Tattooing in prison: Not such a pretty picture.' *American Journal of Infection Control*, 35(7): pp. 477–80.

Hellard, M.E., Hocking, J.S. & Crofts, N. (2004). 'The prevalence and the risk behaviours associated with the transmission of the hepatitis C virus in Australian correctional facilities.' *Epidemiology & Infection*, 132(3): pp. 409–15.

Hensley, C., Wright, J., Tewksbury, R. & Castle, T. (2003). 'The evolving nature of prison argot and sexual hierarchies.' *The Prison Journal*, 83(3); pp. 289–300.

Her Majesty's Inspectorate of Prisons and Her Majesty's Inspectorate of Probation. (2001). Through the Prison Gate, a Joint Thematic Review by HM Inspectorates of Prisons and Probation. HMIP: England and Wales.

Herzog-Evans, M. (2011). 'Judicial rehabilitation in France: Helping with the desisting process and acknowledging achieved desistance.' *European Journal of Probation*, 3(1): 4–19.

Hinton, T. (2004). The Housing and Support Needs of Ex-Prisoners: The Role of the Supported Accommodation Assistance Program. Salvation Army: Victoria.

Hirsch, A.E., Dietrich, S.M., Landau, R., Schneider, P.D., Ackelsberg, I., Bernstein-Baker, J. & Hohenstein, J. (2002). Every Door Closed: Barriers Facing Parents with Criminal Records. Washington, DC: Centre for Law and Social Policy/ Philadelphia, PA: Community Legal Services.

HMIE/HMIP, see Her Majesty's Inspectorate of Education and Her Majesty's Inspectorate of Prisons.

HMIP&P, see Her Majesty's Inspectorate of Prisons and Her Majesty's Inspectorate of Probation.

Hobbs, M., Krazlan, K., Ridout, S., Mai, Q., Knuiman, M. & Chapman, R. (2006). Mortality and Morbidity in Prisoners after Release from Prison in Western Australian 1995–2003. Canberra: Australian Institute of Criminology.

Holland, S., Persson, P., McClelland, M. & Berends, R. (2007). 'Intellectual disability in the Victorian prison system: Characteristics of prisoners with an intellectual disability released from prison in 2003–2006', Corrections Research Paper Series, paper no. 2. Melbourne: Department of Justice, Victoria.

Howard, S. (2000). 'Fathering behind bars', paper presented at the 7th Australian Institute of Family Studies (AIFS) Conference, 24–26 July 2000, Sydney, Australia.

Hudson, B. (2003). *Justice in the Risk Society: Challenging and Re-affirming Justice in Late Modernity.* London/Thousand Oaks, CA: Sage.

Hunt, D. & Saab, S. (2009). 'Viral Hepatitis in Incarcerated Adults: A Medical and Public Health Concern.' *The American Journal of Gastroenterology*, 104(4): 1024–1031.

Indig, D., Topp, L., Ross, B., Mamoon, H., Border, B., Kumar, S. & McNamara, M. (2010). 2009 NSW Inmate Health Survey: Key Findings Report. Sydney: Justice Health.

Irwin, J. (1970). *The Felon.* Berkeley & Los Angeles, CA: University of California Press.

Irwin, J. & Cressey, D.R. (1962). 'Thieves, convicts and the inmate culture.' *Social Problems*, 10(1): pp. 142–55.

Jewkes, Y. (2002). *Captive Audience: Media, Masculinity and Power in Prisons.* Cullompton, UK: Willan.

Jewkes, Y. (2005a). 'Men behind bars: "Doing" masculinity as an adaptation to imprisonment.' *Men & Masculinities*, 8(1): pp. 44–63.

Jewkes, Y. (2005b). 'Loss, liminality and the life sentence: Managing identity through a disrupted life course', in A. Liebling & S. Maruna (eds), *The Effects of Imprisonment*. Cullompton, UK: Willan, pp. 366–88.

Jürgens, R., Ball, A. & Verster, A. (2009). 'Interventions to reduce HIV transmission related to injecting drug use in prison', *The Lancet Infectious Diseases*, 9: 57–66.

Kane, S.C. (2004). 'The unconventional methods of cultural criminology.' *Theoretical Criminology*, 8(3): pp. 303–21.

Kariminia, A., Butler, T.G., Corben, S.P., Levy, M.H., Grant, L., Kaldor, J.M. & Law M.G. (2007a). 'Extreme cause-specific mortality in a cohort of adult prisoners – 1988 to 2002: A data-linkage study.' *International Journal of Epidemiology*, 36: pp. 310–16.

Kariminia A., Butler, T. & Levy, M. (2007b). 'Aboriginal and non-Aboriginal health differentials in Australian prisoners.' *Australian & New Zealand Journal of Public Health*, 31: pp. 366–71.

Kariminia A., Law, M., Butler, T., Levy, M., Corben, S., Kaldor, J.M. & Grant, L. (2007c). 'Suicide risk among recently released prisoners in New South Wales, Australia.' *Medical Journal of Australia*, 187(7): pp. 387–90.

Karp, D.R. (2010). 'Unlocking men, unmasking masculinities: Doing men's work in prison.' *Journal of Men's Studies*, 18(1): pp. 63–83.

Kelly, A. (2008). 'Living loss: An exploration of the internal space of liminality.' *Mortality*, 13(4): pp. 335–50.

Kelsall, J. (2009). Harm Reduction Victoria. Presentation to the Community Forum: Post-Release Health Needs of Prisoners Who Use Drugs, Yarra Drug and Health Forum, Richmond, 23 June.

Kemshall, H. (2002). *Risk, Social Policy and Welfare*. Buckingham, UK: Open University Press.

Keyzer, P. & Coyle, I.R. (2009). 'Reintegrating sex offenders into the community: Queensland's proposed reforms.' *Alternative Law Journal*, 34(1): pp. 27–31.

Kinner, S.A. (2006a). 'The post-release experience of prisoners in Queensland', Brisbane: University of Queensland, Queensland Alcohol and Drug Research and Education Centre (QADREC).

Kinner, S.A. (2006b). 'The post-release experience of prisoners in Queensland.' *Trends & Issues in Crime and Criminal Justice*, no. 325. Canberra: Australian Institute of Criminology.

Kinner, S.A. (2008). 'Passports to advantage: Health and capacity building as a basis for social integration.' *Flinders Journal of Law Reform*, 10(3): pp. 581–9.

Kinner, S.A. (2010). 'Commentary on Merrall et al. (2010): Understanding mortality and health outcomes for ex-prisoners – first steps on a long road.' *Addiction*, 105: pp. 1555–6.

Kinner, S.A., Lennox, N. & Taylor, M. (2009). 'Randomized controlled trial of a post-release intervention for prisoners with and without intellectual disability.' *Journal on Developmental Disabilities*, 15(2): pp. 72–6.

Kohl, R., Matthews Hoover, H., McDonald, S.M. & Solomon, A.L. (2008). Massachusetts Recidivism Study: A Closer Look at Releases and Returns to Prison. Washington, DC: The Urban Institute.

Koob, G.F. & Volkow, N.D. (2012). 'Neurocircuitry of addiction.' *Neuropsychopharmacology*, 35: pp. 217–38.

Krieg, A.S. (2006). 'Aboriginal incarceration: Health and social impacts.' *Medical Journal of Australia*, 184(10): pp. 534–6.

Kroeber, A.L. & Kluckhohn, C. (1952). *Culture: A Critical Review of Concepts and Definitions*. New York: Vintage.

Kupers, T. (2005). 'Toxic masculinity as a barrier to mental health treatment in prison.' *Journal of Clinical Psychology*, 61(6): 713–724.

Kuppens, J. & Ferwerda, H. (2008). From the Inside to the Outside: The Aftercare Alignment Project for Ex-Prisoners. Arnhem, Netherlands: Advies-en Onderzoeksgroep Beke.

Kvale, S. (1996). *Interviews: An Introduction to Qualitative Research Interviewing*. London: Sage.

Larmour, P. (2008). 'Corruption and the concept of "Culture": Evidence from the Pacific Islands.' *Crime, Law, & Social Change*, 49: pp. 225–39.

Laub, J. & Sampson, R.J. (2001). 'Understanding desistance from crime.' *Crime & Justice: A Review of the Research*, 28: pp. 1–70.

La Vigne, N.G., Shollenberger, T.L. & Debus, S. (2009). One Year Out: Tracking the Experiences of Male Prisoners Returning to Houston, Texas. Washington, DC: The Urban Institute.

LeBel, T.P. (2007). 'An examination of the impact of formerly incarcerated persons helping others.' *Journal of Offender Rehabilitation*, 46(1/2): pp. 1–24.

LeBel, T.P. (2009). 'Formerly incarcerated persons' use of advocacy/activism as a coping orientation in the reintegration process', in B. Veysey, J. Christian & D.J. Martinez (eds), *How Offenders Transform Their Lives*. Cullompton, UK: Willan, pp: 165–87.

LeBel, T.P., Burnett, R., Maruna, S. & Bushway, S. (2008). 'The "chicken and egg" of subjective and social factors in desistance from crime.' *European Journal of Criminology*, 5(2): pp. 131–59.

Lecercle, J.-J. (2002). *Deleuze and Language*. Basingstoke, UK, & New York: Palgrave Macmillan.

Liebling, A. & Maruna, S. (eds) (2005). *The Effects of Imprisonment*. Cullompton, UK: Willan.

Liebmann, M. & Braithwaite, S. (1999). Restorative Justice in Custodial Settings: Report for the Restorative Justice Working Group in Northern Ireland, Restorative Justice Ireland Network.

Lindquist, C., Hardison, J. & Lattimore, P.K. (2003). Reentry Courts Process Evaluation (Phase 1), Final Report. Prepared for the National Institute of Justice, Washington, DC.

Link Out. (2008). Training Manual. Melbourne: ACSO.

Lockhart, G., Ullmann, B. & Chant, J. (2008). 'You're hired! Encouraging the employment of exoffenders.' Policy Exchange Research Notes, September 2008. London: Policy Exchange.

Logrip, M.L., Zorrilla, E.P. & Koob, G.F. (2012). 'Stress modulation of drug self-administration: Implications for addiction comorbidity with post-traumatic stress disorder.' *Neuropharmacology*, 62(2): pp. 552–64.

Lorraine, T. (2005). 'Lines of Flight' in A. Parr (Ed.) *The Deleuze Dictionary*. Edinburgh: Edinburgh University Press.

Lösel, F. (2012). Risk and Protective Factors in the Resettlement of Imprisoned Fathers with their Families: Final Report. UK: Ormiston Children and Families Trust/ University of Cambridge, Institute of Criminology.

Lusher, D. & Robins, G. (2006). 'Hegemonic and other masculinities in local social contexts.' *Men & Masculinities*, 11(4), pp. 387–423.

Lynch, J. & Sabol, W. (2001). *Prisoner Reentry in Perspective*. Washington, DC: The Urban Institute.

Lynn, P. & Armstrong, G. (1996). *From Pentonville to Pentridge: A History of Prisons in Victoria*. Melbourne: State Library of Victoria.

McCarthy, B. & Hagan, J. (1991). 'Homelessness: A criminogenic situation?'. *British Journal of Criminology*, 31(4): pp. 393–410.

McEwen, B.S. & Seeman, T. (2009). 'Allostatic load and allostasis', Allostatic Load Notebook, Macarthur Research Network on SES and Health, University of California, San Francisco, CA.

McEwen, B.S. & Stellar, E. (1993). 'Stress and the individual: Mechanisms leading to disease.' *Archives of Internal Medicine*, 153(18): pp. 2093–101.

McGregor, C., Ali, R., Lokan, R., Christie, P. & Darke, S. (2002). 'Accidental fatalities among heroin users in South Australia, 1994–1997: Toxicological findings and circumstances of death.' *Addiction Research & Theory*, 10(4): pp. 335–46.

McGuire, J. (2002). 'Criminal sanctions versus psychologically-based interventions with offenders: A comparative empirical analysis.' *Psychology, Crime & Law*, 8: pp. 183–208.

McNeill, F. (2011). 'Supporting desistance from crime: Reconfiguring penal practice', screencast produced by the Institute for Research and Innovation in Social Services (IRISS), Glasgow, UK.

McNeill, F. (2012). 'Four forms of "offender" rehabilitation: Towards an interdisciplinary perspective.' *Legal & Criminological Psychology*, 17(1): 18–36.

McNeill, F., Batchelor, S., Burnett, R. & Knox, J. (2005). 21st Century Social Work – Reducing Reoffending: Key Practice Skills. Edinburgh: Scottish Executive.

McNeill, F. & Maruna, S. (2007). 'Giving up and giving back: Desistance, generativity and social work with offenders', in G. McIvor and P. Raynor (eds), *Developments in Social Work with Offenders*. London: Jessica Kingsley, pp. 224–39.

McNeill, F., Raynor, P. & Trotter, C. (eds) (2010). *Offender Supervision: New Directions in Theory, Research and Practice*. Cullompton, UK: Willan.

Makkai, T. & McGregor, K. (2003). Drug Use Monitoring in Australia (DUMA): 2002 Annual Report on Drug Use among Police Detainees. AIC Research and Public Policy Series no. 47. Canberra: Australian Institute of Criminology.

Makkai, T. & Payne, J. (2003). Drugs and Crime: A Study of Incarcerated Male Offenders. AIC Research and Public Policy Series no. 52. Canberra: Australian Institute of Criminology.

Mann, L., Dall'Alba, G. & Radcliffe, D. (2007). 'Using phenomenography to investigate different ways of experiencing sustainable design', in *Proceedings of the American Society for Engineering Education (ASEE) 2007 Annual Conference*. Hawaii, 24–27 June 2007.

Marcus, G.E. & Saka, E. (2006). 'Assemblage.' *Theory, Culture & Society*, 23: pp. 101–6.

Marmot, M. & Wilkinson, R.G. (eds) (2006). *Social Determinants of Health*. Oxford, UK: Oxford University Press.

Martin, S. & Stermac, L. (2010). 'Measuring Hope: Is Hope Related to Criminal Behaviour in Offenders?' *International Journal of Offender Therapy and Comparative Criminology*, 54(5): 693–705.

Marton, F. (1981). 'Phenomenography – Describing conceptions of the world around us.' *Instructional Science*, 10: pp. 177–200.

Marton, F. (1986). 'Phenomenography – A research approach to investigating different understandings of reality.' *Journal of Thought*, 21(3): pp. 28–49.

Marton, F. & Pong, W.Y. (2005). 'On the unit of description in phenomenography.' *Higher Education Research & Development*, 24(4): pp. 335–48.

Maruna, S. (2001). *Making Good: How Ex-convicts Reform and Rebuild Their Lives.* Washington, DC: American Psychological Association.

Maruna, S. (2005). 'Restorative re-integration: Helping offenders rebuild their lives.' Presentation to NIACRO, Belfast, Ireland, November 24.

Maruna, S. (2006). 'Who owns resettlement? Towards restorative re-integration.' *British Journal of Community Justice*, 4(2): pp. 23–34.

Maruna, S. (2011a). 'Judicial rehabilitation and the "clean bill of health" in criminal justice.' *European Journal of Probation*, 3(1): pp. 97–117.

Maruna, S. (2011b). 'Reentry as a rite of passage.' *Punishment & Society*, 13(1): pp. 3–28.

Maruna, S. & LeBel, T. (2003). 'Welcome home? Examining the "reentry court" concept from a strengths-based perspective.' *Western Criminology Review*, 4(2): pp. 91–107.

Maruna, S., LeBel, T. & Lanier, C. (2004). 'Generativity behind bars: Some "redemptive truth" about prison society', in E. de St Aubin, D. McAdams & T. Kim, (eds), *The Generative Society*. Washington, DC: American Psychological Association, pp. 131–52.

Maruna, S., LeBel, T., Mitchell, N. & Naples, M. (2004). 'Pygmalion in the reintegration process: Desistance from crime through the looking glass.' *Psychology, Crime & Law*, 10(3): pp. 271–81.

Maruna, S., Matravers, A. & King, A. (2004). 'Disowning our shadow: A psychoanalytic approach to understanding punitive public attitudes.' *Deviant Behaviour*, 25: pp. 277–99.

Maruna, S. & Roy, K. (2006). 'Amputation or reconstruction? Notes on the concept of "knifing off" and desistance from crime.' *Journal of Contemporary Criminal Justice*, 22(2): pp. 1–21.

Mason, P. (2006). 'Prison decayed: Cinematic penal discourse and populism 1995–2005.' *Social Semiotics*, 16(4): pp. 607–26.

Matthews, B. (2008). 'A view from the inside', Our Patch, viewed 17 January 2009 at: www.ourpatch.com.au/australia/users/intractable/blogs/247-a-view-from-the-inside

Mauer, M. & Chesney-Lind, M. (2003). *Invisible Punishment: The Collateral Consequences of Mass Imprisonment.* New York: The New Press.

Maurutto, P. & Hannah-Moffat, K. (2006). 'Assembling risk and the restructuring of penal control.' *British Journal of Criminology*, 46: pp. 438–54.

Mentore, G. (2009). 'Interview with Edith Turner.' *AIBR Revista de Antropologia Iberoamericana*, 4(3): pp. i–xviii.

Merrall, E.L.C., Kariminia, A., Binswanger, I.A., Hobbs, M.S., Farrell, M., Marsden, J., Hutchison, S.J. & Bird, S.M. (2010). 'Meta-analysis of drug-related deaths soon after release from prison.' *Addiction*, 105: pp. 1545–54.

Messerschmidt, J.W. (1993). *Masculinities and Crime: Critique and Reconceptualization of Theory*. Lanham, MD: Rowman & Littlefield.

Messerschmidt, J.W. (2001). 'Masculinities, crime and prison', in D.F. Sabo, T.A. Kupers & W.J. London (eds), *Prison Masculinities*. Philadelphia, PA: Temple University Press: pp. 67–72.

Miller, E.J. (2007). 'The therapeutic effects of managerial reentry courts.' *Federal Sentencing Reporter*, 20(2): pp. 127–35.

Mills, A. & Codd, H. (2008). 'Prisoners' families and offender management: Mobilizing social capital.' *Probation Journal*, 55(1): pp. 9–24.

Moore, R. (2012). 'Beyond the prison walls: Some thoughts on prisoner "resettlement" in England and Wales.' *Criminology & Criminal Justice*, 12(2): pp. 129–47.

Morse, J. (2000). 'Determining Sample Size.' *Qualitative Health Research*, 10: 3–5.

Mukamal, D.A. & Samuels, P.N. (2002–3). 'Statutory limitations on civil rights of people with criminal records.' *Fordham Urban Law Journal*, 30: pp. 1501–18.

Nadesu, A. (2009). Reconviction Patterns of Released Prisoners: A 60-Months Follow-Up Analysis. New Zealand, Department of Corrections.

Naylor, B. (2011). 'Criminal records and rehabilitation in Australia.' *European Journal of Probation*, 3(1): pp. 79–96.

Naylor, B., Paterson, M. & Pittard, M. (2008). 'In the Shadow of a Criminal record: Proposing a Just Model of Criminal Record Employment Checks.' *Melbourne University Law Review*, 32: 171.

Neuman, W.L. (1997). *Social Research Methods: Qualitative and Quantitative Approaches* (3rd edn). Boston, MA: Allyn & Bacon.

Newell, T. (2001). 'Restorative practice in preparing prisoners for resettlement, integration and return to their communities.' London: Restorative Justice Consortium.

Newell, T. (2002). Restorative Justice in Prisons. Paper presented at the Restorative and Community Justice: Inspiring the Future conference, held in Winchester, UK, 28–31 March.

Norden, P. (2008). 'Prisoners' Aid', eMelbourne. Available at: www.emelbourne.net.au/biogs/EM01196b.htm

Nugent, B. (2008). Life after Prison: Resettling Adult Offenders. Report on the Conférence Permanente Européenne de la Probation (CEP), April, University of Glasgow, Scotland.

O'Brien, M. (2005). 'What is cultural about cultural criminology?' *British Journal of Criminology*, 45(5): pp. 599–612.

Ogloff, J.R.P., Davis, M.R., Rivers, G. & Ross, S. (2007). 'The identification of mental disorders in the criminal justice system.' *Trends & Issues in Crime and Criminal Justice*, no. 334. Canberra: Australian Institute of Criminology.

Olivares, K.M., Burton, V.S. & Cullen, F.T. (1996). 'The collateral consequences of a felony conviction: A national study of state legal codes 10 years later.' *Federal Probation*, 60(3): pp. 10–17.

Oliver, S. & O'Brien, M. (2003). From Corrections to the Community: The Need for Transitional Support Services for Offenders with a Cognitive Disability, The Office of the Public Advocate, Victoria.

O'Malley, P. (2004). 'The Uncertain Promise of Risk.' *The Australia and New Zealand Journal of Criminology*, 37(3): 323–343.

Oppenheim, F.E. (1955). 'Control and unfreedom.' *Philosophy of Science*, 22(4): pp. 280–8.

Ortner, S.B. (ed.) (1999). *The Fate of 'Culture': Geertz and Beyond*. Berkeley & Los Angeles, CA: University of California Press.

Paterson, M. and Naylor, B. (2011). 'Australian spent convictions reform: A contextual analysis.' *University of NSW Law Journal*, 34(3): 938–63.

Patillo, M., Weiman, D. & Western, B. (2004). *Imprisoning America: The Social Effects of Mass Incarceration*. New York: Russell Sage Foundation.

Patrick, K. (2000). 'Exploring conceptions: 'Phenomenography and the object of study' in J. Bowden & E. Walsh, (Eds). *Phenomenography*. Melbourne: RMIT University Press, pp.117–136.

Peacock, M. (2008). 'A third space between the prison and the community: Post-release programs and reintegration.' *Current Issues in Criminal Justice*, (20)2: pp. 307–12.

Pew, see the Pew Centre on the States, the Pew Charitable Trusts.

Pew Centre on the States, The (2008). One in 100: Behind Bars in America 2008. Washington, DC: The Pew Centre on the States.

Pew Centre on the States, The (2009). One in 31: The Long Reach of American Corrections. Washington, DC: The Pew Charitable Trusts.

Pew Charitable Trusts, The (2010). Collateral Costs: Incarceration's Effect on Economic Mobility. Washington, DC: The Pew Charitable Trusts.

Phillips, Jenny (2001). 'Cultural Construction of Manhood in Prison.' *Psychology of Men & Masculinity*, 2(1): pp. 13–23.

Phillips, John (2006). 'Agencement/assemblage.' *Theory, Culture & Society*, 23: pp. 108–9.

Pinard, M. (2010). 'Collateral consequences of criminal convictions: Confronting issues of race and dignity.' *New York University Law Review*, 85: pp. 457–534.

Polit, D.F. & Beck, C.T. (2005). *Essentials of Nursing Research: Methods, Appraisal, and Utilization* (6th edn). Baltimore, MD: Lippincott Williams & Wilkins.

Polizzi, D. & Arrigo, B.A. (2009). 'Phenomenology, postmodernism, and philosophical criminology: A conversational critique.' *Journal of Theoretical & Philosophical Criminology*, 1(2): pp. 113–45.

Pratt, D., Piper, M., Appleby, L., Webb, R.T. & Shaw, J. (2006). 'Suicide in recently released prisoners: A population-based cohort study.' *Lancet*, 368(9530): pp. 119–23.

Presdee, M. (2004). 'Cultural criminology: The long and winding road.' *Theoretical Criminology*, 8(3): pp. 275–85.

Pryor, S. (2001). *The Responsible Prisoner: An Exploration of the Extent to which Imprisonment Removes Responsibility Unnecessarily and an Invitation to Change*. London: UK Home Office.

Richardson, J.T.E. (1999). 'The Concepts and Methods of Phenomenographic Research.' *Review of Educational Research*, 69(1): 53–82.

Robbers, M.L.P. (2009). 'Lifers on the outside: Sex offenders and disintegrative shaming.' *International Journal of Offender Therapy & Comparative Criminology*, 53(1): pp. 5–28.

Rodriguez, S. (2011). 'The challenges of successful reentry programming.' *Offender Programs Report*, 14(5): pp. 65–80.

Rolfe, P. (2011). 'Wife killer back in business.' *Sunday Herald Sun*, May 29.

Rose, N. (1989). *Governing the Soul: the Shaping of the Private Self*. Oxford, UK: Routledge.

Rose, N. (2000). 'Government and control.' *British Journal of Criminology*, 40(2): pp. 321–39.

Rose, N. (2010). '"Screen and intervene": Governing risky brains.' *History of the Human Sciences*, 23(1): pp. 79–105.

Rosenberg, J. (2009). Children Need Dads Too: Children with Fathers in Prison. Geneva: Quaker United Nations Office (QUNO).

Ross, S. (2003). Bridging the Gap: A release Transition Support Program for Victorian Prisoners — Final Evaluation Report, Melbourne Criminology Research and Evaluation Unit for the Office of the Correctional Services Commissioner, Department of Justice, Victoria.

Ross, S., Brown, M. & Henry, N. (2006). Successful Transitions: Mentoring as a form of post-release support for women exiting prison. Paper presented to the Reintegration Puzzle Conference, Brisbane, 15–16 June.

Sabo, D. (2001). 'Doing time, doing masculinity: Sports and prison', in D.F. Sabo, T.A. Kupers & W.J. London (eds), *Prison Masculinities*. Philadelphia, PA: Temple University Press, pp. 61–6.

Sabo, D.F., Kupers, T.A. & London, W.J. (eds) (2001). *Prison Masculinities*. Philadelphia, PA: Temple University Press.

Saliba, A. (2012). 'Beyond the prison walls: The role of a criminal record check in balancing risk management and reintegration through employment.' PhD thesis, School of Global, Urban & Social Studies, RMIT University.

Säljö, R. (1997). 'Talk as data and practice: A critical look at phenomenographic inquiry and the appeal to experience.' *Higher Education: Research & Development*, 16(2): 173–190.

Sampson, R.J. & Bean, L. (2006). 'Cultural mechanisms and killing fields', in R. Peterson, L. Krivo & J. Hagan (eds), *Race, Ethnicity, and Crime in America*. New York: New York University Press, pp. 8–36.

Sampson, R.J. & Laub, J. (1993). *Crime in the Making: Pathways and Turning Points through Life*. Cambridge, MA: Harvard University Press.

Sampson, R.J. & Laub, J. (2005). 'A life-course view of the development of crime.' *Annals of the American Academy*, 602: pp. 12–45.

Schmid, T.J. & Jones, R.S. (1993). 'Ambivalent actions: Prison adaptation strategies of first-time, short-term inmates.' *Journal of Contemporary Ethnography*, 21(4): pp. 439–63.

Scott, D. & Usher, R. (1999). *Researching Education: Data, Methods and Theory in Educational Enquiry*. London: Cassell.

Schulkin, J. (2011). 'Social allostasis: Anticipatory regulation of the internal milieu.' *Frontiers in Evolutionary Neuroscience*, 2(111): pp. 1–15.

Scottish Executive. (2004) Supporting Safer, Stronger Communities: Scotland's Criminal Justice Plan. Edinburgh: Scottish Executive.

SCRGSP, see Steering Committee for the Review of Government Service Provision.

Seaman, S.R., Brettle, R.P. & Gore, S.M. (1998). 'Mortality from overdose among injecting drug users recently released from prison: Database linkage study.' *British Medical Journal*, 316: pp. 426–8.

Semetsky, I. (2005). 'Semiotics', in A. Parr (ed.), *The Deleuze Dictionary*. Edinburgh: Edinburgh University Press, pp. 242–4.

Senate Select Committee on Mental Health, The (2006). A National Approach to Mental Health – from Crisis to Community, First report. Canberra: Commonwealth of Australia.

Sentencing Advisory Council. (2013). Reoffending following Sentencing in the Magistrates' Court of Victoria, Sentencing Advisory Council, Melbourne.

Sewell, W.H. (2004). Comments on James P. Boggs, 'The culture concept as theory, in context', p. 202. *Current Anthropology*, 45(2): pp. 202–3.

Seymour-Smith, C. (1993). *Dictionary of Anthropology*. London: Macmillan.

Shewan, D., Hammersley, R., Oliver, J. & Macpherson, S. (2000). 'Fatal drug overdose after liberation from prison: A retrospective study of female ex-prisoners from Strathclyde region (Scotland).' *Addiction Research*, 8(3): pp. 267–78.

Sisters Inside. (2005) Building on Women's Strength: Developing community-based service models for women in prison and released from prison in Victoria. Discussion paper prepared by Sisters Inside Inc and the Aboriginal Family Violence Prevention and Legal Service, Melbourne.

Slowinski, K. (2001). Crisis Accommodation and Support Needs of Women Exiting Custody. Research report prepared for the South Australia Department of Human Services, Adelaide.

Social Exclusion Unit. (2002). *Reducing Re-offending by Ex-prisoners*. London: Office of the Deputy Prime Minister.

Solzhenitsyn, A. (1974). *The Gulag Archipelago: 1918–1956*. New York: Harper & Row.

Sparks, R. (2001). 'Degrees of estrangement: The cultural theory of risk and comparative penology.' *Theoretical Criminology*, 5(2): pp. 159–76.

Stagoll, C. (2005). 'Arborescent schema', in A. Parr (ed.), *The Deleuze Dictionary*. Edinburgh: Edinburgh University Press, pp. 13–14.

Standing Committee on Social Issues. (1997). A Report into Children of Imprisoned Parents, Legislative Council, Parliament of New South Wales: Sydney.

Steering Committee for the Review of Government Service Provision. (2012). Report on Government Services 2012, Productivity Commission, Canberra.

Steering Committee for the Review of Government Service Provision. (2016). Report on Government Services 2016, Productivity Commission, Canberra.

Sterling, P. & Eyer, J. (1988). 'Allostasis: A new paradigm to explain arousal pathology', in S. Fisher and J. Reason (eds), *Handbook of Life Stress, Cognition, and Health*. New York: John Wiley, pp. 629–49.

Stewart, L.M., Henderson, C., Hobbs, M.S.T., Ridout, S.C. & Knuiman, M.W. (2004). 'Risk of death in prisoners after release from jail.' *Australian & New Zealand Journal of Public Health*, 28(1): pp. 32–6.

St John, G. (2000). 'Alternative cultural heterotopia: ConFest as Australia's marginal centre.' PhD thesis, School of Sociology, Politics and Anthropology, La Trobe University, Melbourne, Victoria.

Stoové, M., Kirwan, A., Winter, R. & Quinn, B. (2010). Hit and Miss: Results from a Post-Prison Release Cohort Study of People who Inject Drugs, Centre for Population Health, The Burnet Institute, Melbourne.

Stowell, J.I. & Byrne, J.M. (2008). 'Does what happens in prison stay in prison? Examining the reciprocal relationship between community and prison culture', in J.M. Byrne, D. Hummer & F.S. Taxman (eds), *The Culture of Prison Violence*. Boston, MA: Pearson, pp. 27–39.

Sutherland, R. (2005). 'Throughcare: Rhetoric or reality? The policy and practice of throughcare in Australian community corrections', Honours thesis, School of Social Science and Policy, University of New South Wales, Sydney.

Svensson, L. (1997). 'Theoretical Foundations of Phenomenography.' *Higher Education Research & Development*, 16(2): 159–171.

Swidler, A. (1986). 'Culture in action: Symbols and strategies.' *American Sociological Review*, 51(2): pp. 273–86.

Sykes, G. (1958). *The Society of Captives: A Study of a Maximum Security Prison*. Reprinted as the First Princeton Classic Edition, 2007, Princeton, NJ: Princeton University Press.

Taylor, S. & Bogdan, R. (1996). *Introduction to Qualitative Research Methods: The Search for Meanings*. New York: Wiley.

The Argus (Melbourne, Victoria: 1848–1954) (1872). 'Prisoners' Aid Society', 1 August, p. 3.

Toch, H. (1998). 'Hypermasculinity and prison violence', in L.H. Bowker (ed.), *Masculinities and Violence*. Thousand Oaks, CA: Sage, pp. 168–78.

Toch, H. (2000a). 'Altruistic activity as correctional treatment.' *International Journal of Offender Therapy & Comparative Criminology*, 44(3): pp. 270–8.

Toch, H. (2000b). 'Commonality in prisons.' *Relational Justice Bulletin*, 7: pp. 1–3.

Tomkin, J. (2009). Orphans of Justice: In Search of the Best Interests of the Child when a Parent Is Imprisoned: A Legal Analysis. Geneva: Quaker United Nations Office (QUNO).

Travis, J. (2000). But They All Come Back: Rethinking Prisoners Reentry, Washington, DC: US Department of Justice, Office of Justice Programs, National Institute of Justice.

Travis, J. & Petersilia, J. (2001). 'Reentry reconsidered: A new look at an old question.' *Crime & Delinquency*, 47(3): pp. 291–313.

Trigwell, K. (2006). 'Phenomenography: An approach to research in geography education.' *Journal of Geography in Higher Education*, 30(2): pp. 367–72.

Tripodi, S.J., Kim, J.S. & Bender, K. (2010). 'Is employment associated with reduced recidivism?' *International Journal of Offender Therapy and Comparative Criminology*, 54(5): 706–720.

Tubex, H., Brown, D., Freiberg, A., Gelb, K. & Sarre, R. (2015). 'Penal Diversity within Australia.' *Punishment and Society*, 17: 345–73.

Tudball, N. (2000). Doing It Hard: A Study of the Needs of Children and Families of Prisoners in Victoria. Melbourne: VACRO.

Turner, V.W. (1967). 'Betwixt and between: The liminal period in *rites de passage*', in V.W. Turner, *The Forest of Symbols: Aspects of Ndembu Ritual*. Ithaca, NY: Cornell University Press, pp. 93–111.

Turner, V.W. (1969). *The Ritual Process: Structure and Anti-Structure*. New York: Aldine de Gruyter.

Turner, V.W. (1982). 'Liminal to liminoid, in play, flow, ritual: An essay in comparative symbology', in V.W. Turner, *From Ritual to Theatre: The Human Seriousness of Play*. New York: Performing Arts Journal (PAJ) Publications, pp. 20–60.

Turner, V.W. (1986). 'Dewey, Dilthey, and drama: An essay in the anthropology of experience', in V.W. Turner and E. Bruner (eds), *The Anthropology of Experience*. Champaigne, IL: University of Illinois Press, pp. 33–44.

US DOJ, see United States Department of Justice.

United States Department of Justice. (2011). 'Attorney General Eric Holder convenes inaugural cabinet-level reentry council', US Department of Justice press release, 5 January.

VAADA. (2003). Drug Services and the Prison System – a Special Issues Discussion Forum, Forum Report. Melbourne: Victorian Alcohol and Drug Association (VAADA).

Van Gennep, A. (1909). *The Rites of Passage*. Chicago, IL: University of Chicago Press.

Van Ness, D.W. (2005). 'An overview of restorative justice around the world', presented at the United Nations 11th Congress on Crime Prevention and Criminal Justice, Bangkok, Thailand, April 22.

Victorian Ombudsman. (2015). Investigation into the Rehabilitation and Reintegration of Prisoners in Victoria. Victorian Government: Melbourne.

Vinson, T. & Tehan, M. (2001). Repairing Relationships behind Walls: An Evaluation of the Me and My Family Program in Two Victorian Prisons. Report prepared for The Family Relationships Services Program, Commonwealth Department of Family and Community Services on behalf of the program providers, Jesuit Social Services and Caraniche Services, Melbourne.

Visher, C.A. (2007). 'Returning home: Emerging findings and policy lessons about prisoner reentry.' *Federal Sentencing Reporter*, 20(2): pp. 93–102.

Visher, C.A., Debus, S. & Yahner, J. (2008). Employment after Prison: A Longitudinal Study of Releasees in Three States. Washington, DC: The Urban Institute.

Visher, C.A., Debus-Sherrill, S.A. & Yahner, J. (2010). 'Employment after prison: A longitudinal study of former prisoners.' *Justice Quarterly*, 28(5): pp. 698–718.

Visher, C.A., Yahner, J., & La Vigne, N.G. (2010). *Life after prison: Tracking the experiences of male prisoners returning to Chicago, Cleveland, and Houston*. Washington, DC: The Urban Institute, Justice Policy Center.

Wacquant, L. (2001). 'Deadly symbiosis: When ghetto and prison meet and mesh.' *Punishment & Society*, 3(1): pp. 95–133.

Wacquant, L. (2002). 'The curious eclipse of prison ethnography in the age of mass incarceration.' *Ethnography*, 3(4): pp. 371–97.

Walker, L. (2010). '"My son gave birth to me": Offending fathers – generative, reflexive and risky?' *British Journal of Social Work*, 40: pp. 1402–18.

Wan, W.-Y., Moffatt, S., Jones, C. & Weatherburn, D. (2012). 'The effect of arrest and imprisonment on crime.' *Crime and Justice Bulletin*, no. 158. Sydney: NSW Bureau of Crime Statistics and Research.

Ward, T. (2002). 'The management of risk and the design of good lives.' *Australian Psychologist*, 37(3): pp. 172–9.

Ward, T. & Brown, M. (2004). 'The good lives model and conceptual issues in offender rehabilitation.' *Psychology, Crime & Law*, 10(3): pp. 243–57.

Ward, T. & Maruna, S. (2007). *Rehabilitation: Beyond the Risk Paradigm*. Oxford, UK: Routledge.

Ward, T. & Stewart, C. (2003). 'Criminogenic needs and human needs: A theoretical model.' *Psychology, Crime & Law*, 9(2): pp. 125–43.

Warr, M. (1998). 'Life-course transitions and desistance from crime.' *Criminology*, 36(2): pp. 183–216.

Watkins, S.C. & Swidler, A. (2006). 'Hearsay ethnography: Conversational journals as a method for studying culture in action.' *Poetics*, 37: pp. 162–84.

Watson, P.J. (1995). 'Archaeology, anthropology, and the culture concept.' *American Anthropologist*, 97(4): pp. 683–94.

Weatherburn, D. (2010). 'The effect of prison on adult re-offending.' *Crime and Justice Bulletin, No. 143*. NSW Bureau of Crime Statistics and Research (BOCSAR).

Webb, G. (1997). 'Deconstructing deep and surface: Towards a critique of phenomenography.' *Higher Education*, 33: pp. 195–212.

Wedeen, L. (2002). 'Conceptualizing culture: Possibilities for political science.' *American Political Science Review*, 96(4): pp. 713–28.

Weiss, G. (1973). 'A scientific concept of culture.' *American Anthropologist*, 75(5): pp. 1376–413.

Western, B. (2002). 'The impact of incarceration on wage mobility and inequality.' *American Sociological Review*, 67: pp. 526–46.

Western, B. (2008a). 'Reentry: Reversing mass imprisonment.' *Boston Review*, 33(4).

Western, B. (2008b). From Prison to Work: A Proposal for a National Prisoner Reentry Program, Discussion Paper 2008–16, the Hamilton Project. Washington, DC: The Brookings Institution.

Whitehead, A. (2005). 'Man to man violence: How masculinity may work as a dynamic risk factor.' *The Howard Journal*, 44(4): pp. 411–22.

Willis, M. (2004). Ex-Prisoners, SAAP, Housing and Homelessness in Australia, Final Report to the National SAAP Coordination and Development Committee. Canberra: Australian Institute of Criminology.

Willis, M. (2005). Shifting Sands: Conducting field research with ex-prisoners. Paper presented to the Australian Institute of Criminology Conference, 'Safety, Crime and Justice: From data to policy', Canberra, 6–7 June.

Willis, M. (2008). 'Reintegration of indigenous prisoners: Key findings.' *Trends & Issues in Crime and Criminal Justice*, no. 364. Canberra: Australian Institute of Criminology.

Willis, M. & Moore, J.-P. (2008). Reintegration of Indigenous Prisoners. AIC Research and Public Policy Series no. 90. Canberra: Australian Institute of Criminology.

Wittenberg, P.M. (1996). 'Language and communication in prison.' *Federal Probation*, 60(4): pp. 45–50.

Woodward, R. (2003). 'Families of prisoners: Literature review on issues and difficulties.' Occasional Paper no.10. Canberra: Australian Government Department of Family and Community Services.

Wormith, J.S., Althouse, R., Simpson, M., Reitzel, L.R., Fagan, T.J. & Morgan, R.D. (2007). 'The rehabilitation and reintegration of offenders: The current landscape and some future directions for correctional psychology.' *Criminal Justice & Behaviour*, 34(7): pp. 879–92.

Yahner, J., Visher, C. & Solomon, A. (2008). Returning Home on Parole: Former Prisoners' Experiences in Illinois, Ohio, and Texas. Washington, DC: The Urban Institute.

Young, A. (2008). 'Culture, critical criminology and the imagination of crime', in T. Anthony & C. Cunneen (eds), *The Critical Criminology Companion*. Sydney: Hawkins Press, pp. 18–29.

Index